Joy Ride

My One-Legged Journey
to Self-Acceptance

Karen Witt Daly

D1275086

DANCE GYPSY PRESS

JOY RIDE: MY ONE-LEGGED JOURNEY TO SELF-ACCEPTANCE
Dance Gypsy Press
www.karenwittdaly.com
karen@karenwittdaly.com

The events and relationships recounted here are my most true head, heart, and gut memories. My collaborators in these happenings may have wildly different truths. That is precisely what makes the human experience so rich and exciting. Some, not all, of the names have been changed to protect the innocent—and the guilty.

ISBN: 978-1977815446

Front Cover artwork: *Out and About*
© 2008 Karen Witt Daly

Back Cover artwork: *Who Am I?*
© 2008 Karen Witt Daly

Photo Credits
pp 391-393: Phil Miller,
p398, top: Karen Nelson

Editing, Book and Cover Design, and Production
Long On Books
www.longonbooks.com

Printed in the United States of America

- To my dancing body -
She saved my life by softening the harsh tendencies of my mind
and freeing my joyful spirit.

FOREWORD

JOY RIDE IS AN EVOCATIVE STORY OF a hero's journey through inner landscapes of the human psyche, the internalized narrative of early messages and interpretation of events that change lives. A true story of how one's dragons are born and mature into fire breathing monsters. It is a personal account of coping skills that can offer refuge but eventually can turn into dangerous patterns. Karen's writing touches me so deeply that I feel as if each thought, each occurrence is alive within me. The myriad emotions take me on a ride that is chilling and poignant, touching and distressing, romantic and heart-rending and in the end distinctly inspirational. It is a pilgrimage of one woman's quest to find a sense of peace and harmony within her own skin.

As I read Joy Ride, I am struck with the momentous events that altered Karen's life in such a crucial way. Yet she never gave up the search for self-healing even if the search was sometimes buried deep in the unconscious. She took incredible chances, even desperate chances, to move forward to find her way. She attracted all kinds of people. She opened herself to exhilarating experiences even though fear permeated most circumstances. The dichotomy of her inner life and her external persona continued to be in conflict and yet the tenacity with which she approached uniting the divide is proof of inherent wisdom. I feel we all have that wisdom. Karen's story models how the universe assists us. Many of the people who were drawn to Karen offered some direction toward her path to art, movement in Nature and dance. Her story motivates me to continue my own journey and to continue to help and facilitate others on their journey.

Based on my personal and professional experience, I believe that most of our human suffering comes from feeling unworthy. How do messages and events that are out of our control create this deeply seeded sense of not being good enough or pretty enough or lovable enough? How do some people cave under this burden and some rise above? Karen's honesty in the telling of long held 'secrets' and her willingness to bare all in the courageous act of writing her memoir is truly inspiring.

For ten years, Karen and I have practiced and continue to practice Authentic Movement together on a weekly basis when travel and workshops allow. Through movement and witnessing each other in this form, we share the journey toward self-love and compassion. Because of the intimacy and the foundation of trust practicing this work requires, I have come to know some of Karen's story. Yet reading her memoir opens me to much more than her story. It offers a glimpse of the intricacy of the human psyche and how complexes develop. It gives me hope that even under the direst circumstances it is possible to heal and it is never too late. It gives me encouragement that the personal work each one of us dedicates ourselves to offers more healing to our community and our world as a whole.

We learn from each other's stories. It is possible to recognize ourselves in the details of others choices and behaviors perhaps seeing our own potential for good or ill. Compassion grows out of understanding and understanding comes from the willingness to take in another's reality, to live it for a moment. Karen's offering of her journey is a gift to take in and learn from, to experience as a testimony to the healing potential of the moving body.

———◆———

Mary L.Seereiter is a Somatic Movement Therapist and Educator (ISMETA), a Certified Teacher of Bod Mind Centering®, a Certified Body-Mind Centering® Practitioner, a Certified Laban Movement Analyst, and a Certified Authentic Movement Facilitator.

She is the program director of the Moving Within Somatic Movement Educator Program at her residential Studio In The Woods in Lorane, Oregon. Mary has taught dance and Somatics at the community college in Eugene, Oregon and she served as the Director of the Dance Program there for almost 25 years.

PROLOGUE

The most important and enjoyable thing in life is doing something that's a complicated, tricky problem that you don't know how to solve.

/ William Vollman

LOSS AND GRIEF, AND MY LONG AND winding road to self-acceptance are the essence of *Joy Ride*, for it's about the power a mind stuck in denial can wield over a being, the ability of a body to survive years of self-inflicted abuse, and the unwavering tenacity of a spirit that knows it's lucky to be alive. It's about peeling away the layers and welcoming the cracks in the armor, and slowly coming to know that my true strength is equal to my willingness to be vulnerable.

When I was eleven, following a three-year bout with bone cancer, I had my right leg and pelvis amputated. The year was 1962. My parents dealt with this situation practically rather than psychologically, just as they had dealt with many other devastating events in their lives. Because poverty, mental illness, suicide attempts, and alcoholism were present in both my mother's and father's extended families, I remember my mother saying more than once that we don't dwell on those things, rather we accept them and move on.

When it came to my family's reaction to the loss of my leg, it was not surprising that there was little talk about it. Our tacit agreement was that nothing had changed—I was the same person and the whole family was the same, as well. We never discussed it as a family, and I never talked about it with my friends or schoolmates. It was assumed we would all accept it and make the best of it.

Although it seems unimaginable now, this was not an uncommon approach in the 1950s and 1960s. Those were years, before the focus on feelings that swept the nation sometime in the 1970s, when families kept difficulties to themselves, and there was very little talk about anything other than how to put the best foot forward as an individual and a family. My best foot was the only foot I had to stand on, the only one I had to wash, and the one that led to my life-long search and rescue mission for solo socks that had been separated from their twin.

I refused to acknowledge the reality that I had lost a leg—in one breath I told myself it hadn't happened and in another, I believed I'd fully accepted it. I wouldn't or couldn't see myself with one leg, and had little sense of the jolt others experienced when they saw the big emptiness where there should have been a leg. My inner masquerade was not so difficult to hold onto since I was given a wooden leg within a year of the amputation and I looked like I had two legs. Eighteen years later, when I gave up wearing the wooden leg, it was less about embracing my body as it was, and more about getting rid of that fifteen-pound burden.

For decades I denied the very fact of my body and did everything by and for myself. My staunch independence was a counter to my childhood fear that I would be seen as crippled—or worse, as retarded—and relegated to the special education class. Out of this pretense were born some functional but unhealthy coping patterns.

Functioning on one leg has never been difficult. My body seemed to innately know how to adapt itself to any challenge that arose. Without a thought, I'd find myself balanced on one leg or climbing a flight of stairs on crutches with grocery bags, or riding a two-wheeled bike. Improvising in the physical realm came naturally, and I've enjoyed the game of finding the most efficient way to move about. I discounted people's awe and curiosity, and their claims that I was "amazing" in what I could do. I couldn't acknowledge that, in fact, I was living on one leg. My mind was a master at denial and deception.

Projection, rationalization, and intellectualization were my mind's best friends. They refused to allow any unpleasant feelings to exist for more than a few seconds, always dismissing them with a rational argument for why they needed to be banished from my consciousness. They could twist any crazy behavior or unpleasant feeling into something that ultimately made sense to me. They convinced me that I could grow my leg back if I would focus my energy properly. For decades my mind rationalized my addiction to eating and purging as a way to purify my soul, whispering in my ear that E&T—my name for my eating and purging addiction—was my best friend, and a perfect way to eat and socialize without gaining weight. My mind is clever, cunning, and bright, and has been a harsh critic of any attempt to acknowledge the honest facts of my life or my emotional responses to them. Taming my mind, while embracing it, has been my biggest challenge.

My life began with parents who loved me, something I knew intellectually, but didn't always feel. Nonetheless, it was their love, and knowing that I was a wanted child, that primed the strong spirit that kept me alive in spite of myself. There have been many mentors who loved, inspired, supported, and encouraged me along the way. Most of those relationships were short, deeply-felt connections that seemed to appear out of nowhere exactly when I needed what they had to offer.

In my forties, I was introduced to a form of improvisational dance, which allowed me to open the communication channels between three strong, yet deeply divergent aspects of myself: my body, mind, and spirit. Dance took me inside to the place where these three collaborate as I move about in life. All that came before I discovered dance had helped crack the shell of fear and bravado that allowed me to function, but would never be a path to joy. Dance connected me to a playful, and reverently irreverent part of myself that was free from the tyranny my mind had held over my body for so long.

When I began writing this book, it was for the simple purpose of telling my story. I never imagined the power that reliving the story of my life in words could have. In revisiting myself in all stages of this journey, I've developed compassion for myself and, subsequently, for others. It's been an affirmation of my deeply felt sense that the journey unfolds on its own when I continue to show up.

It's my wish that this book inspires you with hope so that when faced with your own difficult experiences you'll know that the simple act of showing up and participating in life as fully as is possible can open doors to life-changing adventures, joyful moments, and a deep, profound sense of inner peace. And I hope you find a friend in the girl I write about.

As Mark Twain famously said, "A few fly bites cannot stop a spirited horse."

1   The Early Years

A sacred illness is one that educates us and alters us from the inside out, provides experiences and therefore knowledge that we could not possibly achieve in any other way.

/ Deena Metzger

I STAND ALONGSIDE MY BROTHER BILLY IN his pram. I'm wearing a summer dress, anklets, and red T-strap shoes. My blonde hair is chin length, with inch-long bangs cut straight across my forehead. Billy's one-and-a-half and I'm three. We're at the foot of the steps that lead to our Hoboken, New Jersey apartment, which sits atop a candy store. Mom has put me in charge of watching Billy for a few minutes while she runs up to lock the door. I love being the big sister helping Mom. When she comes down, we go for a walk.

As she tells it, whenever we're out walking, I stop at other babies' prams and grab the angora blankets between my thumb and the first two fingers of one hand while I suck my other thumb. I love the soft, fuzzy feeling of the fluff that slides across my fingertips. Mom backtracks to retrieve me.

"Karen, you have to stay with me. One day you'll get lost and be all alone somewhere in the middle of the sidewalk." She pulls my thumb out of my mouth and, gripping my wrist, leads me back to the side of my brother's carriage. She mutters apologies to the other mother and tells me, "Now keep that thumb out of your mouth and stay with me."

I hold onto the carriage and try my best to forget about my thumb, but before long, it's back in my mouth. To me, my thumb comes first. Angora fuzzies are a distant second. When there are no fuzzies around, I pull and twist the silky hair at the nape of my neck.

For a few days, I've had a nasty scab, like a mustache, on my upper lip from falling a few days earlier. I was running back to Mom from the swings in the playground we go to almost every day. Mom says I'm a clingy child. I stand with one arm wrapped around her legs and my thumb in my mouth while she holds Billy on her lap until she shushes me away.

"Go play, Karen—I'm holding your brother." I like to run and skip and jump for a few minutes in between clutching Mom's legs, and the scabs on my knees prove it. She says they ruin my pretty little girl appearance.

Mom wears pretty clothes and red lipstick. I want to be like her when I grow up. Sometimes she lets me hold Billy and feed him his bottle. But I'm afraid of her, too, especially when she screams at Dad or me. Mom knows everything and that's something she tells me all the time. "Because I'm the mother and I say so," she says, staring at me with her wrinkled forehead if I ask why I have to do something. "You better do what I tell you to, or you'll be sorry. Don't for a minute think you can lie to me, either."

I do sometimes lie when I think she'll be mad about something, like sticking my finger in the frosting of a cake or the butter dish in the refrigerator, or sneaking my thumb in my mouth when she tells me not to.

"Calm down, Dor," Dad says when she yells at him for coming in late. "What did she do?" he asks when she tells him to punish me while he's taking his coat off.

"Tell her not to talk back to me. You're out at work all day. You don't know how much trouble she gives me sometimes."

"Listen to your mother. Do what she says, or you'll be sorry," he says in his stern voice as he glances at me with furrowed brow. Then he goes to his chair in front of the TV.

She's a stay-at-home mom. We do lots of things on schedule, like eating and baths and naps and walks. I'm always meticulously dressed and expected to stay that way. Mom stays busy with dusting, vacuuming, sweeping, and running the clothes through the wringer washer and hanging them out to dry. I always want to help.

"I made my bed, Mom," I smile wide, happy to be helping.

She takes one look and pulls the covers apart. "You got the pillow all wrong. Let me make the bed. Go," she says, shooing me out of the room, "get out of here. I can do it faster by myself." I hesitate. I know she'll yell at me if I ask her anything.

Dad works day or evening shifts running the big printing press that prints the paper tea bag covers and tags in the Lipton Tea factory in Hoboken. He loves his job. When he works evenings, his favorite shift, he likes to sleep until ten in the morning and have a big breakfast of eggs and bacon, cooked by my mother. When I'm older, she tells when they were first married she'd sometimes break a whole dozen eggs before she got two that were good enough for over-easy. I wondered how that could be. Dad was not a fussy eater.

When he works days, Dad likes to go out with his buddies after work, usually to the tavern across the street from our apartment. When I'm old enough to cross the street, maybe five, Mom sends me there with Billy to remind Dad to come home for dinner. The place is dark and when the weather is warm, they leave the door wide open. The TV is always on, usually with sports or news. Before I even get to the doorway, I can smell the beer that flows out of the taps behind the bar. Inside, the men sit on high stools with shiny red seats and lean on a wooden counter.

As soon as they see us, Dad's friends invite Billy and me in and lift us up onto the stools. The bartender slides a bowl of peanuts down the counter and brings us sodas.

Billy and I love going to the bar. Dad knows why we're there, but he usually finishes his beer before we leave. Arriving home in his own time, he'd sometimes be met by Mom screaming.

"You don't appreciate me. Someday I'll be gone when you get here," she threatens. One day when I'm about six, she really does leave while Billy and I are playing outside. We try the door but it's locked. When Dad gets home that evening, we're running back and forth across the side street. He's furious. He grabs us, drags us into the house, and makes us eat Franco-American spaghetti and go straight to bed.

Mom comes back later that night. While they argue, Mom goes through the apartment closing all the windows so the neighbors won't hear. When Mom comes through my room to close the windows, I close my eyes and pretend I'm sleeping. Mom says she doesn't want other people knowing our business, especially when we're mad at each other and arguing. I never get mad, though, because it makes her mad and sometimes she puts soap in my mouth or grabs my ponytail if I talk back or say a bad word.

In the fall of 1956, Mom and Billy walk me to my first day of kindergarten. I cry hysterically, clutching Mom's leg, thumb firmly planted in my mouth. They turn to leave, and the teacher gently drags me into the classroom. She tells Mom to go. After they leave, I quickly warm up to my teacher and have fun listening to stories, drawing, and learning new things with the other kids. This morning scene is repeated several times over the first week of school. Eventually, I look forward to the attention I get for being smart and well-behaved, and I miss going to school on the weekends.

One day my class makes a big United States flag on the wall with individual pieces of construction paper. When it's my turn, I climb up the stepstool, all proud and confident, to put my piece in place.

"You put it upside down, Karen," my teacher says. "Go back up and fix it."

I burst into tears. I feel my insides tighten into a ball. Ashamed and scared, I want to disappear. I know my teacher's mad at me. It takes her several minutes to reassure me that life will go on after an error, but I hope she doesn't tell Mom.

Mom and Billy pick me up every day after school. Sometimes, before we head home, we stop at the candy-apple man's cart on the corner. The cart is a small wooden box frame with shelves, a piece of white cloth draped over the top and two wheels in the front. There are two shelves, the bottom for the big ten-cent apples, and the top shelf for the little five-cent ones. We get the little ones, though we plead with Mom for the big ones almost every day. The candy coating is a soft, gooey red that smells like hot sugar and pulls off in long strands that melt in my mouth.

"Be careful with those. I don't want you getting stains on your clothes," Mom says. She whips out the wet washcloth she always keeps in her bag and wipes our mouths a few times before we even finish eating.

In the summer Mom takes us for swimming lessons at the YMCA pool, in a dingy brick building a block from our house. It's a small indoor pool with yellowish blue water that smells a little like the bleach Mom puts in the washer. It's always crowded and noisy. I love to jump in off the side, swim across the pool, get out and jump in again. Mom doesn't get in the pool. She seems happy to sit out and let the teenage swim assistants take care of us. Sometimes on the weekends, Dad takes us to the small outdoor pool at Hudson County Park, with clear blue, cold water. It's a pool for little kids. You have to be shorter than a line carved on the wall by the entrance. The sun is bright, and the grass is very green outside the fence. Dad splashes with us or throws us up, and we make lots of bubbles as we sink to the bottom, holding our noses.

When I'm seven, in May 1958, my second brother, David, is born. Mom loves having a new baby and so do I. I feed him from a bottle and carry him around in the house, and when we go on walks Mom lets me push the carriage. I still suck my thumb, but mostly just at home. I don't get distracted by the other carriages anymore. In August 1959, my third brother is born. Mom hoped for a girl, and it takes a few days for Gerard to finally get a name.

It's pretty busy in our five-room apartment that summer. I'm eight, Mom's helper, her big girl, and I love it. I look after my brothers while she cooks and cleans and I walk to the grocery store, a block away, when she needs something. There are two other identical brownstones with eight apartments each, connected to ours so we have lots of other kids to play with. When I'm not helping Mom, I love bouncing ball games, where we throw our legs over the ball, and jumping rope on the wide concrete sidewalk, and roller skating down the uneven, bumpy slate hill that is perpendicular to our street, skate key on a string around my neck.

Soon after third grade starts, I begin to have terrible pains in my right leg.

"Why aren't you ready for school?" my mother asks.

"My leg hurts," I cry. I'm lying on the living room couch.

"C'mon, get up. It's probably sore from that bruise you got on your knee the other day," she says. "Why can't you be more careful? Now go get dressed for school. Dory will be here to pick you up."

Dory, my new best friend from Mrs. Smith's third-grade class, lives a block away, over top of a rug store, with her older sister Judy, and her mother, Ann. She's skinny like me and has long dark hair. Her mom lets her wear nylon stockings and shoes with the straps buckled around the back. Her sister, Judy, at ten, is a couple of years older and sometimes she's allowed to wear makeup.

Mom lets me play jacks, pick-up sticks, and jump rope with Dory outside our house but doesn't let me spend time at her house.

"Those girls are too grown up for their age. You're too young for strapless shoes, stockings, make-up, and boys," she says when I ask why.

"I don't care about Dory. My leg hurts too much when I stand up. I don't want to go to school today." I love school and playing with Dory, but that day my leg hurts whether I move or not. I lie on the couch staying as still as I can.

14

The next day the pain is just as bad. That night I hear Mom and Dad talking about me, and the next day my mother takes me to see Dr. Spath, our family doctor.

He reassures my mother. "It's probably growing pains, Doris. Try to relax. Let her rest a few more days. Give her baby aspirin. The pain will go away."

Still, the pain persists. I go for an X-ray, and as soon as Dr. Spath sees it, he knows something is very wrong.

"I think you should go see someone at Memorial Hospital in NYC," he tells Mom. "I've called the pediatric department, and they're waiting for you to call."

A week or so later, in early November 1959, we see a pediatric doctor. He refers me to Dr. Francis, an orthopedic surgeon. In mid-November, the same week we see him, he admits me to the hospital.

As soon as I get there, I have blood tests, X-rays, and a bone marrow test in my chest, close to my heart. I scream and kick. A few big people have to hold me down while the doctor pushes and pushes until the big needle jabs right in the center of my chest bone.

A few days later I have an operation called a bone excision. When the bandage comes off, my right thigh is skinnier than my left and twenty stitches that look like railroad tracks run from above my knee to the top of my thigh.

"We took out the bad stuff and left the good stuff. You'll be fine after a month of radiation treatments," Dr. Francis tells me. I have no idea what this means. What bad stuff? No one talks about what's wrong with my leg, and I don't ask, but everyone seems very worried. The good news is, the pain is gone. It hurts some around the stitches where my skin is tight and red. I'm weak but, after a few days, a nurse helps me out of bed. I can stand without pain on my skinny right leg.

———◦———

For the next month, I have radiation treatments in Manhattan every day. Dad takes the mornings off to drive me there. Riding with him in his car, just the two of us, is a treat. We hardly talk, but I like sitting on the wide front seat of our green Chrysler, my feet hanging over the edge, watching my father maneuver the Lincoln Tunnel traffic. Cars speed by us and red brake lights flash on and off. Sometimes horns beep. When we get close to the hospital, Dad searches for a spot on the street. He's a good parallel parker, spinning the wheel with his left hand as he stretches his right arm over the back of the seat, turning his head around to see out the back window. We always find a spot close to the hospital. As we walk through the streets on the upper east side of Manhattan, amidst the early morning hustle and bustle, he holds my hand. I'm happy to be with him.

In the radiation room, I lie on a cold, gray metal table under a big machine that hangs down from the ceiling. No one's allowed in there with me because it's dangerous for them. Dad waits outside drinking coffee and reading the New York Daily News.

"This is going to help your leg get better. Now hold your breath," the radiation man says through a speaker. He's a husky, dark-haired guy wearing green drawstring pants and a green top. His shoes are covered with paper booties. He stands outside a big window watching while the machine makes its radiation noise as it moves back and forth above my leg and chest.

The treatments are supposed to prevent my leg from getting more bad stuff in it. I don't really believe this. I heard about what happened to some of the kids I met in the hospital. I imagine that what happened to them is going to happen to me since they had the same bad stuff as me (some people called it cancer) in different places in their legs. Take, for instance, Sally. She was four and had cancer in her knee. She had her leg cut off. Jimmy did, too. He was older than me, and I don't know where the cancer was in his leg.

"Is that gonna happen to me?" I ask Mom, as we pass Jimmy and his mom in the hall, with a nurse pushing one-legged Jimmy in a wheelchair.

My mom and his mom stop for a moment to talk. They hold hands and my mom's face gets all scrunched up and sad looking.

"No, they caught yours early. You're going to be alright. I feel bad for Helen, though." As she mutters the words, she's looking away and up toward the ceiling. Maybe she's praying and I should pray, too. Even though Mom tells me everyone is praying for me, I pretty much think I'll have my leg cut off one day, too.

Gloria, one of my hospital roommates while I was recovering from my surgery, had leukemia.

"Her blood is getting eaten away. Those mayonnaise and pepper sandwiches are not good for her," my mother tells me while she's visiting. "She hardly eats anything else." I have no idea why mayonnaise and pepper sandwiches would be bad for someone, but I don't ask. Mom usually tells me not to ask so many questions, and it's even more that way since I'm in the hospital. She paces around the room and in and out while she's visiting. She leaves whenever the nurse is doing something with Gloria and me. She asks the nurse to get me up in a wheelchair so we can go to the playroom.

One day when visiting hours are over, Mom takes me back to the room.

The nurse says, "Let's leave her up, Mrs. Witt. Take her back to the playroom. We'll come get her for supper."

"Can Gloria come, too?" I ask the nurse. We like to make finger paint pictures together sitting at a big, low table. The paper is shiny on one side, and the paints are thick and gooey. We make pictures of our houses and families and flowers and animals. Gloria loves cats. She always puts them in her pictures.

"Gloria's not feeling strong enough to go today. She needs to stay in bed and rest," the nurse says. She wears a cap like an upside down cupcake liner on the back of her head and a white dress with big, deep side pockets. She keeps everything in those pockets: scissors, tape, Band-aids, a clamp that looks like scissors with a bent over point, and even lollipops. She offers me a red one that day.

"Can I stay here with Gloria? We can watch TV, or maybe the cart will come by, and we can make something together." I'm worried about her.

"It's best if you go to the playroom. Gloria's mom and dad are coming to keep her company," the nurse says.

I want to stay with Gloria. She's my friend and we have fun laughing at cartoons and eating ice cream Dixie cups, the kind that are half vanilla and half chocolate split right down the middle. When I come back to my room a few hours later, the curtain is pulled around Gloria's bed. I can't see her.

"Can I go in there and say hi to Gloria?" I ask a different nurse, one with a pointy cap that looks like a paper airplane's landed on the back of her head.

"Not tonight. Gloria's not feeling well, and the only people she wants to see are her parents."

"What's wrong with her?" I ask.

"She's tired. Now be quiet so she can rest, " the nurse says sternly.

The nurses go in and out of the curtain, but they won't tell me anything else about Gloria. Later that night they get me up in a wheelchair and take me out to the nurses' area. When they take me back to the room, Gloria's bed is gone.

"Where'd she go?" I ask.

"Gloria died. She was very very sick. Now she's more comfortable," the nurse says as she helps me up into bed.

It's hard to sleep that night. I'm thinking about Gloria and where they took her, what it means when someone dies. I wonder about Sally and Jimmy, too. I feel cold in my bed. I lie very still, looking straight up at the ceiling. I suck my thumb and feel the soft hair at the back of my neck, but nothing helps the big fat hole I feel in the middle of my chest. My right leg throbs as I imagine the stitches opening up and bad stuff pouring out all over the bed. I'm afraid to go to sleep. I keep thinking I just want to go home.

I think about all of this while I lie on the radiation table. It makes me really sad and I know that someday I'll have my leg cut off and I might

18

die from the cancer or whatever the bad stuff is. I don't tell anyone. They'll just tell me it's not true. But I know it is. The operation place on my leg heals up and it doesn't hurt anymore. My mother buys me knee-length skirts and shorts to cover the big scar on my right leg. My third- grade class welcomes me back after Christmas. Nobody asks me anything about where I was. I settle in as if nothing happened.

Every year I look forward to watching Miss America on TV. I sit on the couch or the floor with my brothers, Mom and Dad each in their own chairs. My parents pick their favorite girls, usually different ones. To me, all the girls are really pretty, even the ones Mom says are a little chubby look beautiful to me in their swimsuits and high heels. We sing along to "Here she is, Miss America...". I imagine being Miss America, thinking I would learn to tap dance for my talent, even though I've never taken dancing lessons. I know my mom would be proud of me if I were Miss America.

Every couple of months Mom takes me to Manhattan for an X-ray and an appointment with Dr. Francis. I always wear one of my best dresses, anklet socks, and patent leather shoes with straps across my feet. Mom wears a nice dress and high heels, red lipstick and eyebrow pencil that shapes her eyebrows the way she likes them. We take a bus from Hoboken to the Port Authority, walk a few blocks to board another bus that takes us close to the doctor's office, then walk the streets to his building. It's a glass skyscraper with a doorman who gets the elevator for us. The man in the elevator wears a blue uniform with red stripes on the shoulders and pockets, and a stiff cap with a brim. He welcomes us and pushes buttons that make the elevator go up. I love going to New York, but Dr. Francis scares me. I just know one day he'll say he wants to cut off my leg. My mother seems to love seeing him. She smiles and offers her hand, which he takes in both of his.

"Have a seat Mrs. Witt. You, too, Karen." He escorts us to two brown leather armchairs positioned in front of his enormous desk. They have gold-colored round buttons running up one arm around the back and down the other arm. The chairs are so big I get lost in them. When I grip the arms and slide back, my feet don't touch the floor. There's enough room for another whole person to sit beside me.

"Everything looks good today," he says. I had an X-ray the week before, and he says it's fine. Whew! I slide out of the chair and take big steps toward the door. "Let's see her in another six months, in December. Have another X-ray before you come." He turns to me with a smile. "Hold on, you." He comes over and gets down on one knee, facing me. "You're doing great, kiddo," he says, looking me square in the face. He hugs my shoulders. I squirm and turn away, ready to bolt out of the room as fast as I can.

"Thank Dr. Francis," my mother tells me.

"Thank you," I mumble. I'm already halfway out the door.

In August 1962, we move to Flemington because the Lipton Tea Company, where Dad works, relocates and asks him to go along. My parents are delighted for two reasons: Dad worries it would be hard for him to find another good job and Mom will get a house, something she's always wanted. She's so anxious to move that they buy a house a whole year before the company actually moves. Mom moves with us kids and Dad stays in Hoboken with his mother, coming to his new home on weekends.

Our house has a creek running down the hill behind it and I see cows in a yard just beyond the creek. I'd never seen a cow close up or lived in a house. In Hoboken, we lived in buildings with eight apartments on four floors, and most of the trees grew out of holes in the concrete near the street. Our new house has lots of grass and trees all over the place. We can walk to the store, a good thing, too, because we only have one car and Dad has it all week while he's working in Hoboken. It doesn't matter about the car anyway—Mom doesn't know how to drive.

I'm ten when we move there, and my mother lets me have a bike for the first time. My cousin Bernadine gives me her old one, with hand brakes and skinny tires—just what I want. One day while I'm riding around a curve, I slide on some gravel and tumble to the ground. The hand brake pushes deep into my left thigh. I lay there in the gravel with the bike on top of me, praying that nothing bad has happened to my good leg. I'm in a fog of fear, convinced I hurt my bad leg and my good leg, until a car stops in front of me and I see a man walking toward me.

"What happened?" he asks as he bends down to take a look.

"The brake is stuck in my leg," I wince, trying hard not to cry.

"Here let me help." He pushes gently on my thigh while moving the bike away from my leg. The brake slides out along with purple, gooey stuff, but no blood. I wonder if it's the same bad stuff I had in my other leg.

"It's not too deep, but we better get you to the emergency room, see if you need stitches. Where do you live?"

I know I have to go to the hospital but I don't want to. I'm scared to go to any hospital, especially to have them do something to my legs.

"Around the block." I point toward my house as he's carrying me to his car. We stop for my mother, who gets our neighbor to watch my brothers.

"I hate that bike," she says as she gets into the car. "Thank you so much for picking her up," she repeats and repeats as we drive to the hospital. She barely looks at me and doesn't look at my leg at all.

"It's a puncture wound, they rarely bleed," the emergency room doctor says as he puts in two stitches. My mother and the man wait in the waiting room.

"It'll be fine in a week." The nurse shows us how to clean it and the man takes us home. Mom wants to pay him but he refuses.

After that Mom doesn't like me riding that bike, but I still want to. Sometimes, if I plead with her, she lets me ride it in the backyard and to the corner of our street. I guess she's scared I'll hurt myself again and get another scar somewhere. I am, too, but I really like how free I feel when I ride.

―――――◦―――――

In September 1962, I start sixth grade in a new school in the town we moved to over the summer. Billy and I walk together in the mornings and sometimes Mom comes by with David and Gerard, my two younger brothers, to walk us home as she did in Hoboken. The building sits back from the road, and there's a big circular driveway the school buses drive up to unload. My old school sat right on the sidewalk, and everyone walked to school.

In my classroom, the desks are in pairs. Two boys named Barry and Steve sit at the desks in front of me and a girl named Mary. On the first day, as we're all getting settled, Barry turns around and drops what sounds like a marble onto my desk.

Mary and Steve exclaim almost in unison, "Barry! Why'dya do that? It's her first day."

The hard round thing rolls across my desk. It's not a marble. "What is it?" I grimace as I shrink down in my chair.

"It's his eye," Steven chimes in with a sort of eerie glee. "See?" He points to the sunken area on Barry's face where his eye should be.

Barry wears a spooky grin. "Yeah, see, it goes in here…like this." He picks up the orb and pops it back into the socket. I lean forward, amazed. He smiles and pops it out again. The two boys burst into hysterical laughter, while Mary sits there watching. She leans over and whispers, "Don't worry, they're really nice. Really."

Our teacher, Mrs. Denbigh, looks up. "Steve, Barry—turn around NOW and face the front of the room." She pauses. "NOW. I mean it." She rises from her perch behind her desk. Barry pops his eye back in.

Later Mary tells me, "Somebody threw a scissor that got stuck in his eye when he was younger and they had to take the eye out. That's why he has the glass eye."

22

"Yuck. Who threw the scissors? That must've hurt a lot." I'm thinking about the kids without legs and arms I saw at Memorial Hospital. Now I know someone without an eye, too. I hope that soon I'll forget about all those kids and that I'll stop worrying about having my leg cut off.

"I don't know who threw them. He never told me."

As the weeks go by, Barry pops his eye out when I least expect it. No matter how many times he does it, I get chills when I see the eye rolling around on my desk and glance up at Barry's sunken face. Still, it's a way we connect. We're four eleven-year-olds, clueless about how to engage the opposite sex.

No one in my class, including Mrs. Denbigh, knows I had cancer. I try not to think about it. What if it happens again? My big secret leaves me feeling like a bag of mush. I pray no one finds out.

I love my new school and Mrs. Denbigh. She makes us work hard, with homework every night except Friday, but she lets us go outside to play every day. There's a big playground with swings and slides and monkey bars and lots of grass and trees. Sometimes the boys organize races and invite us girls to join, even though we're wearing skirts. I love running, and I'm pretty fast, so I win a lot. When I do, I throw my arms in the air and yell "yahoo!" Playing tag is like that, too. It's fun to run fast and dodge whoever is "it," laughing out loud and collapsing onto the grass when the bell rings. Three times a week we have gym, with volleyball and girl's hockey, my favorite. Some of the girls hate the one-piece blue gym suits with the short legs and snaps up the front, but I feel ready for anything when I put mine on.

Even though we've moved more than an hour away, Dad and Mom continue to take me to see Dr. Francis in Manhattan for X-rays and blood tests. The X-ray taken on December 13, 1962, makes everyone very nervous.

Dr. Francis looks straight at me from behind his fancy desk. "I think there may be more cancer inside your leg. I want to do some other tests in the hospital." Mom and Dad sit on either side of me.

I protest. "But my leg doesn't even hurt. Not even when I run. I don't want to go to the hospital again. I hate it there," I squirm in my chair, wanting desperately to run away. "I want to go home!" I shout as forcefully as I can, holding back tears. My insides are sliding out of me, like I'm melting into a big puddle on the floor. What about my new class? My new friends? If I go back into the hospital, they'll cut off my leg, like they did to those other kids.

I have no choice, and I know it. I have to do what they say. No matter how loud I scream or how fast I run, they'll get me and take me to that awful hospital. When we leave Dr. Francis' office, my parents drive straight to Memorial Hospital.

As they're leaving, Mom looks at me and then glances away. "I'll be back tomorrow. Everything will be fine. Maybe it'll just be for a day or two. Be a good girl, keep your chin up." She's trying to be positive, but she looks worried. Dad pecks me on the cheek and says a quick goodbye. He stands near the door, with his head down and his hands on his thighs, like he's propping himself up.

I'm in the hospital for a week having all kinds of tests before anyone tells me what's going on. Mom comes every day and stays for the entire period of visiting hours. When I'm not being subject to blood tests, X-rays, and tests where they put needles in my arm and inject something before the X-rays, I spend my time in the playroom making things like potholders for Mom and Christmas cards and decorations. I make Dad a belt with interlocking strips of soft brown leather. He wears it every day for years, until it falls apart.

On the evening of December 19, Dr. Francis comes to my room. "We're going to do another operation tomorrow. I have to take your leg off. It looks like there's more cancer growing inside. If we leave it, the cancer could spread to other places in your body and you could die," he says. "I wish I didn't have to do this. Do you understand?"

I just look at him and nod, my entire body limp. I don't understand, but I knew something like this would happen if I stayed in Memorial Hospital again.

"I brought you a present," he says, holding up a shiny gold bracelet with a heart charm. It's got a pearl on one side and is inscribed To Karen Love Dr. Francis on the back. "Let me put it on for you." He fastens it around my wrist and hugs me. I can tell he feels bad, that he doesn't want to cut off my leg. I feel sad for him and me, but I don't question anything. I have to be a good girl. He and my parents know best.

Mom and Dad are pacing in the hallway outside my room, watching as Dr. Francis talks to me. I wonder if he asked to talk to me alone or if they didn't want to be there when he told me. As Dr. Francis leaves they walk in and, moving from one to the other, he holds their hands in both of his for a long time and says things I can't hear.

Mom comes to my bedside, admiring the bracelet, the one bright, shiny thing in the room. "Oh Karen, that's beautiful." She looks tired. From the doorway, Dad puts one hand over his eyes and pulls his handkerchief from his back pocket.

I don't cry. I can't. I'm just there, in that big hospital bed, with the gold bracelet hanging from my skinny wrist.

"The operation will be very early tomorrow morning. I'll be here when you wake up from it. Everything will be fine." My mother also doesn't cry but her face scrunches up and her lips quiver. She hugs me tight, turns and rushes toward my father. They wave as they disappear from sight, holding onto each other.

Not long after they leave, a nurse comes in to shave me. She puts a basin of warm water on the table, soaps me up and shaves everything from my chest down.

"You're a very brave little girl." She sits me up and squeezes my shoulders. "We'll take good care of you, I promise. Everything will be okay."

I'm in a daze, like a limp noodle in her arms. Still, there are no tears. It's like I'm frozen inside. She cleans up from the bath, leaves and comes back with a needle.

"This will help you sleep tonight, Sweetie. I'll try not to hurt you." I hate needles but I don't make a sound. I drift off to sleep.

25

In the morning, the nurse walks me to the bathroom, changes my gown and helps me onto a stretcher. A big man all in white rolls me into an elevator. In the room he wheels me into, every surface is shiny steel. The nurse slides me onto the table in the middle of the room.

"Hi Karen," a man standing at my head says. "I'm going to put a mask over your nose and mouth for a few minutes. You just breathe normally, and it'll put you to sleep."

———◆———

When I wake up, I'm a mummy in a bed of white. The bed rails are up, the sheet is pulled up to my neck, and my head is exquisitely placed on a giant pillow. I'm a head without a body, lying perfectly still. I can't feel my body or move my head. Mom sits on a chair at the side of my bed and immediately begins talking.

"Oh, Karen! You're awake? How do you feel? Talk to me, let me know you're okay."

More people emerge from behind the curtain drawn around the bed.

"What do you need? Are you comfortable? We've been here all the time, waiting for you to wake up." I hear a cacophony of voices. My dad and one or two of my aunts are there with Mom.

I want to close my eyes and go back to wherever I'd been. My mind races. Where have I been? How long was I gone? Where are my arms and legs? Why can't I turn or move in this bed?

My mother, the nurses and the others keep talking at me, wanting to help, happy to see my eyes open. I feel like I have to respond, to decide what I need, what I want to do. I should know, they want me to know. But I don't know.

"Dr. Francis said everything went well; you'll be up and walking in no time. Things will be fine in a few days, back to like it was." My mother continues talking. I move my head in a nod. I try to smile but I don't feel happy. I don't feel anything. I can't feel my body. It's all tightly wrapped and covered in white.

Over the next hours, the anesthesia wears off. The nurses tend to the bandages around my waist and hip. They sit me up, help me eat, and eventually get me up into a wheelchair. Mom comes every day. Dad takes extra time at lunch to drive over from New Jersey. I get so many cards, from relatives, family friends, from school and our new neighbors, that they cover most of the wall space around my bed. Aunt Jay, my dad's best friend's wife, brings me a Saint Jude medal on a gold chain.

"This will help keep you healthy and safe," she says. The medal is a shiny gold disk with a lacy gold border. It's engraved with a picture of a man who looks like Jesus, and the name Saint Jude in fancy script below his head. I wear it all the time. My mother says it will protect me. "God chose you, Karen, because he knows you're strong." I'm not sure what she means, but right then I wish he hadn't chosen me. Later I learn Saint Jude is the patron saint of hopeless cases. Being chosen because I'm strong eventually becomes a burden.

The next day Mom walks in when the nurse is getting me out of bed. I'm sitting with the nurse supporting my back, just before she helps me pivot my leg around to the edge of the bed.

"Oh, I'll just wait out here until you're done. I don't want to be in the way," Mom says nervously and quickly turns away.

"You can stay, Mrs. Witt. It'll just be a minute. It's only Karen's second time up, but already she knows what to do."

"No, it's fine. You girls finish, and I'll be right out here. Love you, Honey," she waves as she walks toward the door.

As I slide my foot down the side of the bed, I see my changed body. A big bandage covers what's left of my right hip. My right side is round from my waist into where the crease of my other leg starts. Below that there's nothing, just a big empty space. My left leg hangs down over the side of the bed, all alone. I'm unbalanced on the right and fall over to that side if the nurse doesn't support me. As my foot touches and I put weight on it, the ankle wobbles. It sends waves of fear up through the leg and out my mouth.

"I'm afraid I'm gonna fall," I yell out, grasping for any part of the nurse's body I can reach.

"You're fine, Karen. I've got you. Slide your foot around and slowly sink down into the chair." She's calm and strong and guides me into the chair where she's propped a pillow for my right side to rest on. It balances me. Some of the terror flies out through my skin as I sink down into the wheelchair.

"I can still feel my leg there," I say to the nurse, worried something is wrong.

"That's pretty common in people who have missing limbs. As long as it doesn't hurt, it's okay. You'll get used to it." I wonder if I'll get used to the big empty space. It's the only thing I can focus on, like the rest of me doesn't exist.

The nurse summons Mom. "We're all done. Karen did great. She's a good, brave girl," she says as she heads for the door. "Call me if you need anything."

For Christmas that year I get a watch, which I'm wearing in the only picture I have of myself from those weeks. I'm sitting in a wheelchair in the playroom, looking fuzzy from exhaustion and the unknowable work of healing. I'm holding one of my favorite dolls, a pudgy baby with a plastic head and painted on brown hair. She's wearing a soft, white baby kimono. It'll be another week before I get up on crutches for the first time.

"It's called an amputation, Karen," Dr. Francis says, halfway sitting on my bed with his hand on the covers over my good leg. My parents are there. "We took out all the bone we could to make sure you don't get cancer again. And we checked inside, where your lungs and belly and liver are, to make sure there was no cancer in there. That's the big scar down the front." It's the first time I hear the word amputation. To me it is still better to just say my leg was cut off. He says they pulled my right butt skin up and around to seal up the hole. I imagine a whole chicken with the drumstick missing.

For a week or so, there's a tube in an open area along the hip incision that drains blood and yellow fluid into a bag. When the tube comes out, there's a scab about the size and shape of an egg. The nurse shows Mom and me how to soak it in the tub and cover it with a bandage, but we try not to look at my scar. It's ugly, with a long purplish red line and lots of little red puffy spots on either side, where the stitches were. If I do look, it scares me. What if they have to cut the other one off? What if the whole thing pops open and my insides come falling out?

I just can't believe my leg is really gone. Maybe I'm in a dream or something, just waiting to wake up. I didn't watch while the doctor took the stitches out the other day, but I could feel the string coming out the holes as he cut and pulled. It pinched as he pulled each stitch up to get the scissors under the loop. I didn't cry and I swear I won't, that's why I'm not looking. I know I have to be strong so no one worries about me.

———————

I'm sitting on the side of my bed, finishing my breakfast. My new wooden underarm crutches are propped up in the corner of my hospital room. A night nurse put them way over there so I can't get up by myself. I got them a few days ago, and a couple of times a day a physical therapist takes me to a special room to practice walking.

Nancy, my therapist, demonstrates, holding her right leg off the floor. "See, Karen, you move the crutches ahead and lean down on them while you lift your foot off the floor a little and swing it through." I'm between bars, but because I have to hold onto the crutches, I can't use them for balance. I wobble and fall sideways into the bars or backwards, where Nancy moves right in to catch me.

"You're doing great," she says. I hate that I can't do it right away. I'm shaky, my arms tremble and hurt, and my head is full of tears wanting to burst out, but I tighten myself up all over and hold them in.

"It's okay, Karen, you'll get it. You're just tired. You'll see, when we practice again later, after you rest and have lunch, it'll be easier." She's right. After a day or two, I'm walking outside the bars, slowly and still shaky, but a little stronger.

We spend two sessions practicing on a box with four stairs on either side and a flat space between. I balance on the crutches while I lift my foot onto the step, then pull the crutches up to meet my foot and start over. It feels like I'm on top of the world after I climb the last step onto the flat top. It's really hard. I wobble and stumble. Nancy assures me it will get easier, but I want to do it right now. My insides are moving around like ants on a hill. I want to stop them immediately and make everything like it used to be. I want all of it to go away and I know it won't. There's nothing I can do.

———◆———

On January 4, 1963, after a three-week stay, I'm going home. My room is bare this morning because Mom took all my cards and presents home yesterday. I'm listening for her high heels in the hallway. I can't wait to hear their clap clap on the shiny, tiled hospital floor. I check my new watch every few minutes. It feels like hours go by. Finally, around eleven in the morning, my parents walk in with Susan, my nurse for the day.

"Today's the big day." Susan musses my hair and turns to my parents. "She's been awake since five wanting to get out of bed," she chuckles as she looks over at me, grinning from ear to ear. "We had to put her crutches over in the corner for fear she'd fall trying to walk by herself."

Susan is one of my favorites. She brings me extra Dixie ice cream cups, the kind that are half chocolate and half vanilla, divided right down the middle. When she's here in the evening, she lets me sit out by the nurses' station and listen to my heart through her stethoscope. Sometimes she plays Go Fish or Checkers with me or helps me with something I'm making from the art cart. I'm going to miss her, but I really want to go home.

"What's the first thing you're gonna do when you get home?" Susan asks.

"Say hi to my little brothers," I say. They're ten, four and three. I've been away for three weeks, and I miss them. I hope they remember me.

Susan and Mom help me get dressed while Dad stands around looking uncomfortable. He's got his hands in his pockets and his head bowed. He kisses me hello, walks to the doorway and paces in and out.

"I'll go down and bring the car around." He seems relieved as he heads out the door.

It feels funny putting on only one sock and shoe. What did Mom do with the other one? I don't ask.

"Wow, what a pretty red dress," the nurse says as my mom buttons up the back. "Here, let me steady her while you put her coat on, Mrs. Witt." It's an A-line, grey wool coat with big white buttons in front. I'm weak and wobbly on my one leg. I have to hold onto Susan while my mother gets my arms in the sleeves and buttons me up. I'm excited, but something feels different on the inside of me. It's like I'm trapped or all tied up. I'm not fighting, just scared. It's as if I can't move or speak, even when I'm talking and doing things.

Susan pushes me in the wheelchair, to the elevator and out to the street. It's a cold, grey wintry day and the first time I've been outside in three weeks. After I get used to the cold and the noise from the cars and the hustle of people, I realize everything is different now. As people pass or stop to let us through to the curb, they study the three of us: me, a skinny little girl with one leg in a wheelchair; the crisp, white-outfitted nurse; and Mom, chattering at us non-stop, carrying a pair of crutches and the baby doll I got for Christmas. I imagine the passers-by wondering what's wrong with me. They stop to watch me wobble as I stand, and look away quickly as the nurse and my mother shout directions as I step off the curb.

"I can do it myself," I protest, on the verge of tears and trying hard to push away anyone who might notice. I'm weak and struggle to get my foot from the gritty, littered curb to the street. I just want to be out of here, far away from Memorial Hospital.

31

Cars and buses whiz by our double-parked car. Dad stands at the car door, takes the last puff of a Phillip Morris cigarette, and drops the butt on the ground. He stubs it out with his foot like he's doing the Twist. As I get closer, I see more butts on the ground. He glances up at me and quickly looks away. Is he fighting back tears, too?

I take my first steps on crutches outside the hospital, but I have no idea what's happened to me. Although I am physically present and performing all the tasks of moving, I'm not at all connected to the reality of my one-legged body. I'm lost deep inside myself, scrambling in a maze with no outlet. All of my mental and physical energies are concentrated on staying upright while hobbling the few steps to the car. In that moment, I realize the hospital was a shelter, a place where time and the realities of everyday life were suspended. Now that's over.

My silent father and chattering mother seem to be distracted. They barely watch as I attempt to find my way to the car. The pain I see on their faces is broadcast to passers-by, while they struggle to hide that pain from me. We three wordlessly connect. I feel drawn into a silent pact: to act as if nothing has changed and everything is exactly the same as before Memorial Hospital.

Mom slides the crutches into the back seat, and I pivot my new body in to sit beside them. Crutches are pretty important now, my only way to walk around.

"It's so good to be going home all together," Mom gushes. "How do you feel?"

She reaches back to squeeze my hand. Her eyes are slits and her mouth is scrunched up. She's crying but I don't see tears. "I always cry when I'm happy...these are tears of happiness," she sobs. It's something she's said many times before.

"I'm happy," I say. Her happy tears sicken me and feel like a burden. I want to push her hand away and scream that I'm scared and tired and miss my leg, but I don't. The wind whooshes in the open wing window and lightens the heavy grey cloud that settles inside the car.

As we pull into the driveway, my brothers are waiting with Grandma Straub. Curtains move aside as the two youngest peek out the front window. Grandma's holding them back from running out to greet me. They watch as my father helps me get the crutches under my arms and as I slowly move first my foot and then the crutches, precariously balancing with each step. I need Dad's steadying arm to make it up the three concrete steps into the living room.

"Sit down boys…let Karen get inside…go on, go sit down over there," Grandma says to the boys. She can be stern. She's not gushy or sentimental like Mom, but she's kind and has stayed with my brothers for the last three weeks so Mom could stay close to the hospital.

Dad holds the door open as Mom and I move into the living room. My brothers are perched in a line in front of the Christmas tree. I hobble over and slide my body down the crutches onto the edge of the couch, facing them.

"We left the tree up for you…and you have presents. Here, it's from Santa Claus." David, my four-year-old middle brother, hands me a Barbie doll, with a blonde ponytail, wearing a black and white bathing suit, hoop earrings and black high heels. He turns away quickly and runs back to his seat on the floor.

"I'm so happy to be home, everything back to normal," Mom gushes again. Her mouth is scrunched down, and it looks like she's trying hard to turn it into a smile. She buries her head in my grandmother's shoulder.

"I got a new bike," David says. "It has training wheels, and I can ride it myself." He's standing, jumping up and down, grinning from ear to ear.

These words slam into my chest and suddenly I want to leap up and run outside, to get away, to stop knowing what I know. It takes a lot more effort to get up now. My heart sinks to the floor as I realize I won't be leaping or running anymore. And what about my bike? And roller skates and jump rope? I'll never be able to…

Ten-year-old Billy hands me a red-and-white flannel nightgown. "Here's your Christmas pajamas." He quickly glances down at my one

33

leg and turns away. We get new pajamas every Christmas Eve and have our pictures taken sitting on the floor in front of our tree.

"Did you take pictures?" I try hard not to think about my bike.

"No," Billy says. "Mom said to wait till the real Christmas when you come home."

I'm surprised by this and feel delighted. Seeing my brothers makes me happy.

"We'll do it tonight," Mom says, "before Dad and Grandma leave to go back to Hoboken."

I can't think about bikes and roller skates. I can't be sad. Not now. Everyone's happy I'm home. I'll be happy, too.

There's lots to settle once I'm home. No one asks me about what happened, how it is to have crutches or be missing a leg. Mostly we focus on the practical, like what to do with the empty leg of my pants. Do we cut it off and sew it up, let it hang loose, fix it in a way it could be undone when I get my new leg? Dr. Francis says I can get a new leg about a year after the surgery. We settle on pinning the empty leg up and tucking it inside the back at my waist.

There's the important issue of my still healing body. I have two incisions. One is a long straight cut down the middle of my abdomen, from below my navel up to my ribs. This is where the assisting doctor looked around in my belly for signs of more cancer. The scar is bright red and puffy. The stitches are out, it doesn't hurt, and everyone says it's healing well. The other is the open area along the side of my hip that still needs soaking and bandaging.

"Get in so you can soak," Mom says as the water is running in the tub. She helps me in then walks to the door.

"Are you leaving Mom?"

"You can be in here for fifteen minutes by yourself. I have things to do, and the boys need me. I'll come in when the time's up."

I sit in the tub with my scabby hip and missing leg. I hadn't really looked at it much. I don't look much that day either.

When the time is up, Mom comes in and helps me stand and pivot onto a chair.

"Pat your hip dry with this towel, put some of this Nivea cream on like the nurse showed you and cover it with the bandage there on the sink. I'll be back in a minute to put the tape on."

That's the routine for the next couple of weeks until the scab is all dried up. I get so good I can do the whole thing without Mom's help.

The next few months are a challenge in adjusting to my altered body. I'm still weak from the surgery. There are many unspoken anxieties about whether this will be the last bout, whether I will live or die. When will the next shoe drop? We settle into some semblance of ordinary existence. If for nothing else, my two youngest brothers demand it. They need Mom, and she loves a routine.

I stay home from school for two months. I'd already missed several days in the fall and the three weeks in the hospital. I'd been too sick for tutoring in the hospital, and it was Christmas vacation. Now there are worries about my being able to keep up with my sixth-grade class. My teacher, Mrs. Denbigh, who I'd known for only a few months before the surgery, volunteers to tutor me three times a week. She comes to the house after school.

Several weeks after we start tutoring, the Flemington phone company offers to put an "Executone" in my bedroom and the classroom, so I can hear and talk with the class. It's like a walkie-talkie, half the size of a cereal box, with slits down the front where the sound comes out. I push a bar on top to talk and let it up to listen. For the next few months, I can hear everything that goes on in my classroom. All my classmates want to talk with me. I can hear their, "Oh me, please me, me!" in the background and imagine different ones stretching their arms way high into the air and calling out for Mrs. Denbigh to pick them to talk.

"We saved your seat behind us," Barry says through the intercom. "I'll pop my eye out for you when you get back."

"OK," I say, as I hear Mrs. Denbigh telling him to get away from the box. I like hearing Barry; his voice brings a smile. Maybe I have a crush on him.

School is a welcome challenge. I love having the right answers and being liked by Mrs. Denbigh and my classmates. Even with all the communication, though, no one asks where I'd been or what happened while I was gone. Mostly that's fine, I'd rather not have to talk about it. It's like a dark secret, something I have to keep to myself, even though I know everyone who sees me can see I have just one leg now. We just never acknowledge it.

As the months go by, I become quite the expert at walking on crutches. One morning, I stand at the foot of my bed and notice that I'm balancing on one foot.

"Mom, Mom, come here. I'm standing on one leg. Come quick." I'm so excited I can hardly contain myself. It's a big discovery, a magic moment.

"What do you want, Karen? Stop yelling. I'm busy."

"Look," I burst out, "I can stand on one leg without my crutches. I can balance." I'm teetering, my arms stretched out, and I have to catch myself on the bed post, but I'm mostly balancing.

"That's nice. Just be careful you don't fall and hurt that hip." She quickly turns and leaves the room.

Months before I had the surgery, one of my cousins asked me to be a junior bridesmaid in her summer of 1963 wedding. Plans are still on. I'm fitted for a custom-sewn, long, green satin and lace dress. It's beautiful and I feel pretty when the lady making the dress fusses over me as she adjusts it. Mom and my cousin's mother, have words over whether I need a bra. I hear them talking during one of the fittings.

"She's too young," Mom asserts. "She's hardly showing at all."

"There're little buds there. It will look foolish if there isn't something to cover them," my aunt insists.

"She can wear an undershirt like she always does. Eleven is too young for a bra," Mom retorts.

Finally, Mom gives in and my aunt buys me a training bra. How fun. I'm even more excited.

The day of the rehearsal, we meet at the church. As we practice the entrance, my aunt tells me I won't walk down the aisle. Instead, I'll be standing at the front of the church, with my crutches and flowers, watching while the others walk in.

"Why can't I walk in with everyone else? I'm good on my crutches. I can hop without them and skip with them. See." I use the church vestibule to show my aunt how good I get around. "I hardly ever fall."

"We don't want to take the chance you might trip on your skirt. The long dress is tricky to walk in and you'll be nervous walking in first. We want you waiting at the front." My aunt says this in a tone that makes me know it's absolutely final—no more discussion. Children are to obey and not ask questions.

Mom agrees. I wonder if maybe they don't want everyone looking at me with my crutches. I look too ugly, I'm not elegant like a bridesmaid should be.

The day comes and it goes smoothly. I stand in front of the church, looking up the aisle as the others walk in. The groom stands near me and rests his hand on my shoulder. I can tell from the way his eyes look and his mouth puckers that he feels sad for me, but he doesn't say. At the reception, I wander around talking with my cousins, aunts, and uncles. One of my older cousins invites me to dance and I join him shaking my body in between the crutches to the rock-and-roll tunes the band plays.

A few times that summer Mom takes us to the new Flemington Community Pool. I'm amazed, as is everyone else at the pool, that I can swim with one leg. I jump and dive off the side, swim under water and do laps across the pool. I convince Mom to let me hop up the slide ladder and, although she insists the lifeguard will say no, he agrees and stands behind me while I pull myself up, step by step.

I beg Mom to get a summer membership so we can go every day, but she refuses.

"It's too expensive, and I won't have time to take your brothers every day. We'll come once or twice a week. That'll be enough." She tells me not to bring it up again.

———◆———

Toward the end of the summer of 1963, I see a local family doctor who we met briefly the summer before. Dr. Franklin is a big, gruff, yet kind man whose office is a few blocks from our house. The office smells like a hospital and as soon as I step in, I want to run out of the room. Instead, I'm the polite little girl I'm expected to be.

He does a brief exam, looking at my hip and belly scars and my good leg.

"Mrs. Witt, there's a Shriners Hospital in Philadelphia that could provide Karen with a new leg. The care is free until age sixteen. I'm a Mason; we're connected with the Shriners. I'd like to recommend her for admission. Is this something you'd be agreeable to?" He's sitting across from Mom leaning forward and looking straight at her.

"Really, Dr. Franklin, that's very generous of you. I'll have to ask Karen's surgeon, Dr. Francis, if it would be okay," Mom says hesitantly.

"I can call him if you like and get back to you in a few days."

"OK, that would be good. Thank you, doctor," she says. "Say thank you to Dr. Franklin, Karen. He's offered to help you get a new leg."

I thank him, we leave, and I wonder how exactly I'll get this new leg and what it will be like. Most of all, I'm glad to get out of there before he pokes around and tells me something else is wrong with me.

2   At Shriners Hospital

A journey of a thousand miles begins with a single step.

/ Lao Tzu

IN MID-SEPTEMBER 1963, WHEN I'M A MONTH from turning twelve, my family piles into the car for the trip to Shriners Hospital for Crippled Children, where I'll be admitted. It's in Philadelphia, more than an hour drive from our house. Mom and Dad are excited about my getting a new leg. I'm more worried about having to stay in another hospital.

Mom turns to look over at me, sitting between her and Dad in the front seat. She grabs my hand. "It's exciting. When you leave Shriners, you'll have a new leg." She smiles and shakes our clasped hands up and down on her lap. I'm surprised there are no tears of happiness.

Since it's a special day for me, I get to be up front between my parents. In the back, it's Grandma with Gerard, four, on her lap, Billy, ten, and David, five.

"Yeah, I guess it's exciting. I really don't want to go to another hospital." I'm sitting straight up with my back propped against the seat.

My one leg hangs over from my calf on out and there's a big empty space next to it, between Mom and me. I feel frozen. My outside body is only an outline, but inside me someone has scribbled and smudged with black crayons, in all directions and in crazy patterns. If I move, all the black will burst out of the lines. I'm not supposed to color outside the lines.

Mom says, "It'll go by fast and, just think, you'll have two legs again, right Dad?" She looks up at him. She has no idea how worried I am that some doctor will say I have to have another operation. What if they find something wrong with my other leg? Mom wants everything to look normal. Maybe I'm a little bit excited. What will my new leg be like? I can imagine myself with two legs, but in my mind I have my old one back again.

Dad mutters, "Your mother's right, Karen. You'll see." He smokes cigarettes, one after another, and flicks the ashes out the open window. He looks straight ahead at the road.

"I guess so," I say.

Even though I'm scheduled for admission that day, Mom, Dad and I have to wait in the clinic waiting room until my name is called. It's a wild and crazy place. Kids with all kinds of deformities wait to be seen. A boy, about eight months old without any arms, lies with his head on his mom's knees and holds his bottle with his feet. Many kids have varying degrees of curved spines, some so severe, it looks like their bodies are bent in half. Others have badly misshapen arms or legs. Some are here for initial assessments, their parents hoping they'll be accepted into the hospital for the extensive treatment they need. Treatment is free for all kids until age sixteen. In a way, it's hard to look, but most seem happy and normal, except for their bodies. They smile and play with the toys in the playroom and their parents scold them, just like regular kids. I'm one of the luckiest. I walk and skip with underarm crutches and stand and hop on one leg without them and, I'm already accepted into the hospital.

Mom excuses herself. "I'm going out to check on the boys," she says hurrying to the door. She can barely hold her head up enough to look around. Dad finds a magazine to study, and I sit there, still afraid to move, trying to imagine myself with a new leg.

When my name is called, we three go into a small room where a nurse, older than Mom, asks my parents questions and writes down their answers.

"It's all set, then," she says matter-of-factly. "Say goodbye to your parents and come with me." She turns to Mom and Dad. "Visiting is every other Sunday for two hours. The Sunday after next is girls' visiting. You can see her then if you like."

"How long will I be here?" I ask.

"I have no idea, but probably at least until the next girls' visiting day," she says, then turns to my parents. "They'll have more information for you, then."

After some back and forth about that, Mom and Dad each hug me. I can't believe they're leaving me here, in another hospital. "I guess we won't see you for a couple of weeks," Mom says. "Be good, do what the doctors and nurses tell you to. Just remember, you'll have a new leg and everything will be back to normal when you leave."

"Be good," Dad says, as he pulls my stiff body close to his. I can't hug back. I'm disappearing into some awful place, with all those crippled kids. No one understands. Everyone just thinks it's fine and easy and great.

I watch as they leave the room. I don't know if I'll ever see them or my brothers again.

The nurse takes me to an isolation room, a routine procedure for all new patients to ensure a new child doesn't spread some infectious disease among the twenty or so other kids who live on the various wards. It's a tiny, square space with big windows covered by blinds lowered to the floor and slatted open. The room is empty except for the bed, a small table and a TV. Everything else is disposable, including my light blue oversized gown, tied in the back at the neck and waist.

The nurse hands me a postcard and pen to write a note to my parents. I finish and pass it back.

The nurse skims it. "Sorry honey, you can't send this postcard. You'll have to write another one." She reaches into her pocket and hands me another blank card.

"Why not?" I'm scared and lonely and want to go home. That's what I tell my parents in the postcard.

"Tell your parents you're well and doing OK," she insists.

"But I'm not, I hate it here," I shout.

"It's only because it's your first day and you miss home. Most kids like it here after a few weeks. Just tell your parents you miss them and you're doing fine. Otherwise, they'll worry and there's no need for that."

"I don't want to write a postcard," I exclaim in a pouty and defiant tone.

"Write the postcard like I said. Now."

I take the blank card, ashamed and even more scared. I do what she says.

I spend three days in isolation. The nurses help me with a bath in the mornings, bring my food in, and offer books and crayons and other things that can be thrown away or safely passed through an autoclave machine, which the nurse says is hot enough to kill infectious germs. They insist I write a postcard to my parents every day.

Around twenty beds, lined up along two walls and in an alcove off the back of a large room, make up the older girls' ward. There's a small table next to the head of each bed and maybe three feet between beds. Despite the hospital feel, the isolation nurse is right—a week or so after I arrive, I feel better and only think about home a few times a day, because I make friends and we're kept busy all day long.

The ward is mostly full. I'm the youngest at eleven and the oldest is sixteen. Quite a few of the girls are encased in plaster from their necks to their upper thighs. A few are covered in plaster to their feet, with bars between their calves holding their hips open. Most have free arms below the shoulders, and big metal triangles hang by a chain from above their beds, which they use to pull themselves up. They're bedridden for months like that so their spines can heal after surgery. Karen, a twelve-year-old, has one regular length leg and a shorter one, that reaches to just above her ankle and has a small foot at the end. There's a tall, black lift on the bottom of her shoe and she walks with a limp.

"I think we have the same name," I say when I introduce myself to her. "What are you here for?"

"They say if they cut the foot off my short leg and make me a new leg, walking will be easier and I may be able to run and dance and even play sports. It will look nicer, too," she says as if it makes perfect sense.

"Really, they're gonna cut your foot off. Are you scared?" It sounds awful to me. I'm still terrified something else will happen, and someone will want to cut off my other leg.

"A little," she says. "Why are you here?"

"I had my leg cut off in Memorial Hospital last year. My mother says I won't have any operations here. I'm just getting a new leg." My doctors, whom I imagine are more important than the doctors here at Shriners, promised me that I was only here to get a new leg. Now that I hear Karen's story, I'm not so sure.

She and I are two of maybe five or six girls who can walk with relative ease. The others are either in bed and require help with washing, dressing, and eating, or in wheelchairs.

Jen, almost sixteen, is the oldest girl in the ward.

"I can't wait to get out of here. No more operations. I've had ten already," she blurts out as I crutch and she waddles with a limp to the dining room. The operations started when she was a baby.

"Wow! I've only had two. What for?"

"My hips were dislocated and twisted in their sockets. They were weak and couldn't support my weight when I was a baby."

"Are they better now?" I'm more and more worried. Maybe they will operate on me, even though Dr. Francis said they wouldn't.

"Yeah. I can finally walk after years in those body casts, wheelchairs, and using crutches." Her gait is slow and stiff. She shifts her weight from one leg to the other as she alternately balances on one leg and swings the other forward.

We sit at one of four or five tables in the dining room. It's Sunday today so there's ice cream for dessert, always vanilla. One girl shows me how she mixes the ice cream into her glass of milk to make a milkshake. "We do this every Sunday. I just wish we got chocolate sometimes," she laments.

In the mornings, the girls who can walk wash up, get dressed then help the girls in bed do the same. Once a week, we change our bed linens and help with all the other changes. Three times a day, before we go to the dining room, we help the bed-ridden girls eat. The triangle hoists make it pretty easy. Even though they can't bend their bodies, they pull up in the bed enough to get the sheets changed and to feed themselves if someone, like me, passes them the food and the cups with straws. The nurses take care of the girls who are more sick or just back from surgery. Their beds are closest to the nurses' station.

After we've all cleaned up and eaten breakfast, we help push the beds to the classroom. It's the only place we meet up with the boys, who have the same kind of ward on the other side of the building. The classroom and the kitchen are in the middle, between the two. The teachers get assignments from each of our home schools and work with us to complete them. Some kids may spend a whole school year in the hospital. Jen says she was here for seven months once. Some stay for a year or more. There are crafts and music, and sometimes we watch programs on a TV rolled in from another room. We watch on that day in November when President Kennedy is shot.

Girl/boy socializing isn't allowed, but we manage to find minutes here and there to huddle and make plans to meet by the kitchen after dark. We girls each like one or another of the boys and giggle about them in our beds at night, making plans to marry them and have ten kids or go on fancy vacations. Since I don't have sisters, all of this girl group stuff is new for me and I love it. When we meet the boys in the kitchen, we whisper, share treats we've smuggled in, hold hands and, some girls though not me, kiss and hug with their boyfriends. I'm giddy and only a little scared of being caught.

"What can they do to us, anyway?" Jen asks. She's the leader in all of our scheming, being the oldest and most experienced. "I'll be happy if they kick me out."

Sometimes we're bold enough to open the big freezer and attack the ice cream, digging out big spoonfuls and stuffing our mouths. My favorite part of our evening escapades is plotting to sneak out to the kitchen, getting away with it, and snooping around the forbidden places.

Sometimes when new girls are admitted to the ward, we devise ways to scare them before we let them be part of our group. "Initiation," Jen says. One day a girl the others know from an earlier stay is admitted.

Several chime in at once. "She's fat and complains to the nurses about us. All the time."

Jen's face brightens and her eyes widen. "We can short-sheet her bed."

I have no idea what short-sheeting a bed is, but I want to be a part of the plot.

"I'll hide under her bed and scare her when she sits down," I offer. I want Jen to like me, and I feel a certain powerful pleasure in making mischief.

———◆———

Each week Dr. Wolf, the ward doctor, comes to check on the girls who're back from surgery, talk to the ones who will be leaving, and generally spread cheer. He's young, tall, dark, and handsome and has a relationship with each of us. The ward is cheery and abuzz with whispers when he's around, especially since it's usually the same day the clothes rack comes, and we get to choose our outfits for the next few days. They're all Shriners' clothes, washed and recycled twice a week. The girls in bed don't need many clothes, but we push the rack around to each bed, so they can choose tops they feel pretty in. I'm always among the first to raid the rack, looking for one of my two favorite, colorful, elastic-waistband skirts. I want to be pretty and special. I don't want to be a crippled girl. I'm ashamed to be in a place for crippled kids. It's a dilemma because I want to be part of the group and I don't. I'm mad but have no idea at who. Mostly I think the whole one-legged thing is all my fault and that I did something to make it happen.

The tops are button-down or tee shirts with decorations. Any of those are usually OK with me. I get a new rectangular cloth bag with ties made to tie to the bed frames, to organize the cards. Although we can't write letters (the staff reads the messages we send to our families, so postcards work best), we can receive them after they're neatly slashed open, and searched for anything that won't make it through the heat sterilization machine, such as candy or gum. The clothes are sterilized in the same way to keep germs from spreading on the ward. Some of the nurses are friendly, while others are strict and expect us to do everything by the rules. The friendly ones are willing to mail letters for us. Jen has a favorite nurse whom she's known for a long time.

"She mails a letter to my boyfriend every day," Jen says. "Don't let any of the other nurses know or she'll get in trouble."

———

Every other Sunday we're allowed two adult visitors for two hours. We meet them in the gym, where we've helped set up chairs in groups of three, with the groupings positioned a few feet away from each other, in a big circle around the room. On visiting day, I tie one of the card bags onto my underwear, under the elastic waist skirt. Mom and Dad come, we hug and, almost immediately, I pipe up.

"Did you bring the gum and stuff I asked for in the letter?" Jen's nurse friend mailed it for me.

"Yes, we have some things. Is that all you care about? Aren't you glad to see us?" Mom chides. Dad lets me know with his look that I'd better be nice to my mother.

"Mom," I say with snotty exasperation, "the gym monitor just passed us. Let me have what you brought before she comes back." I slyly slip the gum and candy into the bag under my skirt. The skirt is puffy enough to hide the bulge.

"I don't like that you're sneaking around like this. These people are being very good to you. What if you get caught? Then what? Maybe they'll say you can't stay. Don't you want to have a new leg? What do you think, Dad?" Mom's on a roll.

"It's OK, they won't catch me." I brush her off, almost without acknowledging she's there.

"Listen to your mother," Dad orders, "and don't be so disrespectful."

I hear him, and I know he's right, but I don't care. I'm mad at my mother for leaving me here. I miss my brothers and just seeing Mom makes me want to go home, even though there are so many new things happening here that I don't think about home much. I tighten up inside, and take an imaginary step back from everyone, to avoid tears. I feel like I've been here forever and no one has even mentioned my new leg. Mom and everyone else, except the girls here, want me to be grateful. So, I'm being grateful. I'm not complaining. Why isn't Mom happy?

Less than an hour goes by and Mom wants to leave to check on my brothers who are waiting in the car with Grandma.

"It's hard for me—looking at all these crippled kids," she says. "Maybe you can look out one of the windows and wave to your brothers. They miss you." I wonder if it's hard for her to look at me.

Since we can only move around the room with permission, Dad beckons the monitor and she takes us to a window as Mom hurries out of the room. "I'll come back up in a few minutes," she says.

I love seeing my brothers, but I wonder if they really miss me—or if anyone does. Every time someone leaves this place, it's the same. We miss her for a few days and then we forget she was even here. Maybe they forget about me at home, too.

———◆———

A month or more goes by before I finally begin once or twice weekly van rides to Thomas J. Malone and Sons in downtown Philadelphia, the place where they'll make my new leg. The waiting room has a few hard plastic chairs and a counter too high for me to see over. The van driver leaves me with the receptionist, a smiley, pleasant woman about as old as Mom, who takes me into a small cubicle in the back. "They'll be right with you honey."

On my first visit, I meet Nils.

"Hallo, little girl. Nice to see you today." Nils tells me he's from Germany. He's wearing mustard-colored overalls, with a tee shirt underneath, over his husky body. His hands look like a giant's, and his arms are hairy. He's got a big, round head, a wide smile, and a thick accent.

The back room is a workshop, a big open space with table saws, sanders, other loud machines, and piles of plaster cast material spread out on shelves and the floor. It smells like sawdust and leather. Mannequin-like arms and legs lie scattered all over the room, and a few people walk up and down between bars, while other men with thick accents coach them.

Nils sits on a stool in front of me and looks over my whole body. He lifts my shirt, feels around my waist and the place where my leg used to be.

"Nothing I do should hurt, little girl. I'm just measuring so we can start thinking about how we'll make your new leg," Nils says this as he moves a tape measure all over my hip, waist and butt area, up under my arms and down my leg. He has me walk and sit and lie down. Some of the other men come over and talk with Nils as he's finishing up with the measurements.

"What are you gonna do with all the measurements?" I ask.

"We'll make drawings and put our heads together about how we might make a leg for you. We haven't made one like this before, so we're all excited for the new challenge." He's looking straight at me and smiling as he talks. "Don't you worry, little girl, we're going to make the best ever leg for you." Even though I'm surrounded by wooden body parts, I imagine my new leg will look exactly like the old one.

Mr. Malone, the shop owner, comes over to say hi. He's American, handsome, and looks about as old as my father. "Nils is right. We've never made a leg like this for someone as young as you. You'll be famous here in our shop, and you're going to get a brand new leg." He smiles and puts his arm around my shoulder. I don't feel scared at all. I just wonder how this new leg thing is going to happen.

On the next visit, the receptionist greets me at the door and escorts me back to the cubicle. I feel special, glad to be away from the routine of the ward. I'm the only one I know who gets to leave the hospital. I keep thinking that when the leg is finished, I won't be crippled like all the other girls.

Nils takes me to a place in the room where there's a sink, a big bucket of water, and rolls of dry plaster on the floor. He sits on a stool in front of me as I undress to my underwear as he asks. I'm chilly, exposed, and embarrassed in the open, drafty and noisy room. Men are sanding and grinding at the machines and coaching people at the parallel bars. As soon as Nils starts working and talking to me, I forget about the rest of the room.

"Here, slip this over your head so it covers you from your chest down to the top of your leg."

"What is it?" I ask as I stretch open the thin, tube-shaped fabric and shimmy into it with his help.

"It's stockinette—it helps keep the plaster off your skin." He wets the plaster rolls in the bucket and begins wrapping them around my body. I feel like the kids in the beds on the ward and I'm scared for a minute, until Nils promises that this is temporary, he'll cut it off when he's done.

He wraps the plaster up and under the place where my right leg is gone, around my waist and a little above, down to the top of my good hip and across to my left butt. I'm proud that I can balance on my leg with my arms spread wide all the while he's working.

"What are you going to do with this thing?" I ask while we're waiting for it to dry. He's steadying me with one hand under my arm, and the other supporting me as I sit down a little onto the plaster that goes across my butt. The cast is heavy and it's harder to keep my balance as it dries.

"We'll use this as a mold to fashion you a bucket. You'll sit in it to balance on your new leg and use it as support, like a pivot point, to move your good leg forward. Don't worry, you'll see as we go along."

When it's all dry, he has me lie on my back while he slides giant, ice-cold scissors along my belly, crunching the thick white plaster. I take a big breath and pull my belly in.

"Don't worry, sweet little girl. I won't snip your belly button." He musses my hair and smiles at me.

The next time I'm there, Nils brings out the plaster bucket cut off according to the measurements he took the first day. He's cut the back in half and put strips of leather across the two halves to make it easy to slip on around my torso. On the right, it really is like a bucket, shaped to fit around my fleshy right hip. There are two thick leather straps with buckles on either side of the front. The stockinette is still inside.

"This is it, little girl. This is what we'll attach your new leg to so it will stay on and allow you to walk. Take your skirt and shirt off and let's see how it fits."

He helps me strap it around my waist as I stand there in my underwear. I'm enclosed in plaster from above the bottom of my ribs to my left hip. There's a wide, tongue depressor-shaped piece of plaster that juts out from the bottom of the right bucket to my left butt. The plaster is scratchy and flakes off as I squirm around inside it to get as comfortable as I can.

I had no idea a new leg would be like this. I thought it would be just like my old leg, minus the cancer that made it hurt. I'm embarrassed wearing the big plaster thing in front of the other people in the room. I don't want a leg that is heavy and ugly. I'm disappointed, I feel like crying. I don't want to be crippled or different. Yet, I can't or won't complain or protest. I can't make any more trouble than I already have. All those hospital bills and appointments have been hard on my parents. This is all free and I have to be grateful. I want to get out of Shriners Hospital as soon as I can. I want to be away from all of this hospital and crippled stuff.

"Does it hurt anywhere?" Nils moves all around my body, looking up and down and under every part of my lower half. He slides his fingers between the cast and my skin. "I'm checking for where I need to adjust, fill in or cut away."

I have several more fittings as the weeks go by. One day he brings out a flesh colored, one-piece bucket with leather straps that fasten around my waist. It opens in the front, just wide enough for me to slip it around my side and then all the way onto my middle. The edges are smooth and shiny, and it envelops all of me, from my ribs to my hip.

"This is it, little girl. As soon as we see if it's a perfect fit, we'll start building the leg that will get you walking again." Nils smiles as he checks all the important places, has me sit and stand, bend over, lie down. He helps me put it on and take it off.

I'm mostly glad it's not the plaster thing anymore. This one is lighter, but it still disappoints me. I'm not sure I want a leg if this is what it has to be like. There's nothing I can do, though.

Back at the ward, I don't say much about the leg. The nurses and Dr. Wolf are excited for me—everyone says it'll be great when I can walk normal again.

A couple of weeks go by before I go back to Mr. Malone's. This time the bucket has a leg, made of wood and steel, attached to what Nils begins calling the socket. It's the part of the bucket that envelops my boneless hip. The leg hanging from it looks nothing like my missing leg. The thigh is a skinny piece of wood; the knee has a slit up and down the center that's visible when the knee bends open and closes to a crosswise slit when it straightens. The calf is attached to the thigh on two sides with big, flat circles of shiny steel that rotate around each other to allow the knee to bend. The foot is toeless and bends where the base of the toes would be.

"This is the beginning of your new leg," Nils says as he shows me how the toe and ankle bend and how the knee and hip swing from the bottom of the socket. He helps me put it on and holds me as we walk to the bars.

"How does it feel? Does it hurt anywhere?" I have no idea if it hurts or how it feels. All I know is it's a big, heavy thing hanging off my body.

"It feels ok." I'm a little wobbly but I can stand in it, even without holding onto the bars.

"Let me show you how to take a step." Nils comes over, puts his arm around my waist. "Take a step with your good leg. Good," he says as I do that.

"Now—I'll help you. Move your hips slightly back and up, and then forward to swing the new leg through. We'll do it together."

He has hold of the bucket and moves my hips with me. The leg swings out in front, and he sets it down on the floor. "We don't want to swing it too far out, or you won't be able to balance on it enough to take the next step with your good leg. You'll sit slightly down, into the bucket and onto that piece jutting out across to the left butt—here, I'll help you. Then, lift your good foot and swing it out to start the next step."

After a few virgin steps, he moves aside and I clumsily make my way up and back between the bars. I'm not so sure I like the leg, but I like to be the best at everything. I have to be the best at this, too.

On my next visit, the leg looks different again. The thigh is padded with foam (still skinnier than my good leg) and covered with gold-colored leather. The calf is covered in the same material as the bucket, a flesh-colored, shiny, smooth material that has faint darker stripes running through it.

"It's called fiberglass," Nils answers when I ask what it is. "It's almost indestructible and light—good for this kind of leg."

"Here, I'll help you put it on."

"I can do it myself," I declare, in my most assertive voice. I have to. I have to do it all by myself.

I swallow hard, put it on and begin walking, while Nils calls out suggestions and comes over at times, to walk me through when I get stuck.

"It needs adjustments to the length and a few other places. Maybe the next time it'll be ready to take home, little girl. Ask your parents to bring a pair of flat shoes on the next visiting day. We'll get you all set to take off." Nils is beaming a smile straight at me.

Finally, it's December 14, 1963, the day I leave the hospital. It's one week since I began wearing the leg every day, and almost three months since I was admitted. I celebrated my twelfth birthday at Shriners. Last Christmas I was in the hospital in Manhattan with one leg, and this year it looks like I have two legs again. A lot has happened in one year.

It's the first time my family sees me in the new leg. I'm using two underarm crutches, recommended by Nils for the first few months. He said I could graduate to one and, he hoped to none, as I got used to wearing the leg.

"Wow—look at you, Karen." All five of them, my three brothers and my parents, are staring at me. My two youngest brothers run up to hug me, almost knocking me over. Billy, hangs back, looking away, as if he's bored. I'm wearing a thick cotton stocking over the wooden leg, with tights over both legs, a skirt, a blouse, and a thick wool coat. I feel like a stranger in a strange land. I have little to say; I'm tired. Like when I left Memorial Hospital—everyone is excited except me. I'm embarrassed to be wearing this fifteen-pound wooden leg, walking slow and feeling clumsy. I feel like I'm causing trouble for my family.

When we're a few miles from the hospital, the celebration plans are announced. "Guess where we're going?" my mother asks.

My eleven-year-old brother Billy pipes up. "We're going to a tree farm to cut down a Christmas tree."

I'm preoccupied. How did I even manage to get the leg in the car? I eke out a faint, "Oh, that's nice."

At the tree farm my brothers pile out of the car and run ahead, full of vim and vigor. My parents keep their distance as I maneuver my way out of the back seat, lifting the big leg, and transferring the crutches I need to balance.

"I can do it myself," I insist. Something about anyone getting too close terrifies me. I'm on the verge of tears, and I will not cry.

As soon as I'm out, they begin walking ahead.

"Look at all those trees," my mother says. "Can you smell the pine?" My father, a true city boy, is not impressed. For him, a tree from the local concrete lot, pre-cut, money donated to the Boy Scouts, is the best.

I can hardly keep up with the slowest of the slow that day. The terrain is uneven, and the walk into where the trees begin seems like miles. I struggle in silence, breathless, unable to speak. The overwhelming physical challenge of walking on frozen clumps of grass and dirt, with the weight of the leg strapped around my waist and dangling down to the ground, is consuming all of my energy. It's the first time I'm walking outside. I focus on making everything seem okay, trying to smile, to be grateful and happy.

Fear, rage, sadness are churning—all I know is shame. I'm a stranger in my own body. I should be grateful. I'm lucky to have this new leg. I should be walking faster and laughing. I was looking forward to leaving the hospital—now I long to go back.

———※———

A few weeks after I arrive home from Shriners Hospital, in the winter of 1964, I have my first appointment with Dr. Franklin, our family doctor and the man who sponsored me into Shriners. It was a grand gesture on his part, knowing my family for just over a year. He's a Mason, and I gather it's an honorable thing to sponsor a child.

All care is free until age sixteen, so for my family it was an amazing gift. It would have been financially difficult for my parents to fund the cost of the new leg, even with my father's insurance.

Dr. Franklin's office is on Main Street in Flemington, a five-block walk from our house on East Main. I've had the leg for a little over a month, and I'm still using two underarm crutches for balance and support. The sidewalk is uneven, so I walk with my head down, vigilantly searching for obstacles. I'm quickly becoming a whiz at simultaneous focused attention and broader awareness, so I look up and smile at neighbors as we pass on the street.

"Karen, how wonderful to see you. And you, Mrs. Witt," Mr. Neilson, a neighbor from across the street, says as he takes my hand and looks straight into my eyes. "Looks like you're getting along just fine." His empathy annoys me, and I instantly feel like a cat with her back up. Everyone in this town seems to love me—it's like they see me as a brave soldier returned from battle. It embarrasses me.

"She's doing great," my mother makes eye contact with me, then jumps in before I can speak, as if she's worried I'll say something wrong.

"Well, that's just terrific," he says as he pulls me close and hugs my shoulders. I feel revulsion deep in my gut and want to scream out "mind your own business!" It irritates me that so many people know what happened to me. I'm suspicious of any tenderness—it leaves me feeling exposed, pitied, and like I have to live up to something.

And there's another powerful feeling, coming from the same deep place: I feel special, in a way I don't quite understand, and secretly bask in it.

———

The waiting room is up a short flight of wooden stairs. I go up one-by-one, dragging the wooden leg up each time my good foot steps up. Inside it's crowded with people of all ages. As soon as I walk in, all eyes are on me, darting toward me and quickly away, so as not to stare. It's hard for onlookers to tell what exactly the problem is with my leg. Most people have no idea it's a wooden leg. They see my stiff, limping gait, glance back and forth at me and the leg, maybe whisper to their neighbor about it.

A child yells out "Hey, what's wrong with your leg?" His mother cowers in embarrassment, cupping her hand over his mouth, sternly whispering, "Shush, you don't ask such things." I notice this and feel like I'm causing discomfort for everyone around me.

"How nice to see you, Karen," the doctor says opening his arm to the side to welcome us in. "That leg looks terrific. How are you, Doris? Are things going alright?" I force a smile. I have to be a nice, polite girl. I'm afraid of this doctor. He's big and gruff. My mother says I should be grateful to him for being so good to me. "Karen's doing fine, Doctor. She's wearing her new leg all day. She'll be going back to school next week. The school's arranged for the bus to pick her up. I just don't know how to thank you for all you've done for us."

"Good, good. Come over here, Karen. Let me take a look at that leg. I'd like to see how you wear it," he says as he lifts my shirt up. I'm wearing pants and a sweater that comes down over my hips. "Turn around, let me see the back. Looks like you've gained a little weight. You know, if you get too fat you won't be able to walk in the leg." He turns to my mother.

"We'll get her on a thousand-calorie diet. The food must've been good at the hospital," he chuckles.

I'd been skinny as a rail the last four years. Now, when I tighten the straps on the bucket so the leg stays on, a roll of flesh poofs out over the top of the bucket. No one has ever called me fat and hearing him say it scares me. My father's mother, Grandma Witt, is fat and my mother always talks about how much she dislikes it. When we see a fat girl somewhere she says something like "she has such a pretty face, why does she let herself go like that?" The last thing I want to be is fat—fat is shameful.

The diet is a one-page sample of three meals. Dr. Franklin tells my mother to limit sugary and fried foods.

I take to losing weight like a zealot. My mother helps by buying lettuce and vegetables and the kind of bread and cereal the diet suggests. Over the next several months I lose pounds but the roll of flesh still bulges out over the top of the bucket. I ramp it up a notch thinking if a thousand calories is good, eight hundred, or even five hundred or less, is better. Soon, my daily staple is a few bites of pot roast and lots of lettuce. I weigh about ninety-five pounds with the fifteen-pound leg and miss my period for months at a time.

"You're not eating enough," my mother insists.

"I'm not hungry, I ate lunch," I snap back as I get up to call my girlfriend, Mary. "And don't think you're talking on that phone all night," my mother yells after me, as I pull the long coiled cord on our kitchen wall phone into my bedroom.

3   First Date

Your present circumstances don't determine where you go;
they merely determine where you start.

/ Nido Qube

I TAKE THE BUS TO SCHOOL IN the seventh and eighth grade, even though all the kids who live on my block walk.

"Good morning, Karen." The bus driver gets off the bus, takes my books and waits patiently, as I pull myself up the three high steps. The kids save the front seat for me.

When we arrive at the school, Steve smiles at me as he grabs my books and rushes out the door. "I got your books today."

"I can get them myself," I yell as he's hopping off the bus. He's halfway up the walk by the time I get off. I know he's playing with me. Still, waves of shame wash over and through me at every expression of kindness. I want to do it all myself. I want to be one of the regular kids, not the one everyone tries to take care of.

I'm walking without crutches now. Between classes I carry my books cradled in my arm and resting on my good hip, like all the girls do. My gait is slower and clumsier, but I feel better when I look like one of the crowd though circumstances constantly remind me of my difference.

No one asks me about my missing leg or the wooden one. I keep it covered with a thick cotton stocking under regular pantyhose. My legs are different colors. The wooden one is darker and duller. The pantyhose tear with the slightest knock of the wood against a hard surface, something I don't feel and sometimes can't hear. Some of the girls tell me I'm lucky I don't have to take gym, but never ask how I feel about it. I miss it terribly.

My situation is something everyone knows about and no one talks about.

———◆———

At my eighth-grade graduation I have to climb the stairs to the auditorium stage, walk across to the principal, shake hands and take my diploma. I'm self-conscious about my shape, my gait, my slowness, as I walk alone in front of so many people, on display in my misshapen body. My father takes a picture of me as I make my way.

The next week when I see the picture, I'm mortified at how ugly I look. My wooden leg is thrust way out in front of my body. My shoulders and torso are distorted in a pretzel shape, with my arms flailing out to the side. My eyes are diligently staring ahead, concentrating on the principal and the path and my mouth is in a serious pucker-frown.

"I hate this picture. I'm ripping it up!" I shout as I try to grab at the picture my mother holds. I have to get rid of it so it's not the truth.

Holding the photo behind her back my mother replies, "I like it. What do you think, Dad?" she asks in a way I feel is mocking.

"Give it to me. I look awful. I don't want anyone else to see that." I'm frantic, trying to get it from her.

"Stop it, Karen. Leave your mother alone. It's the only picture we have of your graduation, and we're not going to let you rip it up." My father defends my mother, as usual. He doesn't look at either of us. He's busy changing the channels on the TV. He wants me to stop fighting with my mother so she will leave him alone.

———◆———

In the summer before high school, I give up swimming at the Flemington Community Pool and, instead, sit on a bench in the hot sun, wearing long pants and shirts. No matter that swimming had been one of my favorite things. I'm almost fourteen, a year and a half into my life with a gigantic wooden leg that I take off only when I go to bed. I tell myself (and others if they ask) that I want to make it easy for people by looking as normal as possible at the pool. Kids don't yell out "that girl has one leg!" and that makes it easier on their mothers who don't have to get all embarrassed and flustered. Everyone, including my family, seems to feel more comfortable around me when I look like I have two legs.

Today, while I'm showing some kids at the pool how my wooden leg bends at the knee and ankle, Robbie, the lifeguard, comes over and sits on the bench next to me. He's a tall, cute, tan boy who's older than me. He just graduated from high school. His chest is shiny with sweat, and he smells of coconut tanning oil.

"Can I see, too?" he asks, as I am yanking my pant leg down to cover up the hole in the knee.

"Uh-sure." I'm suddenly very self-conscious. Does he really want to see this leg? The kids are still standing around. They've already asked a bunch of questions, touched and moved the lower part of the leg. But no one sees how it wraps around my waist and covers so much of me that I have to take it off to go to the bathroom.

"What's it made of?" He hesitates, seeming slightly uncomfortable.

"It's real wood," a little boy pipes up. "It's weird."

"Hey, y'wanna go to the movies tomorrow?" Robbie asks as he gets up to go back to his chair.

"Sure, I guess so," I say. He tells me to write my phone number down and bring it to him. A giddy excitement and an overwhelming desire to be loved and wanted by a boy washes over me. My insides are pulsing and sloshing every which way. They want my outsides to jump up and shout "a boy likes me!" but I can't move. I'm stuck to the bench by a panic that is slowly oozing into every cell in my body. Do I look at Robbie and smile? I have to walk over there and give him my phone number. What should I say? I'm back and forth between elation and terror the rest of the afternoon.

At supper that evening I say to my mother, "I'm going to the movies with Robbie, the lifeguard, tomorrow. He asked me at the pool today." This will be my first date.

"Are you asking if you can?" She looks serious like she really wants to know.

"I really want to go. You have to say yes." I'm pleading, on the defensive, and I'm playing on her sympathy. I overheard my aunt and her talking about how they fear that boyfriends, marriage, and motherhood might be difficult for me.

"You'll have to ask your father, see what he says." He's frequently not home for supper. Tonight it's my three younger brothers, my mother, and me.

My brothers chant in unison, "Karen has a boyfriend, Karen has a boyfriend."

Feeling humiliated and enraged, I shout, "Shut up! I don't want to ask Dad. Why can't I just go?"

"Stop it, all of you. That's it until your father gets home." My mother turns to me, points at the table and says, "Now eat something."

Frustrated and scared I defiantly say, "I'm not hungry." My mother and I have struggled around food since the family doctor put me on a thousand-calorie diet a couple of years before. I'm ninety-five pounds now and still want to lose weight.

Later that evening when my father gets home I ask him if I can go to the movies with Robbie. My mother's gone to work for a few hours as a retail clerk.

"Whatever your mother says. It's up to her," he says, never moving his eyes from the TV. This is the first time I've asked him for permission for something. My mother usually takes charge unless she feels she needs backup support, like when my brother Billy gets in trouble. Dad and I have a familiarity because we've driven together to many medical appointments over the last four years. But we've never talked about school or boyfriends or anything personal.

The next morning I do my best to make my case. "You have to let me go. Robbie likes me. I want to go. Please Mom, please." She finally gives in.

Friday evening, as I walk into the kitchen, my mother glances up, rolls her eyes and says, "You're not wearing that, are you?" She's cleaning up after supper. My brothers are watching TV in the living room, and my father is out with his buddies after work.

"It's none of your business." I sass back. I'm wearing faded patchwork, blue-jean bell-bottom pants and an oversized men's white shirt.

"You're going on a date. Don't you want to look..."

"I don't care. Just leave me alone," I snap. I'm ashamed that I can't wear cute, girlie clothes, like cut-off shorts and pretty fitted tops, because I know they'll look awful on me. I try to hide my shame and longing from myself and everyone else. I'm a naive girl who believes babies come out of a miraculous opening in their mother's bellies—and has no idea how they get in there—and I have no clue what to do on a date.

The bell rings.

"Hi Mrs. Witt," Robbie stands in the doorway looking into the living room. My brothers turn their attention to him. They know him from the pool and like him.

"Hey guys. How's it going?" he asks. He turns to me. "Ready?"

I can't wait to get out of the house. "Yeah," I say, head down, eyes raised and looking up at him.

"Where're we going?" I ask as I hobble one step at a time down the front stoop. I'm searching my trembling insides for the perfect thing to say and do.

"The drive-in on Highway 31." He says the name of the movie but it doesn't register. I'm totally focused on unobtrusively lifting my dead-weight leg into the car, a big, two door, green Chevy with a wide front seat and lots of leg room. The inside smells like cigarettes and after shave.

I sit like a statue with a moving head, looking over at Robbie, trying my best to smile through a thick fog of fear. At the theater, he hooks the speaker up to the window. "You've Lost that Lovin' Feelin'" by the Righteous Brothers pours into the car. All the spaces around us are full. Pretty girls, wearing short shorts and tank tops, sit on the hoods and roofs of cars, smoking and sipping drinks of something. I see from the screen ad that the movie is Bikini Beach with Frankie Avalon.

"Wanna come with me to the refreshment stand?" he asks.

"No, that's ok. I'll wait here." I can't walk along next to him with this leg and this body and these clothes. He comes back with popcorn and a soda with two straws. We munch salty popcorn, listening to "Wooly Bully" and the Beatles until the movie starts. He tries to engage me in conversation, asking about school and my family. I want to talk, but can only squeak out one-word answers.

As it gets dark, Robbie pulls my stiff, panicked body across the wide front seat, hugging my shoulders. I hold myself so still I can feel the blood pumping through the veins in my fingers. It's painful to smile. I'm afraid to breathe.

He starts kissing me, rubbing his hands up and down my back. Do I keep my mouth closed or open it? He holds me close for a few minutes and then pushes me away slightly, moving his hands to my breasts and belly. God, I'm so fat. And now he knows about the hard, plastic bucket covering my waist. I suck every ounce of me inward, down a deep, dark hole. I want Robbie to love me. I want to do whatever he wants. I despise myself for being the girl with the wooden leg and the ugly body.

Robbie continues to move his hands around my body. I like the feeling of being caressed. There's a tingling inside my skin, like river rapids coursing up my thigh and into my pelvis. It's warm and wet, a new feeling. It delights and frightens me. He unzips my pants, unfastens the straps on the bucket and pulls me half out of it, rubbing my crotch and thigh. He takes my hand and puts it on his crotch. I move my fingers a tiny bit. My hand and arm are incapable of doing more. It's as if they are not connected to me. My mind and body are not together in this car.

We don't have sex. Robbie's shirt is unbuttoned and his chest is wet with sweat. I can feel his rapid heartbeat. He sighs a few breathy syllables, asks if I like it. I do like it and, I'm stiff with terror at the same time. I eke out a barely audible yes. I feel out of control—not knowing what's happening in my body terrifies me.

We lounge, embracing for some time and then he sits upright in the driver's seat, leaving me to get back into my leg and clothes. Since I can't stand, I slide down so I'm practically lying on the seat and do my best to straighten the wad of ace bandage that's wrapped around my waist over my underpants. I suck in my belly and work on refastening the straps on the bucket and closing up my pants. He looks away, says nothing and offers no help. I'm mortified.

On the ride home I sit close to him, staring straight out, grabbing quick side glimpses of his face with my darting eyes. He seems happy, like he likes me, and kisses me as I leave the car. Maybe this is what a date is. Maybe I did the right thing.

At the pool the next day I want him to greet me with a hug or kiss, something special to let everyone know I'm his girlfriend. He barely looks at me.

"How was the date?" my mother asks that evening.

"Fine." There's nothing else to say.

"Will you have another one?"

I seize the moment, declaring, "I don't even care. I don't like him, anyway." I refuse to feel the pain of disappointment.

4   Prom Princess

We know what we are, but not what we may be.

/ William Shakespeare

THE HIGH SCHOOL IS A SIX-BLOCK WALK from our house. I have the option to ride a bus which will re-route to pick me up. In the summer of 1965, before school begins, my mother tries to talk to me into riding.

"I AM NOT riding the bus. I can walk. The school is only a few blocks away," I'm adamant, leaving no room for discussion.

"Don't raise your voice to me, Karen. Why don't you see how walking is before you say you decide? It looks like a short distance, but there's the long driveway." She's yelling from the kitchen. I'm in my room a few feet down a hallway.

"NO! I'm walking." It feels like a power struggle. I won't let my mother have her way. I have to do my best to look like everyone else, which means essentially denying that I have a wooden leg, which means denying that the real one is no longer attached at my hip. The walking causes abrasions and sores on my right butt and around my waist. I tell no one, take care of them alone in the bathroom.

In the evenings, I spend hours doing exercises that I make up. Things like pounding my butt, my leg, and my belly on the floor to the count of one hundred or more. I'm certain this will somehow re-adjust my shape, make it more like other girls' bodies. I take the wooden leg off only during these exercises, when I'm sleeping, and every time I go to the bathroom.

I meet up with, Leba and Jan, two of my three best girlfriends on the way to school in the mornings. Mary, the third, rides a bus from outside downtown.

"Hey, Leba. Nice skirt," I say as we cross the street. We met in freshman year when her family moved from another town. She's medium height, with tight, curly blondish hair. I'm about as tall as Leba, and still very thin (except all I can see is the roll of skin that bulges out over the bucket of the leg), and I wear my long blondish hair in a tightly curled, chin-length flip, or pulled back high on my head in a ponytail. I have short bangs cut straight across my forehead.

Right before we cross the highway to the school grounds, we meet up with Jan. She moved to town in junior year, and Mary, Leba and I are still deciding how much we like her. She's cute, petite and smart, with longish brown hair. She lives in a big house, and her father is a professional of some sort. Leba's father is not with her mother, and my father works in a factory. Mary lives in a big house, and her family owns a local business.

"Hi, girls." Jan's waiting on the sidewalk in front of her house for us. "Those are really cute culottes, Karen. I love the orange plaid material."

"I made them last night," I boast, nonchalantly. My father's mother, the one my mother calls fat, is a fantastic seamstress. She sewed to support her five children after her husband left her, sometime in the 1940s. I love watching her sew, tat, and crochet. We don't see her much, so I never have the chance to learn from her. In junior high and high school, I take sewing and cooking in Home Economics and am a pretty good seamstress. I buy fabric at W.T. Grant's, the five-and-ten cent store where I work as a cashier on the weekends. I started work there as a floor girl when I turned fourteen and got working papers. Several nights a week, after school, I descend into the basement, to my other grandma's old sewing machine, and whip up something to wear to school the next day. Store-bought clothes don't fit me well: the waist is usually too small to go around the bucket of the wooden leg. Most tops or dresses for girls my age are form fitted for someone with a much different form than I. I like clothes that hide my form, like A-line jumpers, and skirts with elastic waists. I wear oversized shirts to hide my midsection.

Once we get to school, Leba, Jan, and I look for Mary and greet her as she makes her way in.

"Hey Mar," we all three blurt out in unison. "How'd you get here this morning?" Mary is a beautiful, black-haired Italian girl, with a curvy figure and a bright laugh. Her older brothers and father adore her. She's wildly popular with boys—her desirability brings boys into our girl foursome and it grows into a fun coed group.

"My brother dropped me off and I met up with John, that's why I'm later than usual. I think he asked me out."

"John, the football star?" Leba asks, wide eyed. "What about Grover and Terry and Rick?"

"I'm not going steady with any of them. We're all just friends. I haven't dated a boy from outside our little circle. He seems sweet. Maybe I'll say yes. We'll have someone, besides Grover, to cheer for at the football games."

Terry's a cute, tall, crewcut blond, blue-eyed boy with a soft, mellow way about him. Grover's a lanky, dark-curly-haired boy with infectious exuberance, and Rick's a shorter, Ivy league looker with a brain. They take turns hanging out with Jan, Mary and, sometimes, Leba. I'm good friends with all of them but never date anyone. Leba has a steady boyfriend, Jack, for a few months. He's a sweet guy, tall, and skinny. He wears glasses and looks a little nerdy. He's on the fringes of our group, except for the months he dates Leba.

We're all totally and completely involved in high school. Rick is the president of the class for a few years and graduates as valedictorian. Terry and Grover are bright and play sports. I'm on Student Council for two years, on the honor roll every year, and love math and science. Jan and Leba are brainy, social, and are involved in girls' sports. Mary loves all sports, especially wrestling, and is a bit of a tomboy. She's a good student, works in her father's business on weekends. Mary and I, best friends through most of high school (though loyalties shift at times for short periods), keep score for the wrestling team. We ride the bus to away games and sit at a table on the edge of the mat, manually recording points and holds. I would never have had the opportunity if not for Mary, and I love getting to know the boys and learning all about wrestling. Everyone is friendly and accepting of me, but no one flirts with me like they do with Mary. It's something I try hard not to think about.

Mary's much savvier than I am. I'm happy to be second best when I'm with her, happy she likes me. Our team is very good, competing in regional and state meets several years in a row.

We're all in the same grade. Over the course of sophomore and junior years, we celebrate everyone's sixteenth birthday. We arrange a party, usually in Jan's backyard because it's big and close to the school. My sixteenth is on October 12, 1967.

"What do you want for your birthday, Karen?" Mary asks one day as we meet up between classes.

"I want one of those watches that sits on top of the fat leather band that goes around your wrist. Jan has one." Every birthday kid gets one gift from the whole crew, usually ten to twelve kids.

The day of my birthday it's beautiful, sunny weather. I tell my mother the day before that my party is from six to eight at Jan's house, but she forgets.

"Where do you think you're going at this time of the night? It's too late for you to go to work." Her tone is punitive and disapproving.

"I told you yesterday. It's the day of my sixteenth birthday party with my friends. It's at Jan's house, around the corner." My mother's met all my girlfriends. She knows Mary the best. She knows Leba's mother and almost nothing about Jan, except that she lives at the end of Pennsylvania Avenue, one of the streets with the biggest houses. She's met Jan a few times, but she's never met her family. Some kids' parents come to their parties for a few minutes, to say hello and happy birthday. Jan's mom and dad usually pop out of the house once or twice to see how things are going. I don't invite my mother. Our relationship is strained and I don't trust what she might tell people about me.

The party goes as usual. I get my watch and love it. I wear it every day. We dance as a group, a few couples dance together, and we talk and play some games and eat finger food. None of us drink alcohol. Most of us are probably not sexually active.

"How was the party?" my mother asks when she gets home from her shift at the local department store.

"It was fun. See my watch. It's from my friends. I really wanted one. I love it," I go on, almost too excited to stop talking.

"That's nice. You never seem to like the presents we get you."

"Yes, I do. I like the charms you got me for the charm bracelet," I say defensively.

"Yeah, but you never wear it." It feels like an accusation.

"I do sometimes." I turn back to my brothers, father, and the TV. My mother goes upstairs to change. The charm bracelet from Dr. Francis is full of charms my parents and other family members have given me in the five years since the operation. I don't like wearing it. It reminds me of the truth; my right leg is gone. I try to forget that.

———————

I go to all the football games, usually with one or more of my girlfriends or with some other girls I know in school. I'm known to most all of the four hundred kids in the class of 1974. There's always some girl or boy who wants to sit with me on the bus to the games or in the bleachers once we get there. This should be something that makes me happy and proud—my classmates seem to like me and want to spend time with me. Instead, because I wholeheartedly believe that the reason for this is that everyone feels sorry for me, it's something I can't embrace. A tiny survivor part of me, the part that revels in being special, goes with it and only lets on about the feel sorry part in a self-effacing way, like when someone says, "Wow, you're amazing!" I say, "Not really—anyone would do the same. What else can I do—stay in bed?" I have a harshness that I'm not aware of. It's my attempt to hold back whatever pokes at my vulnerability.

Despite my self-protective distancing, I manage to be friendly and outgoing in school. I'm smart, do well in all my classes, and would rather be involved in school than spend time at home around my mother, where I'm usually irritable. Since my teachers and classmates are not as close as my mother, the wounded part of me can hide more easily. I try to anticipate what reactions others will have to my situation and smooth it all over. I want other people to feel comfortable around me, so I do whatever I imagine will make that happen.

———

Several times throughout the four years of high school, I have to go back to Mr. Malone's to get my leg fixed or adjusted. There's always something squeaking or loose or too short. I go to Manhattan for doctors' appointments for what I eventually understand was bone cancer in my right thigh. Those visits come less and less frequently as the years go by and the risk of recurrence decreases. The wooden leg appointments seem never ending.

My father takes off work to take me, not necessarily willingly. I complain and whine and argue about the awful noise or my worsening limp, and finally we make an appointment and go. It takes most of a day, about an hour and a half drive, longer with traffic. My mother never goes. She refuses to drive, despite the fact that she's had her license for a few years. Yet, she bothers me every time to ask Mr. Malone to pad the bucket on the wooden leg so it matches my other butt. There's a bump of foam as big as half a cantaloupe covered with the same gold colored leather that covers the thigh. The men in the workshop are all super nice and try their best to make the back look even and curvy. It's just that when there's enough padding to make it look right, it throws off my sitting, pushing me over to the left and preventing the foot from touching the ground. I hate how it's uneven as much as my mother does, and I've told her a thousand times that they can't make it any better, but she still mentions it every time.

My father and I don't say much in the car on the way down or back. He leaves me at the office and goes off to get himself coffee and a newspaper. He's always there in the waiting room when I'm done. We look at each other on the way home from every trip and decide, without words, to stop at one of the very first McDonald's Golden Arches in Philadelphia. There's no drive-thru or inside seating. My father gets out, goes to the window to order. It's a fish sandwich, fries, and a Pepsi for him and a strawberry shake for me. I eat a few of his fries and refuse to eat anything else for the rest of the day.

I have the same wooden leg through most of high school. As I grow taller, Mr. Malone adds slices of wood, the size of the ankle and half an inch or an inch thick, whatever's needed. The length of the foot to knee gradually gets longer than my good leg, calf to knee. When I sit, the knee sticks up higher than my good knee and looks awful. One day, as I'm walking down the crowded metal stairs between classes I trip, and the calf of the wooden leg bangs into the step and breaks off just above the ankle. When I look down it's hanging off, swaying inside the cotton and nylon stocking covering. I'm ashamed, mortified. Classmates—walking up and down around me—slow down to look.

"Are you alright, Karen? Can we help?" These are the unending chants coming from kids I don't even know.

"No no, I'm fine. Go around me; it's fine. Someone called my mother. She'll be here soon with some crutches." I'm cool, calm and collected on the outside, dying on the inside. Everybody really knows about the wooden leg now.

When my mother arrives she asks, seemingly exasperated, "How did you do that, Karen? Were you hopping down the steps?" She says it in a way I feel it's my fault; I could've prevented it.

"I tripped. Daddy has to take me to Mr. Malone's tomorrow. I don't want to miss school." I spit it all out in a jumble. My whole body is shaking inside.

"He may not be able to get off work tomorrow. You can use your crutches for school tomorrow," she says like it's a fine option. We banter back and forth without even glancing at each other.

"NO, no I can't. I can't use crutches in school. I have to go to Mr. Malone's tomorrow. He has to take me, he has to." I'm desperately pleading.

"We'll see," she says as we get out of the car.

My father arranges to get the day off, and we go to Mr. Malone's. He fixes my leg and begins the process for me to get a new one. "You've had this one long enough. We'll get started on a new one." He hugs my shoulders.

In my high school, the junior prom is the big extravagant event for the upperclassmen. We have a senior ball but that's less formal and less well attended. Everyone who's anyone goes to the junior prom.

I'm one of the organizers on the prom committee, a hodgepodge of random volunteers. We choose a Grecian theme and spend the weeks before making decorations and planning the transformation of our gym into a Grecian garden. We make banners, trees, olive branches, and cardboard pillars with the help of the art department. The home economics department helps with the punch and cookies. We set up a photo booth, manned by a local photographer who volunteers his service for free. There are chaperones to invite. One of our favorite calculus teachers, Mrs. Ziegler, and her husband, were killed that year in a plane crash. We make a special memorial area for her.

All my girlfriends are paired up for the night. I'm not asked during much of the planning phase, but I'm excited to help, holding off my disappointment by keeping busy with school activities and sassing my mother whenever she asks me about school or the prom. I don't give her many opportunities.

71

Then Jack, Leba's former boyfriend, asks me about a week before the prom. We meet up in the hallway by my locker when not too many other kids are around.

"Hi, Karen." He catches me off guard.

"Hey, Jack." I know him fairly well because his mother and mine are close acquaintances. He's not a sexy, popular boy and definitely not someone I dream about going to the prom with.

"Do you have a date for the prom?" He's shy and hesitant. I'd not noticed that before.

"No, but it doesn't matter. I've had a lot of fun planning and getting ready for it. It'll be fun for the kids who go." That's me, ever the denier. I'm dying to go to the prom with a handsome football player.

"Would you like to go with me?" He's looking at me and away.

"Ok, sure. That would be nice." I'm happy and at the same time ashamed that he'll be my date. I hope no one thinks I like him as a boyfriend.

So begins the added frenzy. I'd planned to make my dress so that evening my mother takes me to the fabric store and we pick out green taffeta with a lace overlay. I make a long A-line dress, slightly fitted at the bodice above the bucket of my wooden leg, with a high neck and long sleeves. Shoes are another story since pretty ones never look good on the wooden leg, and heels are out because the foot's flat. I tell myself the dress is long and no one will be looking at my shoes. I'm terrified at the thought of trying to look pretty or sexy, certain that I'll look ridiculous and people will talk about it behind my back. Maybe they already are.

On prom night, Jack picks me up wearing a tux and carrying a pretty wrist corsage. I decline his help in putting it on, afraid of the closeness. It's my second date, and since the first, I've not been touched, hugged, or kissed by a boy who likes me. Jack's mother drives us to the school and offers to pick us up after.

We mingle with our friends, commenting on each other's outfits, corsages, and how great the gym looks. It's high energy and it feels like everyone in our class of four hundred is there. We stand in line to have our picture taken between the Grecian columns. Jack convinces me to dance a few slow dances, promising not to laugh or go too fast. I keep my distance as we move minimally across the floor, longing to be held close and to feel special, but I can't risk the rejection. I tell myself it's Jack, someone I don't really like. Anyway, it takes all my concentration to maneuver the wooden leg with my back, up and down, as we choppity-chop our way in circles.

Toward the end of the evening, the prom queen is announced. The whole junior class had the chance to vote for whoever they wanted. It's likely half the class took the time to cast a ballot. Second and third runners-up are called, two of the prettiest girls in our class.

"First runner-up—Karen Witt." A wave of terror comes over me— instead of being happy, honored, flattered, I feel humiliation. They picked me because they feel sorry for me. I join the other two on the stage. It's all I can do to smile and be gracious as the announcer hands me my flowers. The crowd cheers and is excited and happy for me, but I'm sure they're silently laughing. How could she win a prom queen spot? She's clumsy and that ugly body. I'm sure that's what they're saying.

Finally, Lisa's name is called. She, too, is shocked. She's a very popular girl, one of my better friends, but she's not particularly beautiful or model-like. We all four hug and pose for pictures. There are a few more dances, and then it's time to leave.

When he drops me off, Jack tells my mother about the first runner-up part. If he hadn't, I would've skipped it, said the prom was good and headed off to bed.

"How nice, Karen. So many people in this town really care about you," my mother says. "Did you hear that, Dad? Karen was runner-up to the prom queen."

"Yeah, I heard. That's nice," he mumbles over the TV.

I never mention it again and if someone else does, I quickly change the subject. It's mortifying, and yet somehow it does feel special when I think of it.

5   Off to College

You do not need to know precisely what is happening, or exactly where it is all going. What you need is to recognize the possibilities and challenges offered by the present moment, and to embrace them with courage, faith and hope.

/ Thomas Merton

SENIOR YEAR OF HIGH SCHOOL, 1968-69, IS busy with upper-class activities, SATs, and college applications. My father wants me to go to Montclair State College to study to be a teacher. He says teaching is the best job for a woman for all the obvious reasons: summers, vacations and holidays off, and having the same schedule as your kids.

The last thing I want to do is what my father wants me to do. I fantasize about going to California—the farthest away from my mother I can imagine. I don't know why our relationship is so contemptuous or even that it is. I just know I don't like being around her.

I graduate fourth in my class of four hundred students, and I'm voted friendliest. Another honor that brings with it a mix of secret feelings including delight and humiliation.

Once graduation is over, I hardly see my girlfriends. We're all working to save money for college. I'm cashiering at W.T. Grants, the town's five and dime, and babysitting for the local rabbi's children a few hours a week. I go through the volunteer training at the nearby hospital to become a candy striper. The volunteer department is reluctant to take me on at first, concerned I might not hold up with all the walking. I beg them to give me a try. I want to see how it feels being in the hospital as a helper. Despite the fitted pinafore uniform that barely buttons over the bucket of my wooden leg, I love walking the halls, delivering mail and flowers, greeting the occasional patient, and giving directions to visitors from my perch at the front desk. People seem to light up and smile when they see me, and I have less the feeling of humiliation and more the sense of being special when I'm in the hospital.

Finances force me to settle on Douglass College, the all-girls sister school to Rutgers in New Jersey. My excitement in leaving home comes to a quick and unexpected end soon after I arrive and meet my dorm mate, Janie. She's a cute, petite blond, perky, and self-confident. Her father is a Rutgers' professor, and she feels right at home in the college environment. I'm outwardly confident, yet have no idea how to be with her and the other whole-bodied girls in the dorm. I had no clue I would be so uncomfortable outside my familiar digs.

I watch myself smile on the outside and withdraw deep into a swirling mess of confusion on the inside. As the panic ebbs and flows inside my skin, I hear myself talking about how happy I am to be there, what a great campus it is, how I can't wait to start classes and meet people. I have no words for what's churning inside and even if I knew how to talk about it I wouldn't, because there's no one to talk about it with. I trust no one, least of all myself. I'm ashamed that I'm uncomfortable and I refuse to let anyone see.

One day in the first week Janie informs me that we're having a party in our dorm.

"Hey, Friday we're having a party with some of the boys from one of the Rutgers' dorms. My father helped arrange it," she says smiling and shaking her long, silky-blonde locks around.

"Where?" I ask.

"Here, in the big room. It'll be fun, a chance to meet some cute guys."

A big wave of panic quakes to my bones. What cute boys would want to meet me? What do I wear on this ugly body? All the girls will have on miniskirts or shorts, maybe they'll dance.

"Great. That'll be fun." The words come out effortlessly.

The big day comes. Our dorm is full of attractive, young girls and guys flirting up a storm. I stand on the fringes, smiling with dread that someone might notice me and ask me something. I'm comfortable talking about my leg with oldsters and kids—it's my responsibility to make others feel comfortable around me. I take it seriously. I do what I can to make my situation look like a breeze. In part it is. Adapting to physically being on one leg is easy compared to the inner turmoil I feel creeping up to choke me. Everything feels different here—I'm terrified that someone will want to know about me. I avoid taking the wooden leg off in front of my roommate, waiting till the last minute before bed to unbuckle it, unwrap the ace bandage around my waist, lean it against the wall near my bed and turn out the lights. I hope she doesn't see or ask any questions. She's everything I want to be, everything I'm ashamed I'm not.

"Hi Karen, I'm Janie's father. How do you like it here at Douglass so far?" A handsome man in a neat jacket and tie is standing next to me, smiling. He's friendly, gentle and seems genuine. I'm startled and anxious.

"Oh, it's good," I say, all confident seeming and positive.

"What are you planning to study?" he asks.

"Oh, not sure. Haven't thought about it much." Please stop talking to me, go away, I pray as I stand there stiffly smiling, hoping he doesn't smell the terror building under my skin. We stand there for another minute or so glancing at each other and then away, until he excuses himself to say hi to an old friend.

Truth be told, I had no idea what I wanted to study. I never even really thought much about the college part. I wanted only to get away from home. I'm smart enough, and my high school counselors and teachers said college would be a good path for me. Neither my mother nor father attended college. Only a few of my maternal cousins have gone. I love school and studying, and I must have thought college would be like high school with the added bonus of not having to see my mother. Instead, it's threatening to disrupt my neat little inner package; it's challenging the little self-confidence I have. I know none of this in that moment, of course, I only hope for the party to end so I can bury myself in bed. And I know I have to get out of there.

The next day I call my mother insisting that Douglass is not the right place for me.

"I have to leave, immediately. It's just the wrong place." My tone is forceful and demanding.

"Karen, you've only been there for a few days," she notes.

"I know but I'm sure this is not the place for me. It's not a good fit. I don't want to go to school here," I'm emphatic. I don't mention anything about my roommate or the party or my terror the night before. I merely insist that I have to leave.

"Are you sure?" She sounds perplexed, but she doesn't ask me if I know why I might want to leave.

"It's MY life, not yours. I'm not staying here. You have to come and get me."

"I don't know when I can do that," she barks back. "I think you're making a mistake."

"I AM NOT! I want to leave."

"I'll talk to your father and call you tomorrow."

In a few days, I take care of all the drop-out paper-work and procedures. I'm at ease with others, making lame excuses to the few people I'd met, telling them I want to work for a year to decide what I want to study. I say Janie's father helped me see that. Everyone is very nice and my rational, professional, and distant demeanor keeps people at arm's length, far enough away to not ask questions.

My mother meets me on a large flight of stone steps in front of one of the big campus buildings. She queries me again about my decision, prodding me to change my mind and stay. I adamantly insist I know what I'm doing and want to leave. "I'm leaving even if you don't take me home," I threaten.

She never suggests I might be having feelings about leaving the safety of home, or feeling like an outsider. She banters with me purely around the rational arguments. She never asks what I plan to do when back in Flemington.

When we arrive home that evening, my father is sitting in his TV chair watching some silly show. He barely acknowledges my presence before he comments.

"You better get yourself a job. You're not sitting around this house doing nothing." This feels harsh and spiteful.

I sass back. "I'm gonna be a nurse. I'll get a job at the hospital." It's a statement that truly comes out of nowhere and it shocks me. I didn't think once about what I'd do when home. Something inside takes charge to shoot my father down.

———◆———

A couple of days later I have an appointment with the Director of Nursing at the local hospital. I'd met her when I was a candy striper and, since she'd supported me when I volunteered that summer, I hope she will again.

"Hi, Karen. Nice to see you. I thought you were headed for Douglass this fall." She's sitting behind her desk, leaning forward toward me. Her voice is calm. I have the sense that she likes me.

"I did but it wasn't a good fit. I realized I really want to be a nurse. I thought maybe I could work this year and apply to nursing schools after getting some experience. Do you have any openings for nurse's aides?"

I'm self-assured, positive and almost certain she won't say no. It's like all that Douglass stuff never happened.

"What got you thinking about being a nurse?"

"Working here as a volunteer last summer was really fun. I liked the nurses and helping the patients. I feel comfortable here." The real answer is "I have no idea," but I'm eager and enthusiastic, trying to convince myself and her it would be a good thing.

"To tell the truth I'm not looking for staff, but I am thinking about trying a few of our nurse's aides on a new schedule, 6 a.m.-2:30p.m.. No one seems to be volunteering for those hours, so maybe we could plug you in temporarily on the medical floor as an experiment. See if you like it and if the shift works out for us."

"Really, wow, that would be great. I like to get up early; maybe my father can drop me off before he goes to work." I didn't give a thought to how I'd get back and forth. I want to do it and I will.

"Let me think about it today. I have to talk to some other people, see if they think it will work out. Don't you want to know what you'll be doing?" She turns her head ever so slightly to the side and is looking at me from the corner of her eyes, with a big grin. I hope she believes me.

"Yes, I do want to know. I thought blood pressures, changing beds, bathing and feeding people. Things like that."

"Will that be too much on you?" She's looking right at me again.

"No, no, I don't think so. I'm pretty strong. I think I'll be fine." I'm doing my best to convince her. There's no direct mention of my wooden leg, and I'm happy about that. I want it to not be so.

"Okay then. I'll give you a call in a day or two and let you know what I decide."

"I hope you decide yes. I really want to work here." She puts her arm around my shoulder as we walk to the door.

"So, how'd it go?" my mother asks as I get in the car outside the hospital. "Do you have a job?"

"She's gonna call me in a day or so, but I think I do have a job. She said she wants to start a new overlap shift and try it out with me. I'd work 6 a.m.-2:30 p.m."

"How're you gonna get there, Karen? Did you consider that?" She's annoyed.

"I thought you could drop me off before you take Dad to work. He goes pretty early, too." I expect her to do it. I'm not asking; I'm a tad self-righteous. "He's the one who said I had to get a job."

"I don't know who you think you are. First, you give up a scholarship to college, and now you expect us to change everything around so you can have a job at the hospital. You just better remember I'm your mother, not your servant. And you better watch how you talk to me. And wipe that puss off your face." She's mad.

We ride home in silence. There's palpable tension between us in the front seat of the Chrysler. Thankfully, it's a five-minute ride.

The nursing director calls me a couple of days later, and I go in to begin hospital orientation—a few hours of classes to hear about the way the hospital operates, things like confidentiality, communications, parking, and so on. I'm to wear a white dress uniform, with beige stockings and white shoes. No cap. White stockings and caps are for nurses. I get a plastic name tag that says Karen Witt, Nurse Aide.

My floor is "5 Medical." Kathy is the night nurse; she works midnight to eight in the morning. She orients me to my duties, which include offering mouth, face, and hand care to patients each morning, weighing patients when ordered, placing linens in the rooms for the bed changes later, emptying urine bags, helping with toileting among other things. Once the day shift comes on, I feed patients, help with baths and bed changes, run errands to the lab or kitchen when needed. There are notes to write and emergencies to assist at.

It's a busy eight hours since I cover the busiest times on the night and day shift. I love it, though. I learn how to take blood pressures, temperatures, use a stethoscope to listen to the basic heart and lung sounds. Kathy and some of the other staff teach me about different medical conditions, symptoms, medications. Kathy's a new nurse and loves her job. She takes me under her wing and encourages me to continue in nursing. She's like a big sister.

One early morning, I arrive to find Kathy dealing with an older woman who had died a few hours earlier. Kathy agreed to keep her body on the unit until the woman's husband can make it to the hospital to say his last goodbye.

"We're supposed to get the body to the morgue as soon as possible," she says as we straighten the woman's bed before her husband arrives. "I couldn't refuse her husband's plea to see her before we put her in the morgue. I figure it's the night shift, quiet, with few people around, and she's in this private room. It'll be okay."

We hear her husband walk in behind us. He leans over her body, breathing and feeding tubes removed, kisses her and sobs. Kathy and I leave the room, letting him know we'll return in ten minutes.

"What do we do with the body when he leaves?" I'm a little spooked by a dead body. Other than Gloria back at Memorial Hospital, who's body I didn't see, I've never been around a dead person.

"We'll cover her up with a special sheet, put a couple of tags on her and you and Susan (Kathy's aide on the night shift) will wheel her to the morgue. The funeral people will pick her up from there tomorrow." She's nonchalant, almost like she's talking about transferring someone from a couch to a bed. I'm a little scared, do my best to look nonplussed and confident.

Kathy, Susan, and I transfer the woman to a stretcher after we wrap her in the shroud and attach the identification tags to her toe and finger. Kathy stays on the floor while Susan and I wheel the stretcher to the elevator and down to a dark, stainless steel room in the back of the hospital on the first floor. Susan pulls out the long, flat drawer bed that we'll transfer her to. Thankfully the woman is tiny since neither Susan nor I am super strong, and I'm worried about my balance and ability to move fast enough while holding something as heavy and precious as a human body.

As we slide her between the stretcher and drawer, Susan turns her on her side and awful smelling fluid comes pouring out of her nose and mouth. It's a suffocating smell; it gags us. We look at each other sickened but keep moving, holding our breath for as long as we can.

"Oh my god, that was awful. I've never smelled anything so disgusting," Susan says as we close the morgue door squishing our faces into horrified masks and gasping, trying to fill our lungs with any air besides that air.

"Me either. I'm glad we didn't throw up. What was it from?"

"Probably from letting her sit so long after she died. She had some respiratory secretions, maybe pneumonia, and they turned foul smelling. She was in the room for almost two hours by the time we wrapped her." We head back up the elevator.

It's the start of my day.

Medical students from regional hospitals train at the medical center. They spend a month or two on a floor, working with the doctors, doing physical exams, trying their hands at diagnosing, symptom management, and other doctor responsibilities. Interns actually staff certain floors. Having finished medical school and working to gain experience and decide what they might like to specialize in, they have more responsibility for caseloads of patients. I'm slowly learning about how the hospital runs, the roles and responsibilities of different health care professionals, and some of the fairly common hospital cultural norms. One of those is how flirting and more goes on between doctors and nurses all the time.

There are two young men who take a liking to me. David is an intern from rural Alaska, a small, burly guy with a reddish-brown beard and bushy eyebrows. He covers the patients on another floor but always comes to see me when I'm working. He jokes with me about my shyness, as he calls it, tells me I have pretty blue eyes and gets me laughing almost every time he shows up. He teases me about moving to Alaska with him, wondering how I'd be around bears and other wild creatures.

My other admirer is Pete, a fourth-year medical student studying at a school in Philadelphia. He's assigned to work with the docs on my floor, so I see him almost every day. We exchange pleasantries and banter a bit as we pass each other in the halls or in the cafeteria.

One day he asks to join me in the cafeteria.

"Karen," he says as he passes my table. It's somewhere between breakfast and lunch when the cafeteria is almost empty and I'm alone, "May I sit down?"

"Sure." I motion with my hand for him to sit opposite me. What could he want?

"I like talking to you, wondering if you'd like to have dinner with me sometime? Maybe tomorrow night?" He's relaxed, comfortable, looking right at me.

I'm taken off guard, a little ruffled and feeling lots of buzzing rising up inside. My only other date was with Robbie. I'm over that, but my body doesn't seem to be. All of that old fear, shame, humiliation, and disappointment flood in.

"Uh, I guess so...yes, sure...uh, that would be nice." I'm stuttering, trying not to let myself or him get a glimpse of what's churning around inside.

"Great. I'll pick you up at seven. Does that work? Where do you live?" He's smiling, taking out a pen and opening his notebook.

I give him my address, and he gets up to go back to work.

When I get home from work the next day, my mother and aunt are talking in the kitchen. I say hi and go to my room, take my wooden leg off and begin my regimen of exercises. "What's she doing in there?" I hear my aunt ask my mother.

"Exercises she made up. She won't let me in to see them. If I open the door, she immediately stops and screams at me. I think she takes the leg off and bounces up and down."

A few minutes later the bell rings. I hear them open the door and thank someone, then call my name. "Karen, come out here. There's something for you." My mother shouts and I hear the two of them whispering.

"I'm busy. What is it?" I yell.

"Just come out here." I hear my brothers asking my mother, "Who got those?"

I put the leg on and hobble out. "Karen got flow-ers...Karen has a boy-friend..." my brothers are chanting.

"Who sent them?" I ask.

"Read the card," my mother says.

My aunt asks, "So, did you find yourself a boyfriend, Karen?"

I'm excited and ashamed at the same time. I feel mocked by my brothers and my mother and aunt.

"NO, I did not find a boyfriend. I don't know who sent them. Leave me alone." I'm irritable, yelling. I don't want them to see anything about me. My aunt hands me a vase with the flowers as I stomp into my room. I hadn't told anyone about the date.

It's a big bouquet of mostly yellow daisies with some greens and a couple of carnations mixed in. It's from Pete, the medical student. The card says, "I look forward to seeing you tonight." I love daisies and, if I let myself feel anything, it's a kind of delight in receiving them. Mostly, however, all the good feelings are wiped out by overwhelming terror. I put them on a small table in the corner of the room and try not to look at them. My brothers continue chanting, more quietly.

I hear my aunt tell my mother, "I'm happy to see someone likes her. It may be very hard for her to find a husband."

"I know," my mother agrees. "Bill and I worry about that."

The date is okay. We go to a nice diner where I have a small salad in keeping with my low-calorie diet. He has a hamburger and we share his fries. We have a small cone at the Dairy Queen next to the diner.

"I'll be going back to Philadelphia next week to finish out medical school and decide on a place for an internship in pediatrics," he tells me. "What are your plans?"

84

"Oh, I'll work here while I apply to nursing schools in New Jersey. I've got a few interviews coming up. I want to work with kids, too." The conversation is mostly one-sided, he shares and asks questions. I feel far away from him and tongue-tied.

"Maybe you could check out schools in Philadelphia, and we could stay in touch."

"I don't think so. I have to stay in state for the tuition and scholarships." I'm short with him; I can barely muster up the courage to say thank you for the flowers. It's like someone pushed my mute button.

"Well, maybe I could come up and visit sometime." The more he offers, the more terror and distance from him I feel.

"Sure, I guess so." I'm uncomfortable. I want to go home, but he suggests taking a drive in the country.

He's got a cute blue Volkswagen Beetle. It's just like the car I want and can't afford. We ride around for an hour or so. When we stop, I wonder if it's going to be like the time with Robbie. I'm barely talking, uttering one or two-word answers to his questions and comments. We sit for maybe ten minutes before he starts driving me home. It's a relief. I'm terrified at the thought of another guy finding out about my ugly body with its missing leg and giant wooden leg.

He lets me out at my door, kisses me on the cheek. "See you at the hospital," he says.

"Yep. See you there." I wave goodbye.

"How was the date?" my mother asks as soon as I get in the door.

"Fine."

"What did you do?"

"We ate at the diner, had a Dairy Queen, took a little drive up Thatcher's Hill." I'm indifferent, flat, talking into space.

"Well, does he want to see you again?" She's exasperated with me.

"Maybe but probably not. He's going back to Philadelphia next week to finish medical school. Plus, I'm gonna be busy this next month or two with nursing school interviews. I have three coming up. I told you, right?" I turn to look at my mother.

"Yes, you told me. You always tell me when you want something from me."

———— ✦ ————

I stay busy with work, the nursing school applications and, when I'm not working, I take my youngest brothers, Dave and Gerard, to a miniature golf and ice cream place in a town close by. The boys are the best company—they adore me and we have fun wherever we go. I'm in charge with them, they rarely question or challenge me.

Most of my high school friends are at colleges all over the state and region or working and socializing with their new work friends. I connect up with friends over the holidays, but things are not like they were in school. Everyone is changing, new interests, new friends. Many can't wait to get back to school.

My mother takes me on two nursing school interviews to three-year, hospital-based schools. In these programs, the students take some classes at the local college, but they get the majority of their education in the hospital in classes taught by the nursing instructors and with hands-on duties on the floors. By their second year, students are working more than half their school time staffing the hospital's units. They rotate shifts and floors to get a full hospital-based experience.

I have the same experience at both of these schools. Despite my good grades and year of nurses'-aide experience, the instructors think my disability (a word they use) will be a hindrance and prevent me from performing all the duties of a nurse. I'm crushed and respond by adamantly insisting that I'd be able to do everything the other students do. I have the intelligence, they say, but they're uncomfortable with my physical capabilities. There's no room for discussion. It's a flat out no go from both which is a big disappointment and worries me. I want to do this nursing thing, and I'm mad that they're telling me I can't. It makes me want to try even harder.

Kathy, my nurse friend at work, encourages me to apply to a four-year college nursing program. Those programs include college classes each of the four years and usually two days a week of hospital-based clinical instruction. They focus on preparing nurses for opportunities in new areas of professional, community-based nursing that are beginning to emerge. Students who graduate from the four-year schools have a Bachelor of Science in Nursing degree. It prepares them for going on for a graduate degree, and for working as a hospital nurse.

I apply to Rutgers' College of Nursing, a commuter college in Newark, New Jersey. They have apartment dorms for nursing students, who come from all over the state. When I interview, they're impressed with my academic record, my experience, which they say assures them that I'll be able to manage the two days a week at the hospitals, and my potential for moving on to higher levels of nursing. They offer a full scholarship with dorm fees and suggest I apply for a monthly personal stipend offered by the state to some disabled students.

"I'm not disabled," I tell my mother as we're driving home from the interview. "I don't want to apply for that stipend. I can work if I need money."

"What's wrong with you, Karen? Aunt Lou said you'd be eligible for state money because of your leg. She said we should take it. Your father and I don't have money to give you. What do you think we are?" She's annoyed with me, lecturing.

"I'm not disabled, and I don't want anyone thinking I am," I shout back.

"Let's drop it for now. Let's wait and see if they send you an acceptance letter and we'll see how much money you'll need."

Another silent ride home in the car. I am not disabled. Don't call me that. It's just not true.

6   Camp Counselor

We are given mistakes,
we are given nightmares—
and our task is to turn them into poetry.
And were I truly a poet
I would feel that every moment of my life is poetic,
every moment of my life is a kind of clay to mold.

/ from the Journals of Helen Luke

SOMETIME IN THE SPRING OF 1970, I decide I want to work at a kids' camp the summer before I head off to Rutgers' College of Nursing. I happen upon information about a camp for low-income children with Muscular Dystrophy in a rural town close to Manhattan. I'm hired as a camp counselor for kids with leg braces and wheelchairs. They seem to like the fact that I have the wooden leg. I'd never been to camp as a child and give no thought to what the camp scene will be like.

The counselors arrive a day before the kids. I'm assigned to a dorm with a crowd of attractive, perky high school girls wearing cut-off jeans and tank tops. I'm the oldest of the crew at nineteen, second only to Celie, the girls' head counselor who's twenty-five. She's a soft-spoken, gentle, willowy young woman with short blond hair and a wardrobe of long flowing skirts and tee shirts. A flower child. She breezes around introducing us girl counselors to the camp and our duties.

"You've all seen the dorms. There's a ten o'clock curfew and a strict policy of no boys in girls' dorms or vice versa. You'll all take turns rising early to help dress and feed the campers." She turns to me, "Karen, I wonder if you'd like to be my live-in assistant in the little girls' dorm? The girl who was supposed to be with me at the last minute wasn't able to come this year."

The beds in the counselors' dorm are a few feet apart, and there's one bathroom with a few toilets, three sinks, and two showers with flimsy curtains. Private space is non-existent. Many of the girls know each other from previous years. Many have summer relationships with returning boys. On that first day, there's constant chatter about who's with who, who's new, who's cute. The girls are looking through each other's clothes and, even the girls who hadn't worked there before, seem to easily find a place. I'm totally out of the loop, with my long jeans and baggy tee shirt, and can feel the panic rising inside. It's just like Douglass College. What am I going to do? I can't stay here, and I can't go home this time. Celie's invitation may save me.

"Sure, yeah, that would be good." I jump at the chance to live somewhere other than the dorm, even though I have no idea what the little girls' dorm is like or what I'll have to do.

"Good, then. I'll show you around there and fill you in on what we do after we finish this part of the orientation." Celie smiles at me. I'm still uncomfortable, but I can relax a little knowing I don't have to get undressed and take a shower with all the other girls.

We continue walking the small area that is the camp grounds. There's a swimming pool with a special ramp to roll wheelchairs into the water, and special chairs that we'll transfer kids into during swim period. There are three life guard/swim instructors who all look a little older than the other counselors. There's an arts and crafts structure with a music area, a fire pit for campfires, and a cafeteria with a kitchen staff.

There's a big open area for games and sports and a first-aid structure with a camp nurse.

When the orientation is over, Celie waves the counselors off to unpack and settle in. We'll all meet back for a welcome barbecue dinner. She leads me to the little girls' dorm, down the path away from the counselors' dorm.

"Here's where we'll stay," Celie says taking me into a small room with two single beds and a small, private toilet and shower.

"This is great. You have your own bathroom," I say feeling much more relaxed.

"Well, yes, but in exchange we'll wake up earlier than most counselors and miss some evening schmoozing because we'll be responsible for getting the little girls in this dorm bathed, dressed, and fed every morning, and settled in for bed every evening. One of us will stay in here each night after the kids are asleep. We'll take turns so you can have enough time to do things with the other counselors. Will that be okay for you?" she asks, pressing her lips together and looking at me with bated anticipation.

"Yes, yes, that'll be good. I don't really fit in with the other counselors, anyway. I'm older and I've worked. I'm headed off to nursing school in September, so this will be a good experience." I'm so relieved. I'll have something to do when all that girl-boy stuff is happening. I'm not interested in that anyway.

"Wow, I'm in nursing school, just finished my second year. I love working here, plan to work with kids when I graduate." Celie glows as she speaks, especially when she talks about working with kids.

"I'd like to work with kids, too."

Celie runs off to take care of some organizational planning, and I head up to the dorm to get my things and settle into my new room.

"Hi, I'm Mike, one of the boys' counselors," a boy around my age in a wheelchair calls out as I'm making my way to the new room. "What's your name?"

He's slightly slumped over, with limp looking legs and arms, but able to slowly roll his chair along the path next to me. I'm not so fast myself, especially maneuvering on the uneven, bumpy dirt paths. His speech is a little slurred.

"Oh, hi, I'm Karen, a girls' counselor," I say trying not to look at him and hoping he won't follow me too far. I don't want anyone to think I like him or that I'm his friend.

"Nice to meet you. I never saw you before. It's your first camp?" He's doing his best to engage me by rolling a little ahead and looking back.

"Yeah, it's my first time here. I gotta go get myself set up before the barbecue," I say rushing toward the dorm doorway.

"Glad you're here. I'll look for you later at the barbecue, and we can talk some more." He watches me walk the rest of the way, then waves and yells, "See you then."

The panic that had begun to subside is rising fast again. I hope he doesn't try to talk to me again. Maybe I'll skip the barbecue. I'm not gonna eat anything anyway. He's so disabled, in a wheelchair and his voice—so low and slow and slurred.

Celie won't let me skip the barbecue. "It's the opening of the camp, Karen. The sponsors say a few words, they will tomorrow, too, and it's the only time until the last day of camp that we'll all be together. Over the next three weeks we'll all be coming and going to different places at different times, and you may only ever see some people today and the last day. You have to go."

"Okay, I'll go. I just feel like I don't know anyone…" I feel a little better. Maybe I won't ever see Mike after today.

There's all kinds of food lined up on two picnic tables in a part of the open area: hamburgers, hot dogs, chips, potato and noodle salads, coleslaw, brownies, cookies. It's overwhelming. I see Mike coming towards me and all the other counselors giddy and flirtatious around me. Celie is talking with some of the organizers. I tell myself I can't eat, but standing around the food table feels like the safest place. Suddenly

I'm eating—everything! I can't stop. I'm occupied, focused, and I feel so much calmer.

Mike rolls over to me. "Hi again. How's the food?" He's just there, smiling and cheerful, but to me he looks like a monster I have to get away from.

"Oh hi. Yeah…it's good. I have to go." I grab a brownie and hobble as fast as I can back to the dorm. I'm shaking with fear. What's happening to me? I can't stay here. I have to stay here. And now I ate all this food and I'll be fat when I wake up tomorrow. It feels like any minute my insides will explode through my skin if I don't do something.

Then, out of the blue, I remember an article I read a while back in Seventeen magazine. It told how models throw up after they eat to stay slim. Knowing they can throw up lets them go on dates and socialize over food without losing their model bodies.

I want a model's body. I can throw up. I head into the bathroom, close and lock the door and force myself to throw up. I use my finger some, to gag myself, but it comes up pretty easily, even without the gagging. Maybe it's because the bucket is tight, it pushes against my belly. It takes five minutes or so, and after I finish, I feel a hundred percent better. The panic is gone. I can't believe it. I'm still shaky, but I feel like I can go back to the picnic.

That night, I eat some more and throw up one more time. I feel even better after that.

It's a miracle.

The next day the campers arrive and are assigned their dorms. My dorm will be home for three weeks to a group of girls under age eight, many black or Hispanic. Most have full or partial leg braces and crutches or wheelchairs. Some have respiratory problems and use oxygen some of the time, and most are on medications which the nurse dispenses. In the mornings, Celie and I make the rounds of the dorm, putting on braces, helping the girls wash up, and taking them to breakfast. Most can feed themselves with set up. Some have weak arms and need more help. They're all adorable and sweet, and I love sharing the small dorm room with them.

When activities begin, I go to my post in arts and crafts or sometimes at the pool. I don't swim at all that summer. I don't have a bathing suit or crutches. Boys and girls are together during all activities and in the cafeteria, so I run into Mike a lot.

"Hey Karen, hi," he yells in his slurry voice. "I'm off dinner duty tonight, and I see on the schedule you are, too. Wanna meet me by the fire pit? I'd like to get to know you." He's becoming a nuisance. He finds me all over the camp and invites me to sit with him, take a stroll or have supper. He's friendly with a lot of the other girl counselors, too. They banter and tease each other like brothers and sisters do. Everybody likes him. I'm sure they feel sorry for him. I do, too, but I don't want to be seen hanging out with him. He's disabled and I'm not.

"I can't. I have some reading to do for school in September, and I have to write my mother a letter." I almost never look at him, and I feel more in control knowing that I can throw up when I feel panicked.

"Where are you going to school?" He's really yelling now because I'm walking as far away as I can.

"Nursing school," I yell back as I walk into the dorm.

"Really..."

Celie and I stay up some nights telling each other about our lives and our dreams. I admire her. She's lived in Manhattan, had a few boyfriends and some interesting jobs in hospitals and schools. She's been a counselor at the camp for several years. I tell her about school and my experiences as a nurse's aide. We talk very little about my missing leg or how it is to wear the wooden leg.

"It's not an issue for me, I'm adjusted," I say whenever it comes up. We talk about staying in touch after camp. We never do.

The last few weeks before school starts, I pack my things and take my brothers to the miniature golf place and other fun places around town. I have a shake and burger with them, because I know I'll throw it up. It's become a routine part of my everyday life now, so much so that I refer to it as E&T, eating and throwing up. It's my secret. I tell no one.

I apply for and get the monthly stipend for handicapped students, so I won't have to use much of the money I earned during the year to cover school expenses.

I stop by the hospital on one of my last days in town to thank the director of nursing for hiring me and ask her to keep me in mind for work the next summer. She wishes me all the best.

7   I'm Gonna Be a Nurse

Opportunities, many times, are so small that we glimpse them not and yet they are often the seeds of great enterprises.

/ Og Mandino

IN THE FALL OF 1970, I MOVE into the Colonnade apartments, a few blocks from the college of nursing in Newark, New Jersey. Since Rutgers Newark is a commuter school and the nursing students come from all over the state, the school rents apartments in the building.

In the one-bedroom apartment I'm assigned, the bedroom is shared by our apartment managers Ann and Lee, both juniors. In the four-bed room (ordinarily the living room), where I will sleep, the beds are bunked when I arrive, and two of my three roommates, Sherry and Sharon, turn to face me.

"Hi, I'm Karen," I say as I walk in, my mother behind me.

"I'm Ann, the unit manager and this is Lee, my roommate. We're in the room right here." She points us to the room and we look in. The beds are bunked and there are two dressers and a narrow strip of floor.

"This is where you'll sleep," she points to the big room next to the kitchen. "These are two of your roommates, both freshmen."

Sharon and Sherry introduce themselves and watch me closely as I limp around the apartment. They've each staked out a bottom bunk. I hobble from bed to bed trying to decide which top bunk I want. For sure a lower bunk would be easier, but I'm not about to say that.

My mother leaves to meet my father. She'll carry up the last of my things.

"Is the top bunk going to be OK for you, Karen?" Sherry asks. She's an ordinary looking girl with curly, dirty-blond shoulder-length hair.

"Sure, I think so. There's a ladder at the foot of the bed there." I say, dismissing any utterance of concern they might have.

"I don't mind sleeping on a top bunk..." Sherry and Sharon, a tall, thin, pretty blonde girl blurt out, almost in unison. Ann and Lee are puttering in the other room.

"It's fine, really. You two were here first, you get first choice." I refuse to acknowledge any special needs.

While we're going back and forth, Tricia, a beautiful black girl, with a limp, appears. Her mother and father are with her.

"Hi," we blurt out as we turn to look at her.

Ann walks in to give the manager intro. "You must be Tricia. I'm Ann and these are your three roommates, Karen, Sherry, and Sharon. You'll be sleeping in this room." Ann says as she points to the bunk beds.

"Are the two bottom bunks taken?" Tricia asks. "I have a bad hip and won't be able to get up to the top one."

Ann jumps in, "Looks like all of you would like a bottom bunk. Why don't we put all the beds down? They fit, a lot of the dorms have them that way."

"Sounds good to me," I say. We all four agree. We move our stuff to the sides of the room. Lee and Ann do most of the moving with help from Sherry and Sharon.

"I guess it's a good time to tell you that I have a wooden leg." I lift my pants to show them the calf and my shirt to show them the bucket. "I'll be taking it off when I go to bed and leaving it this corner here." I point to the corner near the head of my bed. "I'm good at getting around when

I don't have it on, which is almost never. I can hop and hold on to things to move forward, like this." I monkey my way between the beds with my arms.

"So you don't have any crutches with you?" Sherry asks.

"No, I never use them," I say as I go back to unpacking my things.

I introduce my mother to all the girls then walk down with her to say goodbye to my father.

"I'm happy you changed the beds around. Climbing up and down the bunk…"

"It would've been fine, Mom. I can climb ladders." I interrupt her, annoyed she thinks things are hard for me.

My father is smoking a cigarette, waiting for my mother outside the car.

"Goodbye Dad," I say as I hug him. He mumbles his goodbye as he pats my back.

My mother hugs me, "I hope this works out. I hope we don't have a repeat of last year."

"We won't. This is what I want to do," I say as I turn to go back up.

"When will you call us?" my mother asks.

"I don't know. Sometime." I turn back and roll my eyes. Maybe never. Just leave.

—————— ◆ ——————

After we unpack and have a chance to catch our breath, Ann and Lee gather up the four of us for an orientation to the basics of the first year and the rules of dorm living in the Colonnades. The four girls in the apartment adjacent to ours are all sophomores and lived together last year. Ann and Lee tried to make a group living plan with them, but it never quite worked out. So the conversation turns to making a go of the six of us sharing the kitchen and one of the two of them sharing our bathroom.

"How do you four feel about sharing chores and food money with us as a sixsome? Chores are basic things like dishes, cooking, shopping, sweeping or vacuuming, garbage disposal, cleaning the bathroom. We can all be responsible for our own food and dishes for breakfast and lunch, and cook and eat dinner together on week nights, maybe even just Monday to Thursday, since at least some of you may want to leave for home early on Fridays." Ann goes on and on with her ideas. Lee sits there as a support, nodding her interest.

After an hour or so of sharing our thoughts and settling in with each other, we come up with a plan similar to what Ann laid out. We'll pool our food money and make a weekly menu together, and we'll rotate cooking and cleaning up chores. There is a dishwasher, for which we're all grateful. Ann and Lee have a car, so they agree to do the shopping.

The talk of food rattles my insides. It's a new group, and I have to establish my E&T ritual without anyone noticing. I'm now throwing up after everything I eat and sometimes I have to eat and drink more to make it easier to start the purge. I often eat something low calorie, like fruit or lettuce, right after a purge. If I stop at the first few bites, I don't have to throw up again. If I happen to eat a cookie or another something I consider off limits, I have to purge again. The bathroom is far enough away from the big room and the kitchen to render what little noise I make likely hard to hear, especially with the girls talking, doing dishes, and fooling around in the other part of the room. I'm confident I'll work it out, and I feel so much better than I did at Douglass. Not one of these girls is cute and sexy the way the girls there were. They're more like my high school friends.

———— ◦ ————

The first year we have all college classes, no clinical, and a Basics of Nursing lecture three days a week.

Our other required classes are western civilization, organic chemistry, anatomy and physiology. I take psychology as my elective. We walk together to classes and meet to go home the first few weeks. After that, Sherry and Tricia begin to branch out, meet other friends and settle into different routines. The only class we have with all the other freshman nursing students is the basics class. There are two sections of chemistry and anatomy & physiology for nurses, and in our electives and western civ classes, we're mixed in with all the Rutgers' students.

Sharon and I share a few classes. She has a steady boyfriend, Jimmy, who comes every Friday to pick her up. They live in south Jersey. Tricia drops out after the first semester, realizing she doesn't want to be a nurse after all. The college doesn't replace her in the apartment, so we have more space. Sherry makes other friends and spends quite a bit of time away from the apartment.

I love my classes and ace them all through the first year. I have lunch every day at the Dunkin' Donuts a few blocks from the campus.

"How ya doin' today, girl? Havin' yer usual?" The black woman behind the counter greets me the same way every day. Sometimes she asks about school, and I tell her what I'm studying or how I did on a recent test.

"Yep, same, with a light coffee today. It's chilly." I'm smiling because she's so nice and she has no idea what I do after eating my lunch every day.

She brings my shrimp salad sandwich on white bread, my coffee, and a giant apple fritter. I scoff it down, pay her and head to the private bathroom in the back, where I drink water from the faucet and purge up every last bit (or so I think) of my yummy lunch. I emerge, still smiling, and feeling good.

It's the start of the 1970s and in the predominantly black city of Newark tensions run high. There are civil rights and war protests, women's lib rallies with bra burnings, and gatherings about other social issues, like free love and sex, happening all over campus every day.

As nursing students, we're told we should stay away from these protests to uphold the standards of the College of Nursing. Ann and Lee complain about this at dinner all the time.

"Why can't we be nurses and activists at the same time?" Ann rants. "This college is pathetic. I hate these rules. Next year when we're seniors and sure to graduate, I'm breaking out of the mold." Lee, who is more quiet and controlled but just as, if not more radical with her long-haired boyfriend, agrees but says little. It seems she'll join Ann next year. Maybe bra burning, as neither of them wear a bra around the house. Sherry is also sympathetic to the protesters and, like Ann and Lee, she finds ways to support the movements that keep her out of the limelight. She collects signatures or volunteers to make posters but doesn't outright join the protests. Sharon is pretty much out of the loop. She and Jimmy are straight-laced when it comes to political issues. They don't seem to feel affected by them and are not part of the struggle.

I, on the other hand, long in some way to be right in the middle of the struggle. My fear of breaking the rules and being punished, and of what people—any and all people—might think of me keeps me locked up. I'm certain if I join people will feel sorry for me and won't recognize me as capable of being a part of the cause. I feel I should keep myself out of the public eye because people don't want to have to look at me. Or, something really bad will happen to me. I know when people see me, they think or say, "What does she think she's doing? She's not a part of this and she never will be. She has that big ugly wooden leg and she's fat." I know this even though no one has ever said anything like it.

My most memorable event that first year is the night before my last final exam. To celebrate the end of a year that was a success in both school and our living arrangement, Ann and Lee treat us to a few bottles of Boone's Farm Apple Wine. They're old enough to drink though none of the rest of us are. Sharon and Sherry had alcohol before, but I never had as much as a sip.

We make a nice dinner and Lee makes a cake for dessert. Then we settled in to sample the wine.

"It's sweet, but I guess you get used to the taste," I say as I down my first cup. Wine glasses are not a part of our apartment's furnishings so we're drinking out of waxed Dixie cups.

"You should taste the strawberry flavor. It's really sweet." Sherry's taking big sips of her second cup.

We drink all three bottles that night. I'm definitely drunk. I can barely walk and I'm animated, talking loudly and nonstop about everything imaginable. The girls offer me a glass of orange juice. I'm thirsty. I chug it. I'm thankful.

A few minutes later I'm in the bathroom, on my knees, puking in the toilet. I'm not in control of it; it simply pours out of me, I'm retching, seemingly without end. I hate it and at the same time I'm eternally grateful. I'm getting rid of all those calories, and it's OK that everybody knows. That's all I remember of that night.

I wake up fully dressed, on the floor of the bathroom. It's a few hours before my western civ final. The shock, jarring fear, and hilarity come when I stand and look in the mirror. My face is covered with pen writing: designs, words, scribbles.

"What did you do to me?" I shout from the bathroom.

"We couldn't resist," Sherry and Sharon shout back. I hear them walking toward the bathroom. "You were so funny last night, so totally different than you usually are, we couldn't resist. Are you mad?"

"No, I guess not. Did I do anything bad? What was I talking about?"

"Nothing bad. You were mostly talking about teachers and different things that happened this year. It was hilarious. We gave you the orange juice so you'd get rid of all the alcohol and be less hung over. We knew you had the final today." I'm sitting on the toilet, and they're helping me get the pen marks off my face.

"I had fun, too. I don't remember much, nothing about this part," I cringe, pointing to my face.

An hour or so later, I'm off to take the final. I ace it. It's been a good first year.

That summer after freshman year, I return to my parents' house to work for a hematologist at the clinic attached to the hospital where I was a nurse's aide the previous year. I escort patients to their rooms, take blood pressures, and set up the rooms for the doctor. Hematologists see people with leukemia or other similar blood disorders. Dr. Hamilton is kind, gentle, and patient with everyone, including me. I feel safe around him, unaware of any connection that I might have to my own cancer journey. It's a delight to work there, and I learn a lot. I'm more and more sure I want to be a nurse.

Toward the end of the summer, when I've saved enough money, I ask my father to help me buy a car.

"Why do you need a car?" Both my mother and father challenge me. "Isn't the school within walking distance of your apartment? Where will you get the money?"

"I have a bunch of money in the bank." I'm indignant that they're questioning me. "I need a car to get to the places where we have clinical practice the next three years. So—Dad—will you help me?"

"I guess so. Start looking in the paper. How much money do you have?"

"A little more than $1000. I really want a VW Beetle. Can we look at the Volkswagon dealer?" I'm dead set on a Beetle. They're small and cute and all the rage.

"They're pretty small. Aren't they all standard transmission, with a clutch? Why don't we just look at some other used cars, too. Some bigger ones." My father is not a fan of small cars. We've had Chryslers and Chevys, all big, long old-people cars.

When I turned seventeen, the age you can get a learner's permit in New Jersey, I asked my father to teach me to drive. He looked around for a way to make the car drivable with a left foot, since my stiff, right wooden leg lay right in front of the gas pedal. He happened upon a left-foot accelerator in a Pep Boys catalog, designed for people who drive long distances over many hours. It's an odd "U" shaped piece of thick, wire-like metal that lays across the floor under the brake. On one side of the brake, there's a thin plate that rests on the gas pedal and is bolted to the floor of the car. On the other side there's another plate, shaped more like a pedal, that rests in position for the left foot. When you push down on the left pedal, it pushes on the gas pedal and the car accelerates. Anyone, right- or left-footed, can drive the car with the contraption in place. Right footers just flip the left pedal down to lay flat on the floor and the right gas pedal is back to itself.

102

At the VW dealer I see a white Beetle, a 1969 with an automatic stick shift and it's love at first sight. It's more than I can afford, something like $1500. My father is surprised they have automatic Beetles. The dealer, a local man whose kids were in high school with me, explains that they made the first automatic Beetle in 1968. "The 69s were built with the knowledge of what needed changing in the 68s," he tells us as we roam the cars. "They're fun to drive, with the engine in the back and trunk in the front, they handle a little differently."

My father agrees to take a test drive, and he drives because I can't slide my leg far enough to the right to squeeze my left foot in to reach the gas pedal.

"I love it, I love it...," I'm excited, smiling, giddy, all lit up inside. "I want to get it, Dad." We're back at the dealer's now, standing with Mr. Denny.

"Let's wait a minute. I want you to look at some other cars first. And if you still want it after that, we can come back and look at this one again."

"What if it's gone? There's only this one with the automatic, right?" I turn, slightly frantic, to ask Mr. Denny.

"Karen, you don't even have enough money for this car. And it looks like it's a little hard to get your leg in the front." My father is annoyed.

"I think your father's right, Karen. Look at some other used cars. Who knows? Maybe you'll see another car you like even better. I can hold this for a week. Come back and see me before next week if you still want this one, and we'll work something out." Mr. D. is the epitome of smooth. We leave, both a little calmer.

"I know it's the car I want," I insist as we drive home. "I don't know why I have to look at other cars."

"Calm down and change your tone or I won't help you find any car," my father threatens. "I want you to see some other, cheaper cars, so you don't have to spend all your money and owe some, too."

We look at a few cars that next week. There's one, a Rambler American for five hundred dollars, that my father really likes and wants me to buy.

"This is a solid car, in good shape. It's not too big, and probably safer than that Beetle. And it's cheaper." It's a no-brainer to him.

"I don't like it. I want the VW. It's my money. I can buy what I want," I stubbornly proclaim. I barely even look at the car. It's boxy and dark brown with that fake wood paneling on the sides. Just plain ugly.

We go back to see Mr. Denny that week. He offers to sell me the Beetle for less, and we set up a payment plan until it's paid off. I'll work the next four weeks for Dr. Hamilton and get a weekend job when I'm back at school. I get money from the college each semester. The monthly payment will be doable.

My father transfers the gas pedal extender from the Chevy to the Beetle, and I've got wheels for the rest of the summer. I drive myself to work and take my brothers on outings when I'm not working. Freedom.

———◦———

Back at school in September, I get a parking space through the school. My roommates, Sherry and Sharon, (still just the three of us) are thrilled about the car. We all go to the same place for clinical every Tuesday and Thursday, and without the car we'd be stuck taking buses and walking long distances, something I knew would be hard for me.

I completely lose myself in the work of sophomore year. The beginning is a little slow since I know the basics of blood pressure, Foley catheters, bed baths, and such that we cover in the first few weeks because I did all of it as a nurses' aide. Early on we begin writing care plans for the patients we're assigned to each week. That involves looking at all the medical data, labs, X-rays, medications and other treatments and writing the physiological reasons and explanations for everything that's being done for them. We explore the diseases and conditions, as well. There's a range of depth we can go into around this and some of my classmates stick to the basics of nursing knowledge, minimally referring to the medical books we were introduced to in A&P the year before. I'm fascinated with the scientific explanations and connections. My care plans are full of scientific theory, things I learn from scouring

104

the textbooks in the evenings. I love to talk about them in class and to read the "very good," "thorough," "thought-provoking,"comments my instructors write on my papers.

All of my roommates have either boyfriends or weekend jobs in their hometowns and leave for most of Friday through Sunday. Early in the fall of 1971, I take a job at Gino's Fried Chicken, a fast-food joint across from the apartment building. I work there on weekends and holiday vacations after I spend the obligatory time with my family. I decide to stay in Newark and work there through the summer after sophomore year.

One night that summer, I'm sitting on the bench outside the lobby when a man appears with a broom, sweeping the sidewalk. With short, swift swipes he quickly makes several piles of cigarette butts.

"Do you work here?" I ask. His shoulder-length, bushy red hair flips around his face as he looks up at me. He's wearing soft, faded jeans with a belt, a form-fitting blue tee shirt tucked in, and sneakers. He's slim, medium height, with friendly green eyes, a large nose, prominent lips, and a red mustache adorning the upper.

"No, I just hate all the cigarette butts. People are slobs." He mutters as he continues sweeping the entire sidewalk in front of the glass building. "Are you a nurse?"

"A student," I say, "just finished my second year."

"Why didn't you go home for the summer like everyone else?"

"I have a job at Gino's across the street, and there's nothing to do at home. My brother took over my room, and I fight continually with my mother. Much better here."

"You work at that Gino's? Are you the only white person in there?"

"I guess so—don't really know," I raise my eyebrows and shrug, "Is that a problem?"

"No, not really. What do you do there?"

"Cashier and sometimes I make fries. I work a few weekdays and Sunday mornings when families come, all dressed up in suits, ladies with fancy hats. They have fried chicken for lunch. Do you go to Rutgers?"

"Me—no—no college for me. I work in Union. I'm a photographer."

"Really, wow. What kind of pictures?"

"Mostly black and white. At work, I shoot brochures and advertisement pictures for flyers. I work in a print shop." He sits down next to me, leans the broom up against the glass wall behind us.

It's a warm Friday evening, and we sit outside talking for a few hours. He's twenty-five and lives with his mother, Adele, in a one-bedroom apartment on the twenty-second floor. He sleeps in the bedroom and she sleeps on a pull-out couch. Neither of them drive. He rides the bus to Manhattan on the weekends to take pictures and asks if I'd like to go the next day. We make a date to meet in the lobby at nine in the morning.

When we get up to go inside, he notices my limp.

"What's wrong with your leg?" he asks, staring.

"It's a wooden leg. I've had it for almost ten years." I say in my most nonchalant tone.

"Cool." He's nonchalant, too.

He asks the lobby attendant for the dustpan.

The husky black man jokes, "Still doing the sweepin', heh, Gene? Do they pay you for that—ha ha?"

The next day, and many more that summer, Gene and I board the bus in the morning and Gene points out landmarks like a tour guide.

"You know everything about everything around here," I comment.

"Yeah, lots of trips on the bus."

We de-board in Port Authority and walk the few blocks to the Herald Square Chock Full o' Nuts across from Macy's Department Store. We find two stools at the crowded counter.

"I always have a cream cheese and walnut sandwich and a plain donut. Sometimes orange juice."

"No coffee? It's a coffee place." I'm puzzled.

"I know. I don't like coffee," he announces.

The waitress recognizes him. "The usual?" she asks.

"I'll have orange juice, too."

"And for you?" She turns to me with a smile. "I'm surprised to see him with someone. For years he's been coming here alone."

"I'll have what he's having, except I'll get a light coffee and no orange juice," I say with certainty. I'm too afraid to ask for a menu or to even look up on the board above. I'm thinking about where I'll throw up, but I act totally in control.

The sandwich is on dark walnut bread smeared with thick cream cheese, cut diagonally in two. The donut is sealed in crinkly plastic with the Chock Full o' Nuts logo. It's greasy on the fingers and crisp with a soft inside when I bite in. I love it. I want another, which as the summer moves on, I indulge in. Gene doesn't seem to notice or care.

Gene pays the bill, and I ask the waitress where the bathroom is. It's a single with a lock, my favorite. I drink out of the faucet to ease the purging and emerge from the room to find Gene waiting by the door.

"It's a pretty nice bathroom," I say.

We walk up town to Central Park. Gene wants to show me all his favorite places. We take a circuitous route to peek into store windows, and alleys with patios, and even a wall of water. We pass the ice skating rink in Rockefeller Plaza.

I tell him, "My parents took us here, pretty much every year to see the Christmas show. We never went ice skating, though. We begged but they wouldn't budge. Maybe because we would've needed lessons. I remember waiting in those long, back and forth lines, seeing the latest Christmas movie and the Rockettes. Sometimes my father would get us hot chocolate from Schraft's. Is it still there?"

"The theater is over that way a block," he says pointing, "and the Schraft's is still there. When it gets colder, we'll go down to the rink. There's a cafe in there that has good fish sandwiches." Gene knows everything about Manhattan.

As we walk on, crossing many streets, Gene yells at the cab drivers who turn into us when we have the walk sign. They're aggressive, almost pushing people who are crossing so they can make the turn while they have the green light. When the light turns red, they have to wait to turn until it's green again even if there's no cross traffic. The traffic cops are on them, ready and waiting to issue a ticket.

Gene bangs on one cabbie's car hood as he barely misses hitting me. He yells some obscenity at him, shaking his fist. When we're on the curb he asks, "Are you okay?"

"Yeah, I'm fine," I say. "I don't think they'd really hit me. They'd get a big fine and feel bad about it for the rest of their lives."

"I doubt that. I hate those cabs. That's why I don't drive. I know I'd get so mad I'd want to ram into them. If I ever do get a car it'll have big thick wooden bumpers, front and back, so they'll know to stay away from me."

As we enter Central Park at Columbus Circle, I tell Gene I was born on Columbus Day.

"Well, this is your circle, too, then." He points to the big statue in the middle of the green circle. "Are you tired? Wanna sit down on a bench when we get inside the park?"

"I'm not tired, but let's sit down and watch the people walk by." I am tired and sore around my waist where the edge of the wooden leg rubs up and down around my ribs. My butt hurts where the piece of fiberglass juts out and chafes my skin as I slide in and out of the bucket with each step. I'm having fun, a guy likes me, so the discomfort is something to grin and bear.

Somewhere around Sheep's Meadow, the home of outdoor concerts throughout the summer, we find a bench and sit for a bit. Endless streams of people pass: roller skaters, bikers, families with baby carriages, and kids running wild on the grass. Couples loll on the grass, making out, reading. The park is green and alive with humanity. Gene takes his Nikon camera out of his army-green canvas shoulder bag every so often all throughout the day. It's a small bag, big enough for two or three lenses and the camera, plus incidentals like filters and different lens pieces. Things I never fully understand, just like I never really get all the F-stop and shutter speed business he fools with.

"What are you taking pictures of?" He's contorting his body in all different ways: bending down with the camera facing up, lying on the ground, sitting close to trees, pointing the camera toward the sidewalk.

"Shadows, details, the place where the buildings and the sky meet. Different things. I like wide angle shots," he says as he fiddles with putting the camera in the bag. "I'll show you next week after I develop them."

Our next stop is the Boat House which sits on the edge of a big pond near the center of the park. There's a little snack bar where Gene meets up with a few camera buddies.

"Who's the girl, Gene?" one of the men asks.

"My new friend, Karen. She lives in my building. We met downstairs yesterday."

"Be careful of this guy, Karen. He's a lunatic," he says as he pats Gene on the back and chuckles.

The other man offers his hand. I shake it. "He's a talented photographer, Karen. Maybe you can encourage him to show people his work. He won't listen to any of us."

We eat plain cheese sandwiches and under-cooked fries with gobs of ketchup. Gene says the cheeseburgers are greasy and may be made with horse or dog meat. He's serious and refuses to eat them. "I hate the smell of them," he says. His pals shake their heads and roll their eyes.

Central Park is huge. I'm in awe. I hope I can come with Gene again and see more of the city. Leaving, we head toward the uptown museums. Gene points out the Guggenheim Museum and The Metropolitan Museum of Art. We walk over to Madison Avenue and pass by the Whitney Museum of American Art.

"I go inside sometimes, more in the winter when it's cold on the streets. I try to go when they're free. They should be free all the time. It's art. Everyone should see it." There's a hint of self-righteousness in his voice.

I haven't thought much about art or museums or what should be free. I have no comment. Gene doesn't seem to care.

There are stores galore along Madison Avenue. It seems like we walk forever. Then Gene says, "Let's take the subway to Little Italy. I know a good little place there, Luna's. They have the best ravioli."

We walk directly to the subway. Gene knows exactly which train to take. He buys both our tokens, and we enter to wait for the train. "This is a shithole," he says, "the city doesn't do enough to keep these places decent." There's garbage all over, people sitting around begging for money. "I only take the train when it's faster than walking. Little Italy is pretty far and it's getting late now."

The train comes. We get out in a totally different looking place. We could be in a whole different city. The buildings are no taller than three to four stories, all concrete with fire escapes outside the back windows. They're crowded together on streets with narrow sidewalks, and many of the stores are open to the sidewalk with goods on the street. It's noisy, all kinds of people are out walking. Some places have neon signs or colored lights hanging in front.

"Wow, this place is great, so different from downtown," I say wide-eyed.

"I hate the crowds down here and it can be dirty, too. Good food, though, and a good place for pictures. I love all of Manhattan because there's so much to see, so many places to walk."

We're on a mission to get to the restaurant. He grabs my hand so we don't get separated and weaves us through the crowds to Luna's.

It's no more than a storefront, no fancy sign or anything that would alert you to a good Italian restaurant. We walk in and the waiter, a tall, stocky, grey-haired man immediately knows Gene.

"Gino," he exclaims as he walks toward Gene with open arms. Where you been hiding, man?" He loosely embraces Gene and pats his back.

"Not hiding, Sal. Just not in the area. Can we sit in a booth?"

"How about right here?" It's a booth a few in from the vestibule inside the door. "You used to like this one."

"This is good," Gene says.

"Who's your lovely friend?" Sal asks, gesturing to me.

"Karen, a girl I met in my building."

"Nice to meet you, Karen." He offers his hand and squeezes mine when I extend it. "Would you like some wine? Your buddy Gene never drinks here. The house red goes good with the food."

"Uh, sure. I'll have some wine." My drinking experience is still minimal, but I've been able to drink without getting sick. Besides, I'll find the bathroom and purge it all before we leave. The last thing I can allow myself to eat is spaghetti without a purge.

The wine comes in a small juice glass. It's dark red and rich. Sal tells me it's Chianti. I like it.

Gene has ravioli and I have eggplant parmesan. We're facing each other in the booth. It's the first time I've been out to dinner with a man since the medical student. He tells me he lives with his mother, Adele, on the twenty-second floor of our building. He comes to Manhattan to get out of the house. She and he have been together since childhood. His father left them, and his two older brothers were out of the house as soon as they were old enough to work. He sees Todd, the middle brother, once a month or so. Todd's a cop in Union, New Jersey, with a wife and two kids. His oldest brother, Ernie, is more distant. Married, too, but Gene hardly sees him. There's an indignant tone in his voice as he speaks.

"Yeah, my brothers hardly ever visit my mother. She is a pain, complaining about all sorts of things all the time. She gets to me, but she can't live by herself, so I just stay with her. I'd really like to move to Manhattan."

"Why can't she take care of herself? Is there something wrong with her?" I ask.

"No, it's just that…well we've been together for so long now, it's just hard to change that situation. There's no real reason for me to leave." He tells me he's twenty-five and has never really had a girlfriend. I tell him it's the same for me and that I'm twenty-one.

The food is good. I find the bathroom, another single with a lock. I purge, feel relieved, and meet Gene at the door. He insists on paying.

We take the subway back to the Port Authority and the bus back to the apartment. We don't hug, kiss, or even touch.

"I had fun. Thanks for inviting me." I say as we stand outside my door.

"Wanna go again next week?" he asks. "We can go to my favorite steak place. I'll even have a drink there, Jack Daniels. You can meet me downstairs at the same time."

"Okay, sure."

—————— ⸙ ——————

The summer goes along like that—I work, Gene and I go to Manhattan on Sundays, and sometimes on Fridays if I'm off. He works ten-hour shifts Monday through Thursday. He buys me little presents—a small stone lion, a yellow flowered blouse, a chenille-like yellow hat with a brim—when he's in the city alone. Sometimes we hold hands, but it's hard for me to walk holding hands, and walking with someone's arm around me is impossible. It interferes with the swing through motion I have to do to move along. My steps are out of proportion with other people's.

We visit all sorts of different places, eat Weiner Schnitzel in Germantown, bagels at the Bagel Nosh (a favorite), and drive to Friendly's in New Jersey for the french fries and ice cream. I become bold enough to ask Gene for two orders of fries and/or ice cream and hit the bathroom in between. We explore lower Manhattan, where Gene fantasizes about living someday, stop for outdoor concerts in Washington Square Park, Bryant Park behind the library, and sometimes Lincoln Center. Some days we spend the mornings around 10th Avenue Midtown, home of camera shops that sell used and new equipment. He buys lenses, filters, and other gadgets.

He comes to New Jersey to meet my family. My brothers like him and my parents are happy a person of the opposite sex likes me. I'm not sure they see him as a man, I can't say I do either. He and I are like kids, brother and sister. We don't make out and there's only passing mention of sex, which I completely ignore. It terrifies me.

I learn more things about him when I meet his mother and see his darkroom in the closet, and the photo station he sets up on a board between the stove and the kitchen counter. The space above the projector/printer in the darkroom is lined with shelves full of canisters of negatives and boxes of developed pictures, spanning more than ten years.

"Do you ever take color pictures or pictures of people?" I ask.

"I used to take lots of people but the last few years I've liked the contrasts and detail I get working with shadows, angles, water, buildings...that sort of thing. And, I don't have the set up for developing color. I don't like it as much, either."

We go back to the living room and Adele turns to me.

"I make his lunch every day," Adele tells me. "I know just what he likes and how he likes it packed." It's like she's proud she's such a good mother to her twenty-five-year-old son. "I do all the laundry downstairs, too. Gene likes his jeans and tee shirts folded a certain way." She walks me to the low bench-like place in front of the floor-to-ceiling windows to show me the shirts. They're each folded perfectly, like you would a good dress shirt, and there's a thick phonebook on top of the stack of four or five shirts.

"What's the phonebook for?" I ask.

"It keeps them neatly pressed," Gene says from across the room. "In the drawer, they move around too much and get wrinkled." His pants are folded without a crease and hung from the bottom of the leg on a wooden clip hanger.

He tells me he's never had a bank account or a credit card. He gets paid in cash. He pays for everything with cash or money orders and keeps all the money he has in a certain place in one of the two or three closets in the apartment.

That fall Gene meets my roommates. Sherry moves into a place with friends and Sharon and I, now juniors, are happy to invite sophomores, Claire and Joan, to join us. We met them the previous year when they lived in the adjacent apartment. They all like Gene, and over the course of the year, bestow upon him the nickname, Gene-o. He finds things to lovingly tease each one of them about. We're pretty much the only females in his life, aside from his mother, sister-in-law, and the wives of some of his photo buddies. He works until late each evening, and we're studying, so we rarely see him during the week. He comes by on Thursday nights sometimes or sees the girls on Sundays as they come back from weekends home.

School is mostly the same as the year before. We have pediatric clinical, which I love, and various other medical and surgical experiences. I continue to excel, fascinated by the scientific knowledge I'm absorbing. I begin to think about possibly working in pediatrics when I graduate.

Claire and Sharon both talk about marrying their boyfriends after graduation. Joan is single that year, hoping to find a suitable partner for marriage. Ann and Lee, both graduated, married their boyfriends over the summer. I wonder if Sharon and Claire are having sex or if they've decided to wait until they're married, like my mother told me to do.

She said, "Remember, Karen, if you have sex with someone before you're married, he'll think you're a fast girl and probably won't marry you. So, save yourself until you're married."

I have no idea what having sex is. I still believe what my mother told me, that babies come out of a miraculous opening in the woman's belly. Later that year, in obstetrical clinical, I learn the truth about the uterus, vagina, and the mechanics of sex and childbirth. It all makes so much more sense than my mother's stupid explanation. I can't believe I believed her for so long. That part of my body is foreign to me, and I feel scared just thinking about what sex would be like with my one-legged body.

8   I Marry Gene

Risk itself is a process of constant unfolding. And taking risks is the process of peeling back layers of what you are and who you want to be.

/ Phoebe Eng

TOWARD THE END OF JUNIOR YEAR, I get my Practical Nurse license and apply for a paid summer internship at Memorial Hospital in Manhattan, the place where I had both surgeries. My hope is to work on the pediatric unit.

"I was a patient here in 1959 and 1962, and I've always wanted to come back and work here in pediatrics," I say to the woman interviewing me, not sure it's true, since I never thought about it until this year after having the pediatric rotation. It sounds good, though.

"Well, that's amazing, Karen. You have some good experience and excellent recommendations. You'd be a good addition to our staff." The woman interviewing me is the Director of Nursing, a middle-aged prim looking woman meticulously dressed in a tailored suit. She tells me she's been a nurse for many years and especially likes working with nurses who are committed to cancer patients. "Unfortunately, we don't have internship positions in pediatrics. Would you be willing to work in another ward?"

"Oh sure. I really want to work here. Maybe I can visit the pediatric unit or talk with a nurse who works there while I'm here. I'd love to see a leg amputation surgery, if that's possible." I'm eager and excited—there's no hesitation.

"We'll see about that. I'll arrange for you to meet with the pediatric educator/play therapy nurse specialist and she can let you know what's possible. Meanwhile, I'll get you assigned to the Head and Neck unit. You'll learn a lot there and be a big inspiration to our patients. Throughout the summer, you'll have a chance to work for a week at a time on some other units, as well." She's looking at me intently, with an ever so small smile in her eyes. She likes me. I want her to like me more.

———◆———

The school year ends. My roommates flee for their hometowns, various jobs, and boyfriends. Gene and I are a couple. He worries about my driving into Manhattan every day for work.

"It's not safe for you to travel back and forth alone. Why do you have to work there? Couldn't you get a job at one of the hospitals around here?" He's annoyed. He tells me repeatedly he doesn't like me driving without him in the car, no matter how far.

"It's fine Gene. It's only for six weeks. There's a parking lot right where I go into work, or I could live in a dorm there if driving doesn't work out. I want to work there. It'll be a great experience. I hope I can spend some time on the pediatric unit." I don't understand what he's so mad about and I'm a little afraid if he gets too mad at me he won't be my boyfriend anymore.

"I'll meet you there on Fridays, and we can drive home together," he concedes.

The Head and Neck unit is a real education. Most of the patients are men, former smokers or tobacco chewers who developed cancer of the head, neck, face, or throat. Most have major pieces of their lower jaw, lips and/or tongue, trachea, and esophagus removed. They have tracheostomies for breathing and feeding tubes hanging out of their bellies so they can eat. We visit each one every morning and afternoon, open the over-bed table, so the mirror is usable, and assist them with washing up, suctioning and dressing their trachs, and we practice talking with them. After that, we roll the IV pole with the bag of liquid food to the bed, watch as they hook it up to the tube and allow the thick, pasty beige food to flow in. I'm amazed they can look at themselves with their cut away faces and holes in their necks. Most are good-humored, blaming their misfortune on their smoking and, in some cases, drinking habits. Their voices are low and distorted, as they cover the neck hole to create the throat vibrations that translate to sounds.

I quickly get used to their gruesome appearances and begin to see the men as individuals, all different, many delightful despite their misfortune. One week, I work on a gynecological unit. There the women have radical genital surgeries, called vulvectomies. Many have the entire pelvic floor cut away to lessen the chance any cancer cells are left behind to grow and spread. It's 1973 and chemotherapy is relatively new. Radiation has been around for a while but is still somewhat crude and non-specific to its target. Surgery is the first line of defense for many cancers.

A few weeks into my time there, the pediatric play therapist finds me for a chat and a tour of the pediatric unit. She's a middle-aged woman with a graduate nursing degree in child psychiatry. She's studied Jungian analysis, the basis of the play therapy she does with the children. Hers is a new position, begun sometime in the years after my 1962 stay.

"You must be Karen," she says, extending her hand to me. "I've heard nice things about you. How's your internship been so far?"

"Terrific. I love it here. The people are all so nice. I'm learning a lot. Who are you?"

She introduces herself, and we head off for a tour of the unit.

It's different than I remember it. There are some private and semi-private rooms, many with floor-to-ceiling glass walls. The kids are sitting on their beds or with their visitors on small, built-into-the-wall couches in each room. Many kids are hooked up to IV poles with fluids infusing. There's a big playroom, like the one I remember, and a nurses' desk in the middle of the space.

My tour guide, Ms. Taylor, introduces me to the charge nurse.

"This is Karen Witt, she'll be a senior this year in a bachelor's nursing program in New Jersey and is in the internship program here."

"Karen Witt, is that really you??" She's looking at me, especially at my leg, shaking her head. "It can't be, can it? You were a patient here about ten years ago! I was the new head nurse then. I remember you like it was yesterday." She's gushing as she hugs me.

"Yes, it's me. I was here then." I don't really remember her but it's nice to meet someone who knew me then.

"We treat so many kids who don't make it. It's a joy to see you. You're healthy and beautiful and going to be a nurse, too." She tears up. Other staff start to notice us.

"You're pretty lucky, sweetie. Only a few kids with bone cancer like you had, live to tell about it. I'm feeling pretty lucky today, getting to meet you. It's been over ten years. They must consider you cured?"

"I guess so. I don't have to go for appointments or tests anymore." I remember the kids I knew who died and have a sense of how lucky I am.

She shows me around, introduces me to other nurses and some of the kids with bone cancer in their legs. The older kids and parents ask all kinds of questions about my wooden leg and where and how I got it. Many look weary, their bandaged stumps much shorter than their cancer-free leg. I learn the chemotherapy is keeping kids alive longer, but it makes them sick. The surgeons are reluctant to depend on it too much. They continue to do semi-radical amputations.

When we're done on the unit, Ms. Taylor takes me to her office for a short chat. I ask if I can watch a leg amputation from the viewing area in the operating room.

"I'm not sure that would be such a good idea. I'm concerned you may have more of a reaction to the sight of it than you think. It could trigger a big emotional outpouring." Her tone and look are serious. She's worried about me.

"I don't think so. I've watched some abdominal and back surgeries during school clinical this past year. It was fine." I'm hoping she will, and pretty sure she won't, let me do it.

"I'm sure you'd be fine, but I feel the need to be cautious." It's the last mention of this. I have no idea what she's getting at. I'm certain I'd have no emotional reaction. I'm well-adjusted. My one leggedness is not problem.

I ask her about play therapy and Jungian analysis. She talks about learning how to watch children play with toys or make art or act out plays, to find clues to what's deeply troubling them, things they would never talk about or don't even really know about. Since kids learn through play, with guidance from a trained professional they can work out challenges, dilemmas, and difficult relationships without having to really understand what they're doing. She introduces me to the book, _Play Therapy_ by Virginia Axline and offers me a copy from her bookshelf.

"It's an extra. You seem interested. You might be more so after reading it."

We say goodbye, and I return to my head and neck patients in time for afternoon care.

———— · ————

Sometime late that summer, after a Saturday in Manhattan, Gene and I are walking down the apartment stairwell from his mother's place to mine. He's halfway down one section and I'm halfway down the one behind and we can see each other through the space between the two railings. He stops suddenly, turns to me as I hop down one step at a time, and says, "I want to have sex with you. How about tonight?"

Neither of us has had sex. He has a gay woman friend he hasn't seen for a few years who promised to do it with him but then backed out. He and I smooch and hug and cuddle, all rarely and very innocently. There's a platonic chemistry between us. I imagine we love each other for the companionship and the relief from day-to-day loneliness we provide one another. There's never been anything hot and heavy between us, no necking or French kissing. I don't even know what either is.

None of this is apparent to me at that moment. I can only think of what my mother's told me—that if I have sex with someone before we're married, he'll think I'm a fast girl and probably won't marry me.

I'm terrified to have sex. I have no idea what it entails, aside from the anatomy I learned in school. Fearfully and impulsively, I look at Gene. "I'll only do it if you promise to marry me," I say.

We continue down the stairs and into my apartment. No one's there that weekend, and there's very little chance anyone will return before Sunday night.

"Okay, hon-o, we can get married. Let's do it tonight," he says as we're putting our stuff down. We exchange a few mundane words as we undress to get into my dorm bed. There's no mention of birth control—it never enters my mind. Gene's never seen me with my leg off, nor has he seen the enormity of the wooden leg. I'm sure he'll back out of marrying me after this.

He timidly rolls on top of me and pulls the covers up. I have no idea what to do. There's no foreplay. I'm clueless what that is and likely he is, too. He fumbles around with my help until we achieve the right alignment then the bouncing up and down begins. It's over in less than five minutes.

"Where are you going?" I ask as he jumps up and leaves the bed. I'm sure he's leaving, just like my mother said.

"To the bathroom," he says, as he pulls on his jockeys. "Harold told me to go right away after sex." Harold's his best buddy.

I sit up, pull the covers up and stare into space. If that's what having sex is, it's not much at all. I slide to the edge of the bed, put my underwear and tee shirt on and sit there waiting for Gene to come out of the bathroom.

We sit on the bed, snuggling. "Thanks, hon-o. I better head upstairs before my mother thinks we're up to something."

I show him how I hop around the place without my leg on. He's impressed. He'll head to Manhattan alone tomorrow. I'll stay home getting ready for the week ahead at the internship. "See ya tomorrow. We'll go to Friendly's for supper," he says as he closes the door.

The next evening he shows up with a beautiful yellow-flowered, soft cotton blouse he bought me at his favorite store on Fifth Avenue. "I saw this today. It'll look nice on you, hon-o."

We head out to Friendly's, where I have my usual second order of fries and ice cream after whatever it is we order. I make two runs to the bathroom, one after the sandwiches and the other before we leave. I have to make sure all I ate is cleared out before we get home.

A few weeks later, we make a trip to the Diamond District in West Midtown Manhattan. Gene says it's the best place to buy good diamonds for a good price. We browse several stores. I know I want a solitaire setting in white gold. I want the ring to show my roommates when they return in the fall. Marriage is another thing, something most people I know seem to think is a good thing to do. Gene will marry me. I may have no other offers. I'll get married. Besides, we had sex and now it's too late to change my mind.

Gene buys me a ring with cash. I'm happy to have it but don't like wearing it. It's too fancy or something. I'm embarrassed to have people see it on me. I'm certain everyone is judging me, my choice of husband, my deservedness.

———◆———

My roommates are excited and surprised when they return in the fall. Two of them have weddings planned for after graduation. Including me, it's three of us who'll be married by next year. Neither of the others are formally engaged with diamond rings. I'm the one and only. Still, I rarely wear the ring when I'm not with Gene, and even then, I find excuses not to.

Senior year we have our psychiatric clinical at a state hospital in New Jersey. We go there twice a week for several weeks and are each assigned a patient who we interview for twenty minutes, writing down everything we say and they say. Our instructor is a young blond woman, maybe ten years older than we are. She has a master's in Psychiatric Nursing and claims to love the chronically ill population as well as the healthier patients she sees in clinics. We see only the state hospital patients, though our lectures and assignments are focused on both populations.

On arriving for our first clinical that semester, Sharon and I are nervous. We've heard, and anxiously laughed at, stories of people in psychiatric hospitals. As we enter the building in our crisp blue uniforms and white shoes, I feel helplessly self-conscious among what seems like a hundred people, men and women, all ages, mulling around. Some are falling asleep slumped in dingy chairs and sofas, some are attempting to play games, only to be distracted and walk away, some are pacing, or sitting in corners on the floor. Many look old, but when I get closer, they seem to be much younger than they look. We were told to read *To Kill a Mockingbird* over the summer. The scene is similar to those described in the book.

I'm assigned a white man, in his fifties, who's been there for most of ten years. He's an alcoholic who fell on hard times, unable to get sober due to life circumstances, and descended into depression and hopelessness. He was living on the street, in jail a number of times, and when he began to show signs of alcoholic dementia, was sent to the psychiatric facility for medication and safety. He's toothless, with yellowed fingertips on his right hand from years of smoking. He searches for butts in the ashtrays and asks for smokes all day long. Patients can smoke on the ward with supervision. All the cigarettes are kept at the nurses' station. In our twice weekly talk sessions, my gentleman talks about how it's a skill to find unsmoked butts. He tells me all the important jobs he had as a young man, before whoever it was "put me in this place." He gets up and walks around during our twenty-minute sessions, telling me all about what the others are doing, thinking, and saying. He's medicated with Thorazine to keep his behavior and hallucinations in check. In class, we learn how years on psychiatric medications can strip individuals of their will and ambition, while helping them maintain socially acceptable behavior—a kind of double-edged sword. We're told these are the best treatments currently available for unpredictable people with chronic mental illnesses, and may help patients avoid psychosurgery, like a lobotomy.

Sharon's patient is a whole different sort of man. He's younger, in his thirties, African-American, with thick, curly black hair and eyebrows. According to his hospital records, he had a psychotic break in his early twenties and needed medication and hospitalization. He recovered enough to be discharged with support, but then became violent, was deemed insane and a danger to others by the courts, and was admitted for long-term care. He, too, had been on several strong antipsychotics and tranquilizers for many years and continued to have repeated, though infrequent, violent outbursts. He'd been on the less restrictive ward for several months and was thought to be doing well.

One day as Sharon and I walk onto the ward to find our patients, one of the woman patients greets us. "He's over there," she says to Sharon, "combing his eyebrows to get ready for you. Are you his girlfriend?"

Sharon and I are a little nervous, but our instructor reassures us Sharon's time with him would likely be fine. She suggests Sharon explore his thoughts about her without asking many questions, just allowing him to talk.

The day goes smoothly. In class we discuss the concepts of fixed delusions, and transference, where patients sometimes project their own feelings onto others who interact with them. "It's common in psychiatric circles to let people express their delusions, hoping they would look at them and see their part in the creation of the delusions."

The next time we visit Sharon is assigned a different patient. As we walk onto the ward, we're told that Sharon's patient climbed on a chair and pulled the TV off the wall, believing it was saying bad things to him. He'd been moved to a more restrictive ward, and he was too ill to talk. Her new patient is a woman. The rest of the semester passes without incident.

I'm curious about psychiatric nursing, and my instructor encourages me. She says my care plans and insights into what's happening with people are strong, and she's noticed that the patients seem to gravitate to me. I admire her. She tells us in class that many people who work professionally in the psychiatric field, including herself, engage in personal psychotherapy to better understand how the mind works, and to experience the process from the point of view of the patient. I read more about psychiatry as the semester goes on. I remember being curious in my freshman year psychology class and the experience in the hospital sets me to wondering why some people are able to overcome life challenges and others aren't. My thoughts are purely intellectual, and it is from that analytical place, that later the same year, I begin personal psychotherapy with my former Psych 101 professor.

In June 1974, I graduate first in my class with a Bachelor's in Nursing. I accept a job in Jersey City on the pediatric infectious disease ward. It's a big room with cribs lined up on two sides. The babies are mostly under a year old suffering with diarrhea and vomiting. As an RN, I manage the IV fluids each receives adding medications as prescribed, and help the aides change diapers, which is an endless task. As we finish diaper rounds on the lot, the first is soiled and screaming again, and we begin the next round. Sometimes parents come, but because this is an infectious disease ward, visiting hours are limited and the parents are encouraged not to touch the babies.

Because of my interest in psychiatry, I visit the mental health department to ask about what they do. I apply for a position as a nurse-counselor in the Child Day Treatment program. They're interested in hiring me because I have an interest in psychiatry and pediatrics, and I have excellent references. When they ask about my personal psychotherapy experience, which I shared in my application hoping it would be seen as an asset, I say I'm hoping to gain an understanding of the process from the patient's point of view. At that time, I have no clue that I have an interest in my own mental health. I start working there in late August 1974.

I marry Gene in September of that year, three months after graduation. We pick the date in the spring, and I spend much of the second-semester planning and making favors for the wedding. It's a simple service at the Catholic Church in Flemington, even though we're both disinterested Catholics. I wear a self-made white dress, embroidered across the bodice by a friend's mother, and a wreath of flowers in my hair. Gene wears a tux. Mary, my best friend in high school, is my maid of honor and my three college roommates are bridesmaids. Gene's brother is best man, and my three brothers, ages fifteen to twenty-one, are ushers. We leave the church in my decorated VW Beetle with me at the wheel.

At the reception, I surprise Gene and everyone else when I yank my skirt up to expose the garter and a red and white patterned knee-sock. The crowd roars as Gene sheepishly smiles at me with his lovely green eyes. We're both happy to deflect the attention from the intimacy of him touching my leg to the hilarity of my antics.

I hear my mother, looking mortified, say to my aunt, "That's Karen for you. Full of surprises." My aunt looks perturbed, and she glares at me. I feel like I'm spoiling something.

We leave for our apartment later that evening, with Gene's mom, Adele, in the car. No honeymoon after the service. Instead, Gene and his buddies are planning a trip to the southwest, Ansel Adams' territory, hoping to capture something close to Adams' *Moon over Half Dome*. I'll tag along for what will be a honeymoon we both can endure—one with little focus on romance.

Our premarital living situation switches: Adele takes over my studio apartment on the eighth floor, and I move into the twenty-second-floor apartment she shared with Gene. We sleep in the same bed he slept in when he lived with Adele. With me as tag-a-long, Gene's buys new Danish-style furniture in tones of orange, yellow and brown. I weigh in, but he knows exactly what he wants and I'm indifferent. He chooses a long pile Rya rug, a sleek upholstered couch and teak tables and lamps.

All very modern and bright. We buy a thick, round, oak butcher-block kitchen table, something I especially want.

I settle into a full life. I'm worker bee by day, as is Gene, and an Adele replacement in the off hours. Gene is accustomed to having things a certain way. For example, Adele shows me how to fold his teeshirts just so and place them under a phonebook for natural pressing. I learn how to prepare the perfect lunch each morning, and to make his favorite evening meals, like an easy Pasta E Fagioli, made with canned beans, tomatoes, and pasta. Each evening we have ice cream from Baskin-Robbins bulk gallons, something Gene bought a chest freezer for. I pig out then throw up at least twice each night, seemingly without Gene's knowledge.

Gene likes things neat and tidy in our living room space and he spends upwards of an hour each evening after work with the vacuum chasing fuzzballs shed from the Rya onto the black tile floor, and straightening the magazines or do-dads on the two square tables in front of the couch. He likes edges and corners to be lined up perfectly. We follow a kind of schedule each evening—some nights he develops pictures in the kitchen, which he prints in the small hallway closet. Weekends I putter at home or go with Gene to Manhattan, which he wants me to do every weekend. Unfortunately, those outings are more of a chore and less exciting than they were when we first met. We argue over my driving when he's not with me.

"I don't want anything to happen to you when I'm not with you. Please promise me you won't drive alone." He's serious. What he's afraid of, except accidents, I don't know.

"I know how to drive, and I've driven plenty of places alone and without you. You can't control me, Gene. If I want to go places, I will. I've invited you to come to Jim's when I go there with Peggy and Jerry, and you always refuse. I'm not staying home because you want me to." I'm adamant and mad. I feel like he doesn't trust me and wants to control me. In a way, I'm happy he doesn't come when I invite him. He'll be judgmental and critical and want to leave as soon as we get there.

Peggy, Jerry, and Jim are my co-workers in the Child Day Treatment center.

We work together providing a safe environment for elementary school-aged emotionally disturbed children. We structure each day's activities, set limits, reward good behavior and learning, play with, and love them. My duties include giving out medications, taking care of simple medical problems, and being an all-around team member like my three pals. A psychologist, Ronnie, works closely with us. She's a few years older than the three of us—smart, funny and takes a liking to me. Her husband, Kenny, is a newly licensed dentist.

Peggy is studying for a doctorate in neurolinguistics, Jerry and Jim are working on doctorates in psychology. Jim, a true seventies hippy, has long hair, an apartment with walls and windows draped in tie-dye and floors covered in pillows and mattresses. He questions everything about society and says he smokes pot to chill out and tune into a clearer perspective. I begin taking graduate classes at New York University, working towards a master's in nursing.

Our work group gathers at Jim's place every couple of weeks to chatter about how we could make things better for the kids if the establishment would only stop this or do that. We're all very serious twenty-somethings. We haggle over how to respond to different kids and how to get their seemingly disinterested families more involved in their lives. We use our psychiatric book learning to make diagnoses and talk about the complexes we decide plague the higher-ups we work with. We talk about each other, too, playfully arguing about our own psychiatric symptoms. We smoke pot and drink beer and wine out of bottles we pass around for sharing while lounging in close huddles on the floor—except, I can't really lounge or huddle in my non-pliable, waist-high, wooden leg. Instead, I sit legs stretched out, literally half my body inaccessible to lounging.

Everything about this is new to me—exciting and terrifying, though I don't let on. Instead, I settle into fantasies of how Jim wants to be my boyfriend. In my head, I play over and over things he's said, times he's brushed into me while lounging, and how I imagine he's sending me signals with his eyes. The alcohol, which I've rarely consumed in the amounts I drink at these parties, spaces me out and the pot agitates me to a kind of paranoia. I manage my hyper-aware inner state by purging everything I put into my mouth in whatever bathroom is around. It's noisy at Jim's, but if I worry I'll be heard releasing the contents of my stomach, I run water and flush in succession. It works every time, sending me back for more of the same indulging and fantasizing.

One night while I'm driving home I have a minor accident with another car. There's some damage to the car, but it's drivable. I call Gene.

"Gene, it's me. I had a little accident coming home. I have to wait for the police to get here…"

"Are you ok? Where are you, I'll be right there. Don't drive home without me." He's riled, sounds worried and, not angry but upset.

"I'm fine. You don't have to come. I can drive home. How will.." I'm annoyed. I can take care of my self. I don't need him.

"I'm taking a cab. Wait there for me." He hangs up.

Now I'm mad. I finish up with the person whose car I hit, the police leave and I sit in the car waiting.

We argue on the way home and then sink into a palpable silence. I hate being controlled. Things haven't been going well, and we've been married just a little over a year. We don't like the same things. I blame him for all that's wrong—socializing, sex, my lack of independence. I know I've changed and I expect him to change with me, exactly like I change. He refuses counseling, he doesn't want me to go to graduate school—he says it's too soon that I just graduated from college. I don't want to go to Manhattan with him anymore; his friends bore me. I find them dumb and tasteless. The marriage is a big mess.

To add to it all, one day soon after the accident, I decide to go home with a man I met in the halls of New York University. It's a planned rendezvous, so I tell Gene I'll be home late because I'm going out with friends. We walk to his place, a small apartment, up a few flights, with a loft bed, which he invites me into immediately. I've never been in a bed with anyone but Gene, and we usually have quick sex, cuddle a bit and sleep separately. It's all I know. I'm terrified yet curious. I take the wooden leg and my pants off at the bottom of the ladder and pull myself up into the loft. I lie down, stiff as a board, afraid to speak or move. He begins undressing me, we have sex and I leave. It's a little more than an hour start to finish, and I never see him again.

I feel mean—and scared. Gene doesn't deserve this.

A few days later, I'm in the bathroom at work, washing my hands, and I take my wedding ring off—a ring I wanted more than anything just a short year ago. It accidentally falls into the sink and rushes down the drain with the running water. I'm scared because I recognize it as less of an accident and more of a sign that I don't want to be married to Gene anymore.

At home that night, I tell him about it. "My ring fell into the sink today while I was washing my hands, and went down the drain before I could grab it. I feel awful."

Exasperated he asks, "Why did you take it off?"

"We're supposed to wash our hands really well at work. I've taken it off before. It really was an accident. I've felt bad all day. I loved that ring."

"Me, too. I remember the day we picked it out. You said it was just what you wanted. You always liked it more than the diamond, which you hardly ever wear."

"I know. I'm afraid it'll break off or I'll lose it somewhere."

That's all that was said that night or for the next few nights. It's a relief not to have the ring and not to talk about it.

Come Friday, I go to work and Gene heads out to Manhattan. We meet up that evening at home. He has a surprise for me.

"Hon-o, open this," he says as he scoots closer to me on our couch.

It's a small box, perfect size for a ring. I open it.

Before I say anything, he says, "I couldn't find the exact ring. I hunted all over the jewelry district. This is pretty close, right?"

"Oh, Gene, wow." It's almost exactly the same, a squishy gold chain with an interesting pattern. I slip it on, wishing he didn't buy it. I feel so bad.

That week, I tell my therapist everything: the night with the man, losing the ring, not wanting to be married to Gene anymore. I'm self-righteous, he's so hard to live with…

My therapist, John, is in his late fifties with a shock of white hair, a thin, tall frame and an elegantly distant manner that attracted me my first semester in nursing school when he was my Psychology 101 professor. Though some months ago when I began meeting with him I thought of it as an adjunct to my studies and work, I quickly took to complaining to him about my mother, and lately Gene. Both my mother and Gene disagree with my seeing him. They believe therapy causes problems rather than helping to solve them.

"Should I tell him about the guy I slept with?" I ask John.

"What do you think? Have you told him that you're unhappy and don't want to be married anymore? Have you talked about it with anyone else?" He's sitting back in his fancy black leather chair, totally still, staring straight at me.

"No, I'm too scared. I'm confused. Please, just tell me what you think." John rarely offers advice. He listens as I ramble on through most of our meetings.

"If you're certain you're going to leave him, I'd suggest not telling him about the other man. It would be hurtful and there would be nothing he could do. Maybe if you tell him how you feel, he'll agree to work on it. I could see the two of you or recommend another therapist."

"Gene disagrees with therapy. He's already told me he'd never see a therapist."

130

I'm a mess inside, but I tell no one else. I go along acting as if everything's fine, except for the eating and throwing up. I decide to tell Gene and my mother about that. I have not told John. I worry he'd suggest I need more intense therapy or say he can't see me anymore. I know it's awful to keep doing it. Maybe it's contributing to how awful I feel inside. I don't tell Peggy because I don't want all my new friends to know about it.

The next week I arrange a trip to my family's place, telling my mother I want to talk with her. I'm scared but I have an edge that keeps things in control.

"I'm unhappy married to Gene," I tell my mother. "I'm thinking about getting a divorce."

"What? Are you serious? He's a good guy, Karen. He loves you and he'll take care of you. There won't be many other men who'll want to marry you with your problem. You'd better really think about it before you do it." She's shocked and clearly not happy. My back goes up.

"I have this eating and throwing up problem, and I think being married to him is making it worse." I say as if I was telling her about my day. It's like it's nothing big, but it's his fault.

"I know about that. You've lied about it whenever I've asked you. It's your problem. You have to just stop, that's all, just stop." She's yelling, walking around closing the windows so the neighbors don't hear.

Suddenly, all my defensive armor finds its way to the surface. She doesn't understand. No one understands. I have to do everything myself.

"Yeah, you're right, you're always right. It's all my fault. Everything's my fault. You've never helped me with anything, not even when I was sick with cancer."

"It's all that therapy that's making you this way—angry, selfish, ungrateful. Don't you think we were hurting, too, when you were sick?"

"Therapy is helping me figure out who I am and what I want to do. You don't know anything about it." We're shooting accusations, like arrows, straight into each other's heart. Neither of us is hearing or seeing the other.

I storm out of the house and drive back to Newark. That night I talk with Gene.

"I'm unhappy, Gene. I think I want a divorce." I say it as if I were telling him about my day at work.

"Really. What's so wrong?" He's surprised, like he has no idea.

"We don't like the same things anymore. You won't come to therapy with me and never want to meet my friends. You don't want me to go to graduate school even though I've been accepted and have a full scholarship and a stipend. I'm tired of spending time in Manhattan doing the same stuff all the time. You don't want to drink wine or try pot. Nothing feels fun anymore." I'm unemotional, detached. I've made up my mind. No matter what he says, I'm leaving.

"Those friends are not good for you. Therapy and all that mental stuff are what makes you unhappy. I told you—I'm not going to any therapy, but I love you and want to be married to you."

"I have another thing to tell you. I throw up all the time after everything I eat. It's getting worse. I think it's because I'm so unhappy." It's like a declaration. I say it as if I'm expecting him to say or do something that will make it go away.

"Well, you just have to stop, that's all. Just stop."

"I've tried, I can't, and I can't live here anymore." Yeah, he loves me but he won't help me. He just tells me to do it all myself.

"Where will you go?" He's puzzled, this is all totally unexpected. He had no clue.

"Peggy tells me there's an apartment across the hall from theirs on Kennedy Boulevard in Jersey City. I'm going to look at it this week and probably rent it."

I do both, and we split up our stuff, and he helps me move in the first weeks of January 1976.

9 Graduate School

Hope is not the conviction that something will turn out well,
but the certainty that something makes sense regardless of how
it turns out.

/ Vaclav Havel

MY NEW APARTMENT IS ON THE THIRD floor of an old brick walk-up. Peggy and Jerry live across the hall. It's a boxy three-room space, with the rooms arranged in a triangle off a short hallway. The windows are small and the ceilings low, so the place is dark most of the time. I want little to do with Gene or any of the things in the Newark apartment but, the one piece of furniture I take is the butcher-block kitchen table. I buy a few things, and Peggy loans me what else I need to have a livable space.

Gene and I agree to file separation papers in January after I move out. We'll have to wait eighteen months to file for a no fault divorce.

My Primary Care Nursing: Child and Adolescent Mental Health graduate program starts in February 1976. It's in the Bronx, at a branch of City College of New York. The ten of us, all women, will finish with a master's in nursing (MSN), and the academic requirements needed to become a Pediatric Nurse Practitioner if we choose to complete the necessary clinical requirements after graduation.

A couple of our professors are known to me from the classes I took at New York University. They're all pediatric psychiatric nurses, with academic and clinical accolades.

Jane, a fellow student, and I become friends over the next few months. She's about ten years older, single, a New Yorker, transplanted years ago from the Midwest, and a long-time Bellevue Hospital psychiatric nurse.

"How'd you end up in this program, Jane," I ask her at lunch one day during the first week.

"I'm so tired of working weekends and off shifts in what feels like a dungeon. I still enjoy the patients, but it's frustrating to see people come back repeatedly and not be able to do much for them. I've wanted to work with children for awhile now, just couldn't afford to get the training. This is such the perfect opportunity."

I tell about myself, too, except nothing about the eating and throwing up. She knows I'm separated and in therapy.

"I've been in analysis for years, with the same person. It keeps me sane," she says.

That reassures me and I like Jane even more.

That first of four semesters, we focus on the nurse practitioner skills, including history taking and physical exam specifics and we practice on each other. Classroom teaching includes a couple of classes on Jungian and Freudian philosophies and the pediatric offshoots of those. I most enjoy the philosophical and psychiatric theories. Jane is well versed in both, and we have great conversations throughout the spring.

Since we all receive full tuition and a $4000 stipend each of the two years, working part-time is enough for me to manage financially. I work full-time through the summer of 1976 in the pediatric day treatment program.

In the late spring 1976, I meet Greg, a sweet, romantic man. He's recently divorced and eager to find a new partner. He dotes on me, calling regularly, willing to meet my friends, all the while trying to convince me to sleep with him. I can't and I don't. I don't trust that he'll like me after he sees what my body really looks like. He asks about my leg but, as always, I sugar-coat all my replies. I don't believe he's truly curious and concerned.

"Is it uncomfortable? It seems pretty tight around your waist. How heavy is it?"

"It's fine. I'm used to it. It weighs fifteen pounds, but it's not a problem. I just use my back muscles to throw it forward. The only thing that bugs me is how I have to climb steps one at a time," I utter nonchalantly, blandly, unemotionally, looking him in the eye. Technically, I'm a liar and I don't know it.

That summer he arranges a camping trip to Canada. Over a weekend we drive to a woodsy place somewhere in the northeast of the country. He plans, packs for, and sets up the entire thing. He woos me. He wants to sit around the fire and cuddle, kiss, and gaze into my eyes. The woods and the wooden leg are not a good mix. Getting up and down from the ground is difficult and the thought of sleeping in a tent, with or without the leg, threatens to upset my tenuous control. Throwing up is difficult because he follows me everywhere I go. His intentions are all the best. He wants me to be his girlfriend, but I tell him I want to leave before the first night is over, blaming it all on him.

"You're too needy—always wanting to touch me and kiss. It's like you can't function unless you have a woman in your life. Well, I'm not that woman. I don't want to be your girlfriend, cuddle and kiss you, or have sex with you." I'm self-righteous, biting and so well defended I have no idea how weak and scared I feel inside.

We pack up and drive home in relative silence. I'm unaware of anything but my relief. I offer no apology and am unable to acknowledge my fears for more than a fleeting second.

Not too long after that, I begin seeing another man. Joe is Italian, late twenties, a sports aficionado, high school and college football player, and a hit with my brothers. He's easy, laid back, sweet and curious about me. Still, I can't allow him to touch more than my distal body. We kiss and he caresses my breasts and leg. Any physical intimacy riles me like a disturbed cat. My skin crawls and my insides feel like I've had gallons of caffeinated coffee. I can't do it. We part without a fight or harsh words. He loses interest and I'm happy. Outwardly, I don't need anyone and can make people believe it, what with my super positive disposition, my sly way of slinging barbs that others don't seem to attribute to me, and the secret eating and throwing up that allows me to rid myself of any unpleasant (and likely many pleasant) feelings. In truth, all those undesirable inner experiences are merely being stuffed down, deeper and deeper. No amount of purging food can touch them.

———— ⋄ ————

We spend most of the graduate school fall semester 1976 in the classroom delving deeper into developmental theory and the writings of some of the major child psychiatrists. I soak up the readings, becoming ever more curious about how life events affect behavior and how different psychiatric modalities explain the workings of the mind. I'm more curious about my own history as well, though I'm still unwilling or unable to look closely at what motivates my self-destructive behavior. I continue to believe it helps me function.

I didn't see Jane all summer and we didn't keep in touch. I'm excited to reconnect, hoping she'll still want to hang out with me. I idolize her: she's older, lives in New York, dresses in an elegant casual style, has a small wardrobe of beautifully fitted jeans, blazers, and classic feminine shirts. She wears smart leather shoes and belts. In addition, she's got lovely curly, free-flowing brown hair and is pencil thin. My hero, really. I want to be just like her.

She teaches me all about quality fabric—wools, cottons, silks—and tailoring. She has all her clothes tailored by a professional she's known for years. We talk a little about my body and the kind of clothes that might work.

"Mostly, Karen, the key to good looking clothing is fabric. Tailoring for a fitted look is important, too, if that's a look you want. Looser

136

fitting, good quality clothes will hang better and feel nicer on than cheaper clothes made of polyester." We walk through department stores like Bonwit Teller and she has me feel fabrics. I love it. It's like having a big sister.

We grow much closer that semester. We sit outside and talk about school. She shows me some of the inexpensive places to eat and shop. She loves Manhattan, and I experience the city again, in a way not so different from when I was with Gene. He, too, seeks quality and scopes out less known and unusual places in the city. Jane is interested in hearing about Gene and what went wrong. She's never been married and wants to have children. Despite having had a number of relationships, nothing ever worked out. She's curious about why I'd let go of someone who loves me and is good to me.

She and Gene meet once or twice that semester. Jane awakens a desire in me for nice things, and I begin hassling Gene about stuff I want from the apartment since everything in the apartment we shared is of the best quality and style thanks to Gene's impeccable taste. Our interactions are not pretty. I can't be in the same room with Gene without feeling agitated and uncomfortable. I manage those feelings by criticizing and interpreting everything about him, using psychological theories I've recently learned. I expect him to take it and agree with me. He does take it, but he refutes all of my psychobabble.

Over the next year, Gene begins dating a freshman nursing student. I meet her and am happy for him. We agree to share more of the apartment furnishings. I have no contact with him after the first few months of 1977. He stays very much with me though, stuffed way down in the dark recesses of my cells.

———— ◊ ————

Winter semester 1977 Jane and I plan our required project, a six-week group play therapy session at a private school in Greenwich Village. Jane and a professor in the program know the Headmaster and he welcomes us. We have a group of six to eight boys, selected by the school with permission from the parents and we base our weekly sessions on theory from Virginia Axline's book, *Play Therapy*. We meet with the parents and the Headmaster to discuss our progress throughout the project.

It's a difficult, though enlivening and educational experience for us. We can only hope the boys are learning and having fun. Our planned activities sometimes capture the boys' attention. At other times we have a bunch of unruly, scattered, overly energized eight-to-ten year-olds running around the small room we work in. We manage to complete the project without any major incidents—no major altercations, no injuries, no parental complaints—and grow lots closer sharing the ups and downs. Our paper earns us an excellent grade.

———— ◆ ————

Early in the 1977 winter semester, I have an appointment for a fitting for a new wooden leg. I have insurance, which will pay for most of it. As I wait to see the prosthetist, I overhear talk about skiing in the next cubicle and knock on the wall.

"Hi, I'm Karen. Heard you talking about skiing. With one leg?" I'm skeptical as hell.

"Yeah, that's right," a man's voice answers.

"Where?" Truth be told, I've never had a conversation with another amputee. My only interaction with disabled people since Shriners, has been in passing at the prosthetist's office. I've never considered skiing.

"Come over to our room, and I can tell you more."

He's about my age, mid-twenties, tall and lean. His left leg is missing above the knee. The man and woman with him each have two legs. He introduces them as his "normie" friends.

"There's skiing for gimps in New Hampshire, a place called Mt. Sunapee," he says, "and in Canada, Colorado, and Pennsylvania."

"Do you know anyone in Pennsylvania?" I ask.

"No, but I know a guy in Boston," he says as he flips through the address book he takes out of his bag.

I ask how long he's been skiing and if it's hard to learn. I'm intrigued and have lots more questions. Maybe skiing is the thing that will make my life perfect. I don't acknowledge it to myself or anyone else, but what that means is that my leg will grow back, I'll have a model's body and will stop throwing up. Like magic.

"Not too hard. You'll be able to learn if you don't mind falling in the snow a few times. Here, call Steve. He's a great guy who loves to turn new gimps on to skiing."

We talk for several minutes more. He and his friends are from Canada, passing through Pennsylvania on a longer trip. He stopped for a wooden leg tune-up. I ask him what gimp means, and he tells me it's what amputees call themselves and each other. A term of endearment.

I call Steve the next week. We talk for half an hour, and he invites me up for a long weekend in April 1977. Skiing season will be over, but he'll introduce me to some amputees and show me around Boston.

—————— ٠ ——————

Steve lives in Charlestown, the home to Bunker Hill. It's mostly a working-class, Irish town with pricy condos lining the water's edge. His ground-floor apartment is in a row house on a street a few blocks from the water. He talks me through directions to his place and greets me with a broad, welcoming smile. We're total strangers but for a few short phone conversations. He's a stocky guy, arms outstretched for a big hug. We carry my things in, and he offers me a drink. We share a beer in his messy kitchen, and he tells me about himself.

"I lost my leg a few years ago in a sailing accident. You can see it's below the knee, so not such a big deal. It's a radical BK (below knee), though, so I don't have the stability I'd have if I had a longer stump." He says all this while taking off his leg, showing and inviting me to touch his stump and taking a few steps after he straps it back on.

"The suction action in the socket is not the greatest because the stump is so short." Almost immediately, I decide that Steve's disappointments—losing his leg, and then not having the best situation for a highly functioning prosthesis—limit him in his physical abilities and, maybe more, in how he feels about himself. Although, I don't chime in with my self-righteous judgments, like how I think he's making excuses, that first day, over the next couple of days those judgments grow and extend to others I meet.

The next day Steve introduces me to Cale, an avid, experienced skier, and a few of his sailing buddies. Cale's a curly-blond-haired woman, about the same age as me, who lost her leg several years earlier in a motorcycle accident. She and her boyfriend, both nineteen, were driving to the place they would consummate their relationship. They crashed. He was killed and her leg was ripped off at the groin. After extensive medical and surgical care over many months, she was left with a hemipelvectomy amputation, a reconstructed pelvic area, and a tremendous amount of scar tissue. She has a wooden leg, a fancy endoskeletal modular, like the one I'm being fitted for, which she rarely wears because of the pain, phantom and other, that she experiences constantly.

"I'm much happier without the leg. I try to wear it but the pain is so bad, I end up taking it off and leaving it in a corner. I can't believe you can wear yours all day and walk in it so well. Doesn't it hurt and drive you crazy?" She's lying back on a beanbag chair, her back extended, wearing a long, flowing dress, her signature style. Her hair is a curly, free-form bob. It suits her cherub face. She's full of wild energy which she shares with me as we drive around downtown Boston in her Audi. She yells out the window to people and sings as loud as she can to the music. All without her wooden leg which she calls a prosthesis. She's a pro on underarm crutches, fast moving with a skipping motion.

I'm in awe and, also, somewhat mortified. How can she show herself like that, without her leg? I have many more judgments—she doesn't want to work, likes being on the dole (as she calls it)—which I keep to myself.

The next day I tour a forty-eight-foot sailboat with Steve and meet several of the crew members. The owner of the boat is an amputee doctor,

140

Al. He has an AK—above knee amputation—with a long stump which he inserts into a socket atop a wooden log-like thing that substitutes for a wooden leg, something like Captain Ahab wore in *Moby Dick*. He and the crew compete, mostly for fun, in summer races in the Boston Harbor and beyond.

"Come back this summer and join us," Al says, his hand on my shoulder. "We'll introduce you to the pleasures of sailing and get you up to snuff with crewing. We have a blast, though we rarely win a race." He tells me it's being out on the water with friends, and the barbecue, and gin and tonic parties after the racing that make it all the more fun. "Come back! Love to have you, a fellow gimp!" He's a big presence and overwhelmingly welcoming in a totally believable way.

Sunday, as I pack to leave, Steve hugs me and invites me back for the summer. I'm my true wooden-like self through all the physical affection and I feel self-conscious being seen with an amputee man. I'd love a boyfriend—just not one with one leg.

"Come live here with me. I'll introduce you to more skiers; we'll sail and see more of Boston." Cale's there with us as I'm getting in the car for the drive home.

"Yeah, come back. We'll hang out, cruise around, do wild things. It'll be so much fun." She's sorry to see me go. I'm the first person she's met with a hemipelvectomy and a functional prosthesis. She's the first amputee woman I've met, and I'm shocked and curious that she's OK not wearing her leg.

"I'd have to get a job," I say, thinking maybe that would be a good excuse not to join this seemingly rag-tag group of amputees that I self-righteously feel superior to.

"I'm sure you could find something here. Think about it and give a call if you decide to come. Open invitation," Steve says with a big smile and his arm around my waist, squeezing me toward him. My body stiffens, and simultaneously I feel cared for and special.

Driving home, I'm full of excitement—maybe learning to sail and ski would be a cure for the E&T. I worry that Steve wants to be my boyfriend, though it was never mentioned. I'm full of who's-better-than-who confusion, as well, and whether it would be okay to spend time with all these one-legged people. Isn't that the opposite of being adjusted? Will I be judged as handicapped and lazy by normal people?

———

Back at school, Jane is beside herself with interest in what the weekend was like.

"So—how was it? Did you learn anything about skiing? Did you like Steve? Meet anyone else?" It's like she's on the edge of her chair with anticipation.

"Well, it was great. I met a woman skier, Cale, who never wears her wooden leg. She says it hurts too much and she takes it off and puts it on anytime, anywhere, on a whim. I can't believe she can walk around without it and feel OK. Several of the amputees I met do the same thing..."

"Really? That's great. It's brave to show yourself as you are." Jane's totally serious.

"Don't you think it's kind of lazy not to at least try to look normal?"

"Not at all. Besides, you probably don't know the whole story. What about Steve?"

"He's nice. He introduced me to some sailing people and they invited me to come sailing this summer. Steve invited me to live with him. It was a lot of stuff for a short weekend." I'm excited. I had an adventure and Jane's interested.

———

I do some research that spring and find a job as the nurse at a camp in Essex, Massachusetts. It's a camp for middle and high school boys and girls, with a nurse and a doctor on site. That makes it perfect for me since I'm not confident enough as a nurse to assume total responsibility for anyone's health and safety.

I'm overjoyed. I'm going to Boston for the summer. I call Steve and Cale.

"I'm coming..."

10 Adventures with Fellow Gimps

Opportunities are also everywhere and so you must always let your hook be hanging. When you least expect it, a great fish will swim by.

/ Og Mandino

A COUPLE OF DAYS AFTER I ARRIVE in Boston, I know I have to talk with Steve about our living arrangements. He's friendly in a way that makes me uncomfortable—I can't imagine allowing myself to have an amputee boyfriend. I worry about what people will think of me.

One night early in that first week Steve and I meet for dinner at the house.

"Steve," I say without a hint of hesitation in my voice, "I really like you and it's great living here, but I'm confused about what you expect of me. It doesn't feel right to be in a relationship with anyone right now. With working at the camp and new friends to meet, places to see—I wouldn't have enough time to spend with you. I'm wondering if we could live together as friends for the summer? I can pay some rent..."

"Sure, platonic is good. I didn't know what to expect either. No need to pay rent. I like the company," he says before I finish. Maybe he never considered anything else and I just imagined it all? It doesn't matter. It's a big relief.

"Wow—really? So I can live here and we can be friends, maybe do some things together?" I'm excited; it seems like it will all work out.

"Yeah, that'll work," he says in his Boston twang. "I'd like to take you sailing sometime. I think you'd really like it. I have some friends with a big sailboat. We'll set it up for some weekend."

Soon after I begin my camp job, Cale and I meet up regularly after work to hang out. One evening I confess about my newest infatuation.

"There's a guy at the camp I really like," I say.

"Well, what's he like? Tell me the rest." Cale loves men and is unabashedly certain they all like her. She dresses in skirts and fitted tops, has a nice cleavage and the most beautiful curly blond locks I've ever seen. She knows how to flirt.

"His name is Kevin. He's around my age, maybe a little younger, really cute and soft-spoken. He seems to seek me out for company when he's not on duty." I say sheepishly, always afraid to talk about liking a man for fear he'd never like me, and I'd be humiliated for even thinking someone might like me.

"So, does he have a girlfriend? Has he asked you out? Have you touched?" She's super excited, wanting to hear all the details of which there are few. I'm a wreck around men on the inside. I'm stand-offish and judgmental on the outside.

"Well, I haven't talked to him that much..."

"How do you know you like him, then?"

"He's just nice, and he seems to like me," I say, unaware that what I really like is the aloofness that dominates his interactions with me.

"You've got to talk to him more, see if he likes things you like, see if there's any chemistry," she says. "And keep me posted about the developments."

The camp job is relatively easy. Kids and staff like me, I do a fairly good job as the nurse giving out daily medications to kids who need them, applying Band-Aids, and consoling the occasional homesick camper. I do as Cale suggests and find time to hang around with Kevin. I share stories about my escapades with my new found friends.

"What's your roommate like?" Kevin asks one day while we're sitting by the water at the camp. I never swim there. I don't want anyone to see me without my wooden leg.

"He's a nice guy, an amputee. I don't know much about him except that he loves sailing and skiing. He seems to go out on the water only when other people invite him."

"Maybe he's depressed about losing his leg. How'd it happen?" he sounds truly interested. He'd asked me about my missing leg during the first week of camp and accepted my pronouncement about how well-adjusted I am. He asked a few questions then, none since.

"A sailing accident. Apparently, he was a pretty good sailor. Still, it's been a few years. He should be over it by now." I'm low on compassion and don't want to talk about Steve.

"A few years is not very long. That sounds like a big loss," he says, then changes the subject. "Have you ever sailed?"

"No, but Steve says he's going to take me sometime, on a boat some friends have. Do you sail?"

"I love sailing, especially small Lasers. They're fast, one-man boats, though two people can fit in. How about we go to the Anisquam bay—it's a few miles away—after camp this week. I'll take you out." He's excited, and I'm scared and happy. I'll have something to tell Cale.

"I'm little scared…" I say.

"You'll be fine. I'll sail, you sit and watch."

That night I tell Cale I'm going sailing.

"So he asked you out. He must like you then."

"I'm not sure. He just likes sailing and wants me to see. I told him Steve wants to take me. Have you ever been?"

"When I was a kid, and once or twice with Steve since his accident."

145

Later that week Kevin and I drive to the Anisquam bay. He rents a Laser for an hour. It's a small boat with one sail and a mostly flat deck with a shallow cut-out around the mast for the sailors' feet.

"Don't worry," Kevin says as he sees me cringe while staring at several boats on the bay. Some are up on their side with the mast almost parallel to the water. Many are part way tipped, with water splashing into the shallow cut-out. All are going fast. "We'll stay close to the dock and I promise not to tip it too far."

I'm horribly self-conscious as I sit on the dock and slide my wooden foot into the boat. I quickly catch myself with my good foot. The boat rocks side to side. Kevin's in the boat, doing his best to steady it. We're up against the dock so I can hold on as I bend the wooden leg and slide down to sit on the edge.

"Good, you're in," he says as he sits and adjusts the sail. There's very little room for all four feet in the cut-out. My wooden foot is inflexible and juts out taking up much of the space. Kevin says nothing about it.

"Ready?" He looks at me across the narrow deck. There's an electricity between us here and when we're at the camp, but we don't touch or acknowledge it. I'm both happy and frustrated to feel it. Happy because he's a cute guy who maybe will save me from myself, and frustrated because I have no idea whether Kevin likes me and I'm pretty certain he just feels sorry for me.

"Yep," I say as we take off floating along the water. Kevin adjusts the sail as the wind shifts. I have no idea how, although he's telling me everything he does as we sail around the bay.

"It's not too windy right here, close in, today. Go out a little further and you can see how much fun those guys are having."

"You can drop me off, if you want. I can watch while you go out further." I offer, certain I'm a drag, spoiling his fun.

"No, not unless you want to get out."

"No-no, I like it."

As we sail back and forth, Kevin makes some quick turns but never once tips the boat to the point that we get more than a light spray. It's a bit of a challenge getting out, muscling my torso high enough on the dock to swing my good leg around and then hoisting the wooden leg up. I feel exhilarated when I'm on the dock again, looking out.

"Fun, huh? Next time maybe we can go to Community Boating on the Charles River and you can try sailing. The boats there are small and easy to maneuver, and the river's calm."

I spill my guts to Cale the next time we're cruising the streets of Boston.

"The whole time you were in the boat he never touched you?" Cale is shocked.

"No, it's okay. I'd rather just be friends. I'm perfectly fine without a boyfriend," I say with my usual detached air. I'm a good actress. "What's Community Boating?"

"A place on the Charles River, where they teach people to sail small, one-man boats. Why do you ask?"

"Kevin said we would go there next time and I could do the sailing."

"Does he have a membership? I think you need to sign up for the summer. They have different plans based on how much you're gonna sail."

"I'll ask him about the membership. Maybe I can get a membership." I'm thinking so I can impress Kevin.

A couple of weeks later, before anything happens with Community Boating and after a few Laser rides with Kevin, Steve invites me to join him for a day on the forty-eight-foot sailboat owned by his friend.

"Al's looking forward to meeting you. He's a one-legged surgeon. Lost a leg in the war, I think. He uses a peg on the boat."

"I think I met him when I was here last time. Remember, you took me to the place he keeps the boat."

"Yeah, that's right, I remember now. Well, he's invited us for a sail."

"How did all you one-legged people meet? Seems like you're a big club or something."

"There's a pretty good network here in Boston, mostly because of skiing at Mount Sunapee where's there's an amputee program."

"You all like each other just because you're amputees?" I'm thinking: is that a reason to like someone?

"Sort of, yeah. You'll see when you meet more people. Lots of these guys and ladies are really great people: fun-loving, friendly, generous. It borders on a wild bunch sometimes. Maybe because we've all had something that makes us realize life is not in our control."

I feel perfectly in control of my life, I think, as I excuse myself to purge the chips and candy I just ate.

As we approach Al's boat at the dock in Charlestown, I see him and a few others moving around on the deck and in a sunken place at the back end. Al pops up to welcome us.

"Karen, glad you made it back," he says extending his hand. I sit on the edge and hold my wooden leg up to swing it over the side. "I'm Al. Do I remember right? You've never been sailing?"

"Not on a boat like this. Just on a Laser up near the camp where I'm working. A friend there took me out a few times."

"Those are fun. Did you try sailing it?"

"No, I have no idea how to sail. I love the water though. I used to swim a lot so I think it'll be fun." I'm excited. Sailing on the ocean seems so ritzy and sophisticated, yet everyone I've met is so nice. I notice Al's peg again. It's a wooden log sort of thing attached to the socket that covers his stump. He walks with a stiff leg limp, similar to Steve's. Something about it is very attractive, even though I'm shocked he feels OK looking like that. I get the sense it's a macho thing, like a medal earned through valor. He and Steve are wearing shorts, smartly so on this warm day. I'm in my usual long pants and long tee shirt, hoping to cover up all my lumps, bumps and hardware.

Soon another couple, Julie and Tim, arrive. They each have two legs. Julie's a nurse who sells medical devices, maybe six or seven years older than me, blonde, curvy, sassy and very attractive. She flirts with Al and he reciprocates. Tim, her boyfriend, is a laid back guy with a blond crewcut and beard. The guys banter. I learn we five will take the boat on a day cruise several miles up the coast. They'll show me the ropes of crewing.

"Have you been sailing a long time?" I ask Julie as we tour below deck. There's a kitchen, called the galley, with stove, fridge, sink, a table with long cushioned benches on either side which reconfigure to make four beds for overnighting; a bedroom with a double bed; and a bathroom, the head in sailing lingo, with shower and sink.

"Since I was a child. I did some racing in one-man boats, and I've crewed with a few different captains. Tim has a boat smaller than this. We go out whenever we can. It's always fun on this boat, though, with the people Al knows and his adventurous nature. He's only had this boat a few years, so it's like a new toy. He got it to try his hand at racing. No medals yet, but a whole lot of fun and partying." She obviously likes Al. I learn they worked together in the past.

We motor out of the harbor with only the large, central mainsail up. It hangs on the mast that rises from the center of the deck and attaches to the boom that is parallel to the boat and extends back to a few feet shy of the helm, where Al steers while sipping his morning coffee.

"Let's walk up on the deck while the guys shoot the baloney here. Since we're motoring, the ride is pretty smooth, a good time for you to get a feel for your sea legs." Julie leads me around the boom to the front of the boat. We stand, then sit, watching the city pass by. Being out on the water is magical and freeing—breathing the air, soaking up the sun, and gazing into the beautiful blue water.

She points to a large bag stuffed against the bow of the boat. "This is the jib, a sail we'll take out when we get out far enough to catch some nice wind. You'll see how we raise it. You'll be able to do it yourself after a few sails."

I feel pretty stable on my feet, but I wonder if I'll meet up to the expectations she seems to have of me.

"There's another sail we use when the wind is light and we're trying to catch as much as we can. It's a big colorful, balloon-like sail called a Spinnaker. You'll see lots of boats with spinnakers during races."

Julie and I talk about lots of things besides sailing. She's impressed that I wear a leg with such a high amputation. We're both nurses, so we share about nursing school, doctors, salaries, alternative jobs for nurses. She's assertive and stands up to the men on the boat when she thinks she's got more experience or a better idea about how to do things. I learn a lot from just being around her—it's like she's a big sister showing me the way to become a well-rounded woman. She shares about her relationships and has no difficulty talking about sexuality, a topic I shy away from in any personal way, though I can hold my own in intellectual bantering.

I watch as the sails go up when we're far enough out of the bay to catch some wind. The sails balloon out and the boat glides, sways and twists on the gorgeous blue water. Al, Steve, Julie, and Tim take turns steering. We all graze on the snacks below in the galley. I'm concerned about E&T. How will I manage in such a small space with so many people and the teeny tiny bathroom? I can't resist the food, and once I eat a bite, I feel the urge to purge. I check out the head and find it securely locks. I'm confident that the noise of the boat moving and the lively conversations will overpower the sounds of my purging.

"Time to bring out the grill," Al announces as we head into the bay after several hours out on the ocean. The grill hangs over the stern. We grill burgers with onions and peppers that evening. We've been drinking gin and tonics through most of the afternoon since we were out for a day sail, not a race. "We run a much tighter ship when we're racing," Al says.

"It's a little tighter—Al is more into having fun than anything. We've been known to start pouring the drinks halfway through a race sometimes." Julie winks and whispers to me.

I sail with Al, Julie, Tim, Steve and various others many times that summer. During one of our long days racing, as we're heading home, I faint on deck. "She's dehydrated," Julie and Al declare together. "We have to get her to the emergency room for some IV fluids." I'm awake, drowsy, cold and shivering. One too many purges, maybe? I'm scared. Not really for the fainting, but what if they find out?

We motor in quickly. I'm wrapped in blankets and lying with my head on Julie's lap. In the emergency room, they give me fluids. "What happened?" the nurse asks.

"I got seasick and threw up a couple of times." I lie. Truthfully, I ate and threw up throughout the day.

"That'll do it," she says.

"Why didn't you tell us?" Julie asks.

"Too embarrassed. I didn't want you to say I couldn't come anymore."

"Everyone gets seasick at times, even the heartiest of sailors. We're just glad you're okay."

I never quite get the hang of sailing on my own. Part of it is the clumsy way I have to maneuver in the small Community Boating boats, something I'm aware of but would never express. Another part is my anxiety, the fear that I won't be good enough. That expresses itself as indifference. "It's no big deal," I say to anyone who asks about how it's going. "I'm happy just sailing on the weekends and with Kevin when he asks me." I'm in control. Nothing bothers me.

———— ‡ ————

Toward the end of the summer, Al announces he'll be moving to New York to start a new job, a welcomed promotion. "Who will we sail with?" we all lament.

"Julie and Tim have a boat," Al offers.

"Sure we do, nothing like this, though. We're going to miss you, Al, and not just because of the sailing, even though you are the best captain to crew for." Julie gives Al a big hug.

A party is planned for one of the last weeks of the summer. It's a day sail with several more people than usual. Jane, an amputee I'd met a few times earlier that summer, sails with us that day. There's food galore spread out all over the galley counters and benches. We're sailing slowly, chatting, eating, and drinking. I gorge and find myself in the head more than a few times. The last time, it's too much baked ham—a wadded blob of meat and starch that won't flush. As I emerge from the bathroom to look for something to scoop it out so I can throw it overboard, amputee Jane is right outside the door.

"Are you alright?" she asks. "Sounds like you've been throwing up."

"Oh, yeah, I got sick on the ham, I think. The toilet won't flush," I say as nonchalantly as I can. I have no doubt she'll believe me.

"Are you bulimic? I've seen you use the bathroom several times today. My sister has the problem, so I'm aware of what people do." She's standing close and looking right at me.

"No. I just drank a lot today and had to pee a lot. Then, all of a sudden I felt sick. Maybe from the alcohol." No one has ever asked me about E&T. I feel cornered, exposed, scared. She's onto me.

"Okay then. Still seems like a lot of bathroom time, and running the water..." She turns and goes up on deck. I find an empty food container and get the ham out of the toilet and it eventually flushes.

Up on deck, I act as if nothing happened. I'm a tad worried inside, but the denial is so powerful and my rationalization ability so honed, I have another bite and the worry is shoved way down inside.

One beautiful sunny day, Cale and I park the car and stroll the streets of downtown Boston. We stop in front of the library, standing against a wall, watching the people walk by.

Cale spots a tall, dark-haired, handsome man wearing shorts, with a camera strung around his neck. "Hey, you with the peg, come over here," she yells. I never notice the peg. She notices the hunk.

"What's your name?" she asks while she pulls up her floor-length dress to show him her lone foot. "I'm Cale and this is Karen. We're gimps, too."

"I'm Phil."

"Well, hi there Phil. What's a cute guy like you doing walking the streets alone today." Cale is flirting, flirting, flirting.

"Looking for photos. What are you two doing here?"

"Looking for guys—no not really—just hanging and watching people. What happened?" she asks as she looks down at his peg.

"Motorcycle accident and the leg wouldn't heal. After more than a year of antibiotics and surgeries, they suggested amputation and I said okay," he says with a poker face.

"How long ago?" I ask.

"A few months since the amputation. I'm still getting used to the peg. How about you two."

Cale and I tell him our stories. "We're pros by now—we'll show you the ropes," Cale jokes. "Have you been skiing?"

"Not yet. I've heard about it, though. You?"

"Cale's a renowned skier—medals and all. I haven't been—hopefully this winter," I say.

We hang out the rest of that day walking the streets. Phil says he's into taking artsy photos and asks if we'd let him take pictures of the two of us. I hate pictures, Cale loves them. We agree to meet the next week.

Phil takes us to a street in Boston with brownstone row houses. We choose one and Cale and I sit on the stoop, next to each other. We're both wearing our wooden legs. Mine is the wood and metal one I've had for several years. Hers is a new-fangled endoskeletal modular. It has a narrow, metal shaft of workings covered by a nude-colored, leg-shaped foam sheath. Phil photographs us with the wooden legs covered, and again after we pull up our pants and expose the wooden legs.

Next time we meet, Phil brings a sheet of proof photos, each little shot is a two inch square. They're Diane Arbus-like. We're in exactly the same positions in the two poses, but our faces are wildly different in each. In the ones with the legs exposed, we look dour and pained. In the ones with the legs covered, we're smiling.

We have several more photo shoots with Phil. He takes full front, back, and side shots of me in a bathing suit with my bare wooden leg strapped around my waist. Another time in Cale's apartment, he has her lying seductively, her head hanging and her torso draped over her favorite beanbag chair. She's without her wooden leg, so her body is lithe and slinky. He places me so that he can capture my face in a mirror as I gaze at Cale.

My sense that Cale and I are alter egos, connected by our one-leggedness, grows as the summer rolls by. Though I don't know it at the time, I'm in the midst of one of the most important summers and relationships of my life.

11 Unexpected Complications

One must have chaos in oneself in order to give birth to a dancing star.

/ Fredrick Nietzsche

BACK IN JERSEY CITY, WORK AND SCHOOL resume. Fall semester 1977 will be my last. I choose The Emotional Needs of the Hospitalized Child as the topic for my thesis and get busy working on the research. Some wise part of my being knows that the topic pertains to me and that's precisely why it interests me, but my functioning consciousness is unable to acknowledge that. I've managed to separate myself from the events of my own history. I'm bright enough to write an excellent paper and fluently discuss the topic of my thesis. I just can't accept that it has anything to do with me.

After my summer in Boston, I decide I'd like to move there. I apply for a few jobs and score one interview for a position as a Pediatric Mental Health Specialist. I schedule an interview appointment for late October.

That fall, my top teeth begin to bother me—they're sensitive to heat, cold and air. They sting when I breathe in over them. For less than a minute I worry it's from E&T, then quickly decide it's from the radiation I had when I was eight. I tell myself it must have damaged my second teeth as they were growing in. I'd read about the little known long-term effects of radiation, one of which is its potential to destroy new cell growth. This becomes the rationalization that overrides what I know deep down to be true: E&T is ruining my teeth.

Lucky for me, Ronnie, one of my co-workers, has a husband who just opened his dental practice. She offers him up for a reasonable price, and I make an appointment.

As I enter his office, he shakes my hand and leads me to the chair. "I'm Kenny. What's going on with your teeth?" He's a tall, lanky man with dark, curly hair —unassuming and friendly. We're the only two in his office.

I tell him about the symptoms, and he begins the exam.

"The enamel is wearing away on your top teeth. Do they seem shorter to you?"

"I didn't really notice, but now that you mention it…"

"Do you eat a lot of acidic foods, like grapefruit?" He looks puzzled.

"Not really. Could it be from the radiation therapy I had when I was eight?"

"I never heard of that, but radiation can have many odd effects on people." He never asks about vomiting.

"Can you fix them?" I ask as if it's no big deal. Denial is a powerful mindset.

"We could drill them down a little more and put crowns on them all. That will protect them from wearing away any more and possibly damaging the roots. How does that sound?"

"How much will that cost?" I have dental insurance, and I assume that will pay for most of it.

He quotes me what seems a reasonable price, though I have no idea what crowns cost. I've done no research. I agree to the treatment figuring if he says I need it, I must need it.

We have a few appointments over a couple of months. He drills my top teeth down, takes impressions for the permanent crowns, and applies temporary crowns while my new teeth are being made. I shove my suspicions about E&T as having caused the problem into the pit of denial somewhere deep in my gut. I continue eating and purging all through the process. Whatever pain I feel is soothed. After all, I muse, my real teeth will be covered, so they won't be damaged anymore.

"How's the dental work going?" Ronnie asks.

"Great. Kenny's terrific. It hardly hurts at all. He makes it easy."

"Really? Seems a lot of dental work for someone your age."

"Nah, it's fine," I say nonchalantly. My body and I don't communicate much. It hardly registers that at age twenty-five, I'm sporting an upper mouth full of crowns.

———— ⸭ ————

One afternoon in October 1977 the phone in my apartment rings as I'm emptying two bags of groceries on the kitchen table. It's a black, rotary dial sitting atop a small table in my tiny apartment in Jersey City.

"Hello..."

"Karen, I'm so glad you're there," he says.

"Billy, what's wrong? You never call me. What's wrong?" Billy's my twenty-four-year-old brother who lives in Flemington, New Jersey, about fifty miles from where I live in Jersey City. Flemington is home to my parents, and it's where I went to high school.

"David was in an accident. It's bad. You've gotta come home right away." David, my nineteen-year-old, middle brother is handsome, smart, an amazing gymnast, delightfully social, and in his second year at the Naval Academy. He's the family's golden boy. My parents are certain he'll be president of the United States one day.

"Oh my god. Is he OK? Tell me he's OK. Tell me the truth." I'm yelling into the phone, holding it a foot from my ear.

"He's dead, Karen. You gotta come right away."

I hang up the phone and feel a wave of panic coursing through my body. It's like all the fluid inside is rushing to my feet and pouring out my toes. I don't cry. I won't, or maybe I can't. I know exactly what to do.

I walk back into the dark, dingy kitchen and resume emptying the groceries: cheap white bread, English muffins, a pound of margarine, generic grape jelly, peanut butter, two boxes of mac and cheese, a half-gallon of milk, store-brand frosted flakes (for the milk left over from the mac and cheese), a half-gallon of ice cream, copy-cat Oreo cookies, and a two-liter diet cola.

It's early in the evening of October 22, 1977. I tell myself I'll just have some of this and then get going. I start with the mac and cheese. I fill the pot with water and pour both boxes of noodles into the water when it boils. Meanwhile, I toast the bread and slather it with the margarine, peanut butter, and jelly. The cookies and ice cream are open and I shovel them in mouthful after mouthful.

The table is covered with food. I sit in the one chair, facing the bare wall, and pour the cereal into a bowl. When the noodles are done, I dump in the milk, margarine, and powdered cheese, and bring the pot to the table. My arms and mouth move frantically. I continuously feed myself and pour the soda down my throat.

After several minutes, four or five pieces of toast, a bowl or two of cereal, a dozen cookies, half the noodles and ice cream, I go to the bathroom and bend over the toilet. I have to get rid of the mass of feelings that are threatening to explode my insides right out of me. The soda gives the wadded food liquidity so it comes up easily. I create a muscular wave from my stomach, up through my esophagus, and out into the bowl. It takes several deluges, interspersed with gulps of water, to clean me out. The frightening energy of indistinguishable feelings that was pushed down deep into my guts with the food is gone.

I feel relief, let out a big energizing sigh, and reflexively return to the kitchen to repeat the eating and purging routine before those feelings begin to rise again. The energy generated by any feelings, from joy to horrific pain, is always unbearable, but it feels one hundred times worse at this moment. It's an ugly monster that I fear will quickly take control if I don't continuously act to get rid of it.

I can't leave until I eat all the food I bought. It's my second round of shopping, eating, and purging today. I picked up two bags earlier in the day: soda, cookies, ice cream, a whole chicken, dozen eggs, loaf of bread, margarine, cream cheese. All purged.

On the hour-long drive to Flemington, I stop at four or five fast-food drive-ins, eat in the car, throw up in plastic bags I keep in the pocket of the car door, and dump the bags out on the side of the road.

It's late evening when I get to the house. Billy's there, but my parents have not returned from the Caribbean, their first vacation in twenty years. Their plane is late. Billy will drive to the airport to pick them up when they call.

"David was coming to surprise them before he had to go back to school," Billy says.

"What happened? Did you see the car?"

"No. The hospital called me to come and identify the body in the morgue. He was driving his VW Beetle. They were drinking. He crashed into a stone wall down near Lambertville." Billy inhales cigarette after cigarette as he walks back and forth across the room. He gulps beer from the can sitting on the table in front of the couch.

"Who are they?" I ask.

"John, Larry and Brook, David's best buddies. They're all okay. Brook has a pretty bad broken leg."

"What'd he look like?"

"Not too bad. All smashed up but I could tell it was him."

Neither of us cries. We don't hug or even touch. Billy continues to pace and smoke. I sit motionless on the couch. He calls Gerard, our eighteen-year-old brother, who's a freshman at West Point. He and David are very close, fifteen months apart in age. They did almost everything together in high school. I hear him yelling into the phone, demanding Billy tell him how bad it is.

"He's coming tonight," Billy says.

159

The phone rings. The plane has landed. Billy leaves to pick up my parents at the airport, a forty-five-minute drive from his house.

I'm squirming inside myself, like bugs are crawling up and down my veins, as if poison ivy covers every square inch inside of me. I calm myself by rummaging through the kitchen cabinets and fridge, carefully calculating how much I can eat of everything so as not to raise suspicion about missing food. I swig bottled salad dressing when I've exhausted all other options. In between binges, as always, I visit my most significant other these last seven years, the toilet.

Two hours later, Billy returns with our parents, Doris and Bill. I've taken to calling my mother Doris, something she finds disrespectful and my father chastises me for. Tonight I suck it up and call her Mom. I'm twenty-six with a chip on my shoulder when it comes to anything related to my mother. I'm certain I'm much wiser than her.

"What are you doing here?" she asks in an almost accusatory tone. "I knew something was wrong as soon as I got in the car. What is it, what's wrong?"

"God, Billy, didn't you tell them?" I shout at my brother. "David died in a car accident." My skin is tight, closed up. My lips are pressed together. I can barely speak or move. I feel nothing, I have no thoughts, I don't cry, and I can't reach out.

"What...no...it can't be. How do you know? Where is he now? Take me there; I have to see him."

Billy tells them the story of the accident and the hospital and tries to persuade them to wait until the morning to go to the morgue.

"I have to go tonight! Don't you, Dad?" my mother demands. "I have to see him. If you won't take me, I'll drive myself." She's beside herself, sitting, standing, touching her head, covering her face with her hands, tearlessly sobbing, breathlessly shouting out, "Oh my god...my David, he can't be dead, he can't, he can't, he can't..."

My father sits, stone-like, staring into nothingness.

The three of them leave for the morgue. I stay behind to wait for Gerard. He arrives shortly before Billy and my parents return.

Through the night and into the next morning, we five sit, pace, doze, as we stare through each other into space.

Over the next few days we make funeral arrangements, commiserate with neighbors and relatives, and spend hours going over what happened with the boys who were in the car with David. My mother will not accept that drinking played a role.

"My David did not drink that way," she insists.

My father says very little. He's had a stroke and a heart attack in the last few years. He tears up watching TV comedies, and turns away from most interaction, trying to maintain control. He looks sad, defeated, and distant.

There's food all over the house, and I'm eating constantly.

"She has a terrific appetite," my mother tells everyone. If anyone suspects anything about my binge and purge behavior, they don't let on. I run water or flush several times to cover up any sounds. I'm a quiet, efficient, and creative purger. I do it behind trees, in bags, or right out the car door when necessary. It's a challenge to stealthily scope out every situation for the ins and outs of its purging options. There's a kind of panic inside that drives the constant maneuvering and also, a perverse delight in finding ways to make it work.

There are two days of viewing, with the burial in the afternoon of the second day. My mother and father stand like soldiers at the foot of the casket. None of us have cried during the viewings.

A bus full of cadets arrives the morning of the burial. David's three friends, and my brothers and I are behind the crowd of young men making their way up to say their final goodbyes. Gene, the man I am married to and separated from, shows up. The air in the room is dripping with love, sympathy, empathy, grief, but I cannot connect with a single molecule of it. I'm walking on my wooden leg one minute and collapsed on the floor the next. David's friends are lifting me, holding and supporting me as we trudge up to my brother's dead body, on display in the open casket.

"She and David were very close." This is how my mother explains the scene to those in need of explanations.

I ride to the cemetery with my parents and brothers. The driver helps my mother and father out, then turns to help me. I'm catatonic. I honestly cannot move or speak.

"Come on Karen." My brothers and Gene gently try to coax me. I'm literally unable to respond.

"Leave her," my mother says. "She'll be alright. She can see from here."

At the gathering after the burial, I eat and purge and eat and purge.

The next day I drive to Boston to interview for a pediatric mental health nurse position.

———— ◦ ————

A few days later, I get together with my friend, co-worker, and next door neighbor, Peggy.

"Sorry about your brother. Gee, that must've been sad. How are your parents doing?" Peggy asks as we share a beer in her apartment across the hall from mine.

"Yeah, pretty sad...my parents are OK, I guess. Everything about it was hard, especially being around my mother. It's like I'm dead around her. I can't do or say anything that's really me. The way she looks at me—I suspect she's accusing me of something...I collapsed during the funeral. Really, I just turned to mush and slid down to the floor. I have no idea why, but I wondered if she thought I did it on purpose."

"You probably collapsed from shock." Peggy looks at me with sad, puppy eyes. "It was unexpected and all the stress with your family...it's part of the grief reaction."

"Yeah, I guess. I'm much better now, though. Back to school tomorrow. Gotta get to bed."

"Wait, how about the interview?" she asks as I get up to leave.

"It was good and I liked the people I met, but they're looking for someone to start now, and you know I don't finish school until February."

"Are you disappointed?"

"Oh no, it doesn't matter," I say, cavalierly dismissing her concern. "There will be plenty of jobs around after I graduate."

"Sure, but I thought you wanted to go to Boston to meet up with your new friends."

"I do, but it's okay. See you tomorrow," I mutter as I run off, maybe from the topic, definitely toward the food fix that will blot out the wad of feeling rising up from the depths.

The next week I see my therapist, John. It's our regular weekly appointment.

"I just got back from my brother's funeral." I settle into the big, soft black leather chair in the corner of his office. John sits in a chair in another corner. Sometimes I lay on the couch between the two chairs. I share the details of my brother's death. He sits silently listening.

"Hard to be around my mother," I lament. It's a familiar topic. "I collapsed walking up to say my last goodbye. Good thing my brothers were there with me. They caught me and walked me to the coffin. It was embarrassing. Later, I couldn't get out of the car for the burial. Really, my body wouldn't move. How could that happen?"

He mentions grief and asks if I remember grieving when my leg was amputated.

"No. I didn't have to. I just adjusted to it all. Kids get over things, you know. I never even cried about it." It's the first time in over a year of meetings that we've talked about my missing leg. I never brought it up because I shouldn't have feelings about losing my leg. I should be grateful I'm alive. I shouldn't complain. Lots of people are worse off than me.

John still knows nothing of the eating and throwing up either. I'm afraid if he knew he'd think I'm disgusting and refuse to see me or commit me to a mental hospital. There's a part of me that doesn't want to stop, and if I tell him, he'll try to make me. I consider John a support, yet don't tell him about things that trouble me. I can't allow myself to acknowledge such things as my hatred for the wooden leg, insecurities about how I look, envy I have for anyone with two legs, or any sadness or disappointment. I may get vague hints of these things moments before

I stuff myself with food, but I can't tolerate the helplessness and out of control panic they evoke in me. Eating and purging are my constant relief. I know it's not right and I'm sure it will stop when I find the right job or boyfriend or when my leg magically grows back. I need John to listen, and not question or challenge me, which is exactly what he does. I need him because I was told people who want to work in mental health fields should have their own therapy experience. But, secretly I want him to fix everything with one word or look, and at the same time, I know it doesn't work that way. Holding out hope for that magical fix that will bring my leg back somehow keeps me going.

———◆———

In February 1978, I graduate first in my class of ten from the graduate nursing program. The structure and relationships of the last two years end. Jane and I mean to stay in touch, but life intervenes as it always does. She has trouble finding a job and goes back to working in the psychiatric unit at Bellevue while she continues looking. We live in different cities, both working full-time. Throughout the next year we meet a few times for coffee or dinner, but the time between visits lengthens and we lose contact.

Sophie, the medical director of the pediatric clinic at the hospital where I'd been working, offers me a job as clinic coordinator. I'd be responsible for helping the staff find ways of dealing with the whole child and family, not just the medical problem. It's sort of a dream job, just in the wrong city. I very much wanted to move to Boston after graduation. Sophie and I agree to a start date in April 1978.

———◆———

During my summer in Boston, Steve gave me the name of a group that runs introductory amputee skiing workshops in Pennsylvania. I contact them and set up a week at Jack Frost Mountain after school ends in February 1978. Other than traveling expenses and meals, the week is free: lessons, equipment, and lodging.

Soon after I arrive, a strapping, shaggy blond-haired man, not much older than me, introduces himself as the workshop leader.

"Hi, I'm Adam, the program organizer and one of the instructors. Ever ski before your amputation? Your right leg? A high AK (above knee)?" He looks me straight in the eyes, lifts his eyebrows, and proceeds to scan my body and touch my right thigh.

"Uh, no, a hemipelvectomy," I say, trying to maintain some semblance of control. His slides his hand up to my right hip, encased in the wooden leg's bucket. I wonder if he's flirting with me. He's very good looking. "I've never skied. Cale and Steve, my Boston pals, tell me it's not so hard to learn."

"We'll see," he says looking me up and down. "You look pretty strong. Have you spent much time walking on crutches?"

"Almost none. I hop around when I'm not wearing my leg, usually just at night, before bed."

"How long you been a gimp? What happened?"

"Since 1962, bone cancer," I tell him. "I was eleven. I'm used to it."

"Vietnam for me, lost them both below the knees," he jumps right to the next sentence. "I ski with my prostheses. You'll be using one ski and two forearm crutches with short ski tips on the bottoms. Tri-track we call it. We'll start tomorrow. I'll be your instructor since you're a newbie."

There are several people milling about, but I'm the only woman I see. Cale and Jane have both trained with Adam and fought off his advances. They've told me he has a way of seducing every woman he meets. They think it's something about the combination of strength and vulnerability he projects.

That night I meet Sam, his brother and another man they're with. They've all been to the workshop before and have been skiing for at least a few years. Sam is an amputee. His brother is not.

"I've not seen you here before. There usually aren't many women amputees here. Most of us are war gimps."

"I'm Karen. I heard about this workshop from Steve, Cale, and Jane in Boston. I've never skied, but thought I'd try it." I feel shy and alone. Being around all these amputee men is strange. I feel sad for them and, although it has in no way disappeared, my bravado has toned itself down a notch.

"I've met Cale and Jane, both really good skiers. They race and win. You can ski with us tomorrow if you want. We'll help you learn." Sam's a bit of a flirt. He's a wiry redhead with an AK (above knee) amputation, wearing a peg, his soft blue eyes looking directly into mine. I have to look away after a few seconds.

"Adam said he'd get me set up and start teaching me in the morning. Maybe I can meet up with you all later, if I get the hang of it."

"Oh, you'll do fine. Watch out for Adam. He's got a reputation with the ladies. He's always got a new, good looking normie on his arm. He goes after all the attractive gimp and normie ladies," Sam's friend says.

My ski outfit is white with red, yellow, and blue patches randomly strewn across the jacket and pants. I've cut the right leg off the pants and sewn it up to fit snugly against my boneless hip. It's the first time in over fifteen years that I've been out in public walking on crutches, free of my wooden leg. I fit right in—the slopes are full of one-legged skiers, some with their normie friends. I'm at the bottom of the "bunny hill" waiting for Adam. The slopes are covered in white, packed snow with patches of ice scattered about.

Adam skis up to me. "Hey, let's get you fitted up with boots and skis." He leads me to a room under the lodge packed with boots, skies, and outriggers, the name for forearm crutches with ski tips. An older gent finds me a boot that fits, a beginner's ski, and a pair of crutches we adjust to my height. It's a lot of stuff to tromp around in, especially with the ski suit, gloves, scarf and hat I have on. We leave my crutches leaning on a rack that's packed with the skis of people taking a break in the lodge, and head for the lift.

Every sliding step is a new experience. My body is moving in a whole new way. We make it onto the chairlift and take the short ride to the top of the beginner's hill.

"Here's how it works," Adam says, "you lean your body to the right or left to turn, sliding the outriggers with you. Bend and straighten your knee to assist the turn. For this first run, make big crisscrosses back and forth until you get to the bottom. It's called traversing and helps keep your speed down. I'll be right behind you. Guaranteed you'll fall. Try to relax when you do. I'll be here to help you get up."

With that I head out, slowly at first until I get bored and head down the hill a little straighter. I fall and slide down several feet, losing my outriggers.

"You okay?" Adam's standing over and laughing at me, holding the outriggers.

"I'm great, that was so much fun." It's a bit of a chore getting up. I definitely need the outriggers for leverage. "I guess next time I better hang on to the crutches," I say, beaming at Adam.

I do at least twenty runs—traversing, speeding for short stints, falling and getting up with the help of the crutches, Adam, and other friendly gimps—before we decide to go in and warm up. It takes some work to get the ski off, and my leg is heavy tromping in the ski boot. I see Sam and his brother inside, and Adam and I walk over to them.

"Pretty nice first ski. She's a daredevil—just my type." Adam says to the guys, winking at me. "We can have another lesson tomorrow morning. Have fun after lunch, and practice what I taught you."

"We'll take care of her this afternoon," Sam says looking at me with his baby blue eyes.

And so it goes for the next day and a half. On the third day, Adam takes me up a bigger slope, with longer runs. I ski, I fall and roll, and slide in the snow. It's invigorating, fun, freeing. I am a bit of a daredevil, and foolishly believing I know how to ski after just two days, I push the limits of how fast I can go straight down. Something inside, however, is keeping watch, preventing me from sustaining more than a bruise or scrape, and from crashing into others.

After a few runs, we meet up with Sam and his pals skiing the same hill. It's a beautiful, warm, sunny day and we decide to stay out for lunch. Adam leaves us. Sam offers to go down to the lodge and bring lunch up the slopes.

"What do you want?" he asks us all.

"I don't know...how about a yogurt, an orange, and some tea."

"That's it. Is that enough? You've been out all morning," Sam's brother queries me.

"I'm not very hungry. I'll have a good dinner. That'll be just right for now." I say, fully aware I won't be able to throw up. Eating even that much panics me, but I have to eat something with the others or they'll wonder about me.

Sam and his brother return with the food, and we bask in the sun. Sam huddles close to me, supporting my back and resting his hand on my leg. Eating the yogurt, peeling the orange and sharing the sections while sipping hot tea, I feel warm, cozy, and relaxed. It's another new experience. I don't feel squirmy or like I have to prove myself.

"Eleven years old, eh? That's how young you were when you lost your leg?" Sam's voice is contemplative.

"Yep. It may be better than losing it when you're an adult. Kids adjust to change easier. I haven't had many problems."

"I just feel sorry you had to go through that," he says, softly stroking my leg. "How about we smoke a little weed before we head out again?"

"Sure," his brother says. They light up a partially smoked joint and offer it to me. I take a couple of tokes, worried that it'll send me into a paranoia—anxious, and suspicious of everyone's motives. Sam and his brother smoke it to the end. His other friend, an older man with a family and a good job, refuses.

"I don't touch that stuff," he declares.

I ski with the three of them the rest of the afternoon, then head back to the lodge. I don my wooden leg before heading out to meet up with Sam and his pals for dinner.

"I was injured in Vietnam. A bomb hit near where I was and blew off my leg and part of my privates. I had a long rehab, part of which was learning to ski." Sam shares with searching eyes, seemingly looking inside himself, then at me, and over at his brother. He and I sit close, legs touching and he's stroking my hand. "And after rehab, I took up motorcycle riding. I built myself a three-wheeled bike."

We chat and gaze into the fire for a couple of hours, then decide to head off to bed so we can catch all the sun and snow there is the next day. Two more days and we'll be leaving.

"How about you come to my room and sleep with me tonight?" Sam is totally serious, looking directly at me with his transparent blue eyes. "Really, no pressure, we can cuddle and keep each other warm."

I can't refuse. It feels like he needs me and for the first time with a man, I'm not worried he feels sorry for me. Sex scares me—I'm very inexperienced, and I don't want Sam to reject me for it. The comfort of his touch is something very new for me.

When we get to the room, I realize he shares it with his brother and friend. So there are four of us—he and me in one bed, his friend in the other and his brother on a cot. "I feel a little strange in a room with three guys," I sheepishly mutter.

"Don't worry—we won't look or listen. It's been done before," his friend says sitting on the edge of his bed looking at Sam and me sitting on the edge of Sam's bed. The "it's been done before" goes over my head in the mess of my inside anxiety.

All's well as soon as we lay down. Sam smokes part of another joint and I manage a few puffs. He smokes a cigarette, then we turn the lights out and cuddle under the covers. We have sex. It's quiet and quick and it relaxes me. Sam smokes another cigarette, all the while keeping one hand on my body. I touch his stump and we fall asleep.

The next two days are a repeat of the same, minus the ski lesson with Adam.

"Looks like you've found yourself another teacher. Not sure he's as good as I am, but I'll leave you to him. I don't like teaching someone who's not one hundred percent with me." Adam says this with an air of superiority, as if I've made a choice and it's the wrong one.

"Thanks so much for accepting me into the workshop and spending all that time with me. You taught me a lot." I say with sincerity.

"I could teach you a lot more. I guess you'll learn some things from Sam," he says as he turns and skis away calling to one of the ladies close by.

The afternoon of the day before we leave, I bump into Sam's brother, alone on a stairway in the lodge. "Hey. Where you off to?" I ask.

"Heading back to the room to pack up a bit. We're leaving pretty early tomorrow. It's a long trip back to Washington, D.C.." He hesitates then turns around and comes down the stairs.

"I'll miss you guys. It's been so much fun hanging out with you," I say as he steps down to face me.

"Something I want to tell you, so you know. Sam's married with two children. He's been with several other girls through the course of the marriage. His wife knows, but she loves him. You're the first gimp woman he's been with and he's different with you. Still, I wanted you to know..."

"Oh, thanks for telling me, I guess." My heart sinks to my feet. I'm stunned, having trouble taking a breath.

"I'll see you later, out there on the slopes," he says as he walks up the steps again.

I'm in shock—sad, disappointed. I'm confused—I want to go home right then and, at the same time, I want to find Sam and cuddle with him even more. I feel like he loves me, though nothing even close to that has been said. We've talked about meeting at Winter Park in Colorado later in the winter.

When I see him a few hours later, I ask him about his wife.

"Yes, it's true. I'm glad my brother told you. I couldn't bring myself to do it. You're the first gimp girl I've been with—I'm usually out for the conquest of getting normie ladies to like me. It's different and special with you. We share something I can't explain and don't really understand, but I'm drawn to you."

"Same for me, but you have a wife."

"I know, and I love her. There's something special with us, too, though. She doesn't have to know. Think about it. I hope you'll sleep with me again tonight. And I really hope we can meet up at the handicapped ski races in Colorado next winter," he says seemingly sincere. He gives me a big, soft, loving hug and I feel myself melting with disappointment and resignation. He cares for me. It's something.

In a flash, I'm in the cafeteria stocking up on junk food before I head back to my room to stuff it down, purge and pack.

We spend the last night together and exchange phone numbers before saying goodbye in the morning.

"If you're ever in D.C., give me a call. Otherwise, see you in Colorado next year," he says as he closes my car door and kisses me before I take off for home.

My job as Pediatric Clinic Coordinator begins in April 1978. I'm responsible for making sure the kids and families in our low-income area get comprehensive medical and psychological care. Many of the kids have behavioral issues. I work with the parents around problem solving and getting access to community services. Sophie, my supervisor, is trying to transform the clinic into one that addresses the whole child and family, not just the medical issues. A month or so after I start, she asks if I'd be willing to go to a multidisciplinary conference in D.C.

"It's all about what we're wanting to do here in the clinic. We can pay your way and the fee. You can bring back the information. What do you think?" She's a sweet, gentle soul, maybe twenty years older than me and very dedicated to the kids and families we serve.

"Sure. I'll go," I say, immediately thinking about Sam. "I have a friend who lives just outside Washington. Maybe I can meet up with him while I'm there and learn a whole lot of new stuff about working with our kids all in the same weekend."

After the initial excitement about seeing Sam again wears off, I hesitate to call. Many things about it bother me: maybe he didn't really like me, he has a wife and kids and it's not right to be with a married man, he'll probably not even remember me. Despite my misgivings, I convince myself to call him.

"That's great, Karen," he says when I tell him I'm coming. "Call me when you get here, and we can get together one afternoon. It'll be good to see you again."

Sam shows up outside the hotel on a loud, three-wheeled motorcycle. I awkwardly throw my good leg over the seat that runs across the two back wheels, balancing on my wooden leg and gripping his torso to pull myself up and onto the bike.

"Nice maneuvering," he says, looking back and grinning at me. He's wearing a bandana, black leather jacket, and jeans. The ultimate bad boy, he excites me. My fellow conference goers will get to see another side of me, one I barely know myself.

We cruise, speeding on the straightaways, taking corners with a flair, and stop for an early dinner at a local diner. It's a beautiful evening. Being with him seems strange. We have little to talk about after we exchange a few words about what's happened since we saw each other last. He declines an invitation to stay the night at the hotel.

"I can't. My wife will be suspicious. I'm usually home in the evening with the kids. Especially since I've been off pot and drinking less. I'd like to though," he says kissing me after we get off the bike.

"Good for you for taking care of yourself. I'm sure your kids love that you're home with them more. I understand." I do understand, and I'm resigned. It's just the way it is and I have to accept it.

172

"Hey. Maybe we can meet up in Winter Park next winter, like we talked about during our last ski rendezvous. I'm planning to go. Are you?" He says this as he's climbing on the bike to take off.

"Yeah, sure. That'd be great," I mutter as he's halfway to the street, waving goodbye.

I feel disappointed, sad, and mad at myself for feeling anything. I head back to the room to stuff it all with a food and purge fest made possible with snacks from the hotel store.

————— ◆ —————

In the early spring of 1979, Cale and I plan to meet at Winter Park ski area in Colorado. Jane, the woman who asked me about purging on the sailboat during my summer in Boston two years ago, will be there, too. In the years since that summer, I made a few weekend ski trips to Mount Sunapee, the amputee ski haven in New Hampshire. With the help of Jane, Cale, and other experienced skiers there, I've become a mediocre, novice skier, able make it down a slope without falling.

I meet up with the girls at the lodge, as planned. We hug and share travel stories. Cale and Jane are on crutches, without their wooden legs, but I continue to wear mine whenever I'm not in my ski clothes. All of my street pants still have two legs.

Cale and Jane are excited to get to the slopes for practice before the races.

"Are you going to give it a shot this year, Karen? Maybe the giant slalom?" Jane pokes me lovingly about racing. Cale's right there with her, cheering me on.

"I'm not the greatest skier, guys. You both know I fall a lot," I say half flattered. There's a part of me that thinks I could be a great ski racer, better than Cale or Jane, without doing much work. I think highly and lowly of myself at the same time. But, being noticed for having one leg seems shameful and not a valid accomplishment.

"You'll be fine. We'll run the course every day before the race. You'll see. It'll be a piece of cake," Cale says as we share an energizing group hug.

"I want to find Sam," I say expectantly. "Have you guys seen him?"

"He was here with his brother earlier. They probably went back to their room. You know about Sam, right Karen?" Jane says looking at me, head turned to the side so she's looking out the corner of her eye.

"Yes, I know," I say as if I'm annoyed she's asking. "I'm OK with it. I like him. His wife doesn't have to know." I try not to think about how he didn't want to stay with me when we met up in Washington, hoping it'll be different out here, far away from his wife. He kept saying he wanted to meet me here…

"You're sure you won't be devastated when he decides he wants to be faithful to his wife? It's been a pattern of his. He's been around the ski scene for awhile. We've seen him hurt other girls." I can tell Jane cares about me. Cale is looking at me, nodding her head.

"I'm sure. Besides, I'm the first amputee girl he's been with. Maybe it'll be different with me." I'm unaware of how resigned I am to taking whatever I can get. I could never confront Sam with any backbone. I want to do everything to make him want to keep spending time with me.

"Just be careful," Jane says.

"Yeah, yeah. I know. I'm not expecting anything. I'm good with it, whatever happens, happens. Sam did say he wanted to meet me here when we met up last summer." I say with all my emotional walls secured. I almost believe myself, but neither Jane nor Cale looks convinced. I'm certain that's because they don't know what Sam and I have.

We head up to our room to work out our sleeping arrangements. I'm sure I'll be staying with Sam most nights and be in our room only for dressing between activities, so I claim the cot. We say nothing more about Sam, but I know they know what I'm thinking.

The next day I see Sam on the slopes with his brother and some friends. They're whooping it up, laughing, and poking at each other waiting to get on the lift. I manage to catch his eye. He waves but doesn't come over to me. Instead, he yells he'll see me later in the lodge at lunchtime.

"Okay. See you then." I yell back. He's just having fun with his buddies now. It'll all be different when we meet at lunch. I can't expect someone to drop everything for me—that wouldn't be good for any relationship. This is a sign we're comfortable with each other and can trust time apart. All of this rationally and rigidly lining up in my head, while my heart pounds in my chest and my body wants to run away.

Sam sees me as I come into the lodge for lunch. He makes his way over, hugs and kisses me, as I go through the line picking up my usual yogurt and orange. All's well, I think. Then, he leads me to a table in a corner.

"Good to see you, Karen. How've you been since we met up in the summer?" He's sitting next to me, leaning in. I want to grab and kiss him, but I don't. Something's not right. Why don't we sit with his pals?

"Pretty good. Still working in the same job and wanting to move to Boston. Instead, I'm moving to a new apartment in New Jersey when I get back. How about you?" I feel self-conscious and awkward, afraid I'm not saying the right things.

"I'm good. Listen, I'll come right out and say it. I've decided to be faithful to my wife. It's best for me and my family. I don't want to hurt them anymore. You're one of the most wonderful ladies I've ever met. I'll always remember our skiing adventures and that ride on the bike." He says it all very earnestly. I can't disagree. I quickly pop into my indifferent self.

"That makes sense, Sam. I'm sure it'll be good for you and your family. I've enjoyed hanging out with you." I say, feeling embarrassed that I ever even liked him, and wanting to run fast and far away.

"You can still hang out with us. We're still friends, right?" he asks as if it's true. "Let's go over and join the guys now."

"Okay, sure," I say as I hobble in my ski boot. It's not a big deal. I can't expect someone to leave his wife for me. It's my fault I feel bad.

A short while later I leave, get some treats and head back to my room. I stuff the feelings down and throw them all up into the toilet. It always works.

I see Sam on and off that week. Jane and Cale keep asking how I am and I keep saying, "I'm fine. It makes sense. He can't keep hurting his wife."

"Aren't you mad at him for leading you on?" they ask over and over.

"Not at all. It's my fault. I got involved with him. He's probably not right for me anyway."

I race in the Giant Slalom, come in third of three racers, and win a medal. I feel foolish, like I don't deserve to win anything. I'm embarrassed when people come up and congratulate me. I throw the medal in the garbage when I get home.

More than a decade later in 1991, I head to Winter Park to watch the Paralympics. Cale and Jane compete, as well as a few others I know from my brief involvement in the world of gimp skiing. I meet up with Jane soon after we arrive.

"Hey, glad you made it to Winter Park again, Karen." She pauses and looks at me for a long few seconds. Before I can say anything, she says, "I wanted to tell you before someone else mentions it, and you're not prepared. Sam died of Agent Orange this past year." She reaches out to hug me.

"Really, I didn't know he had Agent Orange. It's something from the war, right? Like a kind of cancer?" I'm in shock. I slide to the ground and hug my leg into my chest. I feel so bad for his kids and wife.

"He didn't tell many people. I didn't know either. His brother told me."

"Is his brother here?" I ask, thinking maybe I can see him.

"No, I saw him at another event this year. He got big into the amputee teaching program because of Sam." She's sitting next to me on the cold ground.

I want to cry but the tears won't come. We sit for a few minutes, then head back to the lodge to meet up with the others.

12 Finding Balance

How we spend our days is how we spend our lives.

/ Annie Dillard

In March of 1979, back from my week of skiing, I resume my responsibilities as Pediatric Clinic Coordinator at the Jersey City Medical Center and move into a nicer apartment. It's on the second floor of a house with a balcony and views of the Hudson River and the Manhattan skyline. I'm certain the new apartment, in the more upscale West New York, New Jersey, will make everything right in my life.

Except for the people I see at work, I'm essentially friendless. Jane, my graduate school buddy, is busy looking for work and Peggy, my neighbor and friend in Jersey City, moved back to Penn State, Pennsylvania, to continue working on her doctorate.

My twice weekly meetings with John, my therapist, and the people in the therapy group I attend each week, are the extent of my social contacts. Since my insurance pays in full (I never get a bill from John) and the sessions are in his home, it's hard to remember that I pay for their company. I desperately want a boyfriend, yet act and talk as if I'm totally happy with my single life. E&T becomes more and more important and remains my shameful little secret.

Out of the blue one day while I'm cruising around a clothing store, I try on a black and white checkered coat and walk out of the shop door without paying for it. It's a totally impulsive move. As soon as I step into the street, limping as fast as I can to my car, looking back and seeing no one following, I feel a rush of excitement and power. I have the money to pay for the coat, but I feel entitled to it somehow. There's a part of me that's disconnected, acting on its own while the rest of me watches and follows.

It's the start of a long and varied stealing career. I stuff food in my pockets, walk out without paying. I ask for deli items, eat them in the store and stash the packaging behind the toilet paper or soap. I eat in restaurants and leave without paying. I steal money from friends and family. While immersed in the rush that comes when I steal things, I'm certain no one notices and, at the same time, I'm certain they do and feel sorry for a pitiful, limping girl like me.

Meanwhile, a war is raging inside of me. One side can think only of taking the wooden leg off forever. The other side is adamantly against it, protesting loudly that I have an obligation to the people who saved my life, my family, and the comfort of everyone in the universe, to continue to look normal. The pro-wooden leg side batters me with declarations of my selfishness and ungratefulness for even thinking of doing such a thing. It insists no one will hire me with crutches and surely, no man would ever love me.

I'm stuck in the back and forth, and then as I walk down a long hall at work one day in late March of 1979, I kinda, sorta fake a fall, landing on my good knee. I've fallen many times, and always get up immediately, declaring I'm fine no matter how much or what hurts. This time is different.

"Are you all right?" a nice young man asks as he kneels down beside me. "Can I help you up?"

"I think I'm okay, but my knee really hurts," I say grimacing.

He helps me up and gets a wheelchair. "I'll take you over to the emergency room. They'll have a look."

"Okay. If you think that's best." I don't recognize myself. I know I staged the fall and my knee is really fine, maybe a little sore. I need an excuse, suggested by someone with authority, to be seen without the leg for even one day.

In the ER they take an X-ray. Nothing is broken. "How does it feel to walk on it?" the doctor asks.

"It hurts a lot when I step on it and even more when I try to swing the wooden leg through."

"Maybe you should take a few days off and stay off it. Do you have crutches at home?" he asks as he softly scans my knee for bruises and tender spots.

"I don't," I say, "I only take the leg off for sleeping and hop around without it."

"We'll get you some crutches and no hopping. I recommend a week off. Keep it elevated as much as you can. I'll make you an appointment with one of the docs here for next week. Do you want me to call the clinic to tell them you'll be off for a week?"

"I'd rather walk over and tell Sophie myself. I have to get my things, anyway."

Elated and full of fear that I'll be found out, I hobble home with the crutches and immediately take the wooden leg off. I've recently used Canadian crutches for skiing, the short ones with the forearm bands, but haven't used underarm crutches since the year before I got the wooden leg. Plain old walking is difficult at first. Stairs and driving are a challenge.

The week off is great and I convince myself and the doctors, that the knee still hurts when I wear the leg. I'm certain I can't work without the wooden leg—it would be too awkward for the patients to have a nurse on crutches. Sophie worries because I say my knee continues to hurt when I'm up on it. After a month without full recovery, she and the other doctors decide I should take time off to rest, while collecting workman's compensation.

My clinic co-workers are worried about me. "We'll hold your position for you, hoping you'll be back with us at the end of August." Each one hugs me and wishes me well. I'm almost certain I'll not return to work there.

By May, I'm receiving monthly checks. With nothing to do in New Jersey and an income, I decide to see about moving to Boston. I remember Julie, who I'd met sailing with Steve, extended an open offer of a room in her house if I ever decided I wanted to give Boston a try. I call her.

"Really, I could stay with you and move my stuff into your place?" I can't believe I'm even thinking of going, without a job, no plans. It's not like me—and the pro-wooden leg side of me continues to voice its disappointment inside my head.

"How much stuff do you have? Big furniture or what?" Julie asks.

"No, no—I just moved in here and have very little. I'll bring only what I can fit in the car." I say expectantly. Something is pushing me to leave quickly. It's as if I have to get away from who I am here.

"Great, then. We'll have fun this summer. Sailing, hanging out. When will you come?"

"In a week or so, as soon as I can. I'll call you the day before I'm planning to leave, if that's okay." As usual, I can't handle the feelings and E&T comes to the rescue.

I call Cale and Jane. They're over-the-top excited.

When I arrive a week later, Julie, her partner Tim, Cale, Jane, and Phil, the amputee photographer, are there to greet me.

"What's with the crutches, Karen? Where's your leg?" Phil asks.

I tell them the story of the fall as if it were truly an accident. "The doctor says I should stay off my leg for awhile. I guess he thinks wearing the wooden leg may be twisting my good knee, causing the pain." I make it up on the spot. "I'm a little scared about finding a job, but I don't have to worry about that for a few months and by then I'll be wearing the leg again. I may even look for a job this summer." I'm still the same, self-assured, always positive girl on the outside. I'm a good talker. I convince people of things. One part of me knows this, and another is certain everyone knows I'm a phony—it's the continual battle of the inner demons I'm minimally aware of. Each has her wisdom and I have no idea how to find the balance or even that I'm searching for it.

A few days after I arrive, Phil stops by and invites me to spend the summer on Martha's Vineyard, an island off the coast of Cape Cod, Massachusetts, where he's rented a house he's agreed to renovate through the summer. For him, it'll be a working vacation. I'd pay a few hundred dollars to live there through August with him, his girlfriend, Chrissy, and college buddy, Kenny.

Julie is listening as he tells me about the house. "It's a Menemsha fishing shack moved to a forty-three-acre lot in Chilmark—three bedrooms so you'll have your own room. I'll be working on an addition to make it a bigger, more modern, space." Not a bad sales pitch.

He goes on. "Chilmark has a private beach for residents only. You need a pass to park in the lot. There are no badges, though, since it's a nude beach!" he says with a grin and a twinkle in his eye. Phil is a charming hunk of a man, seemingly more masculine because of the peg he sports. It's hard to resist him.

"That sounds amazing," I say looking at Julie. I feel like a traitor, thinking about moving to Martha's Vineyard for the summer after Julie so graciously offered me a place to stay. "When would we go?"

"Anytime," Phil says. "I'm leaving in a few days. You could come with me."

"That sounds fabulous, Karen," Julie says. "You've got to go. I only wish I was free to go, too." Julie and Phil are very different. She dresses, talks and acts like a professional adult. Phil seems more like an older college student, although he is responsible. I'm in between—more comfortable with an air of certainty, yet I long for that free and easy, hanging out experience.

"Thanks, Julie," I turn to Phil. "I'm in. I'll go when you go. I'm excited—a summer on the beach with no responsibilities." The nude beach scares me, and I've not been on the beach with one leg. Something about going with another one-legged person, even though Phil wears his peg all the time, makes it okay.

———·———

The house is truly a shack, entirely wood, two floors with a tiny kitchen and one bathroom. There's a partial addition already built with a bigger kitchen, bathroom, and more bedrooms. It's set back from the only road that runs the whole length of the island.

The front yard is flat, spacious, and sheltered from the road by giant trees. The back of the house sits right next to a patch of woods, full of wild huckleberries and who knows what else.

Chrissy, a nurse between jobs, and Kenny, from Manhattan, also between jobs and looking for a girlfriend, arrive a few days after Phil and me. Chrissy and I become fast friends—she's soft spoken, gentle, funny, and unlike me, she's been in many mixed group living situations. I feel safe and comfortable around her. She likes my self-assuredness, and its harshness is able to melt ever so slightly.

"Let's take a drive and explore the island while the guys do whatever it is they're doing with the house." She looks at Phil, and Kenny, who knows little about construction but has come to be Phil's helper of sorts. "You two be careful. Watch Phil on that ladder. All it takes is one fall..."

"Get out of here," Phil says affectionately with a twinge of defensiveness. "I'm fine on the ladder. Have I fallen since you've known me? Huh?" It's the peg Chrissy's worried about—it's a far cry from a flesh calf and foot.

The island is small and outrageously beautiful—we're close to the southwest corner, about a mile inland from the beach. We head northeast to the grocery store and spot the Black Dog restaurant in Vineyard Haven, the town where the ferry docks, which locals tell us is a great place for breakfast. Oak Bluffs, a small town on the northeast coast, is lined with gingerbread cottages, painted all different colors and just steps from the beach. It's the home to many affluent African-American families on the island. Due south is Edgartown, an upscale town, and at the farthest west corner is Gay Head, a beautiful stretch of beach lined with clay cliffs.

We can't believe what we're seeing—it's a paradise we'll spend the whole summer enjoying. Overflowing with energy and excitement, Chrissy and I bombard the guys with our discoveries.

"I know," Phil says dismissively, "that's why I said yes to the job. You guys are just lucky you know me."

We all crack up and crowd around Phil to hammer and hug him. "A woman told us about the backdoor take-out at the Home Port Restaurant in Menemsha. It's cheap, and we can sit on the rocks and watch the sunset. Let's check it out tonight." Chrissy's already decided. "How about we go to the beach before that?"

"Sounds great," Kenny says. "Do we walk there?"

"We'll take a car—we have a pass to park in the private lot," Phil explains. "It's a good hike in the sand to the nude part of the beach. You'll be blown away."

It's true, the walk is far and challenging, trudging through the white, sparkly dry sand. We walk south along a path just to get to the ocean front, and then quite a ways along a wide beach, lined with steep, colorful clay cliffs, before we see multigenerational folks sunning, swimming, walking, socializing—all stark naked and beautifully tanned. Apparently, this part of the beach is difficult to access—there's a body of brackish water running along the back, so the only way in is by walking miles along the beach from east or west.

Unsure of how I'd feel about shedding my clothes (after all, it's only a few weeks since I shed my leg), I wear a bathing suit under them. We put our blanket down amidst all sizes and shapes of buff bodies. We're greeted by many, introducing themselves and sharing tips about the tides and currents of the day. In less than five minutes, I'm out of the suit and sunning my butt. Phil sheds his peg—neither he nor Chrissy wore a bathing suit. They both have beautiful, strong, shapely bodies. Kenny is like me—a little timid at first, despite his outstanding physique, and then fully into the freedom with just a tad bit of self-consciousness.

It takes a while, more than the first few hours that afternoon, to stop looking at anatomy and judging shapes. Kids of all ages enjoy every imaginable beach activity alongside their friends, parents, and grandparents. As the days pass, and we settle into the all-out joyfulness on Lucy Vincent Beach, it becomes the most natural and peaceful place on earth.

One day that first week, as I'm in the glorious outdoor shower, my butt and boobs sting as the water runs over them. Sunburn—bright red and painful. The rest of my body is tanned with a tinge of red. It's so uncomfortable I can't bear to sit. I spend much of next day or two sprawled out on a chaise, face down, my derriere soothed with lotion and exposed to the shade.

If I make it to the beach those days, I stay covered in loose shorts and tee. One of the older gents we've seen regularly asks why I'm dressed.

"Sunburn on my tender parts," I say with a grimace-smile.

"Ah, yes. One of, possibly the only, dangers of the TBT." He shakes his head and smiles knowingly.

"TBT?" I ask.

"Total body tan," he replies. "You're on your way to a beauty once the itchy peeling passes. Even the best of us succumb to it every few years or so when we're so hungry for the sun and freedom we forget."

Chrissy suffers the same fate later that week. Phil and Kenny have either exposed their delicate parts before or are smart enough to do it gradually. Despite our experienced warnings, most of our many visitors have at least a patch of stinging, itchy sunburn while they're with us.

The Home Port backdoor take-out is everything it was made out to be and more. It sits just feet from a long rock jetty that juts out into the Vineyard Sound. The door is an old wooden one with puckered screens in the top and bottom and a half moon shaped metal handle. It's feather-light and slams shut with a distinctive bang after each lucky diner snatches up his dinner.

The fare is fresh-caught fish with a side. The mako shark is delicious, as are the clams, bluefish, and lobster since everything they offer is caught that day. The salads are made from island-grown greens. Truly a gourmet delight without the price and stuffiness of a white tablecloth.

We bring our own beers and feast at least once a week, sitting on the jetty, enjoying the boats and sometimes the sunset. We bring every guest to the Home Port at least once and become true regulars. It's all part of the summer in paradise.

Chrissy's sister, Joanne, and Bobby, a friend of Phil's, are our regular weekend housemates. I meet them that first weekend.

"Hi, I'm Joanne, Chrissy's sister. You must be Karen." Joanne is tall and lanky, with shoulder length, wavy dark hair and a huge smile outlined in red lipstick. She enunciates her words and holds her head high when she speaks.

"Yep, I'm Karen. Have you been here before?" I ask, maintaining my external poise despite the voices in my head proclaiming I'm nothing next to her.

"No, but I couldn't wait to get here. Let's go to the beach." Her energy is palpable. "Where am I sleeping?" Chrissy takes her upstairs.

It seems everyone, except me, knows Bobby. He immediately gravitates to the guys. I go over.

"Hi, I'm Karen." He's got a soft presence and body and seems to merge with the surroundings. He offers his hand.

"I'm Bob. These guys all call me Bobby. Old pals."

Suddenly, it looks like there are two guys, Kenny and Bobby, who may become my boyfriend. I really want a boyfriend, yet I'm petrified to flirt, scared to death of the intimacy, and I can't let anyone know.

The summer rolls on. Weekdays Chrissy and I read, putter and clean, while Phil and Kenny work on the house. I go into town twice a week to volunteer at the library. It's a chance for me to get my E&T fix and stock up on foods that make purging easier. E&T is slightly less intrusive that summer—I eat less because of the day-to-day interactions. We drink our fair share of beer, and this scares me. It's the calories, and the loss of control I feel when I drink. I have close to exclusive access to the upstairs bathroom on weekdays. Weekends we use the bathrooms and the woods. It's easy to slip away for an E&T break when the house is hopping.

Chrissy and I do all the grocery shopping. One day while we're out, Phil slips on the ladder and falls. Kenny is a wreck, trying to help, while Phil pushes away any caring gesture.

When we walk in the door, Phil is laying on the floor near the ladder. Kenny tells us Phil refused to go to the emergency room.

"What happened?" Chrissy shouts as she runs to Phil.

"My peg missed the step. I'm fine." Phil insists as Chrissy reaches to help him up.

"What hurts? What did you land on?" Chrissy pleads with him to tell her.

"I think he hit his good knee then just fell backwards onto his back," Kenny offers.

"Did you hit your head?" I ask.

"NO." Phil is stoic, and he's not giving an inch.

Kenny and Chrissy stand him up and help him limp to the couch. His knee is bruised. Chrissy gets an ice pack and he's sentenced to the couch, with at least one of us ministering to his every need for the rest of the day. He can hardly stand it. By the next day he's up, wearing the peg. Thankfully, nothing is broken or seriously tweaked. He works off the ladder for the next week or so, cringing and flashing a "don't go there" look when anyone asks how he's doing.

———⋄———

We're like a family that summer, especially Chrissy, Phil, Joanne, and me. Kenny takes a few week-long trips to Manhattan where he's courting a new sweetie, and Bobby doesn't make it every weekend. When he is with us, he seems shy and awkward. We spend hours every day at the beach and become a well-known and loved gang of however many we are that day.

One day, on our way home we stop to take a few pictures. We're all naked and perfectly sober—Chilmark is a dry town. For one rather rude shot, my one leg and hip straddle Phil's neck. There's an outburst of outrageous laughter and we draw the attention of many bathers, including a short, cute, curly-haired man. He joins right in, staring straight at my naked body. When Phil puts me down, the man comes closer, chats a few minutes, and invites me for dinner at his place. It's all I can do to remain standing on my crutches. I'm certain he wants to have sex, and I'm certain I have no idea how to manage something like that. My insides quake with fear. If I don't get away from him quickly, I worry something will explode.

"Thanks, but no. I'm going home with the gang." I say with total poise and control as I pull on my tee shirt.

"Why not, Karen. You should go…" My buddies urge me on.

"No, I'm not into it today." I'm rejecting, dismissive, maybe even demeaning, but the monster inside has quieted down.

On weekends, when the house is full, we pick huckleberries in the backyard and make pancakes for breakfast. We take turns showering in the minimally-walled outdoor stall with luxurious water pressure and the warm air surrounding our TBTs. We lounge in the front yard, grill fish—one of our favorites is shark slathered in mayonnaise—drink beer and other yummy concoctions, and smoke pot. Drinking anything encourages purging almost immediately. When I smoke pot, I teeter on the edge of serious paranoia. I'm certain others are talking about how ugly I am, how ridiculous it is that I'm walking around showing off my hideous body, on and on… Somehow I manage to maintain my outer cool: I share little about myself and instead, eavesdrop on and silently judge others. I mistake others' simple friendliness for undying devotion and grow fantasies about how some man in the group loves me and wants to marry me. Bobby is the man that summer.

He's a safe obsession. He's there only on weekends, leaving me free to fantasize all week long about how he's thinking of me and can't wait to see me. When he is present, he's a man of few words around me, seems shy and aloof. I'm certain he just needs loving prodding to come around. I arrange ways to be near him or have an unobstructed view of him. We rarely talk for more than a few minutes, though we exchange words in the group all the time. We never touch, unless it's in passing, an accidental brush of an arm or hand. Yet, any touching excites me and I'm certain Bobby feels the same, and has somehow maneuvered the contact. I speak nothing of any of this. When something happens that pokes a little doubt at my romantic fantasy, it's E&T to the rescue.

This goes on all summer. I never notice that Bobby likes Joanne.

———— ⸭ ————

Edgartown and Oak Bluffs are the only two "wet" towns on Martha's Vineyard, and home to the nightlife. On weekends, when there's music in the bars, we sometimes go en masse, with whoever is visiting, and take over the dance floor in one or another of our favorite places. I'd danced some in high school, wearing my wooden leg—an awkward activity since my entire pelvis was encased in a bucket of fiberglass. Dancing on Martha's Vineyard is an entirely different experience. It takes just one beer for me to drop my crutches and shimmy, shake, hop, and twirl. My balance is good, and I position myself amidst a crowd for those times when my joie de vivre catapults me off center. Falling happens, it's fun and, after the initial humiliation and fending off of stunned and worried onlookers, it spurs me on to more. One evening, in a small gymnasium-type place with a wooden floor and small wooden stage, we dance continually for hours. We're soaked with sweat as we leave to make our way home.

After I change into shorts for bed, Phil exclaims, "Look at that giant bruise on your thigh."

"Where?" I ask as all eyes turn to my leg. It's the size of an open hand, right smack in the middle of my thigh.

Phil can't contain himself. He laughs out loud and in between bursts he shakes his head and says, "Self-flagellation. It's from slapping away at your leg with each beat on the dance floor tonight."

We all burst into laughter. "It doesn't hurt," I say, innocently and slightly embarrassed, wondering if they think I'm stupid. Maybe I had too much fun.

Much of the south coast has "private beaches," designated for residents or guests of a certain home or inn. We're all puzzled by how a beach can be private. Are there certain grains of sand and molecules of water that comprise that particular beach? Gay Head is home to many private beaches and a thriving gay and celebrity community, but it's backed by the same clay cliffs as the Aquinnah public beach, which, like most of the beaches on the southwest end, is never crowded. Chrissy, Joanne, and I frequent the public beach in the often empty mornings, to indulge in clay soaks and rubs. There are small pools of pitch-dark grey clay hidden among the landscape of the cliffs. Chunks of ochre clay with tints of orange, pink, white and even green, line the base. We slide into the pools, fighting over whose been in the longest. We look like monsters, black and shiny from head to toe, as we run into the water, yelling and jumping and diving in the surf. The chunks are perfect for rubbing all over our naked bodies. The texture is grainy—it's like a total body facial. Technically, touching the cliffs is prohibited, in the island's attempt to preserve them. We swear to each other we are obeying the rules by mostly using the clay that has already fallen from the cliffs. There are times, however, when a color is just so tempting, one or another of us has to break off a tiny chunk to indulge in it's unique beauty.

We experience a few good storms that summer, with hearty thunder and lightening. Some evenings, we sit on the Menemsha jetty and watch the clouds pass by so fast they seem to be running. The rain is usually warm and it invites us out to play, with or without clothes. The beach is always magical before a storm and potentially dangerous. I've been "rescued" more than once by a fellow bather who watches as I try in vain to swim to shore against a sneaky current.

One day, storm threatening, I'm certain I have enough time to get to the beach for a swim. I park my car and hurry in along the path and then along the beach, the tide quickly coming up. At the narrowest part of the beach, which we always walk beyond to get to the bathing area, there are only a few feet of sand. The tide is almost lapping the cliffs, but I'm desperate to get in the water despite the danger I know lurks. The urge is similar to the one I have when I'm compelled to purge. Hard to resist.

I huddle up close to the cliffs, drop my clothes and crutches, and hop the few feet into the water. It sucks me up immediately, and I find myself tumbling round and round under the surface. There's no way to know how far out or how deep I am. A sudden calm comes over me and I relax, telling myself this may be the end. Then, in a flash, I'm thrown back onto the shore. It's all of a few minutes. Although I'm gasping for breath, I'm alive, shaking with the chill of relief and disbelief, and exhilarated. Good sense kicks in and I gather up my things and head back to the car. I'm a little sorry it's over. I almost want to run in again.

Sometime in late August, after I receive my last worker's comp check, I call my Jersey City employer to resign. We're all making plans for the fall when our magical summer will end. I'll stay with Julie until I find a place of my own. Chrissy is heading to California for graduate school and Phil's wrestling with whether to follow her across the country. "Women usually follow men," he says with a twinge of self-consciousness. He has nothing solid to keep him in Massachusetts. Kenny found a new sweetie and is returning to Manhattan to work and love.

Up until the summer, Chrissy, Joanne, and Phil lived together in an apartment in Cambridge. With two of them headed off to California, Joanne, who is Miss Frugality, living on an arts/dance instructor salary, is looking for new roommates for the fall.

"What about living with me in Cambridge?" Joanne asks as we all sit around on the beach as the summer winds down. "I'll have to find a third roommate…"

"Sure! I just hope I can find a job. What's the rent?"

"Yours would be about $200 a month. Heat's included, so we just have to split the phone."

"What's the place like?" I ask, certain I'll say yes no matter what. Joanne's fun and we seem to get along. I'd be doing her a favor.

"We have the second and third floors of a house. Two smaller bedrooms on the third floor and a big bedroom on the main floor. There's a smallish living room and a giant kitchen. One bathroom that's pretty big with a clawfoot tub and a shower. It's on a street with lots of houses. We can walk to Harvard, Central, and Inman Squares."

I know nothing about Cambridge, but with her bubbly description, I'm getting excited to see what it's like. "How do we find another roommate?" I ask.

"I know someone—well, I know her boyfriend—who's probably going to be the third. Her name is Merrill."

Joanne is a man magnet. Whenever she's around, men are not far away. She's recently split with a boyfriend of several years—a relationship they both thought would be the one. For her, the summer was partly about getting through the grief of that breakup. She flew solo, her ex visited a couple of times and there were other flirtations, but nothing steady. I'm jealous of her ease with men. I feel twinges of anger when she turns away from me to talk to a man. If I don't have a boyfriend, I don't want her to have one either. And, again, it's E&T to my rescue, when the green envy monster shakes up my insides.

As soon as I decide I'm staying in Massachusetts, I apply for my nurse's license. It's an easy process given reciprocity with New Jersey. I pay a fee and wait for the piece of paper. I look for nurse jobs in the Boston Globe and apply for a Nurse Therapist position in the pediatric clinic that's part of the Boston State Hospital complex using my new Cambridge address as my residence. They call me to come for an interview in mid-September, 1979.

My wooden leg stood idle in the corner of my room all summer. I barely noticed it and, certainly, never thought to put it on. Now, however, I'm going for a job interview and it's back to real life. I've been hiding out, living in unreality these months. No one will hire me on one leg. I have to wear it again.

"You've been fine without it all summer; no one seemed to think it was odd. You did everything we did…" My summer friends encourage me to go without it if that's what I want to do.

"I get it, Karen," Phil says. "No one would hire me without a peg. You're not climbing ladders, though, and you're a pro on those crutches. I'm with them. Give it a try."

"I can't. They'll never hire me. They'll just see me as handicapped and think I can't do anything. It's fine not wearing it with all of you. You get it. Besides, it wouldn't be right to throw it all away after the people at Shriners gave me so much. I'll wear the leg. It makes me look normal." I'm resigned and unhappy, mad maybe, but I don't acknowledge any feeling. I just have to do it.

13 Settling In to 66 Dana Street

Sometimes I go about pitying myself, all the time I am being carried on great winds across the sky.

/ *Chippewa*, translated by Robert Bly

BOSTON STATE HOSPITAL IS IN DORCHESTER, MASSACHUSETTS, a ten-minute drive from Cambridge. The pediatric clinic is on the grounds of the state facility. Bess, the psychiatric social worker who manages the clinic, hires me. She's impressed with my work experience and education.

"You'll be a great addition to our group. Our kids need strong role models. I think you'll enjoy working with them. Craig will teach you lots about childhood psychiatric illness." She puts her arm around my shoulders as we walk out of the office. Bess is warm and personable, dedicated to community mental health, and the staff that make it possible.

Craig, a child psychiatrist, heads my team. He's single, in his thirties, short, with curly hair and a wicked grin. He's quirky and creative in finding ways to engage the kids. He embraces play therapy, talk therapy,

193

snacks, silence, exploring delusions—anything that will help build relationships. Craig's, also, flirtatious, or at least that's how I see it. He's the next man I hope is in love with me. I decide he's flirting because he looks me in the eye, he always sits next to me when our team meets, and he's interested in my assessments and ideas. As always, I'm sure he's shy and will eventually be secure enough to profess his love. I maintain my "could care less" demeanor, while anxious anticipation, and worry that I'm wrong takes over my insides.

Our team provides outpatient follow up to some of the most psychiatrically ill children in the area. Many are on the hospitalization revolving-door plan and on medications for years at a time. Frequently their families are severely dysfunctional, with parents in prison, addicted and/or poor, and marginalized in the racially divided area.

One of my regular clients is Danny, a twenty-year old-boy diagnosed with schizophrenia who functions at the level of an eight-year-old. His father brings him weekly, but aside from a brief hello, wants nothing to do with either of us until I bring Danny out and they leave.

Each week, immediately after we meet, Danny exclaims, "Miss Daly, Miss Daly, can I get a cup of coffee?" as he runs off toward the kitchen.

The kitchen is a tiny space, always a mess with dried coffee stains and grounds on the counter, and other bits of food and wrappers strewn around.

"Sure," I say, although, I know there is no coffee brewed. There never is. We don't have the funding and if someone happens to bring some in, it's gone in minutes.

I follow Danny to the kitchen and watch him make his coffee. "See, Miss Daly, there's coffee," he says as he scrapes whatever grounds he can find into a small pink Melmac cup, adding warm tap water and stirring it up. He takes a sip. "It's good," he says with a smile as we head to my office.

We spend the good part of an hour together. Danny focuses on drinking his coffee, sometimes we talk about his week. He gives little detail, usually chirping, "It's good." He pokes around at the toys and sometimes plays with the guns.

Danny lives in a group home for violent kids. Story is he was an odd child growing up, very active, disruptive, unable to focus in school, couldn't make friends. He had his first psychotic break several years before I saw him: he threatened to kill his parents in their bedroom, wielding a big kitchen knife. He was hospitalized for several months and is on heavy duty psychiatric medications, managed by Craig.

During one of our last appointments, after our coffee ritual, he bursts out, "I had a dream we were flying in the sky together, me and you, Miss Daly. Can we do that some day?"

"Where were we going?" I ask, wanting to follow whatever he brings.

"Nowhere, just flying away," he smiles, glancing for less than a second at me, before he stands and paces the room, "like on a flying carpet."

A few weeks later we hear he's been hospitalized again for attacking one of the group home residents.

"I feel so bad for him," I say in our next team meeting. "He never showed his violent side to me. If I could've worked with him longer, maybe..."

"Maybe so, Karen, but...these are seriously disturbed people, with mental illness. They're unpredictable. They don't form relationships, despite it seeming like they do. If anyone of them is to recover enough to be a part of society again, it'll happen over many years, not just a few months. Thinking you're the one who will cure them can be dangerous for you and the kids." Craig is serious and staunch. I'm taken aback.

"It's just hard to believe he would do that," I say.

Less than a year after I begin working with him, Craig leaves the clinic for a new position after marrying his longtime girlfriend. My fantasies come to a sudden and unexpected halt.

The first months of life at 66 Dana Street are good. Joanne buzzes around, always going somewhere. She works with deaf kids, teaching dance and other artsy things. Her hands move constantly when she talks, signing American Sign Language. She stands tall, holds her head high, and enunciates her speech. Prim and proper comes to mind, though in a friendly way. Sometimes she's all focused on straightening up the house, and other times she's in and out and doesn't seem to notice anything.

One day, soon after we're back from the summer, Joanne and Bobby come home together. As I step from the kitchen to the living room, I see the two of them kissing on the couch.

"Oh, sorry," I say, embarrassed and devastated. I was still hopeful Bobby would someday be my boyfriend.

"It's okay, Karen. We stopped by so I can change my clothes. We're going dancing." Joanne says, as Bobby momentarily glances my way while totally involved with Joanne. She has no idea I had fantasies about him and me. I never told her or anyone else.

"Oh, that sounds like fun. I'll see you when you get home."

The next morning I see them both. He stayed the night.

It's a short affair. Bobby's around a lot for a month or so, and then rarely.

Merrill, our third roommate, is a pretty, petite, bright blond-haired girl who's studying for a doctorate in psychology. She's of old New England stock, polite and gracious, yet fiercely independent and an avid promoter of women's rights. She and Joanne have this in common. Her boyfriend, Ricky, is a dark-haired hunk, also studying psychology. Joanne, Merrill and I spend hours around our round kitchen table, talking about all things psychological. It's the gathering room in our apartment, though we rarely have parties with more than ourselves, and Joanne's and Merrill's significant others.

They have guys; I have E&T.

———— ⸙ ————

Those first few months in Cambridge I struggle with whether to continue to wear the wooden leg. I wear it all the time, like I did before Martha's Vineyard. I tell myself it has to be one way or the other. I have to resolve to wear it or go without it. The decision feels like life or death—with no turning back.

"I don't want to wear this big, heavy, ugly leg anymore," I tell the girls, "but I'm scared I'll lose my job, or never find another one, if I take it off." I'm a wreck inside, but present this as a rational dilemma.

196

"Would you be able to do your job without the leg?" Merrill asks.

"I think so. I mostly just talk to people, sit on the floor and play with kids, or write reports. It's about how people will see me, whether I'll scare them, or make them nervous because of how I look."

"You don't plan on focusing on that when you meet people, right?" Merrill asks, as if she knows the answer.

"No, why would I do that? I just want to walk around the way I really am, without this fifteen-pound leg."

Joanne pipes up, "I say go for it. You did fine and people accepted you on Martha's Vineyard. I didn't even know you had a wooden leg until you took it out those last few weeks. People at your work will forget about it, maybe they'll even think you just wear it sometimes, if you show up without it."

"If you're worried about your job, you could tell your boss before you go to work without it," Merrill adds.

"That's a good idea. She's nice. She'll probably be fine with it."

I do exactly that the next day. Bess, my boss, is OK with it, encouraging, even.

Terrified inside, I begin life without the wooden leg the day after we speak. It means cutting the right leg off all my pants and finding some way to close the hole. Long, tunic tops work to hide my misshaped butt, and E&T helps to calm my insides. I vow never to wear that clunker, chastity belt of a leg again.

After Craig leaves the clinic, there's a reorganization. I begin to work more with adults. Some of my patients are on the inpatient wards of Boston State Hospital. It's a terribly run-down place, swarming with people smoking cigarettes, mumbling to themselves, sleeping in chairs or pacing. The ward nurses pass out medications behind half-doors, locked for safety. Occasionally, there's a recreation person attempting to get people together for some kind of diversionary activity.

My job is to meet weekly with the patients I follow, when they're out of the hospital, to determine what kind of outpatient needs they might have. These are chronic mentally ill folks, the most disadvantaged in the city, most taking strong antipsychotics and antidepressants. Denial helps protect me from feeling the depths of despair that atmosphere calls forth. I'm calm and rational. It's as if I don't see the reality.

Toward the end of my first year there, I decide it's time to look for a new job despite my fears of rejection. I interview for a staff nurse position on the adolescent unit of a private psychiatric hospital in a suburb of Boston. It's a hundred forty-nine bed facility with an eleven-bed adolescent unit. It accepts only patients with private insurance and parents who are willing to participate in a robust family therapy program, which includes two to three single or multi-family meetings weekly. The adolescent unit is in one of the refurbished houses on the grounds. There are three large rooms with accommodations for four boys and seven girls, aged thirteen to seventeen, a living room, a time-out room and an office. There are several other refurbished houses on the campus. The main dining room is in one of the adult buildings and therapy rooms and offices are in the others.

It's a beautiful setting, with big trees, pretty landscaping, and nice paths for walking. My interview with the Director of Nursing takes place in her spacious and bright attic office atop the main building. It's my first interview as a visibly one-legged nurse and, although I'm a whiz on crutches, I'm nervous about how she'll react when she sees me.

"Come in, Karen," she says as she extends her hand. She doesn't flinch at the crutches or missing leg. "Welcome, I've been looking forward to meeting you." I imagine she chose to interview me because of my master's in child and adolescent mental health. In the 1980s, it was rare to find a master's-educated nurse interested in working in a hospital setting. I didn't mention my missing leg on the application.

"So how did you hear about us?"

"I saw the ad in the Boston Globe. Sounded like the perfect job for me. I've been at the state hospital, in the clinic, for just about a year. Time for a new challenge." I'm sitting opposite her, in front of her huge oak desk, looking out into beautiful flowering trees.

"Tell me about how you lost your leg," she says, nonchalantly.

"Bone cancer, I had it in 1959 and lost the leg in 1962."

"Almost twenty years ago. And you've been OK since?"

"Yes, I'm one of the lucky ones." I love talking about the cancer story. I consider myself well-adjusted. It's always been easy to physically adapt to whatever arises. I want to project self-confidence, like I can do anything.

"You have a great attitude. Looks like you're pretty adept on those crutches. Did you ever have a wooden leg?"

"Yes, as a matter of fact, I wore it pretty much round-the-clock until about six months ago. It got me through nursing school and my first jobs and, I guess, it helped me fit in when I was a teenager, though I'm not so sure about that. I wonder if maybe it helped my family feel better about looking at me."

"So what made you stop wearing it?" She's easy to talk to. Her questions put me at ease. It's all out in the open.

"I met some other amputees through skiing and sailing and was amazed at how they felt free to wear or not wear their wooden legs. I always thought it was my job to wear it to look normal and save other people from having to see me as one-legged. Since I lost my right leg and pelvis, my wooden leg comes all the way up above my waist and buckles on with thick leather buckles. After I spent a few days without it I felt so much freer, I decided to stop wearing it."

The interview continues and she hires me as the weekend night nurse on the adolescent unit. Graveyard shift is not easy, but I like the facility and the people I meet when we change shifts in the mornings and evenings. I rarely see the kids since they have strict curfews and, being teenagers, once they're asleep, they sleep like logs until the day-shift rouses them.

A few months after I'm hired the day charge nurse leaves, and I take over her job. I'll be working with a team of psychiatric professionals, including Don, the medical director, mental health aides, various psychologists, teachers, and Noreen, the evening charge nurse. The day team, including Don, who is a very visible and engaged leader, makes rounds with the team every morning after breakfast, stopping at each kid's bed for an update on their progress the previous day. The kids are very involved in their treatment plans, setting daily and longer-term goals. They keep track of those goals with point systems, individually created and revised with their daily staff person. There are school classes, group therapy, recreation groups, and family meetings the kids earn points for attending. They can earn special privileges, like extra sleep-in time or freedom to roam the grounds for short periods of time, for accumulated points.

We have a mix of behaviorally aggressive kids and depressed, suicidal ones. Gender plays a small part in who's in which group, but not much. The admit team screens for serious mental illness or repeated violent behaviors and generally passes on those kids, the theory being: we are able to help children with psychiatric disorders using specific methods when they are part of a group of similar children. The group culture is one of the most important aspects of the therapy: the kids help each other by sharing problems, past histories, hopes, dreams, and generally they quickly feel safe and develop strong bonds in their three to four weeks on the unit. The old pros help the new admits get acclimated. Lots of teen group issues arise in the day-to-day living area, and the staff helps the kids see their part and find healthy ways to resolve internal and external dilemmas. Although I'm unaware of it at the time, I begin to see my own adolescent dilemmas through my work with the teens and begin to feel how hard adolescence can be.

My day staff and I develop strong bonds with the kids, each other, and the evening staff. Our primary goal is to provide consistency of message to each kid and the group as a whole. We have a two-hour staff meeting between day and evening shifts every weekday where we talk about every kid, share experiences, problems, and thoughts about ways to help them move forward.

I absolutely love my job and everything about it. The kids respond to me immediately and constantly. They listen to me and seek out my company. It's as if I'm a big sister or auntie to them, and I feel the same. Noreen, the evening charge nurse, is more of a mother figure, a role she loves. Together, we and our mental health aides, provide a healthy family environment, though we work hard to keep the kids from calling the unit their family. It's challenging, fun, and rewarding. I'm caught up in my role, and cocky enough to believe I'm capable of bonding with every kid and influencing them to do what I ask.

Todd, a fifteen-year-old, is having a difficult day. "I'm not going; I don't care what you stupid, fuckin' morons say. This is all a big waste of time. Nothing's gonna change. I hate that group and all of you."

"Okay, Todd, it's fine if that's how you feel right now. Let's get you in the time-out room. You can calm down in there, and we'll see what's up when you're feeling better," Ben, a tall, sweet, dark haired twenty-something, with a weight lifter's body and a slew of brothers and sisters he adores, says motioning towards the room.

"I'm calm," Todd shouts, with his head down, his body visibly tense. "I don't need you or a time out. I'm fine." His affect is somewhere between rage and sadness.

Ben escorts him into the small bedroom-sized, empty room we use for time-outs. He goes in voluntarily, shaking off Ben's attempt to gently take his arm.

I stand by silently. Ben's in charge; I'm merely his witness and backup. We decide to try a small dose of medication to help him calm down more quickly. Medication is a small part of each kid's treatment plan. Sometimes it can be a big help, but we use it sparingly.

"Do you want me to go in with you?" Ben asks.

"No. I have a good relationship with him. I think he'll be fine. Just stay by the door." I say, certain Todd will calm down immediately when he sees me come in.

I walk to the opposite side of the room where he's pacing. "Hey Todd. Looks like you're having a pretty hard time right now. I brought some medication. It'll help you calm down a little quicker. Here take it with milk, I know you like milk."

Todd takes the cup and immediately flings the milk in my face and all over my dress, a new one I'm wearing for the first time. "I'm calm and

I don't want any of your fucking medicine. I hate milk. Leave me alone. Get out of here," he yells in my face.

I leave the room in total shock. It's the first time a kid has not responded as I asked. Todd eventually calms down on his own and is ready to have a talk with Ben. We talk about the incident in the next staff meeting.

It's not so easy to let go of my sense of myself as able to influence the kids at all times. A month or so later I have a similar incident.

Sandy is a fifteen-year-old suicidal girl from a stable family. She's pretty, smart, well-liked, and yet something inside is not right. She hates herself one minute and is unselfconsciously engaged with boys and other girls the next. She latches onto me immediately, and I become her primary staff person. The week before she's to be discharged, we start discussing what things will be like at home.

"How will you manage when the self-hate and desires to cut yourself come up?"

"I'll remember what we do here, talk to someone, write, listen to upbeat music. I'm scared, though. I wish I could stay longer, or have some way to call you. Can you be my outpatient therapist?" She tugs at my heart strings, and I'm sure I could keep her safe if I could stay in touch, but the unit rules prohibit that.

"I can't. You've learned a lot here and grown up some. You're stronger and smarter. You can remember all the things we talked about, but we won't have any contact after you leave. It's important you get back to life with your family and friends and let them do for you what we helped with here." I know this is a letdown and not enough. She's emotionally shaky. Three weeks is not really long enough to learn and practice such important new ways of living.

Two nights before her discharge date she gives me a gold, forever-heart on a chain. I'm flattered and embarrassed. I don't want to accept it and talk about it in the day's staff meeting. We decide it's something she needs and wants to do and to not accept it would be like a slap in the face.

A few days before her discharge date I work a night shift. While making rounds I see she's awake, huddled under her covers, as if trying to hide. I stand by her bed.

"What's up, Sandy," I whisper, "let me see what's under there." I pull back the covers and see blood. She superficially cut her wrist.

I rouse her out of the room, hoping not to disturb her roommates. "What have you done? I thought you were going to talk, or write when you felt like hurting yourself." I try not to be mad, but I am. I expected her to know better.

"I'm scared to go home. I couldn't help it," she pleads. We hug, I clean her up, and she goes back to bed. I'm conflicted inside—I understand her desperation and maybe can allow myself to sense a tiny bit of my own at that age, yet I think she should pull herself together and get on with it.

I quickly adjust to life in the middle of Cambridge. There's a coffee shop in Central Square that sells gigantic muffins full of chocolate, peanut butter, berries, and in every conceivable flavor. There's a counter where locals sip coffee and gorge on the muffins. I'm a regular, frequently buying three or four muffins to eat throughout the day, or however long they last. A few steps down from there is a co-op grocery store, with aisles of bulk goodies. I become a member and use my discount to stock up on E&T favorites. Joanne and Merrill belong to the co-op too, but I'm the only one who works hours for the discount. I work in the cheese area, cutting and wrapping small chunks from humongous bricks or rounds. My only friends are my roommates, who are usually busy with their boyfriends, so it's a place I go to socialize.

There's another grocery store a few blocks in the other direction and a jazz club, Legal Seafood restaurant and Rosie's bakery, close to the Cambridge Hospital in Inman Square, around the corner from my apartment.

Joanne finds a new boyfriend. Carlos is a handsome, mid-twenties, Hispanic man with a gentle, easy, bright presence. He's several years younger than Joanne, but the chemistry between them is unmistakable. Merrill, Joanne, and I host group dinners with Carlos, Richie and Barbara, a friend of Joanne's, who plays guitar and spent several weekends with us on Martha's Vineyard. Sometimes Bobbie shows up, with or without a woman he's courting. We cook healthy dinners together, share a bottle or two of wine and sit around singing along as Barbara plays popular folk tunes. She sits on a stepstool with a red vinyl seat that lives in one corner of our giant kitchen. Carlos and Richie stay overnight frequently. I like them both, and it pains me to be the only one without a boyfriend. I don't let on. I tell myself I'm too busy for a boyfriend.

It's the early 1980s, I'm thirty-something and other than my ambivalence about having a boyfriend, I tell myself things are good, despite the reality that I'm throwing up and stealing food, other small things, and sometimes money, from stores and people at home, at work, and in the community. The fear of getting caught is overpowered by the compulsion that drives me. I'm certain it will all end when I find the right boyfriend or when I don't have to deal with my mother anymore. I'm more and more certain she's the reason for all my troubles.

———◊———

Working with the teens stirs up internal things that I can't articulate. I find a therapist at the Cambridge Hospital. Chuck's a psychologist who works through the community mental health program at the hospital and teaches at Harvard. He's an ordinary looking man, maybe ten years older than I, who practices a free-association style of therapy. I don't lie on a couch, but he rarely speaks, leaving it to me to talk about whatever comes to mind. My childhood, botched by my controlling mother, is the primary topic. I have no awareness of how sorry I feel for myself. Any self-pity is converted to anger and blame before I have time to recognize it.

"When I ask my mother if she realizes I was suffering inside when I was sick and had my leg cut off, she says, 'don't you realize we were suffering, too?' like her suffering was greater than mine. I feel like killing her," I tell Chuck. "And she was always pointing out how uneven my butt is. I wasn't allowed to have feelings or problems." I'm enraged at my mother—it's my single-pointed focus.

"What about your father?" Chuck asks, in a rare communicative moment.

"My father is not to blame at all. I never had much of a relationship with him. He went to work, came home, and watched TV. He told us to do what my mother said to do."

On and on, over and over, week after week, I rant. Chuck listens, says little. I never once mention E&T.

I have an intellectual rationale for everything I tell my therapist. I label my mother as emotionally distant, and I share unflattering stories about her with my friends. When I feel rage at my roommates, I do the same. I'm unaware that I'm projecting my own sense of inadequacy, disappointment, and rage onto those around me. I want something I can't name from Joanne and from Merrill, from my mother and from everyone else I try to get close to (as close as I can, given I never tell the truth about myself). E&T is the only thing that fills the hole. Everyone and everything else falls short.

———— ✦ ————

Meanwhile, I become friendly with one of the therapists at the hospital. Kathy is single and on the hunt for a man. We generally meet up at a bar in Cambridge frequented by university people and other professional types. Thursday is unofficially singles night always crowded with regulars, which we quickly become, wanting to avoid the more serious Friday and Saturday date nights. One of the regulars is a well-dressed, aloof man, who frequently wears a bow-tie and always smokes awful smelling clove cigarettes at the bar. Pickups happen often, and it's easy to recognize a situation developing as couples flirt while sipping their second or third drink.

I have several one- or two-night-stands over the course of a year or two—most times ending up either in someone's backseat or waking up at their place, in the middle of the night, with something of a hangover. I never bring men home to my apartment and keep the details of these encounters to myself, thinking it's what everyone does when they're meeting new men while shamefully knowing it isn't. The episodes are both educational and demoralizing. It's remarkable that I don't get pregnant—I have plenty of unprotected, meaningless sex.

One evening, a nerdy, casually dressed redhead, close to my age, sits at the bar talking to me for over an hour. He's into science and logic, and I'm flattered that he seems to like me.

"Come with me to my car," he says, motioning for the bartender, "I have some magazines I think you'll find interesting."

"Sure," I say, as I pay my tab. As always, I'm hopeful—maybe he's the one. I'm on crutches so holding hands as we hurry through the streets is not an option, something I lament repeatedly.

I get in the front seat of the car while he opens the trunk to get the magazines. They're full of porn, with splashes of S&M throughout.

"Are you up for some fun?" he asks, eyes wide and expectant.

"Here?" I'm out of my element now—quick, rooting sex in the backseat I can do, but I'm a little scared about what I'm seeing.

"Well, we could go to your house," he suggests as he's feeling me up.

"Not tonight. I have to work tomorrow." I agree to make out for a little bit. He manhandles me, coercing me to do more than I want. I don't protest thinking maybe if I go along he'll call for another date.

———◆———

Early in 1985, my fourth year working on the adolescent unit, Don, our much loved medical director, announces he's leaving for an opportunity in another state. I'm devastated. We all wonder if it's possible to continue without him. He reassures us it is.

The search for his replacement takes most of six months and our new doc, Tom, takes over the unit towards the end of 1985. He's a sweet man, gently confrontational with the kids. We keep the program structure as is for the first few months, but soon after that we expand our census to thirteen, and begin to take kids from the state program for problem youth. Parents no longer have to be involved in the care, and some of the kids don't have willing parents. The kids we get are bigger and more street savvy. It changes the dynamics on the unit.

As it happens, Don knew the change was coming and was not interested in working with kids who were at such high risk. He felt the unit was not set up for it. We have no lockdown facilities or beds that can be used to restrain kids who are out of control. Tom is aware of that, but feels certain our point system philosophy and peer group influences can work for kids with more significant behavioral issues, including those who'd spent time in juvenile detention.

Success in our program would be the last chance for Joe, an older teen who comes to us from juvenile detention, in an attempt to break the cycle of repeated time in locked facilities. If he can make it through four weeks with us and find ways to manage his anxiety and rage, he'll be free to resume life outside of detention. He's a big kid and, at eighteen, one of the oldest we've had. The first week or two he softens some and participates in the unit activities, although he always seems out of his element—like what we ask him to do is beneath him. Nevertheless, he cooperates in those early weeks. Toward the fourth week, it's clear he's merely going through the motions and has no intention of changing. Complicating it all is the sad fact that he has essentially no family support or friends other than those he knows from his life in detention. His aggressiveness is controlled, but palpable.

Our staff meetings focus on ways to engage him, though eventually we realize that we won't be able to change his course. He'll have to discharge back to the youth services facility. We feel it's best not to tell him until the transport van is on the premises.

He's a savvy kid though, and he knows what's going on. The afternoon of the day before he's to leave, while in his four-bed room alone, he begins overturning the eight-foot tall wardrobes the boys use for their personal belongings. The door to the room is closed and many of the kids are outside. Tom, our director, begins talking to him through the door.

"What's going on, Joe? Are you okay in there?" We're in the main room, clustered near the door. One of the aides is outside with the other kids.

"I'm not going back to detention. I'm getting out of here, and you won't stop me." We hear a window break, then the door opens and Joe comes toward us with a large piece of pointed glass.

"I don't want to hurt anyone," he says as he walks toward us holding the glass in front of him. "Just move back slowly, yes, keep going, to the door. Now all of you go out in the back and stay there until I'm off the property. Don't make me hurt you."

We see him run across the road and toward the town. Someone charges inside to call the police. The rest of us, kids and staff, gather in the living room—crying, shaking with fear, hearts pounding—to comfort each other and process what had happened.

14   Cracks in the Shell

I am not discouraged, because every wrong attempt discarded is another step forward.

/ Thomas Alva Edison

MY PARENTS MOVE TO FLORIDA IN 1978 shortly after my brother dies. They're compelled, by the depths of their sadness, to flee the town my brother David grew up in. In the early 1980s, they buy a small trailer in a park in West Palm Beach. My father is retired. He can minimally move the left side of his body due to hemiparesis from a stroke and is home most of the day watching TV. My mother works part-time as a cashier in Sears.

They make friends with people in the park, in particular one man who helps my mother with things my father can no longer take care of around the house.

I visit once or twice a year because I feel an obligation to see them. I can barely tolerate being around my mother, much less talk with her. Though I know it's not her fault, she's the only one I have to blame for what I am coming to slowly understand is the unresolved grief I'm struggling with. Our interactions are heated and accusatory, and our only physical contact happens when we stiffly hug hello or goodbye. My father frequently interrupts our arguments, demanding we stop shouting at each other.

In the mid-eighties my father is diagnosed with lung cancer and, because of his weakness, he's in a wheelchair and does nothing but roll in and out of the house onto their little screened patio. He's frail and tears up at poignant moments in situation comedies, which he's always loved. The doctor says strokes often cause folks to become emotionally labile. I'm sure it's a broken heart. He seems to have become less and less interested in living since my brother David died years earlier.

"Why don't you get one of those spiffy electric scooters, Dad? You could get a job delivering the mail in the park. Or just go out for rides, taking in the scenery." I ask this repeatedly and he barely replies. He shakes his head and says, "Nah, not for me."

One day I call them from Cambridge to talk with my dad. My mother tells me he's worse, having trouble breathing, and says they're considering hospice. I'm sitting on the step between our kitchen and living room, alone in the apartment. Dad gets on the phone.

"Hey, Dad. How are you?" My head hangs, almost to my lap as I hold the receiver to my ear.

"Not so good," he says, breathing audibly into the phone.

"I don't want you to die, Dad. Please don't die. Please, please don't die." I'm sobbing into the phone. "I love you, Daddy. Please don't die."

I can hear my father crying. My mother takes the phone. "You're upsetting him, Karen. If you're so worried, why don't you come down and see him? I'm hanging up."

A week or so later, in August 1986, I fly to Florida. My father is in bed, with a full-time hospice nurse. My mother is minimally involved in his care. She stays in the room with him for short periods.

I see him lying in the fetal position with his back to me and want so badly to lie next to him. I wonder why my mother doesn't. He refuses to face me, and when I walk around the bed to look at him, he closes his eyes. I know I'm sad but I don't cry.

He dies during that visit. The hospice nurse is the only one in the room with him. My mother and I are visibly upset yet can barely look at one another. At one point, after my Dad's body is out of the house, we get into a screaming and flailing fight so intense we almost come to blows.

"Why didn't you stay with Dad in the end? If you had such a wonderful relationship—why would you want to be somewhere else while your husband's dying?" I'm yelling, while my mother frantically goes around closing windows.

"Shut up Karen—you don't know anything. You haven't been around, you're so unemotional and selfish, with your therapy and doctors. You've never cared about us and you have no business asking me about my relationship with your father." She's inches away, her eyes wide, and quietly with fierce control, she spits the words into my face. Then, she turns and walks away. I follow, grabbing her arm.

"What? Are you gonna hit me now? Go ahead, hit me, hit me with a crutch. See what happens then." I let go and walk away shaking. We're both overwhelmed with a lifetime of grief and rage so big it consumes every molecule of air in the room. There's not a drop of compassion between us. We are two lonely souls searching for comfort while blaming each other.

A week or so later, we have a small service in New Jersey with my brothers, Bill and Gerard, and other relatives. My father's ashes are put in the grave where my brother David is buried. Bill, Gerard, my mother, and I are not physically estranged—we see each other every year or so—but we couldn't be more emotionally estranged from ourselves and each other.

———◆———

Although I don't return to Colorado to ski again until my fortieth year, I ski in New Hampshire at Mt. Sunapee, once or twice a season. On one of my trips north, the group of Steve, Cale, Jane, and I stop at a favorite breakfast place before heading for the mountain. I meet Posie, a woman forty years my elder and a recent below-the-knee amputee. She's a Cambridge, Massachusetts native, the widow of a prominent local doctor. After college at Smith, she enrolled in the medical school, eventually dropping out to marry and raise a family of six children. I hear all about her from Cale before we meet.

"You must be Karen," Posie says as soon as I walk into the room, as if she's been waiting to meet me. "I've heard a lot about you. Come, sit here next to me."

"I've heard lots about you too, Posie. It's nice to finally meet you. Everyone talks about how amazing you are skiing with one leg in your seventies."

"They're all very generous, but it's hardly skiing like I know it. I stand at the top of the bunny hill and pray I'll make it down without falling. I've skied since I was a child, before any of these places were here. We just took off for the hills. Sometimes there was a rope tow, sometimes we just trudged up the hill for the thrill of flying down. Now it takes so long to get the leg off and the equipment on, I'm lucky if I can make a few runs down the littlest slopes." She's got a true Boston accent, softened with something I think may come from her old Cambridge upbringing. Her diction and pronunciations are just a tad formal on hearing but fully integrated with how she presents herself. There's not a bone of pretension in her body.

She and I are at about the same level on the hills—the difference being, she truly knows how to ski and is limited by her recent physical struggles, where as I have no idea how to ski other than to point the skis downhill and go, toppling and sliding when I can't get my foot to turn quick enough. I'm limited by my resistance to any and all help, which keeps me from being able to learn.

Posie seems to like me despite (or maybe because of) my skiing and my fierce, but not always helpful, independence. We become fast friends, and she invites me for holiday dinners with her educated, professional children who all embrace me. I'm treated to real plum pudding, mincemeat pie, and chestnut stuffing at Thanksgiving. Her house is grand, huge and, at the same time, cozy, and set up for preparing big dinners together and sharing them at the biggest oval dining table I've ever seen. There's matching china for twenty-four or more, real silverware, and drinks and wine offered continually by her adult sons. The furnishings are old and somewhat worn, all beautiful antiques with a comfy and lived in feel.

I come to love Posie. She's like a mother to me and, although we never talk about it as such, I'm sure she knows it. She listens to my frustrations with my mother and shares some of her own with her daughters. She loans me money when I think I want to go back to school, and then refuses to let me pay her back. We have simple dinners together at her humble kitchen table. I visit her in summers on Cape Cod, where we talk and stare out at the beautiful bay.

———————

In early 1986, I decide it's time to look for a new job. My last days on the adolescent unit are bittersweet. I'm unable to admit to the terror I feel each day I walk in the door, or how little trust I have in our new director. Instead, I tell people I'm ready for a new experience while dreading each day, uncomfortable with the changes the unit is going through. Don, our previous doctor, was more than a unit director. He was like a protective and instructive father. I miss him, yet I'm unable to articulate the feeling, even to myself.

Mary, the nurse manager of the Cambridge Hospital inpatient psychiatric unit, hires me on the spot during my interview. My experience and my master's degree once again serve me well. We discuss the reality of my one-leggedness only briefly. It's an open adult unit, on the fourth floor of the medical-surgical hospital. The patients are admitted voluntarily and are well enough to participate in their care. The elevator opens to the nurses' station and a large community room, where patients and staff gather for meetings and socializing. I begin work there part-time, on the day and evening shifts.

Our unit director, Karl, is a young, tall, burly man sporting jeans, cowboy boots, a deep bass voice, and a gentle manner. He's attractive and approachable. Most of the patients, especially our frequently admitted women, like him.

A day on the unit begins with me behind my cart outside the medication room, greeting patients and offering them their morning meds. It's a chance to make a quick assessment of each one. Frequently, I share a few words with them individually, to let them know I'm aware of what's up with them that day. It might be something that was passed on in shift change report or something I'd discussed with them the day before. It's my way of connecting personally, which can help when difficult situations arise.

Community meeting is next, where staff and patients introduce themselves each day and say one thing about how they are. Dr. Karl brings up important unit issues, any notable situations from the day before, things like outbursts of behavior, follow-up on questions, concerns the patients may have (frequently related to smoking, the food, or permission to go on walks to Rosie's, the local bakery, or the convenience store). Each patient has a loosely constructed point system. They earn the privilege of leaving the unit in groups or alone, depending on how they conduct themselves each day.

Finally, staff presents the daily groups and tells each patient which staff person is his or hers for the day. Staff meet with each of their patients for about fifteen minutes during the shift, though it can be as little as a few minutes or as many as thirty. All community meetings are smoke-free, although smoking is allowed in all the rooms and the hallways.

Most of the patients are chronically mentally ill, with diagnoses like borderline personality disorder, oppositional disorder, manic depressive disorder, and schizophrenia. Most receive state disability benefits, don't work, and live in community mental health-sponsored group homes or subsidized apartments. Many are admitted to the unit regularly, for what the staff call tune-ups. It's as if their therapists program in hospital time, anywhere from a week to six weeks, as part of their long-term treatment plans. Although unspoken, it's largely accepted that these folks will never recover and will always be supported by the community and the state. Our job, as mental health professionals, is to intervene in crises and help keep them out of the state hospital.

My apartment is around the corner from the hospital, and I walk to work when I work days. When I'm on in the evenings, I drive so I can hit the grocery store for my after work binge and purge purchases. E&T, as well as my pilfering behaviors, are alive and flourishing. I eat leftover food in patients' rooms and take food from the cafeteria. At home, I eat my roommates' food, always careful to replace it before they notice. I steal from stores, food and other things I don't really want, but can't resist. It's all about ingesting and regurgitating—filling and emptying—over and over and over. I'm never called out.

—————— ♦ ——————

A year or so into my job, I'm encouraged to apply for the newly vacant Charge Nurse position. I decline but agree to work as acting charge nurse until we hire someone into the job. I'm finding myself short on patience and compassion as the months roll on. I'm expected to care about people who, it seems to me, do nothing to help themselves. I talk about this with Cathy, a part-time nurse co-worker who becomes a good friend.

"I'm the one who should be on disability," I'm full of self-righteousness and self-pity I cannot acknowledge. "I'm the one with the physical problems—most of these people could work if they wanted to. They're just lazy. I'm starting to hate these patients. They don't want to do anything but eat and smoke." It's a rant.

Cathy listens and says little. She encourages me over and over to reduce my hours and not to take on the unit charge responsibilities. Things are changing fast in the mental health field. Government money is shifting to community facilities that house aggressive and violent patients, rather than the milder mentally disabled our unit caters to. We begin to admit elderly demented patients with aggressive behaviors, and patients who can be a danger to themselves and others. The hospital begins work on a secure unit, one floor below us, but until then, the unit I'm in charge of is the catch-all. It stresses everyone, staff and patients alike, as we fill our beds with more patients who are unpredictable and potentially dangerous.

One morning during my charge nurse reign, after a seemingly bland community meeting, patients disperse and things quiet down. We have one designated smoking room now due to government regulations, where up to twenty people sometimes crowd in, earphones blasting, to sit for hours and smoke. Jan, a jolly, fifty-plus-year-old woman, a blessed fixture, having worked on the unit for over twenty years, can't find Eddie, one of our most loved regulars. He's a tall, meek, late twenty-something schizophrenic fellow who'd been stable on medications for close to a year. When he arrived days earlier, with mild delusions requiring minor medication changes, we were all, especially Jan, surprised and disappointed. Jan's known him since his first psychotic break, close to ten years earlier. We were all hoping he was over the hump of his illness since he hadn't been hospitalized in over a year.

"I've looked everywhere. I can't find Eddie. I'll go down and check his room again. It's not like him to go missing." She walks down the corridor to his four-bed room on the right.

Before she tears into the room, she lets out a piercing, "I need help NOW, down here in Eddie's room."

Several of us run down to find her short, stout body flung over the bed closest to the door, arms outstretched onto the other bed holding tight to Eddie's ankles. He's belly down, halfway out the ten-inch opening in the fourth-floor window. His torso is literally hanging outside the building, looking down at the street below. We're all shaking as we circle the beds to gently slide Eddie back into the room. He's delusional, mumbling nonsense, limp and passive.

Medical and psychiatric doctors arrive, as we transfer Eddie to our one private room. He's diagnosed with NMS, Neuroleptic Malignant

Syndrome, a life-threatening disorder, caused by an adverse reaction to antipsychotic and neuroleptic medications. He requires medical and psychiatric nursing care. We decide to keep him on our unit, where he knows staff and patients. Our thinking is that he'll have a better chance of recovery if he feels safe. I'm quaking inside for days, certain I was responsible for someone's near death, overwhelmed by the responsibility, enraged, feeling trapped, thinking I have no way out.

I'm nervous about passing medications after that. We give large doses of powerful antipsychotics. Some patients take more than ten different medications, and they're always asking for more.

My therapist, Chuck, knows the unit and the changes it's going through. I rant about my job, my mother, my roommates. I feel an ongoing turbulence inside my body that I can't describe. My words are all intellectual rationalizations. Chuck says little. I can see and hear myself, outside of myself as if I were sitting on my right shoulder, smirking and mocking, calling myself disgusting, worthless, weak, selfish. Talking doesn't really help, so I turn to E&T for physical and mental relief.

I continue seeing Chuck, each week waiting outside his office until he calls me in. One day an exotic looking woman, in her early thirties, dressed in black—an intern of his, I hear—leaves the office straightening her clothes and hair. He's doing the same, as I walk in for my appointment. It happens each week and I begin to wonder if she's his girlfriend, maybe they're fooling around in his office. A disturbing thought, because I have a crush on Chuck. No matter. Somewhere inside my disturbed mind I'm thinking maybe he wants to be my boyfriend. After months of this, Chuck announces he's resigning to be with the exotic woman. He introduces me to another of his interns, soon to graduate. She becomes my new, and first woman, therapist. Her office is miles away. I travel four hours round trip, by car, for my appointment each week. Initially, I think nothing of the commute, relieved she's willing to see me. After a couple of months, I'm tired of her and of talking about psychological stuff, and decide I'm done with therapy.

With the unit still under my day charge, we admit an elderly demented woman who's been aggressive toward her caregivers at home. She's short and stout, and paces the hallway with her cane, moaning and mumbling nasty things to herself. She asks the same questions over and over, calls for help repeatedly when she's in bed, and threatens to pummel everyone with her cane. None of it is in her control, and she's only minimally responsive to the medications she can safely take at her age. Staff and patients are on edge—there's no escape from her frantic, desperate, engulfing energy.

One weekend day when staff is sparse and the unit is particularly busy, this woman is unrelenting. For hours we hear a constant stream of noise from her. At one point, I'm in front of the nurses' station, walking slowly toward her, as she walks toward me shouting obscenities. Something comes over me and I raise my arms, make the shape of a gun with my hands and pretend to shoot her right there in the hall. It's a notable moment. Thankfully, Cathy is working that day and is present to witness and assist.

"I've got her, Karen. You take over my checks and I'll stay with her." With her arm around the woman, Cathy escorts her gently down the hall, whispering soothing words.

Cathy invites me to her house for dinner that evening. It's an old house in Mattapan, a small, predominantly African-American city with rows of beautiful, though run-down, row houses. The interior of her place has dark woodwork, built-in cabinets, shelves, and beautiful hardwood floors. It's cluttered with Cathy's books, kitchen stuff, and her young son, Jeff's, toys. She adopted Jeff, a Central American native, as a single mom when he was an infant.

"I was worried for you today with that woman. Did you really want to shoot her?"

"Yeah, I did. Despicable, huh? I can't stand working there anymore. What am I going to do? I need a job. I don't want to be a nurse anymore.

I'm tired of taking care of people. Who's taking care of me?" I regurgitate, barely taking a breath. "I can take care of myself—I just want to not have to take care of anyone else."

"Maybe you should think about doing something else. What would you like to do?"

"How do I know? I just know I don't want to do that." I'm dismissive, resigned that there's nothing I can do. The voice outside myself tells me to get over it, buck up, and stop complaining.

"Remember I told you about my dream analyst, John. He's a Jungian and a Unitarian minister. Why don't you see him, even once—maybe your dreams could help you figure out what would make you happy?" Cathy and I are friends, but there's something missing. I can't hear much of what she says above the words constantly swirling in my own head. She's accepting, caring, interested in me and a bit of a woo-woo (the dream stuff, and astrology, and herbal remedies, and recycling) and a liberal. I have hundreds of judgments about her, starting with dowdiness and traveling all the way to negativity. I question her parenting choices, all in my self-righteous way. Unbelievably, I'm unaware of my own negativity. I consider myself a positive person.

I poo-poo Cathy's suggestion about the dream analysis—not sure if I'm scared or just oppositional. "I'm done with talking about things in therapy. It's a waste of time."

Later that same year, 1988, I have more trouble with my teeth. The crowns I had put on are falling off, and my teeth are sensitive to hot and cold. I call Kenny, my New Jersey dentist, and he recommends a dentist twenty minutes outside of Boston.

———— ɪ ————

I need a few root canals and new crowns on top. A couple of bottom teeth are now eroded of their enamel and the new dentist recommends crowns for them. Over the next many years, I'm back and forth to the dentist every several months until all the top teeth have root canals with new crowns, and all the bottoms are crowned. Eventually, several back upper teeth need to be pulled. My dentist, who's now a trusted friend, recommends implants and refers me to Dr. F., a short, spunky, Italian man who sports comic-book-character ties. I'm in my late thirties when he introduces me to the surgical process of dental implants: beginning with bone grafts requiring six months of healing with temporary crowns, followed by the implant placement, and another six months of healing before the permanent crown or bridge is applied. I end up with five implants, under two bridges, in my upper jaw over the course of four years.

Through it all not only do I never speak a word about E&T, but I continue it, starting as soon as I leave the chair after any procedure. I know it's insane, but it doesn't seem to matter that I'm threatening my health. The E&T behavior is life saving—I need it to survive.

One of the most wonderful things Posie does for me and the Cambridge disabled community is negotiate with Harvard to let us use the university's pools for a mere fifty dollars a year. There are two pools in Cambridge: a small old, four-lane pool in the basement of an old athletic building and a recently completed pool in a newer building. The new pool is shaped like an airplane: one wing is home to several lap swimming lanes, the other is a diving area and the body of the plane has a higher diving area at its tail end, and a big, open area for free swim, water aerobics, etc. Posie loves swimming and frequents the new pool several times a week. I'm a true regular, swimming one to two miles most of seven days a week. I push myself to near exhaustion and am unforgiving if I miss a day. The small pool opens earlier in the morning and sometimes I swim there, although the basement darkness and smell of chlorine makes it much less pleasant.

Early one morning, I'm in the shower after a swim in the old pool. Suddenly the room is full of chlorine gas—a leak somewhere, we're told, as staff flood the basement rousing everyone up the long tiled stairway. I'm balancing on my one leg, covered with soap and shampoo, moving as fast as I can to rinse off, retrieve my crutches and get my clothes on. My nose and throat are burning, and I begin to gasp for air. An attendant helps me dress and gets me up the stairs and outside where crowds of swimmers, in various stages of wet, dry, and dressed, join the onlookers. Fire and medical vehicles are there and I'm taken to the hospital in an ambulance, oxygen over my nose and mouth. As they wheel me into the emergency room, I yell to the staff, "If I'm dying I want to know. There are a few phone calls I want to make."

It's a spontaneous, impulsive, unplanned outburst that shocks me. The staff chuckle as if I'm joking, but I'm serious. After some tests in the emergency room, they admit me to a bed overnight for continued oxygen therapy and observation. Seems I inhaled a dangerous amount of chlorine gas. I make one call, to Joanne, my roommate.

"Oh my goodness, are you okay?" she asks.

"I'm fine—just a little gas leak at the pool. They want me to stay overnight in case my lungs took a bigger hit than they can see now. They think I may need more oxygen."

Joanne tells me, "Merrill's not around, and I've got a lot to do tonight. I'll try to stop by later."

I tell her where I am. I'm disappointed. I thought she'd hurry over.

When she does come, she brings news. "I'm leaving for Washington, D.C. with Carlos tomorrow morning. He got a job there and my sister Chrissy's working there. I'll find a translating job or something. Maybe I can do something with government arts. We better say goodbye now— we may leave before you're out tomorrow." She's talking fast and seems anxious to get back home to finish packing up.

She tells me the lease is up in a couple of months and she'll pay her share until then. I can get some new roommates or find a new place. "I hope you keep it, though. I love that apartment—I may want to come back to live here again." Then she runs off to begin her next chapter.

Merrill leaves a few months later to continue her own journey. I can afford the rent and decide to live there alone.

I apply to, and am accepted into, Northeastern University's MBA program. I have to do something to get out of nursing. My ability to tolerate my job is waning quickly. It's a work-study program, with a chunk of the tuition paid through an internship, students do the first part of the second year. I'll be paid for my intern work, as well. Posie loans me money to cover what tuition remains. It's an impulsive decision. I haven't considered what I want to do with an MBA or where I see myself working, but it seems far enough away from nursing, and I like the idea of saying I'm getting an MBA.

The first year is easy—classes are pass-fail. It's fun to be in school again, learning new things and meeting new people. In the fall of my second year, I get an internship at a company that's developing DRGs, diagnostic related groups, a new way for hospitals to bundle charges for routine procedures and common admitting conditions. I work with company staff on psychiatric diagnoses, which are in the beginning stages of being considered.

Several times during the internship, I'm asked to take on a project of my own. I decline each time. I don't want to be responsible for anything. School feels like an escape, not a launch pad to something new. I talk to Cathy, who's been challenging me about my choice all along, and continues to suggest dream analysis.

"I don't want to work in corporate America," I say, "especially if I have to start at the bottom salary and be responsible for projects and all that."

"What did you think you'd be doing with an MBA?" She has no patience with my grumpiness. "I told you to think about what you were going for."

"I decided I'm not going to finish. I've already told them I'm dropping out."

"You only have nine months to go," she says exasperated.

"I know but who cares? I know I don't want to work in corporate America and being an entrepreneur is too hard. It's a waste of time to finish." I have no idea how resigned and depressed I am. I think I'm well adjusted because I can care so little about things.

15 An Unplanned Journey

The willingness to consider possibility requires a tolerance of uncertainty.

/ Rachel Naomi Remen

JOANNE AND I STAY IN TOUCH SPORADICALLY, just enough to keep our friendship alive. She and Carlos part amicably. She goes on to meet Josh, a China expert in the foreign service, and eventually marries him.

Chrissy marries a doctor at the National Institutes of Health and has a couple of kids. She's working on the AIDS unit and pursuing a doctorate in nursing.

I lose touch with Phil. Cale, Jane and I talk occasionally. Jane marries, as does Steve. Cale wears her prosthesis for short periods while teaching writing at a local college. Both she and Jane continue to ski. Posie and I are crosstown neighbors. We visit regularly, every month or so.

———◆———

In the summer of 1988, I move into a full-time, weekend job on the psychiatric unit. I work from seven in the evening to seven in the morning on Saturdays and Sundays. I'm paid for thirty-six hours with full-time benefits, while working just twenty-four hours. I have a work partner, a lovely, competent young nurse, married with two small children, who works the daytime hours. We're a good team. We rarely have weekend issues or unit problems. Theory is fewer staff changes, especially on weekend days when staff is sparse, make for a more stable environment for the patients. The mental health workers work regular eight-hour shifts. On the night shift, eleven to seven in the morning, it's one other staff person and me

It's my perfect job. I'm away from the angst and politics of the day and evening shifts and have endless hours of time to myself. I begin making original pattern quilts from muslin and gingham I dye in all imaginable colors with cold-water dye I find at a local craft shop. The upstairs, street-side room, where I have a futon couch, an ironing board set up and a table for cutting, is my studio. I cut the dyed fabrics into two-inch squares and create my own patterns or improvised designs sewing the squares together by hand. It's tedious work. It takes hours to complete a few rows of squares, then hours more to sew the strips together into a full quilt top. I love the monotony, the colors and the feel of the fabric. I love ironing the seams open and pinning the strips together, matching seams. I use the odd shaped extra pieces to make placemats or crazy quilt patterns or round quilts. I take parts of different projects to work and sew while the patients sleep. Brian, the young man who works overnight shifts with me, is a friendly local who fills me in on the city news and his latest escapades.

"I was born right here on this floor," he tells me one night. Right in there was the nursery," he says pointing to the community room. He's a recent high school graduate, competent and kind to the patients, but not in pursuit of a career in the psych field. He wants to get married and have children.

"It's a good job for me now. I'm making money and have time to think about what kind of work I want to do." We sit side by side, behind a chest-high counter that is the nurses' station. Most of the patients sleep through the night with the help of powerful sleep meds. We check each room hourly, some every fifteen minutes and help each other stay awake.

At home, I rarely sleep through the night. Instead, I sit in the kitchen for hours, eating, purging and zoning out. It's a big kitchen, down a step from the living room. On two sides there are eighteen-inch windows lining the walls where they meet the ceiling. One half-wall is lined with open, brown-stained, plywood shelves holding books, the phone, and miscellaneous other trinkets. The sink and a floor-to-ceiling window are on the wall opposite the shelves. The far wall has a long, plywood counter with a fabric skirt that hangs to the floor, hiding the empty space below. Fridge and stove live on either side of that counter. Across the room from the counter, there's a full wall of open shelves, with a fabric skirt covering the bottom half, where dishes, pots, and other kitchen necessities live. A large, inexpensive round table graces the center of the room, surrounded by a mishmash of odd chairs. I slump in the center of the room, in a captain-style armchair, facing the large window at an angle. The counter is to my right. A long, runner rug lines the floor between my chair and the fabric skirt. Most nights I'm joined by a mouse, sitting on hind legs on the rug, his mouth and paws moving the way mice do when they're nibbling. I wonder if he knows he's offering companionship to a lost soul who doesn't really know she's lost?

During breaks from sewing, I swim, always a three-hour activity, and roam the grocery stores to feed E&T. I listen to buskers on the streets around Harvard and Central Squares and work in the food co-op. Cathy and I meet up once a week. I discover Walden Pond, about a half-hour drive from Cambridge, and swim there, always alone, from late spring to late fall. I change into and out of my bathing suit in the car and walk to one of my favorite, secluded entry spots. If I see the beach is empty, I strip and swim nude, way out into the middle, and from shore to shore in both directions. The water is clear, a hundred feet deep, and soothingly silky. I especially love it when it's raining, though I scare myself regularly when caught way out in the middle when thunder and lightning send a warning.

One day in the early fall of 1988, out of the blue, Joanne calls to tell me she and her new husband are moving to China, something they're both over the moon about. After dishing out all the details of his job and their bliss, she tells me about a trip a group of American disabled folks is taking to China. It's being organized by a friend of hers, Susan, who is the founder of Mobility International in Eugene, Oregon.

"Susan's a paraplegic who's passionate about traveling but has found it challenging in a wheelchair. She launched her organization as a way to make travel opportunities and cultural exchange experiences available to disabled people. Anyway, I know her through my work with the deaf here in D.C.. I met her once or twice when I was living in the apartment, too."

"Sounds like a cool person. What's with the trip?" I'd been to Florida and Minnesota on a plane. Never out of the country, so what Joanne proposed next would never have occurred to me.

"Well, it's a three-week trip to east China, three cities, I think. Susan is looking for a few more disabled travelers. I thought you might be interested. It's in November, Josh and I will be there then. We could spend some time together." Joanne's full of energy and encouragement and always up for an adventure.

"November, that's a month away. I can't go—what about work? And the money?"

"Can't you take time off for a vacation? It'd be so fun to see you in China. Imagine? Most people never get to go to China. It can't cost too much. Susan doesn't have much money."

Joanne gives me Susan's number, and although I'm sure there's no way I could go to China, I feel giddy with excitement. Susan's delighted I called and encourages me to join them, the first three weeks in November. She has to know almost immediately to firm up the flights and dates. On a whim, I decide to go, even though the two-thousand dollars Susan expects it to cost, which includes airfare from San Francisco to China, feels like a lot to spend at one time.

I arrange the weekends off from work, and less than a month later I'm in Logan airport walking to the gate for the San Francisco flight, when a man hurries toward me from the very same gate.

"Wait, wait," he calls as I walk by.

"Me...you calling me?" He's behind me, just about to put his hand on my shoulder.

"Hi, I'm Paul. What's your name?" He asks as he extends his hand.

"Karen. Is something wrong?" He's a tall, slightly balding man, close in age to me, wearing a dark gray business suit and carrying a brief case.

"No, nothing's wrong. I just noticed you're an amputee and wondered where you're from. I'm involved with an amputee group in Boston and haven't met you, so I thought I'd ask. Are you from Boston?"

"Cambridge," I say. "What group?"

"It's a group that helps raise money for handicapped ski trips and the like. Do you know Cale?"

"Sure—she's one of the people who introduced me to skiing."

"Where are you going?" he asks.

"San Francisco to meet up with a group. From there, China." I'm happy I have something interesting to tell him.

"I'm just back from Japan."

"What were you doing there?" I ask.

"Business," he says. "Here's my card. Why don't you call me when you get back, and we'll have dinner."

"Sure," I say as he turns to walk away, looking back as he goes. I'm shocked—maybe I just met the man of my dreams in the airport on my way to China. I almost want to turn around and forget the trip. What if he forgets about me or finds someone else while I'm gone? I watch as he becomes smaller and smaller then disappears into the crowd.

I'm greeted by a motley crew of fellow travelers in the San Francisco airport. There's Susan, in a small, speedy manual wheelchair, with a fabricated slot for the two canes she uses when places are inaccessible to the chair. Tom, a big, burly, long-haired teddy bear of a man is her partner, along to check out China and help with wheelchairs or whatever's needed. Evelyn's a tall, charming, able-bodied friend of Susan's who loves all things Chinese and is a seasoned Mobility International participant. Tim's a tall, thin, delightfully outgoing quadriplegic man in a big electric wheelchair, who has minimal use of his hands and arms. His wife, Mary, is along as another able-bodied helper. Carole's a small, bright, funny woman, with a form of muscular dystrophy that progresses slowly, in an electric scooter. There are several other able-bodied people along to lend a hand on the adventure, including Sam, a shy, handsome, blond man, who catches my eye and smiles invitingly.

We board a huge jet with three sections of seats—sets of three seats on either side of a center bank of five seats. There are many empty seats, so we're each offered entire rows, rather than single seats, in a section of the plane that looks to be reserved for our group. The attendants cater to our whims and encourage us to frequent the cart, parked at the front of one of the side rows, stocked with snacks and drinks. The bathrooms are generally free, making it a pleasant journey for me and E&T.

On arrival, sleep deprived and giddy, we're greeted by Bob, our Chinese tour guide for the entire journey, and the bus that will take us around the city of Beijing for the first part of the trip. Pascale, a petite, perky French woman in a manual wheelchair due to polio-affected legs, meets us at the bus. It's a school bus, similar to the ones we all know—no lift or designated place for wheelchairs. Thankfully, I can crutch myself up the stairs and make my way to the seats. For the rest of the three weeks, the able-bodied helpers will lift each wheelchair user—Pascale, Tim, Carole, and Susan—out of their chairs, position them in their seats, load the chairs into the rear part of the aisle and reverse the process, each time we make a stop on our journey.

Except for our hotel, every place we visit in Beijing is inaccessible, but it's never an issue. We all venture up the first bank of the Great Wall of China's amazing stone steps to inhale the incredible view. Our group of unique bodies is an attraction equal to the sites we visit. We hobble up the steps of the Forbidden City and garner stares crutching and rolling around Tiananmen Square, a few short months before the protests in

1989. Our guide is fluent in English, and each of us has mastered at least the Chinese word for hello, "ni hao."

Joanne meets us in Tiananmen Square.

We hug for a few minutes. "I'm so happy to see you," she gushes, as she leaves to hug Susan and introduce herself to the others, a few of whom she knows.

"Me, too." I'm nervous around Joanne. She's popular and beautiful and I want her to like me, but a wall goes up inside of me, and I feel distant. I miss her and remember how abandoned I felt when she left me in the hospital. "How's it been for you here?"

"Hard the first month. Josh was busy with work, long hours, and I knew no one. The embassy people are great, but I want to be out with the locals. I want to learn the language so I can be a part of this place. Many of the embassy wives have never learned more than the basic 'ni hao'. Anyhow, I'm taking private language lessons every day. My tutor takes me to local places and introduces me to people. It's great."

The city of Beijing is noticeably smoggy, its streets jammed with cars, motorbikes and bicycles, many hauling flat trailers piled high with cabbages. Driving looks to be a constant improvisation as cars swerve, zig-zag, turn from all lanes, and stop or go when they want. There are high-rise apartments lining the thoroughfares, many with balconies overflowing with green vegetables. In less congested neighborhoods, food vendors, cooking over fires made in rusted oil barrels, peddle their modest roasted potatoes and meat skewers. Small storefront eateries, serving noodle dishes and soups, abound. Bob, our guide, and various other Chinese helpers we meet up with along the journey introduce us to tastes beyond description, many of the best from the most modest places.

The only meal we eat at the hotel is breakfast, a buffet of watery rice gruel, assorted Chinese dumplings and sweets, bright yellow scrambled eggs and, of course, tasty Chinese tea. Milk is sold on street corners by independent vendors who hawk it at a high price. The bathrooms in the hotel are as we know them in the States. However, most everywhere else we travel, we find pit toilets, some individual size and, many in public places like tourist sites and restaurants, are communal. I find it hard to approach the pits, and with undependable private bathrooms, I eat very little and purge only a few times during the weeks in China.

Pascale and I quickly make friends. She's a pretty blond-haired woman in her thirties, full of joie de vivre and on mission to find good espresso in China.

"All I want is a coffee. Where do I find coffee in China?" She asks everyone we meet and laments every day. "Karen, do you want to come with me today to look for a cafe?" Her accent is full of French allure.

"Sure, Pascale." I'm in awe of her easy acceptance of herself. She wears tight fitting, feminine tops and fashionable leggings on her tiny, misshapen body. Her hair is curly, longish and perfectly messy, whether loose or swept up. She wheels self-assuredly through the streets of Beijing, and as I crutch along side, happy to be part of the duo, we draw stares, and occasional bows, from the people we pass. We find only instant Maxwell House coffee, in little packets or in clumps at the bottom of small jars. No matter. As she smokes and we sip coffee, we bask in the idea of a French cafe in China.

"No smoking for me, Pascale," I say as she offers me one of her long French cigarettes.

"What? You don't even want to try?" She's shocked. Smoking is part of her French identity, although it seems everyone smokes in China, too.

"Not really, but maybe I'll have a puff." She hands me her cigarette after a puff and head toss to the side to seductively blow out the smoke. Everything about her exudes sensuality. I can't imagine being as freely feminine as she is. Her whole body speaks.

I self-consciously take a puff, certain everyone around is thinking I look ridiculous and disgusting, trying to be cool and beautiful. It's dreadful. I choke and wheeze.

"I can't—I don't like it," I say, happy to give the cigarette back. I'm ashamed just holding it, even thinking I could be like Pascale, yet I maintain my reserve, hoping she'll like me even if I don't smoke.

230

Joanne and I meet up once more before we leave Beijing. She takes me for a walk through a park near our hotel.

"I love walking in the parks here. People are always out, alone or in small groups, doing Tai Chi and giving their caged birds a drink of fresh air. Especially the older people—see there, in their Mao outfits—they look so alive." We stop to watch a few men and women in dark blue cotton baggy pants with matching button down, Mao-collared tops, stretching slowly from pose to pose. Birds, chirping away in their cages, hang in the trees.

"Ni hao," one bright, round-faced woman says, walking toward us with a big smile. She bows slightly from the waist.

"Ni hao," we both reply as Joanne mutters a few Chinese words. The woman goes on to say more, with the same fresh open face and wide smile. The language of the body is at work in these moments.

"Why are all the caged birds in the trees?" I ask as we walk on.

"They've cut down thousands of trees in and around Beijing, and the birds have nowhere to live, so people buy them and bring them outside with them. Mostly the older folks, who probably remember when there were birds in the parks. It's probably the smog, too." Joanne says as we leave the park.

"I never thought about how birds need trees to live," I tell Joanne. It's a new conscious awareness of nature and people.

As we walk through an average neighborhood on our way back to the hotel, Joanne points out the dwellings most folks call home. The structure is low and boxy with narrow alleyways running between groups of individual units. People, many in the common Mao outfit, are in their doorways tending food on small, hibachi-like coal stoves used for cooking and heating. There are a few coal bricks stacked near each front entrance.

"This is how most folks live," Joanne says, "breathing in coal smoke all day long. It's pretty unhealthy, but the people are so happy. It's unbelievable how friendly and generous the people are."

"My mother used to shovel coal into a big furnace in the basement of an apartment building we lived in New Jersey," I tell Joanne, "so, the smell is familiar. I can't believe how black everything is though." Despite the conditions, everyone we pass greets us with a joyful "ni hao" and a big smile. Some step back to make room on the narrow sidewalk, maybe conscious of my crutches and one leg, but nonetheless, welcoming us to their humble neighborhood.

"I don't think I'll see you again before you leave for Hangzhou. I have no idea when we'll get back to the States, and if we do, I bet we spend most of our time in the D.C. area where my family is. I'm so glad you came—it's really good to see you." Joanne comes towards me with wide-open arms, embracing me and giving me a tight squeeze. "I'm sorry I left you there in the hospital. I know that was hard for you."

"It was fine. You had plans—you couldn't have known I'd be stuck in a gas leak." I downplay and minimize any feelings I have or may have had in the past. "I'm really glad I came, too. It's good to see you, and I'm glad you're happy here, and with Josh." The wall is up. I feel twinges of jealousy and sadness as she leaves, but a distancing indifference takes over the inside and outside of me.

———

In Hangzhou, our hotel is a couple of blocks from the West Lake, a big body of water, surrounded by a walking path and the most greenery I'd seen since we arrived in China. There's a wide, four-lane street, lined with shops, close to the hotel. Our days start mid-late morning, giving those people who need assistance getting up and dressed plenty of time.

Feeling adventurous, I head out alone, early one morning, to check out the boulevard. I walk a few blocks and run into a man who stops to say "ni hao." He's friendly and knows a little English, but mainly we communicate with gestures and facial expressions.

"Come, come," he motions with his arms. I hesitantly follow behind. He takes me to a Chinese donut shop, a small counter in a run-down storefront, where a few customers are buying sacks of cruller-like, greasy dough. Shelves behind the counter are lined with trays of the donuts and a woman off to the side is scooping them out of a big vat of oil as they rise to the top. The smell is sweet and spicy, different than what I know of donut shops back home.

"Here, for you, try," he says with animation, as he hands me a donut wrapped in paper.

"Thank you," I say nodding and half bowing, as all the people in the shop do after each interaction. I take a bite, knowing I can't have more than that with no place to purge. It's delightfully crunchy and greasy, sweet and savory—an irresistible delight. I have to eat the whole thing, telling myself I'll get back to the hotel soon and sneak up to the room for a quick, quiet purge. Instead, I follow the man to another shop.

"Work here," he says as we stand by a nondescript storefront. We're in an alley-like space with a few shopkeepers entering their places to get ready for the day. The man knows people, bows and speaks to them as they pass. Everyone seems full of energy and happy to be where they are.

My friend walks me back to where we met. "Tomorrow, here?" he asks.

"Okay, yes," I nod, "Hotel?" I ask as I point in the direction I think it is. He corrects me with hand gestures, trying to show me where to go straight and where to turn. His directions take me straight to the hotel, in time to head up for a purge. Too late, only bits of the donut come up, no matter how much water I drink.

The next day he shows me pictures of his family, a few kids huddled around him and his pretty wife. We go to the donut shop again, where he buys me a bag full of donuts to share with my travel mates.

He walks me halfway to the hotel. "Tomorrow, no work. Next day, here? Bring friend?" His face is open and expectant.

"Okay. Next day is my last day in Hangzhou," I say. "I meet you here. Maybe I bring my French friend."

That next day I take a different street up to the boulevard and stroll along an avenue lined with shops of all kinds: clothing, appliances, food, fancy meats, trinkets. It's a cloudy, smoggy, and chilly morning and young people breeze by me without making eye contact. Women have pastel-colored, gauzy scarves tied at their necks under their thick, fashionable coats, and click their high heels on the pavement as they hurry on to their jobs. Men take a large arc around me as they pass.

Time passes as I roam until I realize I have no idea how to get back to the hotel. I can't remember the name of the place, only that it's near a big lake. The group will be worried sick if I'm not there when the bus arrives to take us off on our day's adventure.

I stop and stand motioning to people as they pass. "Do you speak English?" I ask over and over. No one responds. Everything looks the same. I have no idea which way to start walking. I begin to panic inside.

Finally, an older woman stops. "Come, come," she says as she motions for me to follow. I have no idea if she knows what I need. She's my only hope.

She takes me to a group of houses with balconies and says, "Wait here," as she walks around to the side and climbs the stairs. She appears on the balcony with a young teenage girl.

"My daughter...speaks English." She gently nudges the girl forward to the rail of the balcony.

"I'm lost," I say and don't know the name of my hotel. It's near a big lake." I'm scared and desperate but somehow remain calm.

They talk in Chinese on the balcony and then the girl appears. "I think I know the hotel. I walk you." She speaks the words gently, almost humbly, with a distinct Chinese lilt, while looking into my eyes. Her pretty, round face is clear and open.

"Come, here." Her hand brushes my crutch and arm as we begin walking. I ask a few questions and she responds with simple, few word answers. It's like we're on a mission to reach the hotel and her focus is all there.

When we're across the street from the hotel, she points and says, "There. Is this it?"

"Yes, xiéxie," I say thank you in Chinese. I offer her a few dollars.

"No, no," she motions my hands away. "I like to help. Goodbye, I go home now."

The group is gathered in the lobby when I arrive. I tell them of my morning adventure. They're delighted. We take off for our last day in Hangzhou. We each spend lunchtime with a different family, a few have children with disabilities.

My family lives in an apartment similar, I imagine, to the one the girl and her mother live in. It has a balcony, two medium-sized rooms, and a toilet with a string overhead you pull to flush. I ask about it.

"We lucky," one of the kids says. "When it breaks we have to use the outside place."

I have a scrumptious lunch of rice and vegetables arranged in small bowls and served family-style on a lazy Susan built into the center of the table. We each eat a small bowl of soup first and have our own small bowl of rice. As the lazy Susan turns, we reach into any bowl with our chopsticks for something to place onto our bowl of rice. I eat little on purpose because I won't purge there, and because my chopstick coordination is virtually nonexistent. I'm a shoveler, out of my element at this slow, humble, thoughtful table.

That evening, back at the hotel, I ask Pascale about joining me in the morning.

"What time?"

"We meet around eight. I leave here a few minutes before. It's just a few blocks up."

"Too early for me. I'm still asleep in my bed then."

"You sure. He's a sweet man. You'd like him. Maybe he knows a coffee place." I'd like her to go.

"No, you go. There's no good coffee places here. Plus, I have to pack in the morning."

I go to meet him for the last time. He brings me another sack of donuts and a hardcover acupuncture book written in Chinese.

"My work," he says. "Very good for the body and the mind. Maybe you try sometime."

"Xiéxie," I say looking through the book. It's big and heavy. He gives me a bag I can put over my shoulder. I've never heard of acupuncture.

The gesture is touching but, inside, I'm quick to poo-poo it as something I'll never use.

He walks me part way, and we say goodbye. He takes my hand and bows. I smile and nod and turn to walk the rest of the way to the hotel.

On the bus, on the way to the airport, Sam, my young, able-bodied buddy, sits with me. I show him the book.

"Acupuncture is a powerful system of needles used to balance the energies of the body," he tells me. "This is probably a fantastic book. Too bad it's in Chinese," he says flipping through. "The pictures and Chinese characters are beautiful."

"Do you want it?" I ask, thinking I'll probably never look at it.

"No. You keep it. It's a remembrance of your short relationship with him and your time on the trip." It never occurred to me to keep it as a remembrance. If I can't read it or use it, what's the point?

"Okay, yeah, that's right?" I say putting it back in the bag. I'll move it to the bottom of my suitcase when we get to the airport.

That afternoon, we fly to Suzhou, a town south of Hangzhou on the east coast of China, known for its silk factories and fine embroidery. We visit an embroidery workplace where women sit at individual stations with silk fabric pulled over embroidery hoops of all sizes. They hand sew scenes and words onto the fabric with silk thread. It's considered a good job for a woman in China—steady work, good pay. Bob, our guide, tells us the work is hard on the women's bodies. They're hunched over the hoops all day using fine motor muscles in their hands and wrists. Nonetheless, they're cheerful, humble and welcoming, inviting us to watch as they make dozens of small stitches a minute following patterns many of them know by heart.

Bob, tells the women and their male boss about us. They're wide-eyed and curious, only a few asking questions despite our open invitation.

"Women in China are generally dutiful, quiet, and shy. Many are very talented and smart, though, and important members of their immediate families for the contributions they make. It takes a lot for a woman to ask a question, especially of a foreigner," he tells us.

Our last stop in China is Shanghai, where, among other things, we see a show that includes a deaf dance troupe. The program says it's choreographed to music.

How can deaf people dance to music, I wonder?

It's a group of young men and woman, late teens, early twenties. The music is engaging with a catchy beat and good amount of bass. The dancers are mesmerizing. Although their movement is abstract and not expressly with the music, it's clear they are "hearing" the music and in sync with it.

"How are they able to move to the music?" I ask Susan, our tour leader, when the performance is over.

"They feel the vibrations through the floor. Deaf people are generally not only tuned into their other senses, but they have a way of sensing through the body. Sign language, for example, is not only hand shapes. It relies upon body language to communicate subtle nuances in what's being said. The message under the message. We won't see sign language here, though. It's banned in China." Susan says.

We meet the dancers after the show. I can't remember ever meeting a deaf person. These kids are full of life, mouthing words accompanied by odd, guttural sounds as they interact with us and their Chinese fans. Apparently, they attend a school that teaches deaf kids to speak.

"We call it 'hearing rehabilitation'," Bob, our guide tells us. "There are people working to get the government to allow sign language. It's always a big battle here in China. Change comes very slowly."

A few days later, we say goodbye to Bob and Pascale as we board a plane bound for the States. The plane is empty, and I stretch out across the five middle seats and sleep. In California, I say goodbye once more and board the plane to Boston, wondering if I'll ever see any of these people again.

16 An Affair and an Analysis

Psychological work focuses more on what has gone wrong: how we have been wounded in our relationships with others and how to go about addressing that. Spiritual work focuses more on what is intrinsically right: how we have infinite resources at the core of our nature that we can cultivate in order to live more expansively. If psychological work thins the clouds, spiritual work invokes the sun.

/ John Welwood

BACK IN CAMBRIDGE, I RESUME E&T AS if the three weeks free of the ritual never happened. I return to work, share the details of my trip with my workmates and call Cathy.

"You'll never guess what happened to me in the airport?" I gush on the phone.

"What?" she says.

"I met a man, Paul. He came running up to me like he knew me or something. Said he noticed I had one leg and that he was part of some group of amputees in Boston. But he's a normie. A businessman he said." I'm talking as fast as I can, like I have to get to the best part quick before it changes or something bad happens.

238

"So?" Cathy likes men but she never seems enamored. There are more important things to her, like her kid, and dreams, and equal rights, and justice.

"Well, he told me to call him when I get back. I'm little scared. What if he doesn't remember me?"

"Then you say 'sorry to bother you' and hang up. I'm sure he'll remember you, Karen. Sounds like he talked to you first." She sounds a little annoyed with me.

"So should I just call and say who I am and wait to see what he says." I'm nervous—certain it was all a big, mean trick on his part.

"That's what I'd do," she says.

"Ok, then. I'll do it. And how about you, me, and Jeff getting together some night soon? You could come here, and we can make pizza." I haven't seen them in over a month.

"Maybe next week. I'll see you at work this weekend, and we can decide when then."

I call Paul.

"Sure, I remember you, Karen. I'm glad you called. How was your trip?" He sounds really happy to hear from me.

"Terrific," I say. "We went to four different cities and met lots of nice people. How are you?" I'm more nervous than I can ever remember being. I want him to like me. I want him to marry me.

"That's great. Well, would you like to go out to dinner with me some night?"

"Sure, I'd love to. When?"

"How about I pick you up tomorrow around seven? Where do you live?"

I give him the address and we hang up. I'm beside myself with inner rumbling. My mind is hurling a hundred comments a second: he'll never like you, you have nothing to wear, you look awful in everything, you have nothing to talk about, maybe he just knows you're the one, maybe he'll bring an engagement ring, on and on, degrading and encouraging. My body is in an uproar. I soothe myself with a proper binge and purge.

I wear a mid-calf, blue and white nautical stripe, straight dress with a boat neck. It has buttons down the left side, which I open to above the knee. It's my favorite dress, a hand-me-down from Joanne who bought it in a second-hand store. Makeup is not something I know how to do. I wear none, own none.

Paul picks me up at the door, coming up to see the apartment. Dressed in a suit, he looks very professional. He's got a round face and stocky build, is bald on top and wears glasses. He looks perfect to me.

We drive several blocks to Porter Square, to a restaurant I've not been in. It's moderately fancy, and I immediately feel uncomfortable. Most of the women, many at tables with men, are wearing fancy dresses, high heels and attractively applied makeup, all things I tell myself I can't wear. It's ridiculous for me to think anyone would want to romance or love me. I'm a mess of frantic activity inside as I sit opposite Paul, trying my best not to say something that will make him go away.

We eat and drink, and I visit the ladies room to purge. We don't touch. The conversation is a blur as he drives me home. He parks, hesitates, and I invite him up. Without speaking more than a word or two, we're passionately making out on the couch. I'm hot and sweaty as he runs his hand up my dress, caressing my right hip. He carries me up the windy stairs to my bed and we have quick sex. He lingers for a half hour or so, then dresses and says, "I'll call you," as he leaves.

I'm certain he likes me and will call me the next day, and I'm terrified he doesn't and won't. I can't sleep. I sit in the kitchen, talking to the mouse on the rug about my new boyfriend, and eating and purging until there's nothing but swigs of condiments in the fridge.

There's no call that week, or the next. Cathy and I make plans for a pizza night at my house.

"I'm gonna call Paul and invite him to join us. I think you'll like him," I tell Cathy a few days before.

"He hasn't called you?" She's annoyed.

"No, he works a lot. He's a businessman. He said he's pretty busy. But I think he'll be happy to hear from me. It'll take him away from his work."

"Fine. I think you're crazy, though."

Paul accepts my invitation. "I'm glad you called," he says. "I'll probably come late, between eight and nine, if that's okay."

"Sure. I think my friend Cathy and her son Jeff will still be here. We'll save you some pizza."

He arrives with a bottle of wine as we're cleaning up. We sit with him, he and I drinking wine, while he eats.

"Karen says you met at the airport. What were you in Japan for?" Cathy asks.

"Looking for new businesses to invest in. I'm a venture capitalist looking for promising biotech startups."

"Where does the capital come from?" She's skeptical and a tad suspicious.

"Some is my own, and I have contacts. Great pizza," he says turning to me. "Thanks for inviting me."

Cathy's looking askew at him. "We're leaving. Nice to meet you, Paul."

We hug, she says little and is gone.

Less than a minute passes before I'm on Paul's lap, madly kissing him. He's feeling me up. We stay there for less than a half hour before he carries me up to bed and we go at each other. My body is full of desire that feels wildly out of my control. He's more passive, accepting of my caressing and interested in my right hip area.

I have no idea what a female orgasm is and he never asks about my pleasure. My insides feel good when he's inside me. I'm intent on pleasing him, focused entirely on doing whatever it takes for him to come.

We lay side-by-side for a half hour before he leaves. "I like having sex with you, Karen. It's comfortable. I can lay on my back because of how your body is, with the missing leg and soft stump. Gotta go. I have to be up early in the morning."

"Can't you stay? Please?"

"Not tonight, maybe next time. I'll call you." He's up, dressed, down the stairs and out before I can get my crutches to follow him.

A couple of weeks go by without a call. I call him again.

"Hi, Karen. Glad you called. I want to invite you to my place for an amputee group meeting this Saturday afternoon. Cale will be here. You know her, right?

"Sure. Haven't seen her in a while. That'd be great." He gives me the details and we say goodbye.

I'm psyched. I'm going to his house. Maybe he'll invite me to stay after, introduce me as his girlfriend. That he didn't call me first, though? It rumbles around down deep. Maybe he was just about to and I called him first. Sure, that's it. That rationalization and a good round of E&T keep the rumbling to a quiet roar.

I call Cathy. "Paul invited me to his house this weekend for a meeting of some amputee group. My ski buddy, Cale, will be there."

"That's nice. So he called you?" She's skeptical; she doesn't like him.

"No I called him, but he was probably just about to call me and I jumped the gun. I'm excited to see his place—it's a condo in Charlestown, near the water. That's where Steve lives, you know, the guy I stayed with the first summer I lived here." I feel a little cocky—like the invitation means I'm special and more important than Cathy. I wonder if she's jealous of me.

"Sounds like you really like him. Hope it goes well." She's less than interested.

"What's up with you and Jeff?" I ask as a second thought.

"Pretty much the same. He's having some troubles in school. I've been talking to dream analyst John about it. Wish I was dreaming more. I am happy to be working less at the hospital. That place infuriates me." It's what I know of Cathy—slow, thoughtful and socially conscious, committed to dream analysis, easy to anger about injustice and unequal distribution of power.

"You're too serious," I tell her. "Let's have lunch in Jamaica Plain this week."

We meet, I talk about Paul, despite her disapproval, and I dump my advice about how she should handle the problems with her son (I'm an expert, after all, with all my mental health education), and believe I'm being a good friend.

"Sometimes I think everything's about you when we get together. You talk fast, tell me what to do, and act as if you know everything and I know nothing. Like my life is so boring next to yours. I'm tired of it. Maybe we should take a break." She's annoyed. "I think you're making a big mistake with this Paul guy. I wish you'd go see John. I think it would make you a nicer person."

We say goodbye and agree not to be in touch for a bit. She gives me John's number again. It's sobering, but my indifference, rationalization, and E&T allow me to continue to feel the rightness of my position. Cathy knows nothing of E&T, despite my having eaten her food and purged many times at her house.

I meet up with Cale at Paul's place. It's a spacious condo, overlooking the water with a view of Bunker Hill. It's furnished with nondescript, modern furniture, mostly grays, blacks, and whites.

"Seems like a big place for one person. How long have you had this place?" I ask as Paul is showing Cale and me around.

"Oh, I don't own it. I sublet, been here a couple of years." We settle in around the dining room table, a large slab of glass on a metal base. The group raises money for disabled activities. I'm not at all interested, but rather focused on when and how Paul will ask me to stay and how we'll spend the evening. I'm nervous but feel pretty sure he invited me because he wants me to be with him in his place.

He serves snacks. I throw them up later.

Cale takes me aside. "How do you know him?" She asks expectantly.

"He approached me at the airport when I was going to China. Gave me his card and said to call him. So I did. How do you know him?"

"Met him on the street in Boston a year or so ago. He's interested in this amputee fetish stuff. An amputee woman has a website with pictures of attractive, amputee women doing ordinary things, wearing skimpy clothes that show off their stumps. He wants me to contact her, says I could make a lot of money selling pictures and having dates with the men who frequent the site."

"Have you?" I'm shocked and sure that's not what he has in mind for me.

"No, I'd never do that. It's creepy. Paul's a nice guy, though. He's helped me out financially when I was in dire straights. And he bought me a nice typewriter for my writing."

"Have you slept with him?"

"No, not going there. I'm not attracted to him, not at all. Have you?"

"Yes, twice. I think he may ask me to stay the night tonight."

"Be careful; you could get hurt."

She's much more comfortable around men than I am. She jokes with Paul, confronts him, they banter. I sit quietly, afraid to say anything like a lonely puppy dog waiting to be petted.

After everyone leaves, I ask, "What are you doing the rest of the day?" as Paul scurries around the kitchen cleaning things up, essentially ignoring me.

"I've got some work and then I'm meeting some friends for dinner."

The air is thick and tense as I wait, certain he'll ask me to join. "I'll walk you to your car," he says.

"Glad you could come," he says as he turns to go back into the building. Not even a kiss.

He's preoccupied with work, I tell myself. He'll call sometime this week.

Weeks pass and he doesn't call. Eventually, I call him and it's the same scene: he comes late in the evening with take-out Chinese and wine. We eat and drink, I purge. He pulls me into his lap in the kitchen for hot and heavy making out, carries me upstairs. We have sex almost immediately; he lingers at most an hour then leaves.

The ritual continues, unchanged, for a good part of five years, during which time I continue to tell myself he's interested in me. This, despite his telling me about a house in Nantucket, a beautiful island off the coast of Cape Cod, he owns with a woman and frequents often.

"Maybe I can come out to Nantucket with you sometime," I say on many occasions.

"Sure—maybe—we'll see if it works out with my co-owner friend." He never commits or even sounds slightly enthusiastic.

He regularly tells me what an attractive woman I am, encouraging me to check out the fetish website. "You'd be a great addition. There aren't any models with an amputation and stump like yours. Your pictures would probably be a hit. You could make some side money and meet some nice men."

Just the thought of looking at the site disgusts me, but I say, "Maybe I'll take a look." I never do and I never ask if he buys pictures or meets women from the site. I'm too afraid to know the answer. It feels better to continue the fantasy that he likes me as his girlfriend and is just too busy with work to see me more often. It feels better to commune with my mouse friend at night as I eat, purge, and ruminate.

A few months after I meet Paul, I make an appointment with John, the Jungian dream analyst Cathy has been bugging me to see. I'm lonely, unhappy, and figure it can't hurt to meet him. He's a big, tall man with greying hair and a professional, yet soft and welcoming presence. His office is in the basement of his brownstone home on a side street off Central Square in Cambridge. There's no waiting room. He greets me at the door and leads me down a narrow flight of stairs, to a cozy space with windows lining the ceiling, booksshelves filled with all sorts of books, and two comfy leather chairs facing each other.

"Welcome," he says. "How did you hear about me."

"Cathy," I say.

"Oh, Cathy—yes. She's been coming for quite a while. I'll have to thank her. What has she told you about dream analysis?"

"That you and she discuss dreams she's had during the time between your meetings. She complains that she doesn't dream much. I'm not sure how much I dream. I usually don't pay much attention."

"Have you been in therapy?"

"Yes," I chuckle, "for years and years. I got tired of all the talking. I ended with my last therapist about a year ago."

"We will talk in here. It's different, though, in that it will all be centered around the dreams you write down between our sessions. You'll have to keep a dream journal—recording whatever dreams you have as best you can remember. I encourage you to keep the journal near your bed so you can write things down in the middle of the night if you wake from a dream."

"What if I don't dream?" I'm worried I'll fail at dream analysis.

"Everyone dreams regularly. It's more about remembering them. There are things you can do, like having the journal handy for even small snippets of a dream, that will help with remembering. It's all about being open to receiving dreams in a way that you can remember. The unconscious, where dreams come from, is alive and present in all of us. We only need to be willing to tune into what's there."

I'm curious and hopeful it will help with my boyfriend issues and E&T, though I never mention either to John. We agree to meet weekly, and my insurance pays John's fee.

Soon after we start, I'm dreaming like crazy. Long, mixed up scenes of houses, groups of people, incidents and relationships that don't make sense. I spend what seems like hours each night writing pages of words with questionable meaning. Visions flood my mind and most of them make no sense, either.

John explains, "When you first start paying attention to the unconscious it frequently sends you lots of confusing information. It's usually related to experiences you've had, or are having, that are stored up inside."

I read verbatim from my journal each time we meet. John helps me make sense of the characters, "Each one is a part of you—even when they appear as someone specific, they are a reflection of some aspect of you that wants to be seen."

Cathy and I compare notes about our dreams and John. She's in awe of the sheer quantity of dreams I'm having. Hers are few and far between.

"If there're two a week I can bring to my appointment, I'm ecstatic. How can you have so many?"

"Got me—they just keep coming. I'm starting twice a week sessions. John says it may help to quiet down the unconscious some." I feel superior, like John's prize client. I want to be the best at everything.

A few months into dream analysis, I begin to have longings to make things with clay. I'm still hand sewing quilts in my dark, upstairs room, swimming regularly at the Harvard pool and Walden Pond, and working weekend overnight shifts on the psychiatric unit. One evening at work, I mention the clay idea to one of the young mental health workers.

"My aunt has an art-making place, a studio and workshop, in Watertown, Massachusetts. It's like a play space—a big warehouse area with all sorts of materials you can play and create with. Maybe you should look into it."

She gives me directions, and I check it out that next week.

"Hi, I'm Kate," the woman who greets me says. She's a small, energetic woman, maybe in her fifties, with blondish-grey hair and an intense passion about the importance of art-making.

"I'm Karen," I say. "Your niece suggested I meet you when I told her I had an out-of-the-blue desire to squeeze and squish clay. I work with her at the Cambridge Hospital."

"Well, we have clay here, and blocks, and paints, and yarn, and lots of other stuff you can create with. Let me show you around."

She leads me into a big open room, with high ceilings, and tall partitions where people have large and small paper tacked up and are busy making images. Another area has a wide wooden plank set up on saw horses with clay piled high on the floor at one end. More toward the center of the room, a few people are on the floor constructing scenes with blocks. There are a couple of smaller rooms, one with a big table. "We use this room for meetings, which we have once in a while. Sometimes people use it for smaller projects," Kate says as we pass by piles of fabric, yarn, cans, sticks, leaves, and all sorts of other materials people use to create stuff.

"I'm not an artist," I confess.

"Everyone's an artist," Kate insists emphatically. "Art-making is inherent in the soul of each of us. It's an expression of the spirit in its purest form. Playing with materials and dialoguing about what you create is an essential need of each and every person. This place is set up to tease out the artist in you or to jumpstart that artist if it's in a dry spell."

She tells me people pay by the month for different amounts of studio time, all materials and coaching included. I choose a one-month option for a couple of days a week. I meet Barbara, one of the coaches, who's finding her way in art-making after a few years working with Kate, and Lynn, a professional painter who's been without inspiration, after many years of painting, showing and selling large, white-based, thickly-painted, abstract canvases.

The next day, after learning how to knead the clay to render it kiln ready, I spend hours at the table making my very first sculpture. It's a six-inch high, rotund monk, in a floor-length robe with a sash at his waist, and his arms, hands, and face raised high toward the sky. It's hardly perfect, but everyone who sees it knows what it is and admires it.

"I have no idea where this came from. I wasn't thinking about making a monk. I don't know anything about monks," I say to Barbara. It sort of scares me, and I'm critical of its imperfections.

"That's what happens when you begin playing with materials with the intention of creating. Art comes out naturally."

"This isn't art—it's just a silly figure."

"It's art. It came from a place in you that's not so easily accessible with words. Something about it is important. What do you like most about it?" Her question is aimed at getting me to put words to what I make. The studio calls it coaching—while I talk, my coach scribes so I have words to go with my creation, whether it be a bunch of scribbles, a block tower I intend to knock down, or a painting I complete.

"It seems so joyful," I say, embarrassed to be saying that I like anything about something I made. It feels like conceit.

"What else?"

I describe how I made it so fast and without thinking, how bright the face is and how the sash looks so real, on and on while she writes every word I say. I feel self-conscious and I barely glance at the pages she presents to me, but I'm curious about the process.

The second clay figure I mold is about the same size, an abstract duet on the order of a mother holding a child. The two are facing each other I title it Being Held.

Again, it just appears as a function of my manipulating the clay. I have no pre-conceived idea of what I will make, because I can't allow myself the hubris of thinking I could make anything worthwhile. And, though everyone who sees the two sculptures is moved, I'm dismissive, unable to overtly acknowledge their significance. Yet, something inside of me recognizes that it's an important process and allows me to continue.

I tell John, my dream analyst, about the art workshop and the sculptures. "I suggest you go every day if you can, Karen. Art and dreams are related. They point to things inside us that words don't seem to get at. The sculptures sound intriguing. Bring them the next time; I'd like to see them." All of this excites and scares the pants off me. I'm compelled to continue—in much the same way I'm compelled to continue E&T.

Over the next months, I move from clay to paint, to blocks. I tell Kate about my quilt making. "That's great, Karen, but it's nothing like what you make here. Quilts are more like crafts. They don't lend themselves to the spontaneity and surprises you get when you play mindlessly with materials. The thick, juiciness of paint and clay allow it to be alive in its own right." She's excited by random brush strokes and swirls of paint on paper. She encourages me to apply paint recklessly, with my fingers, brushes, sponges or thrown directly from the jar, and then to scan the big page with cardboard corners that, when brought together, create small frames around various parts of a big, abstract mess of paint. Coaches help with this, moving the corners around until something inside the frame pops out to delight me. According to Kate's thinking, it's in that small section that I will find clues to what I want to express.

One day, after a particularly vigorous painting session resulting in a mural-sized, multicolored piece of paper full of random strokes, drips and scribbles, I feel tired, overwhelmed, and ashamed of what seems like a big nothing. Why am I doing this? I'm not an artist. I'm just making a big mess and wasting paint, paper, and time. It's the first twinge of despair I've allowed myself to feel. I'm alone with my painted paper. Others are mulling around, talking and creating, but they seem far away.

Then, in a span of a few seconds, I feel a giant arm come down from the sky. It's a vision I can't see with my eyes, but it's palpably there. As it scoops me up, I hear the words, "Lay back, Karen. It's alright, lay back, rest. I'm here." I feel a deep relief as something subtle changes inside of me, despite the fact that nothing outside has changed. I'm not laying back, there is no arm or voice. Yet it feels real. I can trust it, but I'm afraid to acknowledge it. I know it's God, but what is God? I don't think about God, not sure I believe in God. I don't go to church or pray. What does God want in return?

When I scan my painting with Barbara later that day, I see crosses throughout and an area of drippy red paint around what I imagine to be the figure of Jesus. Over the next few months, religious images show up in many of my big, abstract messes of paint on paper. At one point, I see the face of Jesus with the word "LIVE" written recklessly, in big letters across the bottom.

"I'm not making these on purpose," I plead to Barbara.

"I believe you and it is pretty amazing. Even the day when you did that charcoal still-life with the rest of us, Kate said it looked like the tea boxes and mugs were animated by the spirit. Are you still seeing the dream analyst? What does he say?" Barbara's an earnest person, committed to the idea of art-making and, like the rest of us, still teetering around whether it's true that she's an artist, like Kate insists.

"Yeah, I'm still doing the dream analysis—twice a week now. John thinks I should go to church to see if there's anything that comes up for me there."

I take John up on his invitation to the Maundy Thursday service he leads on the Thursday before Easter. It's my first time in a Unitarian church. Something there grabs me and I return the next evening for the Good Friday service, where the church is draped in black and the mood is solemn. I hang on each word of his sermon about how Jesus gave his life for us, how suffering is something we all experience, and how we can rise above it. I remember my aunt telling my mother that God chose me and that's why I got cancer and lost my leg.

"How was the church experience, Karen?" John asks the next time we meet.

"It's a little scary, really. I don't know what's happening to me. I went to the Easter mass at the Catholic church, and I've been to mass there every morning since. I'm thinking maybe I'm supposed to be a nun, but I hate some things about the Catholic church —like confession. Why should I tell some man who doesn't even know me what I've done wrong? And besides, I don't want to be a nun."

"You don't have to go to confession to go to church."

"Yeah, but I have this desire to receive communion, and I have no idea why. All the dreams and the pictures. The other day in a meeting at the studio, I doodled with a black marker on a paper towel. It was all smiley face little circles with all different expressions surrounded by crosses and lines and dots. It extended in a random pattern—black marks all over the paper, like up on a hill and down below. Kate stared in awe when she saw me doing it. "What's happening there?"

"I don't know—maybe a community—a bunch of souls clustered together in a community." The word soul and the idea of souls are pretty new to me. I pick it up in all sorts of books I buy at New Words bookstore in Inman Square, a few blocks from my house. It's full of books on a wide range of topics, most all written by women. I'm drawn to the spirituality section—I devour books about the Greek and Roman goddesses, and women religious and spiritual figures. I read so many I can hardly remember the details of any. It's not head knowledge, although I don't

251

make that connection then. Instead, I'm awash in spiritual images and words that float around inside and outside of me.

For the next several months, I attend eight o'clock mass every morning. I'm one of maybe ten people, including several nuns, seated in the front pews of St. Paul's Catholic Church in Harvard Square. It's a relatively modest brick structure, with high ceilings and beautiful stained-glass windows that represent the stations of the cross. The altar is plain, yet striking, with a massive crucifix in the center and a simple table behind which the priest stands to conduct the mass.

I sit alone, usually behind the nuns, and the few others, mostly singles, are scattered around us. We don't exchange anything more than a glance, and the obligatory handshake paired with a mumbled "May peace be with you" during the part of the mass that follows communion. I'm compelled to receive communion every day, despite never going to confession. I'm eating the body of Christ each time the wafer is placed on my tongue, and I imagine having a direct connection to a God who knows my sins.

After a few weeks of daily mass, I visit the parish priest. I tell him I'm concerned about having to become a nun.

"You'll know if it's right if you keep coming to mass. God will speak to you, and you'll gradually become settled and sure about it if that's what God wants for you. Why don't you join our daily readers? Maybe serving the church and reading more of the Bible will help clarify things for you."

I want so badly to tell him about E&T, but I can't. I can only manage to allude to things in my life that are troublesome, like my relationship with my mother and dissatisfactions at work.

"Jesus will heal you from inside," he tells me.

Over the next few months, I offer gospel readings from the altar several days a week. Those passages, and things I read in other books I pick up at New Words bookstore, convince me that E&T is my spiritual path. It's my way of ritualistically purifying myself, like many past religious figures did, by ridding my body of the pool of polluted feelings and thoughts I have stored up inside.

I have several visions over the course of the next months. At the studio one day, the face of God appears—like a big sun in the sky—looking down on me, in what feels like my little girl body, saying over and over, "everything's going to be alright, Karen."

In the pool, while I furiously swim my miles, I see a movie of my mother and her sister struggling as little girls. I have no idea where it comes from. I'd never consciously thought anything like it, but it makes sense. At our next session, I tell John.

"So I see this movie—I have no idea if it's true. Do I ask my mother? What if it is true and it upsets her?" I feel burdened and confused. I don't want to know that much about my mother, but something about knowing it helps me see things about myself more clearly, especially my struggles with intimacy.

"You can tell her you're wondering about something about her past that may upset her if you bring it up. See how she responds."

I ask her on the phone.

"Yes, that's true. I've never told anyone..."

"Not even Dad or your mother?" I'm shocked—how could she keep that a secret?

"No one. Funny, though, I was just thinking about telling you. We have ESP, Karen. We know what each other is thinking." My mother talks about this ESP thing a lot and it usually infuriates me. I don't want to have ESP with my mother. This time, however, it seems true. She is inside of me, with all of her baggage.

Neither of us brings this up again, but it may be the first feeling connection I've had with my mother since I was a small child. Nothing notable changes about our external relationship, but something changes in me. There's the slightest feeling of compassion for her.

Next time I see John I tell him. "I asked my mother about the movie, and she said it's true. I got to thinking maybe that's why I had to lose my leg—there was so much bad stuff from my family's past inside of me that

I'd be crazy and unable to function if I had to deal with all of it. Maybe the universe, or God or whatever, concentrated it all in the tumor in my leg and it all got taken away when they cut off the leg. All that stuff from the past was too much for one little girl to manage. Losing the leg was a good thing." I really believe it and wonder if maybe I even chose it.

"Could be—no one knows how the universe works. Dreams and art can help us understand deep things about ourselves." John is very professional, and although gentle and kind, he's always distant and neutral. He's affirming, yet I always leave feeling alone with myself.

In the summer of 1989, after I've begun art-making at the studio, I make a reservation at the Duck Inn on Gay Head in Martha's Vineyard. It's a spontaneous act. I hadn't thought about the Vineyard in many years. I want access to the beach with the clay cliffs, close to where I spent my first months in Massachusetts.

I go alone. There's an expanse of a woody backyard with a sandy path up a slight hill, from the top of which I can see what feels like the entire universe. The sea and sky are blue, the sand is white, and the clay cliffs range in color from ochre to pitch dark grey, with hues of green, pink, and orange mixed in.

The innkeepers are friendly, and they fill me in on things that have changed since that idyllic summer ten years earlier. The inn is cozy with a great welcoming room, complete with fireplace and dining area. My room has a fabulous view of the crashing waves.

My first afternoon there, I cuddle and bottle-feed a baby raccoon they've rescued.

"He's so cute—is it a he?" I squeal like I'm talking about a human baby.

"No, a she. See the belly."

"I've never held a raccoon before," I say. I'm generally afraid of wild things. "A raccoon used to visit with me, from a small iron balcony off my upstairs bedroom, when I'd be up late sewing. It stood up, with its paws against the glass doors, peering in. I was glad for the company and terrified he'd break through and attack me. But this little girl is soft and sweet."

One of the mornings I'm there, I get up early, crutch up the hill, excited to see the sand and water. At the crest, I can see myself walking, two-legged, into the sea. I watch as I move farther and farther away, until my head disappears under the waves. It's an amazingly peaceful and satisfying vision. Somehow, I know I will walk into the sea to die. John says the sea is like the unconscious—amoral. It embraces everything and judges nothing. When I tell John about this vision the following week, he explains that dreams and visions about dying are usually not about the body actually dying. Usually, they're pointing out that we're ready to let go of some part of ourselves that doesn't serve us anymore. He says it's about letting that part die so the energy can be used for something new.

I walk down the hill to the beach, strip and hop into the water, leaving my crutches in the sand far enough away so they won't get swept in by the waves. As always, the water is silky and a tad cool. It invites me in, embraces, and rocks me. I swim a little, diving into a few waves, then make my way back to the crutches. Once they're in place under my arms, they take me back from the water to the cliffs.

It's a beautiful morning. The sun's already high in the sky, and it's more than warm with the slightest breeze. I sit in the sand for a few minutes, then spend a good part of an hour rubbing my face and my whole body with all colors of clay. I paint designs on my breasts and belly, and use my fingers to comb clay through my hair, making shapes on my head with the hair that's short enough to stick up and out. I walk the beach choosing seaweed and adorn myself with long strips of all different varieties. I make a skirt and imagine myself a princess. I wrap myself in seaweed bracelets, necklaces, and headbands, as I majestically prance up and down the beach. I run into the sea, dunk my whole self, and head back to the cliffs.

Every so often, someone walking a dog or a couple out for a stroll passes by. They cheer me on in my nakedness, covered with clay and adorned with seaweed. I'm a sea goddess, I tell myself. I think of Cale, my skiing pal, fancying herself a mermaid.

Life moves along at a fast pace the next several months. I continue working weekend nights on the psychiatric unit, which eventually succumbs to the changing nature of psychiatric treatment. We give more medications and spend less time checking in with the patients. The hospital opens a second secure unit, one floor below us, with locked rooms for more volatile patients.

When I arrive for work one evening, I'm told we just admitted a young man from the secure unit.

"They had to send us someone because they had to admit a dangerously psychotic man and needed to free up a bed. Sam was the least worrisome of their patients, even though he just arrived down there this morning." Linda, my day counterpart co-worker tells me.

"So, how is he? Why was he admitted?"

"I haven't had the chance to sit down with him yet. Actually, I hoped you'd do it. He was found grazing—yeah, on his hands and knees eating grass—on the common. He wasn't making sense so they brought him in. I guess he's been manageable so far." She's apologetic for leaving him for me. I'm actually happy because I'll be with him all night and it'll be good to make a connection with him.

I find him walking, extremely slowly, pressed up against the wall. It's almost like he's pulling himself along by pressing his hands to the wall and sliding forward.

"Hi," I say. "I'm Karen, one of the nurses. I'll be here with you through the night tonight. You're Sam, right?"

"Yeah." He stares blankly at me, holding the eye contact as if he doesn't really see me.

"Let's sit down for a minute and check in. You can tell me how you're doing."

I lead him to an interview room. He walks in past me and sits on a chair toward the back of the room. I leave the door open and sit close to it. I want to make it feel safe for him, by not closing him in, and for me, by sitting near the door in case I suddenly need help.

"I'm so glad you asked to talk with me," he says almost immediately, still looking through me with his wide eyes. "There's something I'm wondering about?"

"What is it?"

"Is this life or afterlife?" He's totally serious, sitting on the edge of his chair, looking lost, and anxious for my answer.

I have no idea what to say. It's something I wonder about. From out of the blue, I answer. "To tell you the truth," I say, "I have no idea. But, because I see everyone else around me acting like it's life that's what I do. I just believe it must be life."

Almost before I finish, he answers, "Oh good. I was worried it was a purgatory stop along the way." He says nothing more, gets up and shuffles past me out the door.

In noticing my own dreams, paintings and visions, and continually hearing the religious delusions of psychiatrically ill people, I have many questions about what separates me from someone like him. How is it that I carry the keys and he's on the other side? Why haven't I gone crazy? When will it happen? I worry that if anyone finds out about my dreams and paintings and E&T, I could be committed to a psychiatric hospital. I know deep down inside I'm not crazy. I can't explain it or talk about it, but I'm sure something is leading me down a path where I'll find the things that will make me happy.

17 Something is Moving Me

While we cry ourselves to sleep, gratitude waits patiently to console and reassure us; there is a landscape larger than the one we can see.

/ Sarah Ban Breathnach

ONE MORNING ABOUT SIX MONTHS INTO MY daily church-going, I'm struck by how separate everyone is. I feel connected to no one as I sit in my pew alone. My eyes see them all, we say hello and shake hands every morning, but I don't even know most of their names. This is not the community Jesus talks about in the Gospel. It's an elite group of people, standing in an ornate church, totally separate from the rest of humanity. As quickly as the daily mass ritual began, it ends. I have no idea what Jesus meant by community, but I'm certain it's not the church I'm standing in. In addition, the religious dreams keep coming and they're scaring me. Most recently I dreamt of Thomas Merton, the Jesuit monk. In the dream, we meet at an outdoor art fair where he's peddling his books. He tells me I'm to carry on his work in the form of paintings. I'm honored, terrified of the responsibility, and enraged that this God stuff keeps bugging me. I don't want to be chosen to carry on Jesus' work or

Thomas Merton's or anyone else's. I want everyone to stop bothering me, to stop singling me out because I'm some kind of special. I want them to give me my leg back and leave me alone.

Around the same time, four of my studio friends and I begin to meet monthly to share projects and get to know each other. Ann is the hostess. It's like a women's group with a theme. We talk about everything from art, work, and men, to politics and our current struggles. Ann and Barbara are married and don't work outside their homes, other than what they do at the studio. Marion is retired, and Chris is recently divorced, living off money she inherited from family.

I begin making a series of acrylic apple and pear still lifes. They're boldly colored red, ochre, orange with white and black accents. In some, I position the fruit on the red vinyl stepstool chair that resides in my kitchen, inherited from whoever lived there before me. In some of the paintings the fruit is whole, and in others, it's cut open, baring it's fleshy, seeded center.

"The fruit looks so alive—like it might jump out of the frame," Ann says. She's sweet, gentle, and happy in her role as mother and homemaker, exploring her artistic interests on the side. I'm jealous of her situation. It seems so easy.

"They're all extremely sensual, some bordering on sexual—like the one with the two apples on the chair. Looks like a woman's ass." Marion, the oldest and most willing to explore and express her wildness after many years in a mediocre marriage, says.

"One question—where are these apples and pears? They seem ungrounded; there's no context. Especially the halves on the plate—they look like two open and exposed halves floating in space. I love them— the paint is thick and juicy, colors are great, and they're just abstract enough to make them interesting. It's the lack of context that rattles me." Barbara is a furrowed-brow thinker and the most confident in her artist self of any of us. She's had a career, and currently is a homemaker, charcoal artist, and art coach.

"Huh. I guess you're right. Maybe I don't see them as being anywhere. I really don't know why I painted them that way. I guess I see them as lone objects and I wanted to capture all the details in the fruit without concern for the background." I'd covered part of the floor in the biggest room in my apartment with a dropcloth and painted them on flat, unstretched canvas on the floor. I had no idea how to paint anything before I started, and was fascinated with how I could re-create the look of the fruit by putting brush strokes of different colors and shapes next to each other. It's like they're not one thing, but instead a collection of odd sections, that when placed around each other combine to make the object.

"I see what Barbara's saying. There are no shadows, either. Still, they're really interesting." Ann says.

I love them, and worry they're really awful, and I'm in awe of them, and can't stop admiring them. I'm suspicious of my fellow artists' comments, thinking they're just being nice to me. It's terrifying to see what I make, and to hear the questions about what it means and reveals about me. Still, I want to show them at the city library, where they hang local artists' work for a month at a time. None of us has shown work outside of the studio, although we all talk about wanting to.

"Do you think they're good enough to show at the Cambridge library? They have a wall for local art where the exhibit changes monthly." I ask the group.

"Sure. Why not?" Barbara pipes up. "What's the point of painting them if you don't share them with the world? That's what art's for. Kate says it's a way to share your deepest self, even if you don't know what that is or what you're trying to say."

"I think they're super, Karen. You're brave to put them out there if you do." Chris is the shyest and most soft-spoken of all of us. She's fair-skinned and blond, tall and thin and there's a hesitancy to her—like something big inside wants to announce itself but can't find its way out.

I hang six paintings on the wall of the Cambridge Public Library. Barbara helps me "hang the show," a skill that involves deciding how best to position each one in relation to the others to make the entire wall as artistic as possible. I sell one painting for twenty dollars. Over the course of the next couple of years, I give some of the others away, keep one, and put one out in a free box on the sidewalk. Having them around frightens and confuses me. On the one hand, I love them and think they're fabulous. In an exact opposite way, I'm intimidated by what they say about me, although I have no idea what that is. It's like the energy I captured inside the paint is too much for me to manage. I don't understand it rationally, and that creates inner anxiety that terrifies me.

Shortly after the apple and pear paintings, Chris asks me to try painting and moving to music together with her.

"I just feel so much like drumming and painting at the same time. It seems like it would be fun to put a big piece of paper on the wall, then alternate making marks on the paper and drumming and moving my body. And there's something about doing it together, like a duet. What do you think?" She asks a tad sheepishly, even though she knows I'd been talking about wanting to paint with my whole body and started playing with using my arms and elbows, even my head, to move paint around on the paper.

"Sure, let's try and see how it feels." We meet a couple of times a week, hang a big sheet of paper on the wall, set up paints and ink and drums, tambourines, shakers and other noise makers and go at it. We move in and out of music and mark-making. It's totally improvisational and very satisfying. We build on each other's marks and make rhythms together that inform what colors and shapes we put on the paper.

At the same time, I begin collecting discarded liquor bottles, the glass pint and nip-sized ones, I find in the alleys around Central Square, a haven for street drunks after hours. Out of the blue, I have a tremendous desire to teach myself how to bead. I sit for hours in the upstairs room— the same one that held me while I made quilts—essentially weaving beads together around the bottles. I make checkerboard and diagonal designs, random patterns with different colored beads, that hug the bottles like little sweaters. Some have long strings of beads hanging from different places. Over the course of several months, I make seven or eight beaded bottles. I think of them as "re-spirited vessels," in keeping with the spiritual themes that continue to emerge in most everything I make.

Kate and many of my other studio pals admire them but consider them craft, not art. "I wish you'd take the energy you put into making those and continue to paint. You'd be surprised what you could create," Kate says. "The bottles are beautiful, but they confine your energy rather than let it flow." That may be exactly why I turn to the beading—it feels safer. I have more control over what I make.

I show an elaborately beaded red, black and white pint-sized vodka bottle in a Cambridge Art Association show, secretly believing it's unusual enough to win a prize. The bottle has a black and white checkerboard body with a black, red, and white beaded skirt hanging from an inch above the bottom. At the neck of the bottle, I gather many long strands of mixed colored beads that hang unevenly over the checkerboard. The skirt and the long strands move and sway, making the bottle somewhat of a dancing entity. It has a Native American feel. It doesn't win even an honorable mention, but I love seeing it exhibited on its pedestal, the beads hanging all crazy, and the top of the neck, with grooves for the lost cap, exposed. I love the idea of re-spirited vessels, maybe even just slightly aware it's exactly what I'm doing with myself.

Paul continues to visit every few weeks, whenever I call. He shows up with Chinese food and wine, and despite all the questions I tell myself I'll ask him and all the places I plan to invite him, it's always the same. We have a relationship based solely on sex. He pays lip service to anything I tell him about myself and gives brief, detail-less answers to questions I ask about him and his life. From little things he says, I'm dreadfully aware there's at least one other woman in his life. I'm desperate and needy enough to relentlessly shove those moments of clarity down deep into the ever increasing pool of pollution in my cells.

One night, as I sit at the foot of the stairway to the bedroom watching him fumble around the kitchen for his clothes, I burst out in uncontrollable sobbing.

"Please don't go," I beg through gasps for breath. Real tears are pouring out of my eyes, and my body is erupting in waves. "Please stay with me tonight. Please. I need you."

"I can't," he says, barely stopping to acknowledge me. "I can't. I have to be home in the morning. Calm down. I'll see you again next week. I'll call you." He spends maybe ten minutes trying to console me. I stop sobbing before he leaves, only to begin again immediately and continue through the night.

It's the first I've shed any tears since way before I can remember. I didn't cry at the time of my brother's or my father's death. I didn't cry over the divorce from Gene, my ex-husband. Instead, I rather gloated at leaving him when he wanted me to stay. I didn't cry when I had my leg amputated, because, even at eleven, I knew it was going to happen from the day I met the other kids with one leg. And besides, why cry? I just have to accept things and move on.

Paul calls sometime in the next couple of weeks. He offers to go to an art show at the studio with me. It's the first he's met any of my friends, except Cathy who, upon seeing him again, likes him even less. When it's over, we walk down the street toward my house, barely speaking.

"You're coming up?" I ask, certain it's a given. Now that we've been out together, I feel better, like he really does care about me.

"Only if it's ok with you. I can't stay the night."

"That's ok," I say, desperate not to lose him. "I promise not to cry."

And, so, we continue on as it was before the tears.

In the summer of 1991, the movie Boyz in the Hood is released. I hear the buzz about it at the studio.

"It's a complicated story of what it's like to live in the ghettos in the big cities," someone says. I read a blurb in the paper that says "it's about three young male friends growing up with dreams of one day moving beyond their violent lives in South Central LA. The relationship between one boy and his father, a single parent wanting to help his son escape the horrors of ghetto and gang life, is central." I initially say I'm not interested, then change my mind and see it alone, after a solitary swim in Walden Pond.

It triggers another unexpected outburst of tears. I cry through the film and on and off for most of eight hours after. The movie touches something so strong I have to stop the car along the side of the road and get out for fresh air.

I lean against the car, somewhere on the road between Concord and Cambridge, repeating over and over to myself, "I can't live like this anymore," not even sure what I mean. I'm forty and it feels like my life is one big mess. I feel like killing patients at work, have no boyfriend, except Paul, who I fear will never be a real boyfriend. I'm overwhelmed with wonderings about art. I try to convince myself I'm an artist, but I just don't believe it. I can't stand my mother, hardly ever see my brothers, both of whom have families I hardly know. All my friends have way better lives than I do and it's hard for me to contain my jealousy. Even my amputee friends have relationships and skiing awards and lots more than I do. My best friend is E&T, something I loathe and feel is the only thing I can depend on. I feel cheated, mad at God for choosing me. I haven't the slightest insight into my self-pity. Rather, I see myself as a soldier, racing ahead to fight the next battle.

18 Vision Questing

Practice is like a flowing stream. You make an consistent effort and the consistent effort gives rise to a continuous flow of energy. Certainly from time to time you encounter blocks, depressions and confusion.

/ Ken McLeod, from *Unfettered Mind*

I CONTINUE TO SEE JOHN, MY DREAM analyst, over the next few years and have copious dreams every week. Much of what goes on inside my dreaming body is irrational, disconnected, and confusing. John reassures me it's the way the unconscious works. "Clarity comes in strange ways, frequently sandwiched together between periods of significant un-clarity," he says.

Two of my more cogent dreams come shortly after the crying spells. In the first, I'm greeted by a garishly dressed and made-up wrinkled woman who introduces herself as Baubo. Her smeared red lipstick and generously doughy, yet curvy, body is complimented by the abstract-patterned, hot pink sack of a dress she wears. We meet in the desert. It's just us two, endless space, and a giant, lone tree several feet away.

She approaches with open arms and embraces me, sharing her lipstick with my mouth and chin. "I have some advice for you," she says, twirling her skirt while humming to herself and shifting her gaze from up into the sky to beyond the tree.

I'm unbelievably comfortable around her. Her face is clear and open, and her eyes sparkle while gazing deep into my whole body.

"These are the three things you need to do for a peaceful, happy life. Number one: eat apples. Number two: have as much pleasurable sex as you can, even if it's with yourself. And number three: play." Then she was gone.

When I tell John about the dream, he asks how I felt in it. "Uncomfortable and in awe of her," I say. "Who is she? Where did she come from?"

"And her advice?" he asks.

"Sounds like fun. I love apples and Kate at the studio talks about playing all the time. The sex part is a little scary."

"Could be she represents a counterpart to all the male God energy inside you."

I tell Cathy about the dream, and she loves it. "I think John's right. She's your goddess."

"Even though she's so messy and bizarre?" My idea of a goddess is more proper, like the ones I've read about in the women's spirituality books. Even the powerful ones, like Athena, Hera, Persephone, are not at all as unkempt, free-spirited, and old like Baubo was in the dream.

"That's what makes her so great. She's free, independent, and joyful."

"What about the sex part? Having sex with myself sounds weird and not that much fun."

"Have I told you about Eve's Garden?"

"No, what's that."

"A place that sells vibrators and other things that make sex alone, or with a partner, enjoyable for women. Maybe you should look into getting a vibrator." Cathy loves to help and she's excited about Baubo and about introducing me to more of the earthly pleasures of spirituality. Being

Jewish, and moderately involved with her faith, she's more focused than I am on the here and now. The heaven and hell stuff doesn't mean much to her.

"I think I remember my roommates in college, the ones who took up bra burning and serious women's issues, talking about that kind of thing. I never paid much attention since I barely knew what sex was then." Not that I know much more as we speak.

Cathy gives me an Eve's Garden catalog, and I order an electric vibrator with a little round head for self-pleasure. Hesitantly, over the next many years, I play with it. It packs a powerful punch, and I begin to have regular orgasms. I use it sporadically for weeks or months, then hide it away, feeling like it's a despicable thing to do. I fear being found out—like I was as a child when my mother would make me take my hands out from under the covers when she tucked me in. I had no idea why back then, nor did I ask, or ever think much about it, until now when I feel compelled to shove the vibrator in the back of a drawer.

The other memorable dream I have is about my father. Again I'm alone, walking along a grassy plain spotted with trees, when a fully dressed skeleton appears out of a hole in the ground.

"Hey, Karen? Someone down here wants to say hi to you," he says as he motions for me to follow him down the hole. As I enter, I see a bustling metropolis, just like any city above ground, except all the beings are skeletons. One is rushing toward me.

"Karen! It's me, your Dad," he says as he almost crashes into me with his skeleton body. He's wearing khakis with a casual shirt and sneakers. Sneakers? He never wore sneakers. They weren't even popular when he was young.

"Let's go over there and sit," he points to a bench. "We can catch up."

It's oddly comfortable in skeleton land. People greet us as they pass, some on bikes, some walking with skeleton dogs. My father is more animated and chatty than he ever was when he was alive.

Among other things, he tells me he's studying psychology and belongs to a men's group. He listens intently as I tell him about myself. While we chat, he takes my hand and we lean into each other, shoulders touching. Then suddenly, he looks down at the watch hanging from his skeleton wrist, stands, and exclaims, "Oh, no. I've got to go, or I'll be late for the Robert Bly seminar." He hugs me tight with his skeleton arms and plants a kiss on my cheek with his bony mouth. Then he's off, running on his skeleton legs as he looks back waving and blowing me kisses off his skeleton hands.

I wake up with an overwhelming sense of awe, delight, and unbelievable gratitude. My father is growing and changing in skeleton land. I'd read about Robert Bly's work helping men find lost aspects of themselves through men's groups, and his poetry. It's amazing; I feel so happy. It's as if my father is with me on my journey.

Giddy with delight, and feeling like John's special big dreamer, I ask, "Where are these dreams coming from?"

"The unconscious. Because you've committed to paying attention to the unconscious energy, more of it is available to you." I want him to tell me I'm his best, most interesting client, that he's never worked with someone who had so many unusual dreams. He doesn't, yet I tell myself I really am his one and only client. I need to feel special.

———— ✦ ————

Chris and I continue our moving, painting, and drumming play at the studio. We do a short improvisation during one of the studio showings. I play with blocks and make a few collages over the course of the next months. I love making ink drawings on discarded scraps of paper. It's something about the temporary nature and the non-seriousness of them.

One day early in 1991 a couple of men visit Kate to spread the word about a vision quest opportunity they're hosting in Wyoming in the spring of that year. Tom and John are partners with a friend, Gina, in an undertaking that will introduce more people to the Native American traditions.

John's an ordinary looking man, medium height, soft-spoken and friendly. Tom is a big strapping dude, sporting a cowboy hat, boots, and a humongous belt buckle. He and John have been friends for many years, and both love the Wyoming landscape and the desert. They recently bought a ranch in Savery with the intent of hosting vision quests based on the model presented in Steven Foster's _The Book of Vision Quest._

"What exactly is a vision quest?" I ask. As always, in the back of my mind is the idea that one of them could be the man who sweeps me off my feet and makes my life wonderful.

"This summer we'll offer a week-long experience based on the book. It has three phases: the introduction, the experience, and the integration. We take the group out to a place we're familiar with and each person finds a place for their three-day solo, fasting vision quest. We send you off at first light after a group ceremony and you spend three nights and four days alone, without anything but water, a tent, a pencil and pad to write down any dreams that come, and a few clothes for the varying temperatures in the desert. You ask for a vision or a dream, then wait and listen."

"Wow, that sounds amazing. Could I do it—with the crutches?"

They look at each other. "I don't see why not," John says. "The desert is pretty flat and we make a base camp in the vicinity of the individual questing spots, in case of emergencies. Sure, we'd love to have you." Tom and John are comfortable guys, engaging and very convincing. Who knows—this could be it—the experience that changes everything for me.

"OK, how do I sign up?" John gives me the info. "We recommend you read the vision quest book before you commit. It helps clarify the stages and how the experience is much more than the week-long stay in Savery. It'll help you decide whether you're up for all that we'll expect from you. It's not just a fun vacation—it's a pretty serious foray into the depths of yourself that will likely continue long after the week is over."

I'm even more intrigued. I need to do something drastic to make my life better. It feels like I'm dying inside. I take the application, buy the book the next day and decide right away that I want to go. John, my dream analyst, my studio friends, and Cathy all encourage me. "I want to go, too," Cathy and Chris lament at different times.

According to the book, the quest begins the minute you commit, which for me was the day I sent the check. I was ecstatic—certain everything I was looking for would find me during the week in Savery.

———— ◦ ————

There are several of us partaking in that week in the desert. We meet up at "the ranch," a big, wood-appointed, comfy-cozy house on a giant plot of land, at the foot of a hill where elk visibly roam. The guys fetch me at the airport and Gina, a tall, solidly built, Artemis of a woman, greets me at the house.

"So glad you could come," she says as she hugs me. I imagine she's about ten years older than me. "Welcome to our ranch and the start of your vision quest immersion. I put you in a small room down here for the night. The guys told me you were on crutches and I wanted to make it easy as possible for you." She leads me down a short wood-paneled hallway to a small rustic room with a high bed, draped in a woven spread. The window looks out onto a big garden, full of patches of green.

"Dinner's at six. Make yourself at home till then. Feel free to roam around the house or outside. I'll be in the kitchen getting on with the cooking." She leaves, closing the door behind her. I'm full of anticipation. I can't really believe I'm in Wyoming. It's a place like I've never seen before—big expanses of land and wild animals. The house is like something in a women's "country decorating" magazine, only more messy and inviting.

I wander into the kitchen where Gina's chopping vegetables for a salad. "Can I help?" I ask. There's no one else around. The other questers are out exploring the land, or en-route.

"Sure," Gina says as she hands me a knife and motions toward a cutting board graced with bright orange carrots. "Slice those up thin—we'll add them to the salad."

270

She tells me she, Tom, and John have been pals for many years. They worked together at different times. Her work was in corporate America, something she tired of, as she did living in the big city. Tom and John asked if she'd like to join them as a partner in the vision quest venture.

"I was so done with work and this seemed like the perfect change. I love the community we've established here—with the three of us, John's wife and Tom's girlfriend. I'm excited to meet each group of interesting questers and I enjoy cooking the meals, though it's been a real learning experience. I'm a city girl, not used to being responsible for big, hearty country meals. And the gardening's new, but we all do that. Still, I'm so glad I took the leap."

"So you retired?"

"Yes, and I took a chunk of my money to invest in this venture. Whatever happens, it's already been a great thing to do." She tells me they've been up and running for under a year. Ours is one of their first organized quests. They hope to offer several each spring/fall season.

———•———

That night at dinner we introduce ourselves and share a little about what we hope for. One woman says she's hoping to let go of a failed relationship. Most of us, including me, are less specific, looking for clues about happiness and direction. There's very little socializing amongst us questers. We share bits and pieces, but the atmosphere lends itself to an inner focus. We've already begun our quests and a certain solitary countenance prevails which our hosts encourage.

The next morning we're briefed on what to expect over the next four days. Gina packs the van with food for a campfire dinner, and we head off to the Red Desert. Once there, we set up camp for the night in what will be the home base. Then, it's out into the landscape to find the solitary space we'll call home for the next three days and nights.

We're told to find a place close enough to another quester to allow us to leave a sign for him/her each day—a note, some desert find, whatever. Something to let each other know we're okay. We walk out in a group, then scatter. When I find myself alone and unable to see anyone else, I get serious about searching for a spot, despite my total lack of knowledge about how to do that. Suddenly though, I'm standing in what feels to me like a shallow, mini crater. It's a recessed oval area with three big rocks anchoring one end, a chest high, solid rock wall gracing one side, and a view of the most awesome expanse of desert, that looks like the ocean, I could ever imagine.

"I'm here," I shout out loud to myself, wondering if anyone is close enough to hear.

One of the women questers shouts back, "I'm over here," from what sounds like a perfect distance.

I'm in awe, aware of what feels like my blood, and whatever other liquid stuff is inside my body, pouring slowly through me. It's like I'm melting into the ground. I settle myself by sitting at the base of the three big rocks, looking out into the expanse of desert, imagining the sea. I walk the perimeter of the space once and on my second time around, I see two giant brown and white orbs staring up at me through the brush next to my foot and crutches. The sight startles and terrifies me. I stay still and look closer, careful not to touch the tiny creature. It looks like the eyes of a tiny baby animal. I can see its chest expanding with each breath, its skin almost transparent. I'm so scared I hightail it back to the base camp, worried I'll have to find another place.

Many of my fellow questers are there when I arrive. I was totally unaware of the time—I may have still been meandering if it hadn't been for the baby animal. I tell the group what I saw.

"Probably a baby elk left hidden by its mother while she was gathering food. I'm sure it'll be gone in the morning. Honest—try not to be too scared. It sounds like exactly the right spot for your vision quest. It's a sign of new life," John says as Tom looks on smiling and nodding. They're both so warm and nurturing, so accepting—it's hard to feel anything but restless anticipation and excitement.

We retire early that night to ready ourselves for "first light" awakening. After collecting the few things we'll take into the desert, we meet inside a circle, rimmed with rocks John and Tom gathered from nearby. They lead us in a few chants, we each speak our name and acknowledge the others with our eyes. In unison, we turn to face the outside of the circle, take a breath and each wait for the moment we are consciously moved to step out into our individual quest.

"The conscious act of stepping out of the security of the group and into your own solitary being is essential. Each of you is searching for your place, your dream or vision. It's important to consciously acknowledge that." John says this with a passionate conviction that's humbly convincing.

My pile of things consists of a small, pop-up tent, sleeping bag, three gallons of water, a journal and pencil, a few clothes, and a green brimmed hat I picked up at a second-hand store in Cambridge. I'm wearing calf-length cotton pants, a tee shirt, sweater and a white, lace-up Keds sneaker. Tom walks with me to my space, carrying my things. Jill, the woman who answered my "I'm here" shout yesterday, joins us. She and I stop at a place between our two places to build a stone pile, where we'll leave each other a message each day. I'll walk there each morning, Jill each afternoon.

One of the first things I notice as we walk away from the base camp is my foot and the tips of my crutches crushing whatever lives below them.

"Tom, I'm killing creatures with each step," I say in complete shocked earnestness. I see the corners of Tom's mouth lift his lips into the slightest smile. He says nothing. We've entered the silent part of the journey.

"I want to take my shoe off so I can feel what I'm stepping on," I say, as I stop to do so. "This is not something I've ever thought about before—it never occurred to me to consider life I can't see."

Tom stops, waits, looks wide-eyed directly into my eyes, like he's looking down deep into whatever I am. He puts his finger to his closed lips, reminding me to honor the silence.

My heart is beating hard in my chest as I remember the baby elk and begin to accept what I've signed on for. What if it's still there? I remember John, so sure the mother elk would've come for her baby. "She probably knows you saw her baby and is very grateful you didn't touch it," he said during that conversation the previous night.

The baby is gone. I feel my heartbeat recede from full-on pounding out of my chest to something a tad quieter and less palpable. Tom helps me put up the tent, sets the other things down and leaves without a word. I'm restless, excited, scared, lost—so much stuff is coursing around inside my body and all I have is me and this desolate, yet excruciatingly beautiful place.

That first day I establish a daily routine that consists of sitting at the base of the three big rocks, morning, noon and night, followed by a slow walk around the perimeter of the space, taking care to notice as much as I can. I collect things and make sculptures to decorate the flat top of the rock wall. I sit at the edge of the space opposite the big rocks, sunning myself by the imagined sea, wondering all the big questions. I see sticks I'm certain are snakes. Only one in the three days actually is, and it slithers away as soon as I touch him with a stick I thought was a snake a short while before. Tiny bugs crawl all around me as I sit in the brush, or atop the dry dirt. I feel like an empty vessel—as if there's nothing to me, nothing inside and only the skin outside that makes me visible. I feel God, though I'm not certain what it is or how it comes to me. It's an ease, a freedom from whatever responsibilities I pile upon myself. My brain talks to me, and I repeat aloud what it tells me and answer aloud, as if I were talking to another person.

Sometime halfway through that first day, as I turn to face the big rocks, I see a giant creature, an elk or a deer, standing just beyond the big rocks above the recess of the space, staring straight at me. As soon as I catch the first glimpse, I'm certain it's the mother of the baby. I'm transfixed in space, in awe of her mere presence. She seems larger than anything I've ever seen, majestic, elegant, poised. Either I see or imagine that she moves her head ever so slightly, as if she's nodding to me. I feel more deeply connected than I ever have to another being—one who is acknowledging that I saw her baby and did not disturb it. The encounter

274

lasts less than a minute before she gracefully turns and walks off into another part of the desert.

My rational mind immediately begins making up story upon story about what happened, what it means, what will happen next. It berates me for feeling anything, telling me it's just an animal and doesn't care about me. It shouts warnings about the dangers of wild beasts. Despite the constant chatter, I manage to hold onto the momentary feeling of connection and it settles some of my fears. The desert becomes a friendlier place—I've been seen here, a fellow being knows about me.

I prance, dawdle, meander, sing out loud, sip rainwater from the crevices in the smooth grey rocks, touch as many things as I can—all while nude, wearing just a hat, unless the sun is burning my butt. I put on just a tee and shorts when I walk to the buddy check-in place, considering it to be public property requiring decency. I remember my barely clothed, responsibility-free days on Martha's Vineyard.

The first two nights I sleep soundly but don't dream. I'm disappointed. It's the last day and I really want a vision—for me, and so others will see I've had a successful vision quest. I'm restless, agitated, unhappy with myself. I sit resting my back on the rocks but can't seem to concentrate or relax. The day drags on, but nothing comes to me despite my numerous prayers and requests.

Finally, it's night and I lay in the dark tent, willing myself to sleep. Seemingly, in the next seconds, as so often happens with sleeplessness and dreams, I'm aware of people talking, and metal clanking behind my tent. I look out and see a smooth ramp, leading from a place I can't see down into the recess of my space. Dozens of people maneuvering all sorts of cameras, furniture, and boxes stacked high on hand carts, move down into the space close to my tent. They're facing the desert that looks like the sea, and a lone giant tree I never noticed, is being prepped for removal by chainsaw.

On two legs, I run out of the tent, yelling and screaming, "What are you doing here? What's all this stuff? You're destroying this place. Who said you could bring this awful junk here…?"

"Calm down lady," a short, stocky man with longish dark hair and a bushy mustache orders. "We're making a movie to document the natural beauty of this place."

"You're ruining it with all this stuff. And you can't chop down this tree." I run to the tree and grab a chain and lock lying on the ground. I fasten it around my waist and the tree. "I won't let you destroy this tree or this place."

He's less than happy with me. I refuse to cooperate and threaten to die with the tree if he cuts it down. We're back and forth about how people need to see the beauty of the place and how he's destroying that very beauty by tromping all over it with all the stuff he brought. I'm focused, passionate, articulate, confident, and steadfast in my position. My rational mind is quiet—or maybe it's assisting in the arguments I'm making.

I wake in the midst of it all—before any resolution—full of the same fury and passion I felt while asleep, and in awe of the palpable silence of the dawn. I've never been a tree hugger or environmentalist. I've most always kowtowed to powerful men's wishes and opinions. I rarely, if ever, have felt the confidence and passion I felt in the dream.

As I lay there, allowing the intensity of feeling to settle, Tom shakes my tent. It's time to leave. The immersion phase of the quest is over. He helps me gather my things, and we walk back to base camp together in silence.

When all the questers are back at the camp, we return to the main circle of rocks and again look at one another, take stock of our time alone, and consciously step out of the circle, back into our day-to-day lives. Tom and John suggest we keep conversation to a minimum while we eat and travel back to the ranch. I eat a little fruit and barely a bite of the creamy eggs, smoky bacon, fire-roasted potatoes and crunchy toast, certain this will be the end of E&T. Surely I'm hungry after the three-day fast. However, physical hunger is not a factor in my obsessive craving, and it takes every ounce of willpower and endless silent shouting at the forces inside to avoid stuffing my mouth. I know that the minute

I take one bite of a forbidden food—pretty much anything yummy—I'm doomed.

It's mid-afternoon when we arrive at the ranch and the last day of the experience for everyone. We all leave that night or early the next day. We decide on a schedule for our entry showers and scatter to our rooms to begin the process of leaving. Snacks abound to hold us over until dinner, when we'll gather to share our experiences and talk about what might happen over the next weeks, months, years. I can't continue to resist the food, and I'm outwardly more relaxed, open and available for interaction because of it. The inner bashing continues—you're weak, we knew you couldn't do it, you'll get caught in these close quarters. E&T allows me to ignore those voices.

At dinner we share some details of our quests. One man spent most of every day roaming the desert far and wide, coming in close contact with all varieties of desert life, from bugs to snakes, rodents, elk, and maybe a moose.

"How did you not get lost?" someone asks.

"I had a small compass and, truthfully, I wanted to get lost, to push myself beyond my usual control of everything. There were more than a few times of panic when I thought I wouldn't find my way back, but somehow there was always something that pointed me in the right direction. Usually after a lot of terror and yelling and screaming inside about what a stupid fool I am." He smiles.

A woman begins by telling us she'd just ended a particularly difficult relationship and was having difficulty letting it go. "I fretted and obsessed until halfway when something told me to burn everything I had with me, except the clothes I'd need to walk out. I brought a book of matches, thinking I may want to make a fire if it got cold at night, so I figured why not? It was totally spontaneous. I took things, one by one, until I'd stripped naked and everything but the tent and sleeping bag was gone. The fire was mesmerizing, blazing red hot, and like magic, it just took one thing after another and they disappeared. I walked around naked for the rest of the time. I feel so free today."

A couple of people struggled with what to do with all the time and no distractions. I shared about my surprise at feeling so comfortable, some of the little pleasures, like meeting the mother elk, drinking rainwater and sunning by the desert sea, and told the story of the movie set and my unexpected chaining of myself to the tree, adamant that no one would destroy something so beautiful without killing me first. "I have no idea what it means or where it came from. I never once thought I'd do something like that."

"This last part of the vision quest is really a lifetime thing. It could be years from now before you understand some of the things you got tiny glimpses of while you were solo in the desert. Sometimes we touch on things that we're not quite ready to acknowledge or don't have the inner wisdom to process. Hopefully each of you will continue the quest and allow it to inform you as you make your way back to your day-to-day lives." John seems so wise, even Tom and Gina listen intently, holding on to each word.

The next day there are sweet goodbyes and rides to the airport. My flight leaves later that night so I stay behind chatting with Gina, and wishing I could stay forever. I feel free of all the things that seemingly make my life so troubling. I'm free of responsibilities.

"We host solo retreats, too," Gina offers. "You could come for a week for a small amount of money, everything included.

"I'd love that. Maybe in the winter. Who knows, maybe I could move here. It'd be good to see what the winter's like."

———◦———

I arrange a week-long visit over Christmas 1991. Gina's cousin, Jim, a wildly handsome, laid back man around my age, joins us for several days that week. He's single and takes his place as my next fantasy man. I'm certain he's wild about me and too shy and quiet to acknowledge it. Except for the occasional, perfunctory hug, the only time we touch is when I sit between Gina and him in his pickup, as we make the rounds doing errands. It speaks volumes to me since I'm certain we have chemistry (and we may well have), but it lives only as a fantasy in my head.

The week is magical—with Christmas preparations, the real or imagined flirtations, and the idyllic environs. It snows almost every night, and we wake to fresh, untouched powder each morning. I get up at dawn and head out for a walk several hundred yards up the unplowed road, to a tiny patch of unfrozen water gurgling behind a vacant house. I see elk, and an occasional moose, atop the hill behind the ranch house, and various animal tracks barely breaking the continuity of the powdery white expanse. Some mornings the snow is a foot or more deep, and my crutches and one foot leave the first sign of human life.

Savery is a town of just twenty-five people (or so the sign says) and yet, every morning the plow rolls through, flattening the snow to a firm pack of white. One day as I'm walking back out to the main road after my solitary visit to the singing water, the plow stops and the driver yells to me.

"So you made those tracks! I was so confused...I've never seen tracks like those before. Now I get it." He's leaning out the window of the cab smiling wide and I look up at him, returning the grin. I feel so welcome.

The entire week is warm and full of homey smells and activities. We make meals together and agree to share little presents on Christmas Eve. I help with some basic chores. John's wife is a weaver and has a floor loom. She teaches me how to use it and I spend hours weaving a scarf. They teach me to play pinochle, and I take to it like a card shark. I feel so accepted that I forget I've paid for the privilege of staying there.

A few days before I leave, I tell Gina I have thoughts of maybe moving there.

"Really, are you sure? It's pretty quiet. I'd love it; you'd be great company for me. It's been terrific having you here this week, but what would you do? How would you support yourself?"

"I'm not sure. It's probably not too expensive to live out here, right? How much do you think they'd rent that little house down the road for?" I have fantasies of having a painting studio and becoming a famous artist. "Maybe I could work a couple of days a week at the hospital in Burns?"

Practical realities fly out of my brain while I'm swaddled in the comfort of the responsibility-free week in Savery. Yet, by the end of the week, I'm feeling restless and trapped. Other people's routines are annoying me. I'm tired of everyone being so nice to me. I can't wait to get away for a proper binge and purge.

19 Dancing Queen

Courage is fear that has said its prayers.

/ Anne Lamont

EARLY IN THE SPRING OF 1992, I'M still painting, drumming and moving with Chris, keeping up with other things at the studio and at work, and in the same rut with Paul. One day, I see an ad for "The Festival of Aerial Dance" presented by Dance Umbrella, a small, local arts group that brings unique shows to the Boston area. Quoting Jeremy Alliger, the ad says, "I feel what makes Dance Umbrella unique is that we challenge people's perceptions of what dance can be..."

It grabs me and I buy a ticket, still searching for that something or someone that will make my life perfect. I go alone, as is my usual.

The event is held over four days at the Cyclorama in Boston. I'm told it's the first time anyone's produced a dance event where none of the dancing is on the floor. The area around the theater is packed with dancers in various hanging contraptions warming up, and practicing their choreography. As I walk around eyeing the body slings and trapezes, I imagine myself moving in them, thinking it would be easy, a piece of cake, the minute I slid into the sling. A second later, the fear of how I'd get the equipment and the space, all the work and money it would take, and the terror of failing settles in, and I find myself searching for food and a bathroom until, post binge and purge, I'm once again certain that I could do whatever all these dancers are doing.

The performances are clever, creative, fun, and mesmerizing. There are several solos, a few group pieces and many duets, one of which speaks directly to me.As the lights go up I see a small man lying on a raised circular platform, dressed in black leggings and a poufy white shirt with a sash at his waist. After several seconds, the lights come up on a tall, similarly dressed man standing alongside a rope holding a low hanging trapeze. Using his arms, the smaller man drags himself across the ten feet of stage to meet the rope on the other side of the trapeze. He pulls himself up and hangs over the seat, his legs limp behind him. In that moment, I imagine his legs are paralyzed or, at the least, extremely weak and unable to support his weight. He's handsome, close to my age, and I'm in awe of how he's allowing himself to be seen in such a vulnerable way.

The men come together on the trapeze and create a magical, athletic, tender, exciting dance, moving together and alone. They soar, offering and accepting support from each other, moving in and out of short spurts where one or the other is clearly the star. I'm teary from the moment I see the man on the floor dragging himself to the trapeze. His courage and grace overwhelm me. At times I'm close to sobbing. I wonder how he can show himself like he is, so unabashedly and unapologetically.

At the end of the show, when some of the performers offer to share experiences with the audience, I see him standing, in waist high metal braces, as much a dancer as all the others on the stage. He and his partner work with AXIS Dance, a mixed physical abilities dance group out of San Francisco. He's a scientist by day.

My heart beats hard in the center of my chest, and my entire body vibrates with a jumbled mess of anxiety, terror, anticipation, and delight as I walk out with the other concert goers. I can't believe what I saw. I buy a ticket for the next night and have a full repeat of the first. I cry throughout, shaking with a desire to be that self-accepting.

The next day, I call AXIS Dance Company and have them send me their dancer application form. I wander the streets of Cambridge searching for dance class flyers. I'm determined to explore dancing.

A flyer for a "Composition" dance class, held up two flights of stairs in an old building in Central Square in Cambridge, pops out at me. I imagine it means the class will focus on making a dance. I have no idea how one thinks about that, but I'm certain I can do it. The instructor, a wiry, dark-haired woman with exuberant energy, bounds over to greet me as I crutch up the last of the steps and enter the large open space, complete with wooden floor, and curtains drawn across the mirrors lining one wall. I'm ten minutes early, but there are already a few people rolling around on the floor and leaping through the air.

"Hi, I'm Patty," she says looking at me slightly skeptically.

"Karen," I say. "I saw a dance show the other day and was really inspired to try dancing myself." I'm certain I'm presenting myself full of confidence, yet I feel totally intimidated as I eye the lovely bodies of all the others in the room.

"What show?"

""The Festival of Aerial Dance" at the Cyclorama. I couldn't believe what I saw as I watched the duet with the two men on the trapeze, so I went back and saw it again. After that, I looked for flyers. I thought maybe this class would work since it's about composition, not about learning steps. I guess I could be wrong, though." I feel certain I want to try and scared she won't accept me.

"Have you danced before?"

"Not really, just with my friends at a bar or party. I have been painting and drumming and moving with another woman at an art workshop in Watertown, though. My body just feels like it wants to move, in a different way than walking or swimming, especially after seeing the performance."

"Sure. Well, come on in. We'll start in a few minutes. You can put your things over there and join the others warming up."

I stash my stuff and the crutches, hop a few feet into the space, then sit and stretch out on the floor. I'm wearing leggings and a baggy tee shirt, no socks. Others have on leg warmers with and without socks, and an assortment of perfectly tattered, or deliberately cut up, loose fitting tops and pants. All the girls have bodies I covet.

Patty tells us we'll spend the first part of class warming up, then work on our individual dances. She encourages us to spend some of the warm-up time moving with eyes closed, listening inside for the impulse to move, and then tracking the impulse as it takes us on a journey free of judgment.

"It's not about what you do; it's about how you experience your body moving through space," she says. "Try to keep your judgments of yourself, your inner critic, out of the picture." She calls it "sourcing," a practice she developed for making her own choreography, taken from her work in Authentic Movement. At the end of each class, there will be time for a few of us to show our work in process and request feedback.

I'm excited and terrified. Except for at the studio with Chris, I've never considered rolling around on a floor, especially not with other people or real dancers. And what kind of dance will I make? I have no idea what to do. Still, I want to do something, and there's a part of me that's so staunch, it will not let me back down. It's fiercely determined, and yet there's some redeeming quality softening me enough that I'm able to enter the space at least a tad humbly.

Over the next few weeks I roll around, stand up, hop, sit, find all sorts of movements to do, mostly with my eyes open. Closing them takes me inside, and something about that, in a room full of beautiful bodies, scares me. I'm intrigued with the sensations I have when attempting to move from the place of my missing leg. I can still feel the leg. It's bent at the knee, I can contract muscles up and down the thigh and calf, and move the foot and toes. The sensations are something like pins and needles, and the muscle contractions seem to come from what's left of my right hip, whatever muscles are inside there, but they feel like they're centered in other parts of the phantom limb.

I piece together a few minutes of moving around the room, led by the movement I feel in the missing leg. It's mostly sliding, rolling and scooting along the floor. I add a couple of places where I rise onto my knee or all the way up to standing, only to be pulled down in a fall, when my pseudo leg tries to take a step. Despite my overall self-consciousness, I truly enjoy everything I do in the class.

In the final class, we perform our compositions for each other. I'm envious of the twirling, jumping, leaping and big range of movement the other dancers have. I wonder what I'm doing there, except it feels right despite the constant chatter in my head telling me I'm no dancer and will never be. Patty tells me my "performance" is not as good as the various times I presented my piece during the work in process part of the class.

"Too much thinking—you seemed very self-conscious, and it inhibited the flow and your connection with us. Throughout the class, you were more into your body moving, maybe less aware of us and how we might judge, and more into feeling what you were doing. Good job, though. I'm glad you were here." It's hard to hear. I want to be perfect and amazing and beautiful. Patty is sincere, though. I feel it and I want to do more.

Some weeks after the composition class ends, I join Patty's Authentic Movement classes in her studio in the woods outside of Boston. It's a magical, warm-wood space, surrounded by all sorts of big and little trees you can feel and almost touch through the huge windows lining the walls.

"Authentic Movement is a practice, a little like meditation inside the body." She tells us we'll each move for a period of time, eyes closed, noticing and tracking the movements we make and the feelings and sensations we notice in our bodies. "And you'll be witnessed," she says, "sometimes by one other mover who will track what's happening in her body as she experiences your movement, and other times by a group of movers who hold the space, containing whatever energy might arise from inside any one of us. After each ten to fifteen minute moving and witnessing section, we'll write or draw or move more—whatever you need to do to begin the integration of what occurred during the moving and witnessing time. After that, we'll share, mover first, then witness, trying to speak in the present tense about specific movements and what we noticed inside our bodies. Then we'll switch roles."

It's all very awkward at first. Moving with my eyes closed while being watched, thinking about how I look, what others are thinking about my body, and trying my best to pay attention to what movements I make and how it all feels, is challenging and scary.

And then talking about it, face to face, in an intimate little section of the room. "I am a mover who lifts my arm and swings it back and forth…" It's almost painful to say, and fascinating to observe what arises in my mind about who I am, what I look like and what I think others think of me.

My witness tries her best to speak in the present tense, just like I do. She fumbles with how to stay true to mentioning how my movement resonates in her body—where she felt it, what it brought up for her in the way of images or feelings.

Over the course of several weeks, I become more comfortable, feel freer in movement and happy to be there. I continue to push myself to find the answer, analyzing and thinking hard about everything I say and everything that's said to me. I want to get it right, to be the best, most perfect participant in the class. Then one day, while I'm in the middle of aimlessly moving and doing my best to track, I move into a position where I'm sitting back on the heel of my extended foot, knee and shin touching the floor, my chest and head falling flat onto my thigh. My arms are resting by my side. Instantaneously, I burst into uncontrollable sobbing. No one in the room does anything other than continue with their movement and witnessing. Neither my witness nor Patty approach me. I just stay there weeping. It's amazingly comforting. It feels like something I've craved forever. It's a letting go, a big opening, but I have no words for what it's about. My mind is empty, and my body is melting into the sun shining on the wooden floor. Even my practiced skill at rationalizing and analyzing fails me when I try to talk with my witness about what is happening in those moments when I allowed myself to rest, in silence with eyes closed in what I would later learn is yogic child's pose.

Around the same time in 1992-1993, things at my work are changing. There's talk of ending the weekend position I'd occupied for five years. There are more nurses willing to work weekends and off shifts and rumors are circulating that the hospital is considering returning to the three-shift weekend coverage. I abhor the thought of working any more hours. I'm barely able to bring even ounces of a caring self to work over the two days I'm there. Initially I panic. Then I reach out to the Cambridge Visiting Nurse group at the suggestion of one of my coworkers.

I've been in the psychiatric field a long time; I worry I've forgotten how to administer any other kind of care.

"Don't be silly, Karen," the nurse interviewing me says. "You'll be fine. It's mostly dressing changes, blood pressure monitoring, the occasional blood draw and lots of helping people adjust to their chronic health problems. Your mental health and personal experience will be a big asset. We have some psychiatric patients on our rosters, patients we visit to assist with medication management and overall support after hospitalization. We may have you see some of those folks."

So, after almost eight years as a fixture on the Cambridge hospital psychiatric unit, I take a job as a visiting nurse. I work two to three eight-hour shifts a week, mainly weekends, when things are quiet. I travel around Cambridge visiting patients in their homes to monitor blood pressures and provide wound care, which consists mainly of changing dressings for those folks with lower leg infections. I see the same folks almost every week and, at times, have several patients in the same high-rise senior living facility. It becomes a kind of social activity in addition to a nursing job. The patients look forward to my coming and, after their initial shock at seeing a one-legged nurse on crutches, followed by their seemingly endless questions, we settle in, and my one-legged body becomes a forgotten reality.

———— ✦ ————

As the summer of 1993 approaches, Patty tells the authentic movement class that she's offering a performance workshop as part of that summer's Bate's Dance Festival in Maine. "I'll be making an outdoor performance piece with whoever signs up to take my section at this year's three-week festival workshop. It'll be something we perform on the common in front of the school. We'll make it together. So anyone who wants to check out Bates this summer..."

After class that day I approach her. "Could I be a part of what you'll be doing?"

"You'd have to be enrolled in the workshop—my class is one of several options for students attending." She offers nothing more. I love that about Patty—she's not someone who jumps in to take care of people. She stands back, makes suggestions, and lets the space between remain empty. Today, it upsets me, though. I want her to want me to participate.

"How do I find out about it?" I ask as she's moving constantly around her studio space, sporadically interacting with others as they leave. I feel like I have to drag the information out of her.

"Here's a flyer for the festival. Call the number and ask them to send you an application." She says nothing more, but no matter. I'm going to call. She said I could be in her performance class if I go to the festival.

Over the next weeks, I talk with a few of the people organizing the festival. It's a workshop primarily for college dance majors and attracts dance professors interested in keeping current with what's happening in dance outside of their universities. Occasionally, someone outside those two groups attends. They've never had a physically disabled participant. I'm told there are four class periods a day for the three weeks. There are numerous class offerings to chose from. Three are unstructured enough to accommodate me: a Contact Improvisation class, a Laban/

Bartenieff movement exploration class, and Paula's performance class. The other classes are jazz, ballet, modern technique focused, all with specific choreographic steps to learn, so probably not a good fit.

With this little bit of information, I enroll, sending my deposit and arranging the weeks off from work. I tell no one until I'm sure I'm going. Pursuing movement has become a bit of a compulsion, something I almost can't not do. Despite my head, blabbing its continual negatives, my body has begun its own journey. E&T helps me ignore the critic long enough to get out of my own way.

It's not until I arrive at Bates that I realize what a stranger in a strange land I am. Seventy-five percent of the participants are late teen to early twenty-something, budding ballerinas. Although there are some unconventional dancer bodies, shorter or a tad curvier than your basic ballerina, I see only the tall, lithe, princess-like beauties with bones in all the right places and minimal flesh. It reminds me of my anorexia days and my continuing quest to find my way to that body. I'm full of angst, hoping maybe dancing and the Bates workshop will take me there, and certain I'll make a fool of myself, be mocked and ignored.

Thankfully, I arranged for a private room, so I have a safe place for E&T. The first day, I meet up with several forty-something dance teachers who welcome forty-two-year- old me with open arms at the breakfast table. They say they admire my courage for showing up. We banter about getting older, changing bodies and spending three weeks living and breathing with so many young, beautiful women. I join them from my self-confident place but never feel a part of their little group. They've known each other for many years—some were student dancers at Bates before they were teachers—and they're all real dancers. A few of them are in the Laban class with me. Otherwise, I mostly see them at meals and at the weekend concerts that are part of the festival.

On day one of Patty's performance class, we begin rehearsing a loosely-structured choreography. The piece is set on a grassy slope full of thick-trunked, tall trees spread widely enough apart to allow for movement amongst and between them. We begin the dance with our bodies leaning full weight into the trees, one dancer connected physically to one tree. We're to slowly peel ourselves off over a period of about a minute and begin to run in a large circle, randomly passing each other and stopping at various times to perform dance phrases Paula's choreographed for groups of two to five or six. Much of it is a blur. I have trouble letting go of control enough to allow my body to lean fully into the tree and then, to stay present enough to allow it to slowly and naturally peel itself away. Patty is on me throughout the rehearsals about this—coaching me to relax and allow my body to find its way rather than using my mind to figure out how to move. I never fully get it and, although I do my best in the performance, I know Patty is disappointed, and I imagine she wishes she never said I could join the class.

In the Laban class, we focus on different aspects of movement—things like direction, force, initiation. Most days we do short exercises, alone or in groups and sometimes putting the concepts together to make short phrases of movement using them in either scripted or random ways. I feel OK in the class. The teacher interacts with me around the way my body, including my crutches, adapts itself based on its unique structure. The class is less about performance dance and more about the fundamentals of movement that support choreography.

It's the Contact Improvisation class that holds the most promise for me. Initially, I see beautiful, strong-bodied dancers moving in ways I'm familiar with from the authentic movement classes I'd been taking. It's all very random, moving on the floor, standing, and every level in between. The difference is that people are moving together, leaning into each other, rolling over backs or fronts, at times standing, and at other times, slowly rolling, connecting with any and all surfaces of the body in groups or in piles on the floor. The teacher is a handsome, muscled, fair-haired young man who can move from one side of the room to the other, coming in contact with almost everyone, and using those connections to propel himself into the next shape and contact.

I stay on the outer edges of the group, feeling shy about the body contact and the quick pace of some of the standing movement. I know

I can't move in that way and lament and feel sorry for myself, feelings I'm quick to repress with whatever defense works at the time. The other dancers are polite, even friendly, but I sense their hesitation in moving with me. I'm different, an unknown to myself and to them, and my fear and self-consciousness are big enough to be palpable to others. I don't want to intrude. I imagine the others feel uncomfortable around me, like I've felt at the beach where my physical body and its difference is so much a part of the experience. Still, I act as if I'm perfectly comfortable participating from the periphery.

During one of the Friday sessions, three new dancers join the class. I hear they're part of a New York dance company and will be performing at the Saturday concert. Soon after the class begins, the woman in the trio approaches me.

"Hi. I'm Karen, I'm here with Scott and Jim," she says pointing to the two men who came in with her. "They're performing tomorrow. I'm here for the fun. Can I dance with you?" She comes down to the floor and leans up against me, gently moving my body and then rolling in another direction, still connected by a light touch and, somehow, supporting me as we begin to move, staying in contact with some part of our bodies. We come up from the floor together, without me using the strength of my arms. She moves under me and carries me on her back, gently rolling me off and catching me with her leg or shoulder. It's like magic. I'm effortlessly moving all over the room. At times I feel like I'm flying and yet, Karen is right there supporting me as I fall gently back into the floor.

Scott, another handsome, muscled and fair-haired man, joins in. He leads me on a ride around the room on the floor as we roll over and under each other, lying, coming up to sitting, then up to hands and knees, then back down onto the floor. My entire body has its chance to be in contact with the floor and with another body. My fear dissipates for the hour or so I'm moving with them. I forget myself and I trust them. The self-doubt and self-consciousness resurface at the end of the class when others comment on how amazing it was to watch. I smile big, but I'm certain they're just being nice and they all feel sorry for me.

Before the class breaks up, Karen and Scott huddle around me. Karen says, "I'm planning a workshop for February next year for dancers with all different physical bodies. It'll be called Diverse Dance. I want you to come." She tells me she's been interested in differently abled bodies for several years and has danced with mixed abilities groups in several countries. She finds the variety of movement challenging and inspiring.

"Where is it?" I ask.

"It'll be on Vashon Island, off the coast of Seattle, Washington. I'm trying to find a place—maybe the Campfire Girls' camp." She's jumping up and down with excitement over having met me.

I'm excited, too. She likes me enough to invite me to dance with her again, near her home. I had so much fun in a few hours with her and Scott. Why would I not go?

She takes my address and phone number and we say goodbye. Scott will perform with the New York group later in the evening at the Bates' concert hall, and they'll be leaving the next day. She tells me where they're staying and invites me to stop by in the morning.

The performance is amazing. I'm mesmerized by the exquisite men's bodies, sexily clad in dark pants and white open-collared shirts. I wonder about their lives—imagining them to be full of glamor and excitement.

The next morning I wander over to the building where they're staying. The scene inside is nothing like I thought it would be. Bodies are strewn across the floor amongst sleeping bags and blankets. Couples are spooning; some are snoring. Karen is shuffling around in wrinkled shorts and tee, half asleep. Scott is snuggling the blankets she left empty.

"We had a late night," Karen says. "Don't mind the scene. It's how it is when you travel with a dance company."

I'm embarrassed, shocked, and uncomfortable. It's like everyone's sleeping together, everyone's so easy and comfortable with themselves.

It scares me—the idea of so freely sharing my body. I can't imagine anyone wanting to be like that with me.

We exchange a few words. Karen reads me the address I gave her and says she'll be in touch. "I really hope you'll come to Vashon in February," she says unpretentiously. Her invitation seems so earnest, like an emotional appeal. We share a big hug and go our separate ways.

———— ◊ ————

A couple of months later, when I get the flyer in the mail, I'm sure I can't do it. My body fills with a nervous terror just reading about the communal atmosphere, where we'll share chores and spend hours dancing and making music in a big common space. We'll sleep in the camp dorms with shared bathrooms and spend a few hours each day meeting as a group to discuss the mixed-abilities living and the dancing experiment.

My head tells me I'll never be a dancer. Why would I want to go all the way out there? It's not for me. I'm fooling myself, and they're all just being nice to me. The critic propped on my right shoulder harasses me. My body remembers the energy and excitement of dancing with Karen and Scott, and it knows the pleasure of moving in the authentic movement classes I continue to take. Those are different, I tell myself. Not real dancing. And neither was what I did at Bates. Who am I trying to kid? I don't even know these people.

The chatter is constant until I decide I won't go. Then, Karen calls in early December of 1993.

"I haven't heard from you? Did you get the flyer?"

"Yeah, but I decided it's not for me. I'm not coming."

"No way, you belong here. You have to come. I'll pay your way. The group needs you. Please, please, say you'll come." She's outright pleading with me. There's a twinge of disbelief in her voice, like she never expected I'd say no.

She convinces me despite the insistent monologue in my head. I promise her I'll come for the week in February. When we hang up, I'm left with my divided self— tormented and elated. E&T helps calm both and allows me to go about my daily life, with a detached air of cool, calm, and collected confidence.

20   Diverse Dance

There are many tenets of Wholeheartedness, but at its very core is vulnerability and worthiness; facing uncertainty, exposure and emotional risks, and knowing I am enough.

/ Brene Brown

As the weeks pass before the workshop, I may be my cool, calm self on the outside, but my insides are in more turmoil than ever. I'm terribly unhappy about my ongoing relationship with Paul, yet I continue to invite him over for take-out, wine, and sex. My relationship with Cathy suffers because she so disapproves of Paul, and because I continually offer unsolicited childrearing advice. Dream analysis comes to a halt when John has medical issues and stops seeing his clients to focus on his health. Although E&T still works to divert my attention from my disappointments, it's less effective and I enjoy it less. It feels like another burden—something I must do to continue to function. I worry that I'll never find the thing that will make it end.

I try to talk with my art buddies about these things, but I won't allow myself to tell them specifics about Paul or E&T. I share only vague discontent which keeps me feeling disconnected and alone.

"Yeah, things seem so up in the air these days," I say to Barbara one day at the studio. "I'm dissatisfied with so many things, and now I'm taking a trip to this dancing workshop…as much as I enjoyed the time I spent with them at Bates, something inside me is worried about what it'll be like for a whole week. Maybe I'll hate it and be stuck there."

"It'll be fine, Karen, probably a lot of fun." Barbara is working on a collage she started some days ago, listening but totally absorbed in what she's doing. She looks up. "Remember how excited you were after meeting them. Focus on that. Why would it be any different? Besides, it's a free ride to an island in the Puget Sound. It's got to be beautiful there and you love the beach."

"I guess. I just don't know why all of a sudden so many things are bugging me. I had a big fight with my mother on the phone. She's mad that I never tell her where I'm going or what I'm doing. She worries something will happen to me and people will find out she didn't even know where I was. I know I have to keep in touch with her because she's my mother, but it's never satisfying or helpful to talk with her. I would never ask for her advice. Anyway, it's bothering me more than usual. What is going on with me?" I ask myself as much as Barbara.

"We're all going through things—hang in there. Everything will work out. In a few weeks, you'll have gone and come back from the dance week. You'll know more about things then." Barbara gives me a hug and leaves to find something she needs for her art project.

I arrive at SeaTac airport in the late afternoon to find Karen waiting for me. We drive to Tacoma and take a ferry to Vashon Island, Washington, a large island off the coast of Seattle, smack in the middle of the Puget Sound. It's four miles by ten miles in area, accessible by a half-hour ferry from Tacoma or Seattle. Karen tells me it's a liberal enclave and a bit of an artist's haven. Driving through as we head to the site, it feels rustic and funky, with lots of woodlands, frequent glimpses of the blue-green water, and artsy shops. Along the main street, there's one small grocery store and a movie theater amidst several older small storefronts. Camp Stealth, our workshop venue, sits on four hundred acres, mostly undeveloped, on the southwest shore of the island. It includes a mile of saltwater beachfront which is within a few hundred yards of the main lodge we'll be using for the week.

As we drive down the driveway to the main building, Karen points out the cabins we'll be staying in. "They're dorms that sleep lots of people, but since there are only about twenty of us, we can make it work with just a couple of people to a space. I figure the abled-bodied folks can use the ones furthest away. We'll take a look, and you can pick a place you'd like to be."

It's the first year for this experiment and Karen says she's not real sure how it'll all play out. At the start, she wants to keep it open and spacious so people feel they have a choice in how we do things. "After all, it is an experiment in community living and dancing, so we have to leave lots of room for working things out as we go along. I'm so excited...and so glad you came." She hugs me.

She helps me carry my bags into one of the closer dorms. "Bonnie's already arrived and taken a bed in here. Maybe it'll be just you, Bonnie, and her aide in this cabin. I'll introduce you when we take the tour of the lodge."

"This seems fine," I say wondering who this Bonnie is and what's wrong with her that she needs an aide. I put my things on a bed and join Karen for a walk up to the lodge.

"WOW! The water's so close," I say as we pass an opening just a few yards from the lodge. "Is it cold? Are there tides here?"

"The water's one of the best things about this place. It is cold and not so much for tides. It's salt water but since it's the Sound, the movement is much less than it is in the open ocean. We'll have plenty of time each day to check out the beach. There's a bunch of driftwood beyond the lodge that way," she points, "and the sandy part is pretty wide. The other way is more woodsy, but there's still a nice beach."

I feel more relaxed after seeing the place and connecting with Karen again. She's so welcoming and accepting—she acts as though I'm someone really special. That's a double-edged sword of sorts—it's great that she likes me, except she doesn't know all the awful things about me. And, I wonder if I can live up to who she thinks I am.

The lodge is humongous. It's an open room, one and a half times as long as wide. The floors and walls are old, well-maintained wood that reflects the sun, giving the room a warm glow. Waist-high to ceiling windows line two walls, and a fireplace sits on the long wall opposite the windows. At the far end, several picnic tables with unattached benches sit waiting for our crew to occupy them.

"That end of the room is where we'll eat, pretty obvious. The kitchen is through the door there next to the fireplace and across the hall. Someone will come three times a day to prepare and clean up our meals. We'll eat buffet style." Karen points, as she fills me in on the lay of the land.

She introduces me to Bonnie and her aide, Sandy. "Hi, Bonnie, I'm Karen," I say extending my hand. "Hi, Sandy."

"Hi, Karen," she says in a slow, low, choppy voice as she slowly and deliberately extends her hand. Her grip is light like she doesn't have control of her squeeze.

"I put my stuff in the room you're staying in. I hope that's okay with you."

"Sure, I'm in there, too," Sandy says. "It'll be fun getting to know you. Maybe we'll have the place to ourselves." She's pert, very attractive and likely fifteen-plus years younger than me. I'm not sure about Bonnie's age, maybe thirty to early forties.

"It's okay with me, too," Bonnie cuts in, with a slow, almost a drone-like quality to her voice. She's taller than I am but stooped over a bit at the mid-back giving her an ever so slight arc in her spine. Her body is solid and stocky, yet shapely. Her dark, coarse hair falls just above her shoulders. She's fashionably dressed in colored tights and a bright jersey top, a lovely scarf draped artfully around her neck. She moves like a robot as if she's thinking about every movement before she makes it. It seems she has some sort of disability, but I have no idea what it might be.

"YAY! You two finally meet." Karen says grabbing our hands. "It's one of the meetings I was most looking forward to. You are both beautiful, amazing dancers, with unique dancer bodies and movement. I can't wait to see what happens with you two and all of us as the week unfolds. I'm so inspired by each of you."

We all four let out a "yahoo" as Karen and I continue our tour. She shows me a small gathering place up the hill beyond the lodge, and the wheelchair ramp, which I insist I won't use as "the stairs are good exercise," and I wouldn't want anyone to think I was disabled enough to need a ramp.

I leave her to settle myself into the cabin. Many participants are already there, exploring or setting up. We'll gather a half hour before dinner to introduce ourselves.

After dinner, we'll discuss the logistics of the week and then have the evening free for dancing and revelry.

Later, as I stroll on the path from the cabin to the lodge, what seems like hoards of folks are dancing their way past me. It's a stream of hand waves and hi's and introductions. I wave back and say my name. Just as I'm about to hit the steps, a young man pushing a hefty, reclining wheelchair sidles up next to me. "Hi, I'm Tom and this is Pete. Who are you?"

"Hi, guys. I'm Karen." Pete is a young man, maybe mid to late twenties. He nods and grunts, his head and torso arching upward and toward me. His eyes blink and his facial muscles contract, as if he's making faces at me.

"We're here from Eugene," Tom says as he pushes the chair up the ramp.

"I'm from Cambridge, Massachusetts," I say, my head down as I navigate the steps. I want them to know how mobile I am. "Where's Eugene?"

"Oh, it's in Oregon, about five hours south. There's a bunch of us here from there," he says. Pete lifts his head again, and grunts like he's trying to talk. "Pete can't make words, but he has a letter board. We'll show you when we get inside. Looks like he has something he wants to say."

The room's abuzz with people, mostly twenties to thirties, dressed in loose, worn clothing, scarves draped around their necks, some with hats or headbands covering their ears. There are three or four people in wheelchairs scattered throughout. There's a table with plates, utensils, condiments, and napkins and another next to it with big bowls of salad and bread. The whole place smells like simmering tomato sauce.

I see Scott, the man who was with Karen at Bates, and instantly remember the soft, gentle rolling on the floor we did that day in the class. He sees me, too, and smiles. Maybe it'll all be fine here, I think to myself. Maybe Scott will dance with me again. Maybe one of the other men here will like me.

Karen asks for our attention and explains that meals will be buffet style through the week. Tonight we'll take care of ourselves and aides will take care of the dancer they're here with. After dinner, we'll figure out what we'll do the rest of the week.

My inner wheels are turning, making plans for how I'll eat and throw up without suspicion. There are a few bathrooms close. I'm hoping they flush well—it's always a problem when I have to flush two or three times to get rid of the evidence. Like with every new adventure, I hope this one will take away E&T, but with what looks like abundant food and the mind-jarring mix of beautiful-bodied and very disabled people, I'm already feeling uneasy. I'm remembering the camp in New York where years ago I started E&T. This is almost like that—I'm older and I know E&T is not going to magically transform me into a model—but the inner unease and wishful thinking are the same. I know purging is on the agenda tonight. Still, maybe I can eat just a little after tonight, maybe something here will be the magic answer...

Tom and Pete wave for me to join them at their table. There are three or four others already there. We say hi and immediately Pete wants to talk. Tom reaches behind Pete's chair for a plexiglass rectangle, twice the size of a sheet of paper, with letters and numbers scattered throughout in what seems a haphazard pattern. He holds it up in front of Pete and begins to say letters aloud.

"A, no I, a, m, h—I am happy to meet you?" Tom asks Pete, who's moving his head up and down, his face expressing what I later come to recognize as his awesome smile.

"Me, too," I say to Pete. "How do you do that? It looks complicated."

Pete juts his chin toward Tom, they make eye contact and Tom explains. "Pete can move his eyes, pretty much the only part of his body he has control over. He can lift his head and torso some, but otherwise, his muscles contract randomly, and he has very little control over how and when he moves. He has cerebral palsy, same as Emery, over there at the table by the wall," Tom says, as he lifts the board for Pete to speak again.

"Watch Pete's eyes," Tom says as he positions the board. I watch as Pete's eyes move up, down, and across the board and Tom follows, calling out letters. When Tom gets it right, Pete grunts or nods. Tom guesses at words as he moves his eyes and head from the board to connect with Pete's face to see if he's right. Sometimes it takes many tries, but Pete is patient and adamant enough to stick with it until he gets to say what he wants to say.

In between the bites of food Tom feeds him, some of which fall out onto the bib he wears because his mouth control is haphazard, Pete tells those of us at the table that he has a pottery wheel at home and he makes pots. His face lights up as he sees all our faces make a similar "how could you do that?" expression.

With Tom's help he tells us he holds a stick in his mouth and shapes the pot with it. "WOW, really!" we all say in unison. I can't imagine it—how does he keep the pot on the board? But I'm intrigued by his assertiveness and self-confidence. He acts as if there's nothing different about him, despite his needing an aide for everything he does.

I eat way too much, at least two helpings of everything, and stand in line for the bathroom several times that evening. They're old toilets—flushing is an ordeal because the tank takes so long to fill. I take to fishing out any floating debris and tossing it, wrapped securely in toilet paper, into the trash.

After dinner, we gather near the fireplace where Steve has made a roaring blaze to keep us toasty through the evening. It's February, we're on the water, and the lodge isn't heated. Steve, an unassuming man in his late forties, is the father of Contact Improvisation, a relatively new dance form in which bodies move together around a point of contact, using weight-sharing and counterbalance to extend their range of motion. It's what Karen and Scott introduced me to at Bates. It celebrates the exploration of bodies moving in diverse ways, and is a great foundation for exploring dance in groups with different physical abilities. Steve is teacher and mentor to Karen, Scott, and a number of other people at the workshop who are in awe of his contributions to the dance community and honored to be with him. He's a revered solo performer, as well, mostly for his dance interpretations of Bach's Goldberg Variations. Yet, all is downplayed, as he is not one for any limelight. He has no interest in teaching, organizing or leading any part of the week. Instead, he says he'll tend the fire and be present.

Karen begins. "So happy you are all here," she's smiling and fidgeting, stumbling over her words. I have the sense she's humbled—like she can't really believe her dream is happening. "I want to share with you my ideas for a structure along with permission to tweak it as we feel inclined. Tweaking can happen at any time during the week—this is an experiment and open for input from all. Many different things might happen. Our main task, inside the structure, is to be open to all the possible ways of living and dancing together."

She goes on to say she'd like us all to participate in assisting each other with whatever we need to function each day. She's made sign-up lists for each person who needs help with activities of daily living— bathing, dressing, toileting, eating—and hopes we'll each sign up for a few opportunities. Aides will fill in when needed and are free to participate in all aspects of the week at any time. There's another list for general chores, like sweeping the floor, cleaning the bathrooms, wiping down the tables after meals, tending the fire. Then she says, "We'll have a morning and afternoon session for group dancing, body work, whatever anyone wants to offer the group. I know some of you have ideas to try out—and, of course, participation in any group activities is optional. You can do whatever you want while you're here, but I'm thinking we'll enjoy each other so much we'll want to spend time together." There are some questions, comments. Everybody seems engaged, excited. They all seem to know Karen and many know each other.

"Evenings are free for jamming—there's music-making stuff over in the corner and Scott has agreed to lead us in the evening revelry with any and all participation in making music, dancing—whatever. OK—I think that's it. I'll put the lists up and we'll open the evening for whatever is your pleasure. Breakfast is eight to nine-thirty."

People disperse, exchanging hugs and pleasantries. I head for the cabin to finish unpacking and meet Bonnie, who's in the process of showering with the help of Sandy, her aide. Soon there's music pouring out of the lodge.

"Want to head over there?" I ask them.

"Go ahead—we'll probably join you when Bonnie's done drying her hair." Sandy says.

I'm glad to go alone—I feel uncomfortable around Bonnie. I can't quite figure out what's up with her and my judgmental self is ready to cast her as malingering. I have so many judgments of so many people with so little knowledge of their stories. Even when I know their stories, I notice myself downplaying the severity. More often than not I decide people with any needs are just milking their situations, not wanting to step up to the plate and do things for themselves.

The lodge is throbbing with percussion, harmonica, and guitar vibrations. It's no particular song—just a rush of sound pouring out of the woodwork. I'm surprised when I find only a few people jamming in the corner and another few talking by the fire.

"Come join us," Scott motions to me as I enter. Hesitantly, I crutch over to the bench where he sits with two other guys and a young woman.

"I can't play any instruments," I confess. I'm happy to be where there's noise and stuff to hold and focus on. I feel exposed—one of the disabled people among all these lovely dancing bodies.

"Hey, who cares? Neither can we, except for fun. Grab something— it's easy to join in," Scott says.

In minutes, I'm jamming with the best of them—my whole body expressing the beats and the offbeats. I try various drums, tambourines, bells—then someone invites me out to dance in the space in front of the music area. Before I realize it, I'm in a kind of orgy of moving bodies, minus the sex. One duet leads to another—I roll around on the floor, hop, lean into others, travel on their backs, enjoy the sensuousness of a flowing scarf swooping across my face. I move in and out of music-making and dancing. The evening passes into late night as people leave and join the group. I'm one of the last to head for bed that night. A sensation of total body pleasure registers for a few minutes before the thinking panic overtakes it and I binge on the food I stashed away during dinner to settle the inner turmoil. Did I look ok? Did I do things the right way? What are people thinking of me? It's like a hyper self-consciousness descends after a blissful period of wild abandon.

Each day after breakfast and lunch, someone leads us in a movement score—a simple and loose structure for moving together. Movement scores and contact improvisational dance are most always without music, allowing the body's inner rhythm to be the driver of the dance. The focus is on the inner experience expressed outwardly through movement, the opposite of a more familiar way of dancing to externally provided music. The score might be walking in a circle, noticing people as you pass, walking backward, changing speeds, eyes closed or open. As the movement progresses, groups of any number randomly form, moving in and out of little vignettes with each other. It could be duets taking turns watching each other solo for a few minutes and then playing back the movement with their bodies. Or one person doing a one-minute solo with others watching. When the solo ends, any or all of the observers can enter to replay the solo, not verbatim, but from inside their own bodies. Some days we break into trios and give each other massages, two on one. It's a delightful experience. On nice days, we go outside, wheelchairs and all, to enjoy the sand, water, driftwood, warm sun, and fresh air. It all happens in the moment—everything seems to flow, one thing into the next. Although I'm enticed by the freedom of it,

I'm aware of a voice inside warning me not to get too involved. I worry I could fall over into the nothingness of life like this—no pressures or expectations—something I judge as unproductive and irresponsible, and at the same time crave.

One day I explore the beach with some others and we find a place to dance among the driftwood. I'm in white loose pants and a sweatshirt moving on and around a collection of sun-bleached wood strewn on the white sand under a winter barren tree. We make a sculpture dance—posing in various configurations with the elements. It's a different version of my Martha's Vineyard solo sea goddess dance, this one performed in community with others and witnessed by nature and the universe. Another day, I climb a small, dead tree stump on the wide path from the lodge to the water. It's got a furrow at the top just the right size and shape for my side-lying torso. I hang there for awhile, gazing out to sea, glad when Karen spots me and takes a picture. It's the ultimate feeling of freedom—suspended, held by the tree, caressed by the air and the sky, and I imagine it looks cool. I want people to see me doing things I feel are creative and beautiful. I want to be able to allow pleasure and self-satisfaction, but as soon as I get close, my inner critic pops up to remind me of my ugly, distorted body, and to emphasize that others compliment me because they feel sorry for me. I shouldn't need or want compliments or connection. I should be fine without those.

After dinner each evening, we gather to discuss the day, how things are going, our wishes, dissatisfactions. People share writings, paintings, insights, and we talk about how to make the days flow more smoothly. One evening, Cindy, a lovely able-bodied dancer, shares a song she wrote.

"I'd love to be a singer," she says, as if it were a confession, "but my voice is not great. I wrote "BodyMine" over the last few days to celebrate my body."

The song is about her relationship with her body. She apologizes to her body for not honoring and respecting its strength and beauty, and promises to change her ways.

Her voice is shaky, yet clear and strong. The group listens in pin-drop silence. When she finishes, I'm awash in emotion—aware of my own body battering. Seconds before the group disperses that evening, I'm compelled to speak.

"Cindy's song hit me pretty hard. Suddenly, I'm aware of how much I dislike my body and how uncomfortable I am around so many disabled people," I say, head down, feeling ashamed. "I don't want to be seen as part of a handicapped or disabled or alter-abled group. I loathe myself for having one leg, and for wanting to reject you. My judgments of myself and others are sharp and biting and never ending. I can't escape it this week and it upsets me. Cindy's song put a new crack in my defensive wall—it tapped into a deeper place. Maybe all the body movement and contact with others has got my guard down. Good news is—it feels like a good thing."

The whole group rallies in support. They say I'm brave for sharing and many of the young women tell me they have the same feelings about their bodies. There's a tenacious part of me that wants to downplay what I've said, to dismiss the support and act as if I'm fine with myself. Despite my ability to act as normal as the other guy and do almost everything, I know what I said is true—I loathe my body and I continue to look for, and desperately want to believe, there's a magic pill to change it—something that will bring my leg back so I can be like everyone else. If I can only find that thing.

Emery catches up with me as I head out of the lodge. "Hey, Karen, let's talk," he yells as he propels his wheelchair backward with his feet. His head and neck are wrenched out over the backrest and turned to face me. His grinning face is framed by long, dark hair pulled back into a loose braid.

"Oh hi, Emery. What's up?" I've spent a few hours with him through the week, mostly at meals and in the music area.

"Why be normal?" he asks. "It's more fun to be different. You surprise people."

306

"Say it again, please," I ask. Emery speaks with a halting cadence. His intonation is choppy, and the sounds that emanate are familiar but not easily interpreted. He excels at patience, perseverance, and empathy. He's willing to stick with you until you get what he has to say.

"Don't feel bad about yourself. You're a beautiful dancer and person," he insists. Every time I'm with Emery I have the feeling he's flirting with me. It astounds me—he's abundantly self-confident and humble at the same time. He, like Pete, doesn't seem bothered by his disability. He needs help with all activities of daily living, his body is perched in a wheelchair, lanky, muscular, with feet pointed like a ballerina on toe, his limbs contract unpredictably, he communicates awkwardly— and yet, he's joyful, caring, grateful. I'm afraid that interacting with him somehow confirms my disability—as if it isn't already a fact—and establishes my willingness to be a part of the disabled community.

As the week goes on, I talk regularly with Marion, a German woman in a wheelchair as a result of a car accident several years ago when she was twenty-five. She sustained a mid-back fracture leaving her paralyzed from her low rib-cage down. She's a beauty, with dark, wavy, chin-length hair, a reserved demeanor and impeccable style. There's an air of elegance about her. She's mostly independent, needing some assistance rolling on the dirt path to and from her cabin. She was a dancer, social and active, before her accident. She worked for the German postal service. Following her recovery, her employer tried to accommodate her back into her position, but ultimately, it was inaccessible. She collects a full pension with benefits, lives independently and traveled alone to the states for the workshop. When I ask her what she does, she says, "I live!"

I'm drawn to Marion, maybe because she seems less disabled than the other folks that year. We talk, dance, and make music together. Emery's aide, Irv, spends much of his free time with Marion. It's later revealed they're smitten with each other. Marion moves to Eugene to be with Irv and they eventually marry. Over the next many years, Marion and I develop a close friendship built around dance, art-making, wine-drinking and a German card game, Doppelkopf.

Before the week is over, Bonnie tells me she was moved by Cindy's song and my sharing. "I've been thinking about what you said the other night. It's hard to tell the truth about how I feel. There's no one to tell and sometimes it brings up old feelings that are hard to re-live," she says as Sandy interprets. Bonnie is easier to understand if I pay very close attention and stay with her. She tells me about the attack while she was in college by a man who left her for dead on a roadside. Passers-by found her. She suffered serious brain damage, which left her with a slow-moving body, altered speech, and other subtle disabilities.

"I was a dancer in college and I still love dancing." I hear her, and wonder if anyone will ever see her as a dancer now. It's silly for her or me to believe we're dancers—but we're both here finding exquisite pleasure in the experience. The opposing forces are fighting inside—am I or am I not a dancer, disabled, disgusting, worthy, beautiful?

As part of one of the early Diverse Dance gatherings (an annual February experiment that lasted for seven years), Bonnie performs a solo about the attack and its consequences. We gather at one end of the lodge and watch from seats on the floor as she moves through a series of flowing movement phrases, evoking a myriad of compelling emotions from terror to sadness to awe. We're a rapt audience aware that Bonnie offers us a tremendous gift.

The final hurrah that year is a performance we share in a local middle school gym. Karen leads us in a couple of silent group movement scores, and two or three trios perform short improvisations. For the finale, Karen and Pete perform an unforgettable, unrehearsed duet. Pete's aide lays him on exercise mats set up center space. Karen approaches as raging rock music blares through the speakers. She straddles Pete, lifts him, rolls him, slams herself and him up and down on the mats. Pete howls, his limbs extending and contracting wildly, torso bobbing up and down to the beats. The kids cheer, roar, hoot. It's a sight some might call borderline acceptable—but the experience exhilarates Pete. He's a rockstar and a dancer, witnessed by a huge crowd offering a standing ovation and wild applause. The boldness and humility of the effort astound me. I am part of something I never could have imagined.

Before the end of the week, Bonnie, Emery, and Pete fill me in on another mixed abilities dance workshop happening in Eugene the day after Diverse Dance ends. All three excitedly invite me to attend.

"How will I get there? Where will I stay?" I ask, wondering if I want to go. I'll have to call work and extend my time away, but since I've been working per diem, with no set schedule the work part is not really an issue. Maybe I'll never go back—but I have to go back.

"My friend George has room in his house. I'm sure he'll be happy to put you up for a few days. He'll be going to the DanceAbility workshop," Emery says. I've been with him enough this week to be a whiz at understanding his words.

"Sure. Why not?" Secretly, I'm overjoyed to be continuing my ambiguous journey in the land of improvisation and disability. I feel lighter, like a weight has been lifted. People like me, they support me and compliment me. Yet there's a hole, a longing for something unknown, for some kind of validation I haven't yet felt.

As we gather for our final goodbyes, emotions run the gamut. We hug, cry, lean into one another with faces sad for the ending, and promise to meet back next year. Karen, Scott and Joan, a longtime, active member of the Vashon meditation/dance/arts community, joyfully vow to make it happen again.

George lives in a big, old, wooden house on a busy street in Eugene. The office for his contracting business fills what would be the living room space. There's a long narrow kitchen, front and back porches and a spacious upstairs with several bedrooms, including George's beautiful loft space. Rows of blueberry bushes under bird-proof netting, and raised garden beds, barren except for the few hearty greens and potatoes, grace the backyard. A small wooden house-like structure sits at the far end of the back porch.

"It's a wood-burning sauna," George tells me as he escorts me on a tour of the place. He's a tall, handsome, beautiful-bodied man with golden brown hair pulled back and braided into a thin ponytail that falls to his waist. "We fire it up on Saturday nights—so tomorrow after the workshop. Ever been in a sauna?"

"Not like that. I went on a vision quest a year ago, and we had a sweat lodge in a huge cloth tent. Is it like that?" I'm wondering if George has a girlfriend.

"Hot like that—yes—but different. You'll see. Let's go back inside. I'll help you bring your bag upstairs." He leads me to a small, wood-paneled room furnished with a big bed, small dresser, and chair.

"Thanks for putting me up, George. Emery says you'll be at the workshop tomorrow?" George is very handsome and gracious.

"Yep—I'm planning on it. Emery's a good friend and teacher. I like to check out things he's interested in."

George leaves vowing to pick me up in the morning and offering me full access to the house, yard, and food. I poke around the yard, check out the rooms upstairs and spend most of the evening methodically deciding how to raid the fridge and cupboards leaving as little evidence as possible. The toilet is old—purging takes time. I'm alone, free to continue with life as I know it while full of new, incomprehensible mind and body rumblings.

The next morning, George drives me to the workshop. We walk into a big room already abuzz with people chatting and moving, some spinning and leaping around the room, some on the floor or sitting in wheelchairs. "That's Alito," George points to a short, compact man with dark hair pulled back in a short ponytail. "Hi, Alito, this is Karen. She came down with Emery from Diverse Dance. She's from Massachusetts," George says as he and Alito hug.

"Oh hi, Karen," Alito says. "Nice to have you. So you know Karen Nelson?"

"Yes, I met her once at Bates College last year and she invited me to Diverse Dance. I didn't spend a lot of time with her up there—she was pretty busy. We all were."

"How did you find out about this workshop?" he asks.

"Emery and Bonnie—they were on Vashon. They thought I'd like it," I say. "Will it be like Diverse Dance?"

"Maybe a little—Karen and I were partners until a year or so ago. We got interested in mixed-abilities work while we were together, after many years of contemporary dancing, teaching, and performing. Glad you're here." Alito says, abruptly turning to greet a participant standing behind me.

I spot Emery and Bonnie. I discover they're partners and live in houses next door to each other. Before I can make it to where they are, Alito asks us to gather in a circle to begin.

He instructs us, "Introduce yourself, say something about how your body feels today. Tell us if there's anything we need to know about dancing with you—weak places, pain, like that."

After introductions, we disperse to find comfortable places on the floor. Alito leads us in a long warm-up which starts with eyes closed and an inward focus, and culminates with eyes open, moving together, holding the inward focus while expanding it outward to see and connect with others.

The group is a mix of men and women with a handful of children throughout. There are people in wheelchairs, a few with crutches and many who appear physically normal. Most are dressed in brightly colored, lots of tie-dyed, loose, well-worn clothes—baggie pants, oversized sweatshirts, and tees. The room is cool but not cold. As the warm-up ends and we move out of the groups we were in, Alito offers the next movement score—a basic structure for moving with a partner, without music. Scores are used to facilitate interaction, to get people moving together. They're loose, open structures, lending themselves to broad interpretation. Simple enough for the most inexperienced mover

311

to follow, they challenge experienced movers with the many nuances that can be extrapolated within them.

"Find a partner. One of you will move while the other watches. Watching, however, does not mean sitting or standing and looking. I want you to watch from every angle and position you can find—be creative, challenge yourself. Watch from close or far away, even with your eyes closed or with your back. Emery will you demonstrate with me."

Emery creatively wheels around a small area as Alito watches, moving from standing to the floor, looking between his legs, and upside down rolling on the floor. Although they are moving independently, it looks like a duet as their bodies intermingle, without touching.

Alito answers a few questions then says, "Decide who moves first. You'll each have a chance to do both." Chatter takes over for a moment, until Alito says, "begin."

There are giggles and sighs and grunts, but no words. I hear my breathing, my body sliding, rolling and feel my clothes brush my skin. I'm the watcher, but feel like I'm making a dance of my own and with my partner. Noticing what happens: to me when she moves one way, and to her when I move a different way. I'm curious about how we look together, what images we're making. It feels the same whether I'm the mover or the witness.

Alito moves us through several different scores. We move in a duet with a moving and stillness focus: when he is still I move, when he moves I'm still. We lead and follow with touch, directing our partners where to move. We move in groups of three or more using a mix of the previous scores, including making contact near and far. We learn about counterbalance as a way to support weight in precarious positions. We learn about leaning into our partners, one or more, giving weight to firm up the support we each feel. Alito leads, giving subtle directions, watching what's happening as he dances in and out of groups of movers.

Late in the second day, I partner with George for a duet using any combination of scores we've learned. We decide to leave it open, hoping to find a flow of connecting, separating, slow and fast moves, sharing weight, counterbalance—any and all things we can remember and share through our bodies. It's a longer dance, and although I partnered with George the day before in shorter and more structured scores and enjoyed it thoroughly, I feel nervous, exposed, and afraid I'm making a fool of myself as a would-be dancer. I'm attracted to George and wish that he were my boyfriend. I'm certain he knows and is embarrassed for me. He's not been at his place, except to pick me up, since the afternoon I arrived. He must have a girlfriend.

Despite my obsessing, the dance is magical. George and I float together, in and out of contact, as if we were effortlessly moving through space creating moving images on a Picasso canvas. Our bodies intertwine and burst apart, roll and hop together. I'm transported to another level of consciousness. I feel lithe, nimble, and exquisitely graceful. We end in a connected sculpture, glance at each other and smile, then burst out laughing.

"That was surreal!" George says. "Unforgettable..."

"For me, too," I say. "Do you believe how many different shapes we made, how fast and slow we moved. That was amazing!"

The room vibrates with chatter, as Alito gathers us for the closing. One by one we gush platitudes, gratitudes, laugh together and share individual insights and appreciations. I make eye contact with Emery, Bonnie, Pete, and others I've had the opportunity to dance with during the two days.

I connect with Alito before George and I leave. He invites me to come back to dance with DanceAbility. He and Emery teach and perform in Eugene and in Europe. I'd be welcome to join in classes and participate in whatever is going on. We hug and I realize I have a crush on him, too. Earlier, George invited me back next summer for the Oregon Country Fair. Two men, different from any I've ever met, both handsome, inviting. Maybe Alito's not involved with anyone...

These thoughts and a body full of new experiences follow me home to Cambridge, Massachusetts the next day. The dancing I experienced at both gatherings is nothing like what I was doing in Cambridge. Authentic movement is all about moving alone, with a witness as connection, but without touch. This movement is all about moving in and out of touch. It's about physical and mental connection. It's more touch than I've had my whole life. My insides are a messy mass of movement—similar to but different from the rumblings of the past. I know something different is brewing inside. A small voice tells me it'll all be OK, but I feel the threat of losing control in a way I can't visualize or name, and am thankful I have E&T to calm the mix of pleasure and torment.

21 Moving West

Hope is the deep orientation of the human soul that can be held at the darkest times.

/ Vaclav Havel

WITHIN A MONTH OF MY RETURN HOME, I decide to move west, to Eugene. After my experience there, any thoughts of moving to Wyoming have faded. The workshops, meeting George and Alito, a new place—it all feels hopeful. I write a letter to George asking if I could stay at his place until I find an apartment. He offers me a summer sublet next door to his place. The man who lives there is traveling through the summer. He invites me to camp at his booth at the Oregon Country Fair in early July and offers me a few shifts of work greeting guests or working in one of the concession booths during the fair.

I am ecstatic. Could it be that George truly likes me? It's more than I can do to contain myself. Maybe it was the dance? Never mind that we've spent less than a full weekend in each other's company, we've never had a personal conversation and he made no attempt to flirt with me when there were plenty of opportunities. It's easy for me to ignore what I don't want to see.

Since I'm making such a big move and selling or giving away almost everything but what I can fit in my Golf hatchback, I decide to give up my nursing license, too, thinking I'll never again work in nursing. I tell myself I'll find something else, and until I do I'll live on a little money I've saved and the $20,000 that's accumulated in my Cambridge City retirement fund. Logistics like setting myself up in a new place, daily living expenses, what exactly I might do to earn enough to support myself—these are not concerns. It'll all work out because, secretly, I imagine myself living with George.

Alito responds to a letter I send him with an invitation to join in DanceAbility activities. He offers nothing specific. Still, I harbor a curiosity about what might happen between us.

Part of the planning is letting my mother and brothers know I'm leaving. The boys, busy with their own families and lives, wish me well. My mother is annoyed.

"You're moving all the way across the country—when will we see you? You always seem to think of yourself, Karen, never anyone else. What's in Oregon that you can't do here?"

"I met a bunch of people who dance, and when I was out there last month, I had a fantastic time. I'm tired of my life here—the move will shake things up. It'll be good for me," I say. She never asks about my dancing experiences and I don't share much.

A week or so later she calls to say she wants to ride out with me. "I'll stay with Gerard (my youngest brother) for a few weeks—help him and Pam with the kids," she says. "I don't want you driving all that way alone."

"OK, but it'll be a quick ride. I want to be in Eugene by July 1. We'll drive and sleep and eat—no sightseeing. Did you talk to Gerard?" I ask. I'd rather not make the trip with her. It'll be uncomfortable, the two of us alone in the car for a couple of days.

"Yes, I did. What do you think I'm stupid? You never give me the benefit of the doubt. You're always thinking the worst, ready to criticize me. Why is that, Karen? Why can't you be nice?" It's a familiar exchange.

"I am nice, Mom. A lot of people like me and think I'm nice. You're the only one I have trouble with." I can't seem to control my tone or attitude when I'm with my mother. It upsets me, but I think she's as much to blame as I am. She never sees it that way.

Clearing the apartment I'd lived in for fourteen years takes on the feel of a giant purge. There are two things I obsess over giving up. My cherry platform bed, made by a local furniture maker, which I decide to ship to Eugene; and a solid oak butcher-block table Gene and I bought when we were married. It's one of a few things I took when we split up and I've used it every day since, but I sell it for next to nothing to a young couple who steal my heart when they come to look. It's a bittersweet parting, unlike my feeling of elation as I put my never worn, four-thousand dollar wooden leg, upside down, foot sticking up, in the garbage can on the street. I'd had it for over ten years. It's identical to the one Cale, my alter-ego, skiing buddy, had when I met her, with soft foam shaping the calf and thigh. I could never come to terms with wearing it intermittently—it was all or nothing once I realized I had the option. I don't regret letting it go—dancing would never have been possible had I not felt my body without it.

I give away several framed paintings I'd made over the last two years and leave others on the street with the leg. I tell myself my art is worthless, despite the positive feedback I get from many people at the studio workshop. For reasons unknown, I can't embrace myself as an artist or as a worthy person. Like with purging food, I'm compelled to get rid of things that say something about me. Years later, I regret not having those things to cherish, yet realize the stripping down was what I had to do to move on in my journey.

With the car loaded and my mother and I settled in the front, we take off for Colorado. It's an uneventful trip. We each make an effort to keep things civil and mostly that's how it goes. I wish my mother were different, and I sense she wishes the same of me. We love each other, but we don't have much in common. My disappointment manifests as criticism and dislike of her. I feel expectations from her—she tells me

I'm selfish and angry and spiteful. My E&T compulsion escalates with my discomfort. Keeping it secret when we're in such close quarters is a challenge.

We arrive in Colorado an evening in late June 1994. My brother, Gerard, his wife and two teenage sons live in a house outside of Denver. I feel like a stranger in a strange land. I hardly know any of them. We see each other once a year at most for a few hours. I'm pleasant and cordial and itching to leave. I don't know these people; they're different than me. I don't want to be around them. Something inside me is twisted in knots—while I maintain my distant, controlled self on the outside.

The evening is short—we eat, chat some, and head off to bed. I wake early the next morning and take off without saying goodbye. Later that day I call, "I wanted to get an early start so I can make it to Eugene today," I tell my brother. I don't tell him that I couldn't bear seeing my mother one more minute, or that I felt so uncomfortable with a real family, that all I could think to do was get away. I know these things, but only in some deep recess of myself where it's murky, and there are no words.

"Oh, yeah, okay. I'll tell Pam and the boys." Gerard says. Years later he reminds me of this time—how odd it was that I snuck out without a word.

I make it to Eugene by late afternoon July 1, as planned. Tom, a man who works with George, greets me at the house. "George is traveling in Asia for the summer. He asked me to show you your place and help you unload your car. The country fair crew is expecting you out in Veneta."

"So George's not here—and he won't be at the fair? He didn't tell me," I say, feeling abandoned and alone.

"Seems he didn't tell quite a few people—it was a spur of the moment trip, I guess. Beats me." Tom gets in the car and we drive to the duplex next door. It's a cute, nicely furnished two-bedroom place with a small front yard, a covered porch, and a backyard. We unload and he points me in the direction of the fair. "The fair doesn't start until Friday, but there are lots of workers out there getting things ready," he says. "They'll keep you busy." He's friendly and puts me at ease.

"Thanks so much for helping, Tom. Will you be around this summer?" I ask, thinking at least I'll know someone when the fair is over.

"Yeah," he says. "I work for George. We've got projects happening. I'll be here every day while he's gone."

"OK then, see you when the fair's over." I say, then wonder, "Are you going?"

"Me, no, not for me. Too weird," he says as he goes back to the house.

I drive to the fair wondering what Tom meant by too weird. I realize I'm in a whole new place, all the way across the country from where I've lived all my life. I know nothing about Eugene or the country fair, or about George, or anyone else. I'm a little scared, and mostly excited, about what's next.

The Ritz Sauna booth that George built and operates each year is at one end of the many acres of the Oregon Country fairgrounds. At the entrance road, I'm directed down a windy, unpaved path, and eventually drive into the sauna compound where a man directs me to a parking place between a wooden structure and a field full of tents. John greets me as I get out of the car.

"Hi. Is it Karen?" he asks offering his hand. "George told us you'd be coming. From where?"

"Uh, from Cambridge, Massachusetts. Thanks for guiding me back here. It's pretty unbelievable with all these tents and so many people mulling around. Who are you?"

"I'm John, a good friend of George's and holding down the fort with a few others while he's gone this year. We didn't have much notice—something he said he had to do. We'll make the best of it. We have a great crew."

"So is the fair open yet?" We're walking toward the wooden structure which I see is a kitchen on the side facing the tents and a big open wood deck around a pit on the other side. "Wow—this is amazing," I say. I see two counters around what look like booths for selling things, and a big wooden house-like building that John says is the big sauna.

We look inside at tiered benches around a wood stove. "This looks like a bigger version of the sauna George has in his yard," I say.

"Yep. That one's over there behind you," he points. "Open showers are here and privates over behind that wall."

As he shows me around, others are hustling, carrying wood and other things and sanding, building, cleaning. He introduces me to Barbara and Robbie, who've been working with George for years, Tim and Sam who come down from Port Townsend, Washington, every year for a month to work, and to Ann, Jane and Sara, also old timers at the sauna.

"It takes about a month to get the place up and running after the winter rains," John says. "We have to refurbish all surfaces, and there's always a new addition to be built. George keeps expanding."

I learn that the sauna is open round the clock from Thursday night through Monday morning for fair workers and visitors. In the evenings, there's live music around the big pit where there's always a blazing fire. The entire operation runs on wood—heat, showers, saunas and fires. Sauna crew staff the concession booth, where guests can buy toiletries, tee shirts and other lovely trinkets, and the security booth, where people leave valuables while they're basking nude with their fellow fair goers. Crew members keep the fires going, greet guests at the entryway, and man the ticket booth. The Ritz Sauna, as it's officially named, is one of the most visited booths at the fair. Native American images and symbols, many of animals, grace the wood walls, tee-shirts, and other structures around the main area.

"Gotta get back to work," John says after our short tour. "Make yourself at home."

I wander back to my car feeling overwhelmed, lost, and scared. I've never seen anything like this, so many people, all well-acquainted, working to make something so big happen. I don't have a tent, so George assured me I could sleep in my car. John made reference to it, but said they really rather no cars in the back area—they like to leave cars behind when they're out here. I'm apologetic but happy I'll be alone in my car. I feel intimidated by all the people and activity that I know nothing about.

320

As I'm stepping out from the back of the car I see Emery a few feet away. He's rolling toward me, backwards, with his head turned to look behind him. "Karen, you made it," he says.

It takes me a couple of tries to understand him, but soon we're talking like we did at the end of Diverse Dance. He tells me he's been coming to the fair for a decade or more. George sets him up with a luxury camping spot. He has a big tent, a place for an aide to sleep, and a launch pad for his Flamingo Taxi service. He pedals a manual bike, tailored to his needs, pulling a pink flamingo-themed cart big enough for four passengers. He rides around the grounds after visitors leave until the wee hours of the morning, offering rides to partying fair workers for a minimal fee. He makes a killing each year—people look forward to riding with him. Some nights he can't keep up with the demand. Bonnie has her own tent space next to Emery's, and they spend most of their time at the fair together.

I'm happy to meet up with Emery and Bonnie—at least I know two people. But, my discomfort with the disabled image, me hanging around with them, especially in the company of all these people who don't know anything about me, is troubling. I don't want anyone to see me as disabled, and I don't want the fair people to think I'm friends with them or that I'm like them.

John, and some of the women I meet, find jobs for me to do. Everyone is friendly, although I feel like some people wonder who I am and how I got there. Pretty much, the sauna family is a tight group of folks who've known each other for a long time. They're a mixed bunch—a number of the men working on the construction and refurbishing projects are from Port Townsend, Washington, north of Seattle on the Strait of Juan de Fuca. Many of the women are from various parts of Washington and Oregon, and there's a large contingent of folks from right around Eugene. Everyone chips in to help cook dinner each night before the fair opens. After Thursday dinner, we'll be on our own for food, working odd shifts, round the clock, to fill the numerous three-hour job slots it takes to operate the Ritz. George pays fifteen dollars a shift, and we'll each have three to five shifts through the weekend.

"Most of us will spend the money on food or clothes and other things we can't resist," Linda, one of George's good friends, tells me. "You'll see once the vendors set up. There's amazing handmade art and crafts here, everything from clothes to paintings to herbal body care stuff, to pottery. All original, one of a kind."

Things do change once the fair opens. There's a constant buzz of clothed staff working, and nude patrons lounging in the sauna complex. Behind the scenes, crew members sleep, venture out into the fair proper to catch any of the hundreds of entertainment offerings, and gather in small groups to share food, stories about this and past fairs, and speculate about how George would do things. The folks in charge are busy chasing down problems before they arise. There seem to be continuous issues with water and fire—things I know nothing about.

Everyone is friendly, the sauna crew and the many others I meet as I wander the dirt paths, but I feel more alone than I can remember—similar to how I felt at the coed party before I impulsively dropped out of college, and at the kid's camp, where I was surrounded by beautiful-bodied counselors and the disabled counselor who wanted to befriend me. I'm twenty years older now, but the disappointment I feel about my body and my intense envy of others—believing everyone else is luckier, happier, more beautiful, nicer, and has so much more than I do—feels more acute and urgent. I see it more clearly and I despise myself for feeling the way I do. I reflexively act the part of a super-together, well-adjusted, never lonely east-coaster, relocating because I want to dedicate myself to dancing. To maintain the facade, I spend hundreds of dollars on food I shovel down my throat hoping to keep the feelings at bay, and hours leaning over various public toilets, and the one staff toilet, purging it all up, cleansing myself of the toxic sludge growing in my gut. Despite its amazing powers through the years, E&T is becoming less of a total relief—and although the serotonin rush I feel after purging continues, the unbearable feelings rarely disappear fully, like I imagine they used to. I can only hope and pray that getting to know George or Alito will lead to the magical end of E&T.

Back in Eugene after the fair, I spend most days working in the large garden behind George's house with Lisa, a good friend of George's. I'd never stepped foot in a garden before that summer, and learn volumes about growing all kinds of vegetables, berries, and flowers. Lisa and I weed, plant and harvest every imaginable vegetable as well as raspberries, blueberries, boysenberries, and blackberries. We create flower bouquets full of lilies, cosmos, daisies, zinnias, sunflowers, foxglove, and many more varieties which we sell from a little table at the corner of George's driveway. When George returns mid-summer, he joins us in the garden whenever he has time away from his construction business. John, the man who greeted me at the fair, joins us for Wednesday evening dinners and saunas most every week. I learn through the conversation on those evenings, and glean details when I ask George directly, that he has a progressive, kidney disease for which the only treatment is a transplant. He's known about it for many years. It seemed to be progressing more rapidly in the past year. He vowed he would never have a transplant, but after his summer trip, he considers putting his name on the list of folks awaiting a donor kidney.

"It's a big step," I say, "but just think of all the people who love and would miss you enormously if you were to die. All those people at the fair, your work pals, and so many other people in this town."

"I know. It's something I'm grappling with." I feel closer to George having learned about his long-term illness, and I imagine it's why he feels connected to people with struggles, like Emery and Bonnie, even though their struggles are very different. George isn't a man who talks much about feelings. He's someone who has impeccable integrity and an emotional depth that is welcoming and intimidating. He has big, generous energy that he invests in people and projects he cares about. I hope he decides to have a kidney transplant.

Late in the summer, Lisa and I take a trip to Port Townsend to visit some of the guys who I'd met at the fair. We stay with Jack, who I quickly decide will be my next boyfriend. George and Alito are out, since I'd discovered George was involved with someone, and I saw nothing of Alito that summer. Jack's a lanky, slightly goofy, experienced carpenter with a big heart, chuckle of a laugh, and infectious smile. Lisa and I stay at his place for a couple of nights. We visit with Matt, another fair buddy, and he and Jack introduce us to Port Townsend friends of theirs. Over the course of our visit, I smoke pot for the first time since I skied with Sam, drink beer and eat freshly caught fish with the gang, and fall in love with Port Townsend, much like I did with Martha's Vineyard. I can imagine living there—with Jack as my partner. E&T would surely disappear, and I'd never again have to work as a nurse.

George is disappointed when I tell him I'd like to move north at the end of the summer. "Why there? What's there that's not here?"

"Well, the water, for one. I love being by the water and since I don't have a job here, and won't have a place to live after August—why not?" I'm disappointed that George is not going to be my boyfriend. It becomes clear after I meet Katherine, the woman he traveled to Indonesia with. She visits often on the weekends, and they seem a very happy couple.

George offers me a room in his house, but I decline. It feels like it would be hard to be around him and Katherine, so happily going about their couple thing. I'm envious and my hopes have transferred to Jack, which, of course, I never mention to George, Lisa or anyone else. I harbor many secrets.

22 Life in Port Townsend

The problem, if you love it, is as beautiful as the sunset. The obstacle is the path.

/ J. Krishnamurti

BEFORE THE END OF THE SUMMER, I return to Port Townsend to look for a place to live. I find a tiny, windowless room, much like my childhood bedroom. It's furnished with a twin bed, pineapples carved into the four short posters, a small dresser, and desk. Elgah, my eighty-year-old landlady, asks two hundred dollars a month rent.

"You can use the kitchen and living room whenever you want. I have cats, mostly outside in the yard, but they do come in," she says. She's a tiny, frail woman, with a love of abstract watercolor painting, which cinches the bond between us. She has a desk set up in the corner of the living room where she sits and plays, swirling water and paint on small pieces of thick white watercolor paper. She's hung some of her unframed work around the house. This reminds me of the things I did at the art workshop in Cambridge, and I feel a desire to make some new paintings.

A few weeks after I move in, I find a job as a gal Friday at a small candle factory on the edge of town. The candle shop owners, Jake and Ellen, hire me to come in on days when they need help with various tasks, like bagging candles, sorting mail, searching for items in the warehouse. They offer five dollars an hour, which I secretly enjoy agreeing to. I feel like a rebel, snubbing nursing work that would pay twenty-five or more an hour. I tell myself I'm on a new path, living more simply, needing less. If I have less money, I figure I'll eat less and maybe E&T will leave me.

Jake and Ellen are model employers. They cherish each of us, handing out small bonuses for work well done, holding weekly staff meetings, with all the pizza we can eat, to discuss any issues that might need addressing. The crew of ten or so is a happy bunch and they welcome me with open arms. Ellen invites me to their family property, where they live with their two young boys in a three-room yurt. It's in a woodsy spot, with a separate bathhouse complete with shower, and Japanese-style low squat toilet that has a spray feature for cleaning private parts.

"My first husband is Japanese, and we lived in Japan for a short time. I love some of their customs, like the squat toilet and futon beds on the floor," she tells me as she takes me around the grounds. "Jake seems to like it, too. We both love living in the yurt now that we made the separate rooms for us and the boys. It feels like living close to the land, something we both want to do." I wonder if that's what I want. I'm feeling waves of jealousy towards Ellen—her seemingly beautiful, full life—and I feel lost and alone. What do I want to do, who am I? These are questions that are haunting me. I have no idea how to answer them.

I join the local food co-op and work there for discounts on food. The Port Townsend alternative community is small and very close-knit. The town is comprised of some wealthy folks who own many of the waterfront properties and the wooden sailboats that are a hallmark of the place. There are large contingents of artists and sailors, some of whom have adequate funds and some of whom are struggling to make ends meet. I want to be a part of both groups. I long for the freedom and ease of having enough to not worry about work, to live in a beautiful place on the water. Yet, I want to be artsy and bohemian, too. Mostly, I long to feel like I fit in someplace.

My plan to hook up as Jack's girlfriend fizzles in the first month. I never see him and if I do happen to run into him in town, he's always in a hurry. I see some of the other guys from the fair once in awhile, but all are busy with their well-established lives and don't seem particularly interested in including me.

As the months go by I begin to feel trapped in Elgah's house. Her existence seems narrow—focused on her cats, that she feeds babyfood meats from little glass jars. She saves the empties and they cover many surfaces. She feeds the deer off the front porch, which scares me. I have no idea how to act around wild animals and fear one will attack me as I leave the house. I spend many hours alone in my drab bedroom eating food I sneak in because her rules prohibit food anywhere in the house except the kitchen, which I understand but can't bring myself to obey. I see her as a lonely spinster, lovely but, in my mind, sad and isolated. I try to keep my annoyance under wraps and have little conscious awareness that my projections have more to do with how I feel about myself.

Meanwhile, at the candle factory, I'm promoted to votive candle dipper, a tedious job that involves sitting over a row of buckets full of steamy colored wax into which I dip white votives to make candles that have three colors top to bottom. I dip in one bucket two-thirds up, then over dip the same candle one-third up, then invert and dip the two-toned candle in a third color to meet the first color. I pack them in boxes of twelve and earn nine dollars for each box I complete. False excitement with this new task exudes from my mouth, while the rest of me wonders what I'm doing, where I'm going, how I can keep up the charade? At the same time, I feel I have no options. There's just a small hospital in the area, and it provides mostly emergency care. All of my experience is in mental health, and I loathe the thought of going back to that work. Things feel like they're closing in on me until suddenly it's February 1995, and I get a flyer for the next Diverse Dance on Vashon Island, a short car and ferry ride from Port Townsend.

My fantasies about being a dancer take over. They've partnered with the unceasing negative self-talk inside my head. I tell myself it's ridiculous to think anyone would ever see me as a dancer. Still, I'm less unsure about going to Diverse Dance than I was the first year, and I talk it up to everyone.

"I'll be away that week in February," I tell Ellen after I fill her in on the fantastic time I had the year before. "I met so many super people and everything we did last year was a lot of fun." I stop short of telling her about my disgust with disability experience, certain that's behind me now that I realize it.

It's another amazing week on Vashon—like an idyllic journey to Eden, free of responsibility and worry—although, my mind continues to play the tapes about what I'll do for money and where I'm going to live. I fantasize about what the lives of the dancers I meet are like—full of fun, loving relationships and endless opportunities to dance. I never consider that they may have to scrape for money, may live in crowded and inexpensive quarters and spend much of their time trying to find work that pays much less than I can make as a nurse. I envy them all— they're beautiful, free, and have two legs.

When the week's over, I follow Emery and Bonnie to Eugene for another weekend DanceAbility workshop. I see George for the first time in several months.

"How's it going up there in Port Townsend?" George asks me when I arrive the night before the workshop.

"It's good," I say in my detached and secretive way. "Really. I got a job dipping candles and have a room in the house of a cute, little old lady. I love the food co-op and being near the water."

"We miss you down here in Eugene. If you ever decide you want to move back, you're welcome to stay here in the house. The big room upstairs is free. I'd love to have you." He is so sincere and generous and kind, and there's a strong connection between us that comforts and scares me. Maybe he'll find out who I really am, what I've done and how I feel, and hate me. I want desperately to be close and it terrifies me.

The DanceAbility workshop is fun and satisfying. When the weekend's over I head back to Port Townsend, thinking maybe it would be best to move back to Eugene. I know a few people there, maybe I wouldn't be so lonely. Maybe someone or something will come to my rescue. The only problem is knowing the best way to return would be with the ability to work as a nurse. I can't live with George without paying my way.

Mid-spring 1995, after I tire of the novelty of dipping candles, I face the fact that I don't want to live with Elgah but can't afford anything else in Port Townsend, and acknowledge that I can make more money working a few hours as a nurse than many hours doing anything else, I secure my reciprocal nursing license for Oregon. It's a simple process that involves an application, a fee, and waiting for the card to arrive in the mail. I begin to tell the few friends I'd made in Port Townsend that I'd be leaving. Ellen and Jake wish me well.

"I get it," Ellen says, "there's very little work here and it's hard to find a place to live on minimum wage. I'll miss you, though. Glad we got a New Year's dunk in the Juan de Fuca to start year."

"That was incredible—thanks for taking me there. I'll miss working at the factory and hanging out with you." I say, not mentioning that I'd begun stealing things from the factory warehouse, things I wanted and didn't want to spend the money on. I don't mention how lucky I feel she is to have the life she has. Mine is much harder and I have no choice but to buck up and carry on.

Elgah worries about who will rent the room. "It's been so easy with you, Karen," she says. "Most renters want to have overnight visitors, and leave the kitchen a mess. I hope things work out for you in Eugene." I don't tell her how glad I am to be leaving what feels almost like a prison with many more restrictions than permissions. It was a nightmare for E&T. She's always around seeming to track everything I do. I always wondered if she searched my room when I was out.

"I have to get a real job," I tell Kelly, another woman I'd become friends with, as we sip wine in a place we'd frequented. She's in a relationship with Scott, a man who lives similarly to Ellen and Jake, in a big outdoor space with a beautiful fenced garden, an outdoor kitchen, and a self-built, round, wooden workshop building below a lovely bedroom, tiny kitchen, and bathroom with surround windows atop. He finished the upstairs space after he began spending time with her. Kelly works as a gal Friday for the Wooden Boat Festival, an annual Port Townsend event that attracts sailors and their wooden boats from all over the world.

"I get it," she says. "I sometimes long for bigger city life, but then I realize how beautiful it is here and how much I enjoy Scott. I'd miss this if I moved away." Kelly is more citified than most of the local folks I know. She wears stylish clothes and shoes more often than hang-around flannels, tees, and jeans. She's from Australia and is used to supporting herself. We spent time sipping wine, eating at some of the nicer places around, and seeing movies.

"I'll miss you and your accent," I say jokingly. "You're the person I spent the most time talking with. Thanks for listening to my saga about moving, searching, dancing, and nursing."

"And thank you for putting up with my goings on about Scott and my job. I loved our wine drinking dates and conversations. Hoping you'll be back to visit," she says as we hug goodbye. I'm jealous of Kelly. She's beautiful and Scott is a lovely man who adores her.

23 Back in Eugene

The future is not someplace we are going, but one we are creating. The paths are not to be found, but made. And the activity of making them changes both the maker and their destination.

/ John Schaar

As I DRIVE WITH MY FEW POSSESSIONS to Eugene, I'm happy to be free of the relationships that felt more like work than fun. I act as if things are easy and satisfying, but I'm aware of a growing inner discontent—something that rumbles inside of me and feels deep and dark, something I have no words for. I feel lost and alone, and I'm beginning to know in my bones that it has something to do with the secrets I keep. I tell myself being with George will make things better. Maybe I'll feel so comfortable E&T will leave me.

I settle into George's house, spend much of May 1995 working with Lisa and George preparing and planting the large vegetable garden out back. It's a beautiful month of sunny, cool spring weather. Without telling George or anyone else, I apply for a nursing job reviewing mental health records for a consulting company close to Portland, about an hour and a half drive from Eugene. Anything but working with patients again. I'm hired and rent an apartment in a suburb south of Portland.

"You just got back to Eugene. Why not find a job here?" George asks when I tell him I'm moving north.

"I saw this opportunity in the paper and jumped at it. It's perfect for me; I won't be working in a hospital. I have to make some money. I can't live here without paying rent forever," I say. I feel like I can't impose on George, and I think if I move closer to Portland there'll be more to do and I'll feel better.

"You can live here as long as you like. I don't need you to pay rent. What about the Country Fair? Do you think you'll make it?" He asks like he really wants me to come. Something tells me I have to get away, the stealing I did, what other people might know about me. It's all beginning to worry me.

"I hope so. I'll ask for the weekend off as soon as I start." I say figuring it won't be possible.

A week before my start date, I move my things to a ground floor, one-bedroom space in a small garden apartment complex an hour's drive from Eugene. By the second day, I wonder what I'm doing there. The place is dark and empty of furniture. I've never felt more alone, but I unconvincingly tell myself that I have to work and the job I landed is perfect. Something like desperation—like what I felt a few years earlier when I saw Boyz in the Hood and cried for hours after, telling myself I can't go on if things don't change—is bubbling up inside. The only good thing is that I'm in a void of a space with a private bathroom, where I can let E&T run wild.

The Friday before I'm supposed to start, my supervisor calls to tell me their contract with the consulting company fell through and the job is no longer available. It's like a blessing from heaven, a way out of something I had no idea would be so unbearable. Thankfully, I have a month-to-month agreement with the apartment complex and get my security deposit back. I call George immediately and ask if I can return.

"Sure, you can return," he says, "and don't worry about the rent. You'll find a job here. You can come out to the fair a few weeks early. I'll pay you to work for me."

"Okay, but I'll start looking right away. There's got to be something in Eugene. See you tomorrow."

I move back into George's house and a week later head out to the fair to be part of the crew. George pays me more than I made dipping candles, while I do next to nothing. There are more people than jobs, and the old-timers scurry around knowing what needs to be done without asking. I wait to be given tasks by Lisa, who I discover had been George's partner for many years before their relationship changed when he met Katherine. All the crew knows the details of the split and I feel out of the loop, but I don't ask. George is busy with bigger jobs, and although friendly, he and I rarely interact other than when he asks how I'm doing while passing by on his way to complete some necessary task.

I set up my new pop-up tent joining the campers on the hill. It becomes my refuge when I've exhausted my voracious appetite for E&T and feel uncomfortable with the crew's endless vying for George's attention. Everyone adores George. Many have known him for years, some of the women have had short relationships with him. He's like a benevolent king, although he has no sense of himself as a ruler. He provides opportunities for people to feel special, included, useful, and he shares everything he has with the people he brings into the Ritz family.

As opening day closes in, Lisa and I make a few trips into town to pick buckets of blueberries which will be offerings for the crew. There are close to a hundred blueberry bushes in George's yard. Abundant, plump berries have become one of the perks of working at the Ritz. The day before the fair opens, Lisa and I cut bushels of flowers from other areas of the garden and create dozens of large bouquets to beautify the Ritz for our guests' enjoyment.

I'm assigned several three-hour shifts at the admissions desk. I accept money or food vouchers as barter for the entry fee. Prices are higher for private showers or hour-long clawfoot bathtub rentals—popular with fair vendors who long for a soak after a tiring day selling their wares. All who pay to enter have access to the big and little saunas, the fire pit, open showers, and the entertainment.

"Welcome," I say as I accept their offering, "how's your day been? Is business good? Beautiful weather…" I like interacting with regulars—some people come through twice a day, as a start and an end to their workdays. I see people around the fair and feel a little less alone.

After a couple of work shifts, the temptation to keep some of the food vouchers overpowers my moral judgment. I tell myself no one will notice, and I'm oblivious to the notion that someone might see me pocketing vouchers. I want to eat everything I see and since I find some out-of-the way places where I can purge in bushes, I'm more at ease moving around the fair proper this year. Stealing the vouchers lessens my anxiety about money. A brazen, anti-social part of me that subconsciously feels I'm entitled to have what I want takes over, and I breeze through the weekend. When I'm not working, I wander the fairgrounds alone to escape the other women comparing cute new outfits and talking about their boyfriends and such. It's default mode. I'm friendly, a tad superior, and detached.

When the fair ends, I return to George's place and apply for work at the local hospital. Later in the summer I'm called in for an interview and hired as a per diem nurse on the inpatient psych unit, set to start work in October 1995.

Meanwhile, George tells me he's put himself on the list for a kidney transplant.

"The time in Indonesia last summer and things that happened through the year convinced me it's the thing to do. I'm still not totally comfortable with it, but maybe no one would ever be," he says.

"George, that's wonderful," I say as I reach out to hug him. "So many people are probably more relieved than you'd ever imagine. I'm sure Lisa and Katherine are overjoyed." They're the two most important women in his life.

"Now it's waiting for a donor organ. I want to ask you, though... would you stay with me in the hospital—not as a care person, but as an advocate—to be there in case I have trouble understanding or need something? When it happens, it'll probably be like a week or ten days..." he looks at me and hesitates.

"Really, George. You want me to stay with you?" I'm blown away. "Not Lisa or Katherine?"

"Yes, I want you and I asked another friend who could stay overnights. I want it to be two people I trust, who are not so wrapped up with me, not so intensely involved with me," he says. "You can think about it..."

"Are you kidding? I'm so flattered. I'll be there. You can count on me." I hug George again and feel teary. He's so strong and yet he feels he'll need someone to be with him when he's vulnerable. I'm mixed up inside. I've stolen from George, I feel like a bad person, and yet I know that he truly likes and respects me. The dichotomy of who I am and what I've done, and continue to do, is jarring.

There's not much talk of the transplant through the summer, other than Lisa mentioning that George told her he did not want her to come to the hospital while he's there. She's devastated and, when she realizes he'd asked me to stay with him the entire time, she's annoyed.

"You hardly know him. I've been with him for years. I hope he changes his mind," she says. Things between us become icier, but we still manage to share chores in the garden, though frequently we're out there alone and communicate in passing. I feel bad. I know if I were her I'd feel like she does. There's no easy way to talk about it.

George gets the call about the kidney the week I'm to start my new job. It's much sooner than anyone expected and we speculate that his Portland doctor somehow got his name to the front of the list. I panic for a moment, then call the woman who hired me and explain the situation.

"No problem, Karen," she says. "Be with your friend. Call me when you're back in Eugene we'll get you started then. I'm looking forward to having you. You'll be a big asset to our team."

I travel to Portland with George. His friend, Katherine, puts me up in her house. We get to talking about George's time in the hospital.

"He doesn't want to have to reassure or take care of anyone but himself. He worries that if I were there, he'd be less likely to focus on himself, which he needs to do in order to get through this," she says. "He feels that won't be a problem with you because you're strong and clear. He trusts you in a different way." She says she's glad he has me and Jody, the woman who will stay opposite me.

The surgery is a success and post-op George is a groggy fellow. The morning after, a pharmacist spends upwards of an hour explaining the medications he'll be taking for the rest of his life to prevent rejection of the foreign kidney. I listen from the foot of the bed and watch George nod that he understands. He'd spent days researching the medications and dietary recommendations, hoping with diet and lifestyle adjustments he'll be able to reduce his list of medications from several to a few. When the pharmacist leaves, George looks exhausted.

"Are you alright? That was a lot." I say moving closer to the head of the bed.

"Yeah, but I knew it all. I don't like it. But it's done now," he says looking at me with his tired eyes. "I'm going to take a rest."

I move back to my chair at the foot of the bed, aware of a heaviness in my chest and head. I understand the enormity of the decision he's made and how it sets up a different kind of uncertainty about his future. As George settles, I have a strong sense that his life energy is swirling out of his feet toward me. I do my best to connect with it and redirect it back up to his head and heart. That flow of some powerful force continues for a few minutes before it settles and George appears to sleep. I have an overwhelming feeling that he's grappling with whether to recover or give up and die, before having to face the future uncertainty. It's as if the pharmacist's facts hit home and he clearly recognizes what he's chosen, and is unsure he wants to go through with it. When the flow ceases and he calms, I feel like I've been witness to an amazing example of acceptance despite the many known challenges.

George gets stronger every day. My job of refusing any and all visitors is no easy task. People curse me, asking why I get to decide who sees George. "Because that's what he asked me to do and I want him to be in charge of what he uses his energy for." I tell them.

We have some adventures traveling through the hospital for X-rays or other tests where he says he's glad I'm there to pay attention while the attendants chatter with each other, wheeling his stretcher at what seems like the speed of light. We chuckle about the care and toward the end of his stay, he asks Katherine to visit.

"How are you?" she asks holding out her hand.

George lights up. "I'm okay. Not looking forward to the next month trying to get the medications adjusted. But I'll live," he says with a smile. He's moving to a small apartment close to the hospital where he'll stay with his good buddy, John. There's a post-transplant protocol of appointments they'll manage together. Since Katherine lives close to the hospital, she'll visit.

Back in Eugene, I orient to working on the hospital psychiatric unit, and to work in a facility connected to the county jail for folks in more acute crisis. Although I don't have a regular schedule, I work three to five days a week filling in for vacations and days off. It's all very familiar and I'm happy to be making money. I like the people I work with and they immediately consider me a valuable part of the team. I become their go-to girl for managing difficult patients. Despite my wish to be out of the psychiatric system, I enjoy many of the disturbed patients. I wonder what sets me apart from them. Why are they hospitalized while I, with my many crazy thoughts and anti-social actions, roam free?

I have another round of dental problems requiring a few more implants. I'm operating according to the true definition of insanity—doing the same thing over and over and expecting different results—but I can't see it. E&T is a constant, despite the annoying voice that tells me it's the reason for all the dental problems. Work gives me plenty of opportunities to scoff down patient's uneaten food, and I figure out that if I transfer my credit card balances each year to a new card with zero interest for the following year, I can pay for the dentistry with no interest. Scheming comes easily, and it provides a kind of justification for my insane behavior.

The third Diverse Dance, in February 1996, is as enjoyable as the previous two. I meet new dancers from around the country and from other countries. Emery, Bonnie, Pete and I are regulars. Steve is there every year to support Karen, Scott and Joan. There's the DanceAbility workshop the following weekend. I've become familiar with some of the Eugene dance community through attending the Contact Improvisation Jams, held weekly in an old school building. They're mostly unstructured, though occasionally someone suggests a music-free movement score that the group coalesces around. Most of the dancers are able-bodied and open to exploring all kinds of movement. I'm intimidated by the frequent fast pace of the lifts and jumps and leaps and falls, but find my place rolling around on the floor. I'm always joined by one or two who want to play and dance with me. I find effortless flow and comfort with people through my body and am amazed at the fluidity, delight, and depth of connection I feel with most everyone. Still, when I enter or leave the jams my mind races with judgments and projections I'm unable to stop. I feel stupid and ugly and less worthy of dancing. I'm jealous of others' looks and abilities. I always come away feeling like they all feel sorry for me and are merely humoring me with their complimentary comments and gestures of inclusion. These continue to be secret thoughts, managed only with my secret behavior and packaged, self-confident demeanor.

In early 1997, Alito announces the first DanceAbility Teacher Training, to be held that summer in Eugene. He invites me to attend to learn his method of dancing with groups of mixed-ability people. Emery, Bonnie, and Pete will participate, as well as people from around the States and Europe. It'll be a three-week training, with probably fifteen participants.

The training happens in a local dance hall. We're a diverse group of men and women, twenties to forties, of mixed nationalities and physical abilities. We learn Alito's method, dance with and without the movement scores Alito uses in his classes, and practice teaching over the course of three five-day weeks. At the end of each week we host a jam for the community, all three of which are well attended by many of the same people who attend the weekly jams.

For our ending celebration, we take to the streets of Eugene, inviting any and all to join us in a parade. We wear similarly colored clothing and wander through the streets, stopping at various places to improvise inside of a structured score. We attract willing audiences at most every turn. The perfect ending to a rigorous and rewarding three-week training.

Carolyn, a woman from Portland, and I become fast friends during the training. She runs a small studio with her longtime dance partner, Patrick, where she hosts weekly jams and rents rehearsal space to Portland dancers. She's a seasoned and fiercely dedicated Contact Improviser and she swoops me up during the training, much like Karen did when I met her at Bates College several years before.

"I'm going to miss dancing with you," she says as we say goodbyes on the last day. "There's something between us. It would be fun to explore that some more. Maybe you'll come to my studio in Portland for a jam sometime."

"I loved dancing with you, Carolyn. I can't do all the jumping and leaping and lifting, though. I can hardly even move anywhere unless I'm on the ground." I say, apologizing for myself. I'm in awe as I watch her move with some of the other able-bodied dancers. She's fluid and light on her feet, yet strong enough to lift a burly man and catch someone leaping onto her shoulder. Everything she does looks effortless and graceful. I only wish I could do some of what she does—as much for the feeling inside as for what I could show others. I continue to feel my movement is boring and stupid looking, and yet some part of me knows that I need dancing to find something that's missing. I want to make dances and perform, but I just don't know how and I fear I'll be ridiculed.

When the workshop ends, a part-time position for a charge nurse on the evening shift comes available. I apply, with encouragement from the staff. Another nurse, one who'd been working at the facility for many years, applies, as well. It feels like the right thing to do. I should get a real job, with benefits, and stop fooling myself about dancing. Around the same time, I get a call from the woman who hired me for the consulting job that fell through but was recently finalized, asking if I'd like to work on a per diem basis for them. No benefits, but totally flexible hours, up north, near Portland. It seems I'm headed toward a shift from dancing to working.

Around the same time the job opportunities present themselves, Steve, the Contact Improvisation founder and Diverse Dance regular, asks Alito to join him in Cyprus to teach a week-long workshop at the request of a dance friend of his who lives and works there. Alito asks me if I'm interested in joining him.

"It would be super if you could come along. You'd have to pay your airfare, but everything else will be paid," he says. "We'll be staying in a school for the blind. They'll provide meals and housing. Carolyn is coming along as Emery's aide."

I tell Alito I'm waiting to hear about the part-time job. My head and heart are fighting—my head telling me I'm a fool to think I can continue the dance charade much longer, while my heart longs to believe it's OK to keep pursuing movement. I'm still hoping Alito will declare his love for me despite knowing he has other women in his life and is not interested in me as a girlfriend.

A day or so later I'm told the nursing position is awarded to the other woman. The staff breaks the news hesitantly, expecting I'll be disappointed.

"I guess this means I'm supposed to keep dancing," I say with the widest grin I can fit between my ears. "Really guys, I just got invited to go to Cyprus for a dance workshop with DanceAbility. Now there's no excuse. I have to go. It must be a sign that I should keep dancing. Sandy's perfect for the job. She knows the unit, the patients, and all of you so well. It's a win-win."

24   To Dance or Not to Dance

Darkness deserves gratitude. It is the alleluia point at which we learn to understand that all growth does not take place in the sunlight.

/ Joan Chittiser

PREPARING FOR CYPRUS, WHICH INCLUDES CONVINCING MYSELF that I'm not dreaming, but really have been invited to this exotic island in the middle of the Mediterranean, I cover shifts at the hospital a few days a week and travel to Portland to work Saturdays or Sundays at the other job. In Portland, I stay with Katherine, George's partner, and dance with Carolyn in her studio. We spend hours moving together, frequently with Carolyn directing me to give her more of my weight so our dance can have more depth. The basic premise of contact Improvisation is counterbalance: the notion that the more we are able to move in and out of weight-sharing the more dynamic and creative our duet can become. It's especially important for me given the unique balance of my body.

"You have to really lean into me, Karen, give me all your weight. I feel you holding back and that limits what we can do together." She's

341

relentless and I know she's right but I'm afraid to really give myself over. Something I can't control tightens and pulls away. I can feel it, especially when she points it out. I try to relax, I desperately want to, but I can't, and she sticks with me anyway.

We perform a few places around the city and I make a short solo with her help. It's a four-minute piece featuring me, and a blue folding chair that I use as my support while hopping onto the stage. After setting it down, I move around, through, on and under the chair in all the ways I physically can until I come to standing in front of the open seat, facing the audience. The dance ends as I slowly lower my precariously balanced, one-legged body onto the seat. I'm wearing an A-line, knee-length white dress. As I lower, I give the audience a chance to see the oddness of a body perched on just one leg, and it's unique way of moving from standing to sitting.

In the mid 1990s, I perform the solo at the Hult Center in Eugene during a DanceAbility show, and in Seattle at the Festival of Improvisational Dance, cheered on by Karen, my Diverse Dance pal. These shows are my initiations into the world of improvisational performance. I'm proud of my efforts, and viewers heap on the praise, yet the critic rages inside of me labeling everything as stupid and futile and unflattering. Thankfully, there's a small voice urging me onward, certain that dancing is vital to my eventual well-being.

I travel to Cyprus with Carolyn, Libby, Alito and Emery. The flights are memorable for the free flowing food and alcohol. The flight attendants pass through the cabin continuously offering snacks, nip bottles of any spirit imaginable, pillows, blankets. They offer empty rows of seats for lounging. Though neither of us is a big drinker, Carolyn and I collect and stow the small bottles for future enjoyment. We chastise ourselves for our greediness and justify our behavior by pointing out the goings on with the passengers around us. In the airports between flights Carolyn lounges on the floor in her mismatched, baggy, multicolored clothes, her feet and legs perched on the seats. She wears a makeshift headband that tosses her short, dyed reddish hair every which way. I want to be like her—a real dancer—and I join her on the floor, though my clothes are more staid and my hair less mussed. I feel rebellious and eccentric, and at the same time, self-conscious and foolish. I'm trying on the persona of a dancer on tour, certain everyone watching is judging me harshly.

As we fly into the airport closest to Nicosia, the country's capitol and largest city, I hear people pointing out Mount Olympus, and other well-known areas. Closer to the ground I notice swarths of green and steely industrial areas, seemingly side by side. The ride to the workshop location takes us through busy streets, lined with palm trees, white concrete buildings, old, ornate churches, and dark-haired, tanned people making their way in the city.

We'll be sleeping in the dorms at a School for the Blind in Nicosia, Cyprus' largest city, which is centrally located on the island. It had been a boarding school before expanding it's role to include blind and other special needs children, who attend during regular school hours. School is not in session during our visit, We have the facilities to ourselves with meals prepared by the school staff.

Maria, our dancer host, and Steve join us for dinner at the school the first night.

"I am very excited to have you, Alito. And, of course, Emery, Karen, Libby, and Carolyn," she says, in her beautifully enunciated English while embracing us and kissing our cheeks. Turning to Steve, she says, "I can't thank you enough for making this all happen." She and Steve share a warm hug.

She tells us that her dance community in Nicosia has begun working with disabled children in some of the established dance academies. They've been improvising without direction and are hungry for information from Alito about his methods.

"Several dance teachers, as well as many of our disabled children and young adults will be attending the workshop this week. We're all so ready to soak up whatever knowledge and experience you have to offer us." Maria has a refined and graceful manner. There's a soft assuredness about her, a fluidity, and an approachability that makes it easy to be with her despite not knowing her.

Carolyn, Libby, and I look around our sleeping quarters after a plentiful and hearty dinner—stewed chicken, with potatoes and carrots, milk and juice, cake and pudding for dessert—that is much the same for our entire stay. It's an old building with marble floors and concrete walls. Ceilings are low giving it a dark, almost dungeon-like feel. The bathroom is small and not far from our beds, but I manage to continue my E&T charade without exposure.

We have twenty-plus participants in each of the daily workshops, many older children and young adults in wheelchairs, significantly disabled with cerebral palsy or muscular conditions, who come with aides or family members. Alito invites us to participate in the flow by taking part in the exercises and assisting him with teaching. Carolyn, Libby, and Emery slide easily into both participant and teacher roles. I'm uncomfortable from day one, feeling much like I did during my days as camp counselor years ago in 1970, and at the first Diverse Dance. I don't want to be with so many disabled people. I feel repulsed and hate myself for feeling that way. My discomfort is physical, I'm anxious and antsy and my body wants to escape. My discomfort is urging me to flee. I feign illness and excuse myself from most of the workshop sessions, returning briefly during each to participate in a few exercises.

While I'm away I roam the streets of Nicosia hoping to quell the inner voices shouting many different things: you're just like all of those kids, you're a coward, selfish, repulsive. I should be able to stay and to teach and to be nice to these people, but I don't want to teach or be with so many disabled people. I'm afraid, confused, overwhelmed. While I'm aimlessly walking about, I notice many older women, dressed in long black dresses with black kerchiefs tied under their chins. They bow, with prayer hands pressed to their hearts, and mumble as they pass me hobbling on my crutches. I hear them whisper "oh, god" and "sorry" and "I pray for you" in their broken English. I imagine they see me as crippled and pity me. It's not a new awareness, but it is one I acknowledge with more presence than I ever have. I see it, feel it and take it in. I am crippled and people pity me.

A highlight of the Cyprus trip is an afternoon spent driving to the northwest corner of the island for a visit to Coastal Paphos, an area famed for it's history related to the cult of Aphrodite. It's an hour and a half drive, eighty miles along the south west coast of the island. I get my first glimpse of the clear blue-green waters of the Mediterranean Sea. Our driver zips along past tiny villages and bigger towns, dotted with what he tells us are archeological ruins left from ancient inhabitants, all part of the Republic of Cyprus.

"The island is divided," he says, in amazingly good English, "with Turkey controlling the area north of Nicosia. If you walk in the downtown of the city you will see armed guards patrolling the buffer area between the two parts of the island."

"I wondered what that was about when I was wandering down there yesterday," I say. "I asked, but the guards were reluctant to say much, other than to point out the two fences separated by what looks like a narrow street. City goers were hustling and seemed too busy to disturb, much like people in New York."

Aphrodite's Beach is vast expanse of sand and ocean, spotted with ruins and huge rocks, one of which is Aphrodite's Rock. My inner turmoil sails out to sea for a few hours as Carolyn, Alito, Emery, Libby and I wade and wander the beach freely, with instructions to meet for the ride back. I feel free enough to frolic and sunbathe topless in honor of Aphrodite and my Martha's Vineyard days.

We make an ending performance and share it with some of the local community. Maria arranges for us to attend a performance of some of the top dance groups in the area before we head home.

———◊———

A few months later in 1997, there's another invitation to travel with Alito, Emery and Carolyn, this time to Bern, Switzerland for a performance event at the Tanztager Dance Festival. Alito offers me the same opportunity: free accommodations if I pay my airfare. It's a no-brainer, since my memory of my Cyprus discomfort is short-lived and I'm compelled to continue to move my body and surround myself with dancers. There's no mention of working with a big group of disabled people on this trip. I see the invitation as a sign, another opportunity not to be missed.

In Bern, I stay in a flat on a busy city street. Carolyn, Emery and Alito stay in a different part of town. There are three others in the flat with me, all able-bodied participants in various festival events.

"This is a super nice place," Helen says as she shows me around the apartment on the ground floor of a brick row house. There's a big open bedroom, shared by two women, a couch in the living room, and small bed in another room. The huge window off the kitchen opens to a back yard. There's no door to the small garden, but we sit on the sill or climb out the window to enjoy the patch of green. Across the street there's a market and around the corner a cheese and yogurt shop.

"Wow, you're right," I say. "This is a real European flat, like I've seen in the movies. Who owns it?"

"I haven't a clue. We were just told it was available housing for the festival. I wonder if the other places are as nice?" she says.

I tell her about DanceAbility and she says she heard about Alito's performance.

"Will you be performing with him?" she asks.

"I don't think so," I tell her. "I've only begun dancing in the last few years. Haven't done much performing. Alito and Emery have a couple of duets they'll perform." Helen is sweet and easy to be with. She asks me about my missing leg and I tell her my "no big deal" story.

"It's amazing you're dancing. I admire you," she says sincerely.

The few mornings I'm in Bern, I walk across to the market for a fresh croissant and coffee. I'm amazed to see non-refrigerated milk lining the shelves, which the market folks tell me is a common drink in Europe. At the yogurt store, I buy small glass jars with foil tops full of freshly made yogurt, and return the jars the next day. The cheese is yummy and

346

together with the bread and sweets from the market, and the free meals for performers at the festival, I'm set for indulging E&T.

One morning when Alito, Emery and Carolyn pick me up, Alito says we're going to a small dance studio in Zurich.

"One of their dancers invited me to perform in their space. You can perform your solo if you want. Do you have your costume?" he asks.

"Really? That's scary, but ok. I'll run in and get the dress." Yikes, I think.

The studio is a large open space, with a low ceiling and dim lighting, in an old brick building. Hannah, Alito's friend, greets us.

"So glad you could make the trip from Bern to visit us here," she says hugging Alito and Emery and extending her hand to Carolyn and me. She's a lovely, lithe, dark- haired woman, maybe mid-thirties, wearing loose fitting, flowing white pants and tank top. She introduces us to several similar-aged, beautiful-bodied dancers who are part of the studio company.

"Thank you so much for having us," Alito says. "Nice space—big, heh? Great for me and Emery and the wheelchair." He chuckles.

I perform my solo, borrowing a chair that doesn't fold. Butterflies and self-consciousness out in full force, I move through my short improvisation, hopping with the chair around the space and sliding in, on and around it. I stand still for a few seconds, before slowly lowering myself onto the chair. I hear applause and slide off the chair to the floor, anxious to find my crutches and move out of the spotlight.

"Wait, just sit with us for a moment, Karen. That was nice. You have a genius moment at the end there, where you lower yourself down. We can really see you and don't know what will happen right there. It's a moment that grabbed me." Hannah looks directly at me as she says "genius moment". I hear nothing else. It's an ultimate compliment, though I have no idea what it means or what she thinks of the other moments in the dance. I believe her, and I don't. Still, it encourages me, and some part of me thinks maybe I am a great dancer.

Alito and Emery perform to the usual wild cheers and laughter. We say goodbye and head back to Bern.

When Alito sees the logo for this year's festival, he gets an idea for a one-minute solo for me. He says my chair solo is too long to fit into the performance slot we have, but he wants to show a piece with a focus other than on him and Emery to increase exposure of his mixed-abilities work.

"It's perfect, right?" he asks as he shows me the one, on-point red and white-striped leg, displayed all over the festival. In one place the toe is pointed at a clock, as if the leg was kicking high up from a dancer's body.

"I'm thinking to ask one of the set guys to cut us a leg out of thin plywood and fastening it to your right crutch so when you walk sideways, with the right crutch facing the audience, they see the leg and then your leg as it steps out." He's talking fast, excited with the idea that came to him in the moment. He loves making movement sequences using crutches and wheelchairs. "We can make some moves turning and going to the floor...it'll be so cool."

"Sounds like fun. I have some red and white striped pants with me, like pajama pants. Maybe I can wear them..." He interrupts me.

"Great. And you can wear a festival tee shirt with the logo. Brilliant—it'll be really cool."

It all comes together and I perform the solo in the small black box theatre, with the same butterflies and self-consciousness. I have the feeling I'm in a hole, surrounded by people lining the walls ascending up and out. We decide to forego music, since it's a short piece and Alito says the visuals will be enough to grab the audience's attention. At the time, I have no idea what an amazing thing it is to be a disabled woman, performing in Europe, at a famous dance festival. I'm clueless about the dance world, the dedication it takes to have a career in dance, and the things people sacrifice in so doing. It feels to me like a gathering of young hippies who don't work, but rather spend their time moving and playing and socializing. I want to be part of that way of life, but I have

348

judgements about it—they're my way of maintaining my defenses—and the loose boundaries between people terrify me.

One day, the four of us take a scenic train tour up Jungfraujoch, one of the highest peaks in the Swiss Alps. The train is a rickety old vehicle that travels along open track through the small villages perched in nooks and crannies along the mountain. The weather is cold and sunny and we kneel on the seats with our heads out the windows waving to people along the route. We stop at a lodge close to the top for a short improvised performance on an eight-by-ten foot steel balcony that hangs out from the lodge, enclosed only by grating on it's three sides. The lodge staff finds rubber mats to cover the sharp barbs in the floor grating, designed to prevent visitors from slipping on the ice covering the metal. With an audience of a dozen or so, Emery in his wheelchair, Carolyn, Alito, and I move together, hoping to create an interesting flow between our bodies on and off the floor. It's a comical undertaking in the doing, and I imagine in the watching, as we maneuver among the ice, the slip-sliding mats, the metal barbs, and the breathtaking, and slightly scary, views above and below.

People bundled in their woolen sweaters, scarves and hats watch from one end of the balcony. Some watch from inside the lodge, faces pressed to the glass. They crowd around us as we finish and head into the lodge.

"That was amazing—the agility of each of you, and your daring..." one man says patting Emery on the shoulder. "Nothing like I've ever seen before." We settle in with them, sipping tea and cocoa, and grinning ear to ear with pride and delight, for a short discussion about Alito's ideas.

Close to the end of our stint in Bern, we head to the Aare river for a dip. The river flows swiftly in one direction, so there are steps built into the banks on either side to allow swimmers to get out and return to their upstream starting place for a repeat ride with the current. I'm the only willing swimmer in our group, but Emery and Carolyn volunteer to walk my crutches downstream, so I can have them when I climb out. I take several short floats, bumping shoulders and giggling with other happy floaters. I love the water. It always seems to be inviting me to relax and be carried by it's comforting flow.

Shortly after I return home, Olive B, a dancer I met at Diverse Dance, contacts me about joining a month-long project she's planning as part of the Wellington, New Zealand Fringe Festival in early 1998.

"It'll be a series of outdoor improvisations performed in sites all over the city. My idea is to bring dancing to ordinary people, to take it out of the studio," she says when we connect by phone. "I'm a New Zealander, and my family has a loft space downtown where you and I can stay. The other performers will be locals who will come and go as they can. If you pay your airfare I can put you up and subsidize food with the donations we collect at the performances. Any interest?"

"New Zealand—are you kidding? How could I say no? Dancing with you is always so fun." Olive is a twenty-something, beautiful blond-haired woman with unstoppable energy, enthusiasm and vision. We moved together in the driftwood and sand at Diverse Dance the previous year, She mentioned something about the Wellington Fringe Festival then, but I didn't think it would happen.

Still working per diem and unbelieving of the unending opportunities to travel and learn about dance, I make my way to New Zealand in February 1998. It's the end of summer there, beautifully warm and sunny. Our loft is atop an old warehouse building, sparsely furnished, with an open kitchen/living space and a separate bedroom for each of us. Large windows look out over the bay toward the ocean. The bathroom is out of the way enough to allow me adequate privacy for my E&T routine.

Over the course of the month, Olive, various other able-bodied and disabled dancers and I, perform a waltz improvisation at a busy office complex asking random souls to dance during their lunch breaks; take a partnered blind stroll down a busy commercial street; and dress in crazy bathing suit costumes to perform on a pier, in and out of the water. We inhabit city squares, parks, and beaches in groups of varying size, during busy times, to showcase our improvisational performances.

Although I meet and enjoy time spent with the other New Zealanders, Olive is my main contact and company during my stay. When she and I are not together, I wander the streets, mostly eating to entertain myself. I swim at the city beach a few blocks from our house, always alone. Sometime mid-month, Olive, and a man who joins us frequently in performing, begin to spend time together outside of our performances. I am insanely jealous and lonely, and a dark sense of despair descends. I lay around the loft alone and begin to steal money from the stash of performance donations. I rationalize my actions thinking she'll never miss the money, not caring about how much she may need it, or that it's not mine to take. I spend all the money on food—devouring and purging with a vengeance. I know what I'm doing and I'm close to seeing what's driving it, but admitting I need help seems too risky. After each purge, I feel a rush and a release that frees me from my despair for a short time. I can think of no other way to quiet the monster inside.

Over a particularly long weekend without scheduled performances, I take myself on a ferry ride to Picton on the south island of New Zealand. It's a beautiful day and the three-hour ride on the water distracts me from the overwhelming awareness that something needs to change. I want to have the energy and interest to explore further south in New Zealand, but I can hardly manage anything other than the usual E&T. I join an organized trip to swim with the dolphins complete with rented wet-suit we modify for my one-legged body. It's the highlight of my excursion as our guide steers us to several pods of dolphins who swim within arms length of our bodies. We swim closer to shore to watch huge seals roll themselves in long, green-blue seaweed strands attached to giant rocks in the shallow water near the coastal area. I feel like I'm dancing with sea creatures in yet another, unexplored part of the sea.

The trip ends with my losing my luggage somewhere between Los Angeles where I set it on the luggage roller for the outgoing flight, and Eugene. It's a suitcase I borrowed from Carolyn, one she adored and was upset about losing.

"How could that happen, Karen? Have you done all you can with the airline to try to get it back?" I feel like she's blaming me.

"It's been weeks now and I lost my clothes and an address book with all my contacts. Everyone I ever met and knew was in that book. Don't you think I feel just as bad?" I offer to pay her from the money the airline reimburses me and she accepts, but our relationship is not the same after that. We decide to take a break from each other.

Although it's hard for me to admit it to myself or anyone else, it's a big blow. She's been a main support for my dancing life, and although I was afraid of letting go in the ways she wanted me to, I know her relentless encouragement was helping me see myself more clearly.

I continue to travel to Portland for work a few days a month, staying with Katherine, George's girlfriend. She's rarely home and in my loneliness I take to raiding her fridge, and I even steal a red and white striped flannel sheet from her linen closet, certain she won't miss it. I can't see it or admit it, but I need comforts, and the sheet is soft and worn and I have to have it.

25 Walking Into the Abyss

When there's a disappointment, I don't know if it's the end of the story. It may just be the beginning of a great adventure.

/ Pema Chodron

THE NIGHT I ARRIVE HOME FROM NEW Zealand, George's house is dark and seemingly empty. I make my way upstairs and see Cliff's light on down the hall from my room. I met him at Diverse Dance, and a few months before I left for New Zealand he asked me to ask George if he could rent one of the empty bedrooms. George was reluctant, but he knew I liked Cliff and agreed. Cliff and I spent time together before I left for New Zealand. I thought we were in a relationship, though it was never spoken about. That night, he's in bed with another dancer who I know from the dance jams.

"I didn't know you were coming home tonight," he says when he comes out to meet me in the hall.

"How could you do this? I thought we were a couple. You asked me to get you this room. I thought you wanted to be near me..." I'm hurt, distraught, mad. It's a scene, similar to the sobbing fits I had in Cambridge when Paul would leave me at night.

"I never said that. I never thought that. We're friends and we slept together. That's all it is." He says as he and his friend gather their things to leave.

The next day I decide I have to leave George's place and find a place of my own. I can't be around Cliff and I don't want to be around anyone.

I find a one-room cottage, close to the hospital where I work. It's a place university undergrads would normally inhabit since it's blocks from the school and surrounded by other student housing. I enlist George's crew to pull up the carpet and finish the well-worn hardwood floor. They build me a sturdy staircase (to replace the rickety, aluminum one that George worries will fall apart in my first attempts to pull myself up) to the loft space that will be my bedroom.

"I don't understand why you're moving Karen. I'm never at the house, and you've been contributing to the upkeep. Why do you want to live over here with all these rowdy students, in a place where you have to climb a ladder to your bed?" George is honestly puzzled. His offers of support and assistance are more than genuine.

"I just have to have my own place. I feel irresponsible, like I'm not taking care of myself. And I like the loft. It'll be fun to sleep up there." I tell him. I'm confused, increasingly distraught, not sure what I'm doing or what I want, and afraid he and everyone might find out the worst about me. My only option is to run away.

I buy new furniture and fix the place up. I make a little garden in the tiny patch of dirt in front of the doorway. I know it's all a pathetic attempt to seem happy, but I try to convince myself that things are fine.

Dancing continues to draw me, and inspired by the "genius moment" comment I decide to make another solo. Maybe I have something special. Maybe I can be a dancer in the non-disabled dancer world. I ask David, a man I know from Contact Improvisation jams, to help me. He creates and performs outrageous dances, like one I saw him perform recently, using a scythe as a partner, wielding it with wild abandon while dancing with purposeful intensity around the stage. Although I have thoughts about David as a boyfriend, when I see him at dance jams, he's surrounded by younger, beautiful women. He's got a curious past, having been married, raised a couple of boys with his ex-wife on a small farm in the Eugene area. He talks about milking goats, raising vegetables, and living close to the land. He grew up somewhere in New York, the son of a doctor.

"Sure—let's do it! Let's make you a solo. If it comes to fruition, you can perform it at a Taproot concert." Taproot is David's latest venture. It's a grassroots production company dedicated to showcasing local arts.

"Yeah, that would be fun." I tell him I want to make a piece with black rubber pants, similar to the pants babies wear over their diapers. "I found them when I was looking around the resale place. I want to slip one leg hole over my leg and the empty hole over my right arm," I say as I hold up the pants.

"What's the solo about? What do you want to show people?" He's checking out the rubber pants.

"Not sure, but I want to do something to shock people." I say this not sure what I mean. I feel like something ugly wants to break out of me. I want to scream and fight, but I don't know how to start.

"Well, we can do that. You know me. I always want to shock people," he says with a grin.

We work a couple of hours a few times a week and come up with a dance that starts with me lying on my back, close to the floor, on a square of plywood with wheels—like one of those platforms legless men in the Bowery roll around on. I'm covered with a sheet so only my head and foot are seen. Using my foot, I propel myself around the room until a music cue prompts me to stop. I roll off, dressed in the rubber pants, stretched from my left hip, up and over my right shoulder. My torso is bound and my left arm and shoulder are bare and free. I improvise for a few minutes—hopping, rolling, crawling—to a crazy mix of rock and classical music before I come to standing facing the audience. Balancing on my one leg, I slowly take the rubber pants off my shoulder and slide them down my left leg, revealing a sexy black slip. I slither my hands down the silky material, outlining the shape of my body underneath. I make a full rotation, shimmying around on my one foot to show off my whole body. Then, I bow.

I perform this solo once, at a Taproot concert attended by many of the local dancers. People come up to me after with congratulations and questions—wondering what motivated me and what I wanted to say.

"It's something about my sexual self," I tell them. "It's about letting that part out of hiding." Although I want that to be true, it unsettles me to say it. I have no idea how to feel good about my body or my sexual self. I relate more to the bound up body rolling around on a cart, reminiscent of legless, begging people.

David and I talk about making another solo and I want to, but as the weeks after the performance go by, all my body wants to do is aimlessly walk for hours at a time. Whenever I'm not working or sleeping, I'm compelled to walk.

"I feel like I lost something important—something I can't identify. I want to walk across the country—back to the apartment in Hoboken, New Jersey, where we lived when I got sick to see if I can figure out what I lost. I know it's crazy, but I want to walk back there," I tell David.

"Well, that's what you should do then. It's not crazy. We can think of it as your next solo," he says, like it's totally possible, like I'm not nuts to think I can do it. He encourages me, and with his help I start to plan.

Over the next few months, I write a letter telling people my plan and asking for donations. I've never asked people for money, and I'm not taking the trip for a cause, other than myself, but somehow it feels okay, like I'm entitled to it. In the letter I say I'm looking for something I lost and hoping the solo hitchhiking and walking trip will help me understand what's missing. It all sounds upbeat and positive. It's an adventure. I feel confident. A secret part of the plan I share only with Paul, my Cambridge affair-mate who I hadn't talked to since I arrived in Eugene, is that for the first week I will travel with Carol and Tom, owners of the website that promotes sexy photos of women amputees. Paul encourages the photo shoot, but discourages the walk, telling me it's too dangerous. I tell myself that means he cares about me, though I

356

know better. I want to hold on to the fantasy that some man, somewhere, likes me.

"So glad you let us know about your trip, Karen," Carol says when we talk about the details. "Paul thinks you'll be a great addition to our photo collection. There's likely money in for you, too. I'm sure your photos will sell."

Most of the people I tell about the walk caution me to reconsider. They're afraid for me. My mother won't even talk with me about it—she tells me I'm crazy and selfish and tries to talk me out of it.

"You can't talk me out of it, Mom, I'm an adult. I can do anything I want. I don't care what you think." I tell myself she's just trying to control me. She never knew what was best for me, and I'm high on the excitement of doing something brazen and risky, blind to the internal or external dangers.

The plan is to leave on the summer solstice in June of 1999 and return on the autumn equinox. Sometime in the early spring that year, I get caught stealing food from a supermarket. It's the first time it's happened since I started E&T almost thirty years before, and it takes me by surprise.

In the store one day, I order jalapeño poppers from the deli and eat them all, crumpling the wrapper and stashing it behind the toilet paper, like I'd done many times. At the checkout, I see the deli woman watching me put my items on the belt.

"Where are the poppers?" she asks.

"What poppers?" I say, like I never got any.

"The ones I gave you a few minutes ago. I've watched you several times eating them and not paying for them. This is the bag they were in." She holds up the crumpled plastic.

The manager comes over. They take my picture and warn me to never come into the store again.

"I'm going to post your picture in all of our stores, so be prepared for our employees to be watching you," he says showing me the bulletin he'll put the information in. "I'm going to let you go without reporting you to the police this time. If it happens again, you won't be so lucky."

"Okay, thanks." I say as I leave the store. There's a sinking, empty feeling inside me for a few hours. Later that day, I'm back at it, happy there's only one of those stores in Eugene. The self-disdain I feel takes its place along side all the other pollution piled up barely under the surface of my skin.

I plan to let go of my living space before I leave on the walk, wanting to not be tied down to anything, until a friend convinces me otherwise.

"I want to stay open to all options, maybe I'll want to live somewhere along the route," I tell Julie, secretly hoping that Paul will decide he can't live without me when he sees the pictures Carol and Tom take of me. I plan to take only a backpack with a sleeping bag tied under it, thinking I'll find out of the way places to sleep along the way. Letting go of everything seems perfectly reasonable to me. I'm sure I can do it, though I've never been much of a camper or hitchhiker. I don't prepare in any way other than to walk around Eugene for a few hours each day.

"That dumb, Karen," Julie says. "You need something to come back to, something to remind you you have friends who miss you. How about if I sublet your place for the months you're gone? Now that I met someone, I'd like a place of my own. Maybe something will come of my new relationship if I have some privacy. We can help each other."

I agree, thinking it's fine if I don't have to worry about the rent, and pretty sure I won't want to come back. I keep my per diem status at the hospital, telling them I won't be available for three months. I'd recently let go of my psychiatric position, taking a per diem position in an administrative area.

"Usually, you have to work a couple of shifts a month, but we want you back, so I'll keep you on the books," my new boss tells me.

The local newspaper does a half-page story about the trip, with a large photo of me in the sweatshirt, hat and flouncy pants I plan to wear, backpack strapped on my back and crutches held high in the air above

358

my head. Paul sends me money and several local people, including my dentist, contribute to my cause and wish me luck.

David helps me put together a list of people I can contact in various states along the way, if I need someone to talk with or a place to stay. I'm certain I won't need either. I'm focused on doing it all alone, having it be a spontaneous improvisation—as if that's the only way it would be worthwhile. I can't imagine connecting with others, but I send them each a copy of the letter, thanking them for their offer and telling them I have no planned route after the first week when I'll travel with Carol and Tom.

On the morning of my departure, a small crowd gathers at my doorstep eager to walk the first mile with me. They have questions, advice, concerns to share, and some encourage me not to go through with it. Carol and Tom are there with their van. I tell the crowd they'll be with me the first week, until we get to Steamboat Springs. That information calms the worried ones. Inside, I feel pressured by the attention and want to get far away from anyone who seems to care about me.

During that first week, I walk for an hour or two, a few miles, then the van picks me up and we head to our next photo shoot location. Sometimes it's a shoot in a motel room where Tom sets up his camera and lights, sometimes at a hot springs or park he decides would be a good backdrop for the photos. Before each shoot, Carol and I comb through K-Mart racks for sexy bathing suits, high heels, shorts, dresses and cheap jewelry I'll model. After each shoot, we return all the clothes and get our money back. It's a scheme I'd never think of myself, and the clothes are ones I would never buy or wear. Some of the shots are posed, with me in a high heel and slinky dress, showing off the stump where my missing leg used to be. Some are on swings, with Tom shooting under me, so that my right hip is the focus. He takes some underwater photos, with the same right hip focus. Some are of me walking in short skirts and flirty tops, looking girly and strong at the same time. The week with them helps me ease into wearing clothes that barely cover my body. I keep some of the K-Mart clothes wanting to be sexy and hoping it will make Paul want to be with me.

In Steamboat Springs, we do two photo shoots—one at the hot springs and the other with a fringe and boots and leather cowboy focus. Carol is reluctant to leave me there alone.

"Are you sure you don't want us to take you back to Eugene? We wouldn't mind," she asks when we meet for our final breakfast together.

"No, no, no—I'm on an adventure. If I want to go back I can take a bus or a train." I insist I'm fine and in that moment I am. I have a room in a kitschy hotel in a funky town. "I'll stick around here until tomorrow, then head south to my brother's place near Denver."

One of my intentions for the walk is to let go of E&T. I'm certain it will just leave me. I won't need to do anything because the trip will provide whatever it is I'm missing. Although E&T is full blown during the week with Carol and Tom, my magical thinking persists. I tell myself it's the stress of being with people I don't know and doing things that are not familiar. That first night alone I tell myself it's my last time—a last hurrah celebration of my adventure and the new things to come. I spend most of the day and evening eating and amassing take-out and grocery store food for my final binge in the room that night. I sit on the bed with the map and my cache of junk food looking for a route and ignoring the loneliness, fear, sadness, and rage that I try to extinguish with each bite. I tell myself that night, and all through the trip, that the next day will be different. I'll be ready to stop after this final binge.

Since I have no idea how to find a route that's not along a main road, I begin the next day walking along a busy route, hot, sweaty, and unsure how far I'll have to go until the next sign of civilization. I have the unbelievably crazy notion that I can walk twenty miles a day and it'll be fine to sleep anywhere there's grass along the road. After just a few hours and a few miles that first day, I begin to feel a creeping terror, with visions of being attacked in the dark by wild animals. I'm afraid of hitchhiking, questioning my ability to judge people who might offer a ride. I can barely acknowledge it, but I'm lonely and worried about what I've gotten myself into. I turn around and head back to Steamboat Springs, deciding to take a bus to my brother's place near Denver, where I can map out a better walking route for the rest of the trip.

My youngest brother, Gerard, and his two teenage boys, pick me up at the bus station. Gerard is forty; I'm forty-eight. They're happy to see me, although the reunion is awkward since we see each other at most once a year for a day or two.

"I was happy when I heard you were coming on the bus. There's no way you could walk from Steamboat to here. Are you looney tunes?" Gerard says hugging me.

My nephews, Andy and Casey, hug me and call me Aunt Karen.

"I know it sounds nutty, but I have to do this walk. It feels like I'll die if I don't. Really, I have to find what I lost back there in Hoboken when I first got cancer." I say, surprised by my honesty.

"You lost your leg, you had surgery, and the doctor amputated it. What else is there?" my brother asks, as if it's clear as day.

"I know that, but it feels like something else was taken away. I just have to do it. Something I can't name is pushing me." I never mention my years of E&T or my failed relationships. My brother only knows about my successes and like many other people who know me, he admires my courage and strength. He thinks I'm amazing.

Over the ten days I'm with Gerard, Pam, his wife who works long hours as a nurse, and my nephews, we share a kind of easy living. We watch TV, make meals, do the newspaper puzzles as a group, and play endless board games, a favorite pastime of the whole family. Gerard tells me about his time in the Air Force and his short, non-combat stint in Iraq in the early 1990s, before he left active duty 1992. He's still in the National Guard, hoping to make the twenty years needed for a full pension. He went back to school and is a successful hiring recruiter for a small company in Denver.

I learn about my brother's sobriety, his last drink in 1990, and his continued work in AA. He tells me he was a binge drinker, mostly weekends, and it affected his relationships with Pam and the boys.

"The twelve steps really helped, and I still like to sponsor new guys and keep up with some of the friends I made when I was new. Now I can see how my behaviors and attitudes affect everything in my life. The God part was never big for me, but I do think there's a higher power..." Gerard's vulnerability in sharing touches me. It's as if I'm getting to know him for the first time. I imagine him wondering if I judge his struggles as weakness. I'm not sure, but I know I judge the same struggles in myself as weaknesses.

On the day I'm to leave, we argue about where to drop me off for the next leg of my journey.

"I'm not letting you off on the side of a road somewhere!" he's adamant, almost shouting. Andy and Casey are with us in the car.

"I think he's right, Aunt Karen. Why don't you just take the bus?" the boys seem to say in unison, leaning in close to me from the backseat.

"No, please guys, please. I want to walk. I figured out a route. Please just let me out where I showed you on the map." I did find a road on a map but little else. My next known contact is in Omaha, Nebraska, quite a few miles from Denver.

Gerard and the boys acquiesce and leave me and my backpack with bedroll on the side of a secondary road on the outskirts of Denver. My brother is distraught as he drives away. I have more than a fleeting moment of wondering what the heck I'm doing. Some part of me wants to stay with them forever, but that neediness is too much to allow into my consciousness.

I walk an hour or two before a car pulls up in front of me on the shoulder. I see a young Hispanic man at the wheel, a woman in the passenger seat, and two kids in the back.

"Where are you going? Can we give you a ride?" the woman asks out the window.

"Oh, no that's fine. I'm OK walking," I say waving them on.

"No, please, let us give you a ride. It's too hot to be walking on the road today," the man says. "We can take you to the bus station. It's ten, twelve miles up the road. We go right by there."

After a little more back and forth, they convince me to get in. I learn they're a family, originally from Mexico, living not far from my brother in the suburbs of Denver. They're curious and shocked when I tell them about my walking plans.

"That's pretty crazy," the woman says. "You should take a bus to the next place. That's too far and it's dangerous to be out all by yourself, with your crutches." They're all so friendly and sincere and concerned, it astounds and comforts me.

"Thanks so much for the ride. I enjoyed talking with you," I say reaching forward to give the woman a twenty dollar bill. I imagine they're not the richest of families and want to thank them for their kindness.

"No, no. No way," she says pushing my arm away and insisting I take twenty dollars from her.

"Here," she says, "for your trip. Take it. We want to help."

We're back and forth for a few minutes, until I give in and take the money. In that moment I understand that she sees me as needing much more than she does. I'm alone, disabled and walking. She has a car, a family—much more than it seems I have.

At the Greyhound station, I get on a bus to Omaha after calling one of the women who offered to put me up. Linda, David's current girlfriend and acquaintance of mine, gave me her name.

"Hi Terry, this is Karen Daly, Linda's friend," I say on the phone. "I'm going to be in Omaha later tonight and wondered if I could stay with you?"

"I'm so glad you called," she says. "Linda said lots of nice things about you. I was hoping you'd make it to little old Omaha. Are you walking?"

"Not as much as I thought. I'm finding it hard and scary," I confess. "I'm taking the Greyhound."

She meets me at the station and we head to an urban bar, similar to the ones my father frequented in Hoboken when I was a kid. The place, with red vinyl-covered swivel stools, a pool table and a few wooden tables and chairs, is mostly empty save for a few older men watching TV and talking with the bartender.

"My favorite hang-out," she says as we enter, "though I hardly ever hang out here. Work and living take up more time than I have."

Terry and I become fast friends. We share stories about our lives and have food and a beer at the bar each of the three nights I'm there. While she's working, I aimlessly wander Omaha's streets, checking out the shops and satisfying my E&T desires.

The last night I'm there Terry gives me a beautiful scarab bead that I later have made into a necklace.

"I admire what you're doing," she says, "a journey to find something lost. All alone. It's amazing. You're amazing."

"Not really," I say, thinking how little she knows about me, how really not so great I am, how easy it is for me to fool people into thinking I'm something I'm not.

"You are, but I think you still need protection. The scarab will help you have a safe journey."

I insist on walking to the bus station, some miles from her house, despite her attempts to convince me to take a ride. "This is a walking trip, and I'm hardly walking," I say, beginning to think maybe it's OK not to walk so much. Maybe the trip will be fine even if I don't push myself so hard or spend all my time alone.

From Omaha I take a bus to Chicago, arriving during a torrential downpour. Instead of taking a cab, I walk to a fancy downtown hotel in the pouring rain, thinking it's part of the adventure, something I make myself experience.

"Do you have a reservation, ma'am?" the hotel clerk asks, looking askance at my dripping wet hair and clothes.

"No, but do you have a room for tonight?" I'm so relieved to be out of the rain and off the bus. I don't care how much a room costs. I plan to call a woman I know from the Eugene dance community the next day to see if I can stay with her for a few days.

That night I call Paul to tell him I'm staying in a hotel, like he suggested, and to thank him for the money he sent. He's friendly but distant, saying he's too busy to talk much.

"I can't wait to see you," I say, "and the pictures Carol and Tom took should be up on the site by then." He's unenthusiastically polite. I tell myself he's busy being the successful businessman he is and it'll be different when he sees the new, sexy me. But, I'm deeply disappointed. E&T continues it's dwindling effectiveness at filling the hole.

I connect with Susan, a dance friend of David's who used to live in Eugene, and her live-in partner. She invites me to stay in a room in their small house where I hang out for five days. She invites me to a dance jam, but I can't find the enthusiasm to go. I bow out with excuses of fatigue or other plans, non-existent things I say I set up to do in Chicago. She and her partner work most days and seem to be busy most evenings, so I'm essentially alone in Chicago, where I wander the streets, eating and wondering what I'm doing.

Moving on, I spend time alone in Toledo, where I thought I had a contact, but couldn't make a connection. I explore the rundown, but hopeful city for a few days and then move on to Philadelphia, where I stay in a hotel and wander aimlessly through the streets during the days. I take a taxi past the Shriners Hospital, where I stayed for three months in 1963, but I can't bring myself to get out. I'm filled with feelings I can't sort out: there's sadness for myself which I can hardly stand to feel, and confusion about how my time there was simultaneously a good and horrific experience. Am I disabled or not? Was the wooden leg a good thing or did it contribute to all my current angst about myself?

I call my brother from Philadelphia. "Hey, Bill—I'm in Philly. I'd like to take the bus to New York this weekend. Could you meet me in Hoboken?"

"Karen, you're here already? I thought you were walking the whole way?" he says in his usual upbeat voice.

"Well, I guess I got smart early on. Walking was too much work and I got scared. So, I've been taking buses and staying here and there for a few days. Are you disappointed?" I ask, thinking my big challenging adventure turned out to be not much of anything.

"No, why would I be disappointed. I'm happy you didn't do that to yourself. What are you trying to prove?" He's flat-out honest and direct. It feels like a bit of an attack.

"Not sure, really. I just thought I could figure out what I lost all those years ago when I got sick, what's keeping me from feeling happy in my life," I say, wanting not to talk about it much. It feels silly talking about it with him, like he doesn't get it. "That's why I want to arrive in Hoboken and walk through the streets to 725 Washington, and sit on the stoop in front of our childhood apartment."

"What? You think you're gonna have a big epiphany there or something?" he says chuckling.

"Maybe. I just want to do it. Can you meet me at the train station?"

"Yep—we'll be there."

My hair's long, and blonde from the sun, and I wear a short, stretchy purple dress inherited from Sylvie, a French woman dancer I know in Eugene. The combo of the dress and my black Reeboks makes for a curious sight.

"Hi, hon," my brother says hugging me. "You look great. I like your hair that way."

"Hi, Karen. Long time no see," Rose, my brother's wife says. "Remember Patrick?" she asks, turning to motion him to move toward me. He's her teenage son, my brother's stepson.

"Sure. How are you, Patrick?" I say loosely hugging him. "Thanks for coming along. Thanks for indulging me," I say to them all. "I don't know. It's just something I have to do. I want to see how it feels to sit on that stoop again. It's the last place we lived that I had two legs."

"Okay then, let's go," my brother says grabbing my bag and taking the first few steps out of the station.

We walk along Washington Street from First to Seventh Street, where the old brownstone sits.

"Looks about the same here, except the door's a lot fancier," I say to Bill.

"It's probably a one-family now, or maybe two. Nothing close to eight apartments like when we lived here." Rose and Patrick look unimpressed.

366

Bill and I sit on the stoop and Rose takes a couple of pictures. I'm satisfied. I don't feel anything big or different inside, but I'm hopeful I will. I hope something changes, like I understand something about how the past and the present are interacting inside of me, that helps me move on.

While at my brother's place, a beautiful house he remodeled and expanded on four acres in rural New Jersey not far from where we lived during my high school years, I take a trip into Manhattan to collect my medical records from the old Memorial Hospital, renamed Sloane Kettering Cancer Center. It feels odd walking around the public areas of the building. Nothing looks familiar, and I feel too timid or scared to ask to see the pediatric unit. It's unlikely they'd take an unauthorized person through there anyway.

"So these are your records. From a stay many years ago?" the woman in the health records department asks.

"Yes, I was here in 1959 and 1962 for surgeries," I say looking down at my one leg.

"We had to pull these from the archives, so it's just the bare minimum information. We didn't keep everything from those years like we do now. Sorry," she says handing me a thin manila envelope.

"It's okay. It's the first I've seen of anything official from those days. I'm glad to get it." I say.

After dinner that evening, I share the information in the folder with Bill and Rose. It includes a page about the surgery I had in November 1959 and this description of my leg, amputated in 1962:

Specimen consists of right hemipelvectomy which measures 35 cm to the knee, the calf measures 39 cm and the foot measures 20 cm in length.

"Do you feel better now?" Bill asks.

"Not really better, but it's good to know it really happened and there are records. I know that sounds crazy, but for some reason it matters to me. Having it be on paper, in black and white. Something did happen then, something changed." I say feeling self-conscious and stupid. How is it I need something on paper to verify what I've known all along—something everyone can see plain as day?

"What do you mean? You think it didn't happen. That's nuts. It happened and I felt bad about it all these years." He's animated and talking loudly, like he's exasperated. "But, I guess you're right in a way, nobody ever talked about it with us if that's what you mean. Mom and Dad never even mentioned it. We just saw you when you came home. None of us really knew what happened—even though we did."

"I think that's what made things so hard inside for me. I never had trouble with the physical part, but it was hard in high school—no boyfriends, no sports. I kept up a good appearance but..."

Bill interrupts. "I know. I felt bad for you. I knew it was hard for you in high school." I see his bottom lip quivering and I know his emotions are right on the surface. "I was in pretty bad shape myself. I started drinking even before high school," he says lighting up another cigarette.

"Really, you were thinking about me then?" I ask with tears in my eyes. It's the first time I'd felt emotional around my brother since my brother David died, and it surprised me.

"Well—we ran with some of the same kids—you when they were being studious and school spirited, and me when they were being rebellious," he says laughing.

"I guess that's right. I worried about you in high school, too," I say. "I think you were the one left out after I got sick. Dave and Bub were little and needed Mom, which helped her stay busy and distracted, and I got attention for what I'd gone through. But you—seems like Dad took out all his hurt feelings and frustrations on you, and you just kept doing things that made him mad."

"He and I did get into it. Sometimes I felt like he was mad just looking at me."

"I remember one time he pushed you against the living room wall..." I say, tears welling up again, "and then let go of you and walked away. That was scary."

"Yeah, I got over being scared…" he takes a puff on his cigarette, and I see my vulnerable little brother face to face for the first time.

We change the subject to his sobriety, long overdue he tells me, after multiple DUIs over many years, and a month in jail after the last accident.

"Thankfully, I never hurt anyone. I was close to living in the gutter right before that, right before I met Rose," he says in between puffs. "After my thirty sober days in jail, they sent me to rehab for another thirty. I did the program with Rose's help."

"Are you still in AA?" I ask. We're sitting at the dining room table overlooking the expanse of green that is his backyard, and a beautiful second level deck he built.

"Nah, I knew the stuff when I left the rehab. I'm still sober so it must be working, right?" he says with an impish grin. "And Rose married me, and Patrick is OK with me being his step-dad." Billy was always the mischievous brother with a giant-sized heart. He's a skilled and talented carpenter, specializing in finish work, but able to do any construction task he puts his mind to. My father was like that. He could fix or build anything.

My mother lives fifteen minutes from my brother, in Flemington, the town where my family moved when I was eleven. She's upset that I chose to stay with my brother instead of her.

"I don't know what's with you, Karen. I think you do everything you can to hurt me," she says when I call to tell her I made it to New Jersey. "Why aren't you staying with me? I'm your mother. You never once called me the whole time you've been wandering around. Don't you think I worry about you?"

"I didn't call anyone, Mom. It was a solo adventure. Bill has more room, and you know if we spend more than a few days together we'll be fighting," I say. "I'll come stay the weekend with you."

"Yeah, we'll fight. That's because you're always interrogating me about the past, or disagreeing with me. Even this stupid walk—you wouldn't listen to me. A few people said I shouldn't let you do it, but you wouldn't listen. You make me look like a fool."

I dread spending time with her in her small apartment. She doesn't drive, and there's nothing much to do in the little town of Flemington. We'll just sit in the house and look at each other. She'll be mad that I don't tell her about my life and I'll feel trapped and dead. I'll have to sneak around and run water to purge. I'll get defensive and lie if she asks me about it. It's a familiar rut we'll roll around in together while I'm in New Jersey. My relationship with my mother is another thing in my life that feels totally out of balance, something I'm ashamed of and don't know how to remedy. I know she loves me, but I can't feel it.

Soon after I get settled at my brother's, I call Paul to arrange a time to visit. I imagine a romantic meeting where he'll be excited to see me and wanting me to move in with him. My brothers and my mother know nothing about my relationship with him and I see no reason to tell them.

"I'm very busy these days, Karen," Paul says when I ask about when to come. He suggests I meet him at his place. "The doorman will let you in if I'm not home."

I tell Bill, Rose and my mother that I'm going up to Cambridge for a few days to meet up with old friends. I think about calling some of the women from my old art group, but I make no contact before I leave for the road trip, heading straight for Paul's place.

The doorman lets me into a one-bedroom apartment in the heart of Central Square, the up and coming gentrification area of Cambridge. It's nicely furnished in grey and black and chrome and glass. I look around and see no feminine things, just one toothbrush and only men's clothes. Reassuring!

I'm wearing my shortest skirt, a grey wraparound, and a white v-neck tee shirt. I perch myself on various chairs around the place, searching for the right pose. I feel ashamed of wanting my distorted body to look sexy, like it's impossible, something no one will ever think I am. Still, I hold out hope Paul will be attracted to me.

Paul arrives after nine that evening. I'd been there since early afternoon.

"Hey, nice to see you. How are you?" he says breezing past me, hardly stopping to look at me. He puts a bag of take-out Chinese food and two bottles of red wine down on the counter.

"It's great to see YOU. You look great!" I say moving close to hug him. It's a perfunctory hug, at best, short and hardly close. "I took tons of pictures with Carol for the website. Are they up yet?"

"I have no idea. Haven't looked," he says, moving around the kitchen looking for plates and glasses.

"Oh," I say, disappointed. "Do you like my short skirt?" I ask. "I'm changing my look."

"You look good," he says, but it's awkward. I think maybe it's just because we haven't seen each other.

We eat and drink as he tells me it's not his place or his furniture. He's subletting. He gives no details about his life, says he's still pursuing venture capital and doing well. The conversation is sparse and cool. He eats and drinks a little. I eat a little and drink a lot, most of the two bottles of wine. I sit on his lap, like I used to when we'd meet up at my place years before, but he's distant and physically uninvolved with me. We lay down on the bed and he turns away. We fall asleep on separate sides of the bed.

When I awaken the next morning, he's gone. I slide to the side of the bed to stand and immediately collapse to the floor, full of wine I never purged. I'm horribly hungover. I can barely pull myself up to standing. I try purging but nothing but the water I drink to start the process comes up. I'm shaking scared. It feels like a low point I've not known before. I know Paul cares nothing for me. I'm ashamed of myself for being so needy, for thinking I might be attractive, for wanting to be loved.

I stay in a hotel in Cambridge another night, wandering the streets after I leave Paul's, trying and failing to lift my mood with E&T. Something's changed. I sense it but I'm not sure what to do about it. I tell Bill and Rose it was a good trip. I got things worked out with a friend and it feels like there's good closure between us. I offer few details, and they don't ask.

My brother has an annual outdoor fall party with a washer tournament, a game similar to horseshoes, where people toss large metal washers into pits he's dug. It's an elaborate competition. People contribute to the kitty to play and someone wins the pot. A hundred or more friends attend, and the food is overflowing. That year there's a pig roast. I know many of the people who are there, and I socialize as if all is well with me when I'm not gorging on food of every variety, and purging in one of two small bathrooms serving the crowd. Late in the afternoon, the downstairs toilet stops functioning.

"It's probably from overuse," my brother says. "It's never happened before though, so who knows. Something to do tomorrow."

I know it's from my non-stop purging. I gobbled large chunks of roasted pig, barely chewed and purged in combination with salads, cakes, cookies, ice cream. I'm reminded of the overflowing toilet on the sailboat years before. I worry my brother will discover my secret when he goes to fix it. I fear I've caused some kind of permanent damage to my brother's house, though I say nothing and continue to purge in the upstairs bathroom. Shame, fear of being found out, and the unending compulsion to continue the eating and purging haunt me for days after.

About a week before I'm set to leave, I get a call from my boss in Eugene asking when I'll be back. She called my Eugene phone, and Julie gave her my brother's number. "We need you, Karen," she says. "We've got to get these new Medicare rules implemented this fall. When will you be back? I'd like to offer you a full-time job."

"Great," I say telling her I'll be back the last week in September. "I'm taking the Greyhound bus back. It's a four-day trip. I'll call you when I arrive."

26 Climbing Out

The unendurable is the beginning of the curve of joy.

/ Djuna Barnes

MY BUS TRIP BACK TO EUGENE BEGINS in mid-September 1999. The plan is to touchdown in my humble cottage on September 23, the autumnal equinox. Something about the power of seasonal change and connection to the earthly cycles, as well as my desire to have the trip be book-ended, motivates my desire to arrive on that day, though I never paid much attention to those things before. Eugene, with its hippie and environmentally friendly culture, has rubbed off on me in a few short years. My brother and Rose think I'm nuts for taking the bus.

"Why don't you fly? You'll be there in a few hours," my brother says. "You'll be on the bus for four days. What are you thinking?"

"I feel like I have to make it a full round trip on the ground. I don't know why—maybe I'm punishing myself, but I don't think so. I just have to do it this way," I say. "I took the bus here, though I'm still a little disappointed I didn't walk more, and it seems right to take the bus back. It's only four days."

"Yeah—four days of torture, sitting next to people you don't know and trying to sleep. Not for me," Bill says.

He's right. The trip is pure torture. I'm saved by the fact that the bus drivers offer me the front seat, and unless the bus is full, I'm alone in the double seat. There are a few memorable moments. One day a man in the back of the bus goes on a shouting, raging rampage. A good samaritan seated near him tries to calm him down. The bus driver takes a detour to get him safely off the bus. Another night, a woman in the seat across the aisle sleeps for what seems like hours, with her exposed backside in full view when I turn my head the slightest bit to the left. An upside to the bus is my limited access to food and facilities, which keeps me as free from E&T as I'd been in years.

Julie, the woman who sublet my place, meets me at the bus station. She and her boyfriend enjoyed the few months they cohabited in my apartment and are solidly on their way to a loving relationship. The day after I arrive in Eugene, I call my boss and arrange to start working the next week.

Then comes the surprise—something I didn't contemplate or think about while gone, or on the trip home. I search the phonebook for an Overeaters Anonymous contact and call about meetings in Eugene. I suddenly know it's time and I feel ready. It's a combination of things: the humiliation of the night with Paul; the overflowing toilet at my brother's house; hearing my brothers tell me about their struggles over the years and how they remember never talking about anything that happened when we were kids; getting the medical report confirming that my leg was indeed amputated due to cancer. Or maybe it's finally accepting the fact that things did change in 1962—for me, for my brothers, and for my parents—and after listening to Bill and Gerard's stories, I no longer feel so alone with my feelings. They affirmed something and gave me permission to acknowledge what's been inside of me for years. I remember something David, my cross-country walk advocate, said to me when I first met him. "People come to Eugene to heal." At the time I cavalierly thought I'd already done all that with therapy. Now I think it may be true for me and, though the walk was nothing like I thought it would be, it gave me exactly what I needed to begin the next phase of healing.

I attend my first OA meeting less than a block from my house in a Presbyterian church. As I enter the meeting space, I see chairs set up in a circle and a good number of people mulling and chatting. Someone greets me almost immediately.

"Hi, I haven't seen you here before. What's your name?" the woman says.

"Karen, it's my first meeting," I say hesitantly scanning the room. I see a woman I know from George's country fair sauna booth, but no one else I recognize, which I'm happy about. The group is a mix of men, women, older, younger, thin, overweight.

A woman sitting in one of the chairs gets us started.

"Hi, my name is Gail, and I'm an overeater," she says. "Let's go around and introduce ourselves."

When it's my turn, I say, "Hi, I'm Karen, an overeater and bulimic." It's the first time I used that word to describe E&T. It surprises me when it comes out of my mouth. No one else identifies as bulimic and I feel some shame, but it's mostly a big relief. It's no longer a secret; I said it aloud to a group of people.

I say a few words about my bulimia history in that first meeting, and I hear people talking about sponsors and working the steps. When it's over, Randy, the woman I know from the fair comes over to me.

"Hi, Karen, nice to see you here. Thanks for sharing," she says. "What do you think?"

"Hi, Randy. I think I want to get started. Would you have time to be my sponsor?" It scares me but it feels so right. Something inside of me just knows I must, and I want to.

"I have my full load of sponsees right now, but I think my friend Maria might be happy to be your sponsor. Here's her phone number. Give her a call." Randy says. "See you here next week?"

"Yes, I hope so," I say. Walking home I wonder if I could really stop and not get really fat.

Maria and I meet up the next week before the Overeaters Anonymous meeting to talk about the sponsor relationship.

"I've been eating and purging since 1970." I hold nothing back, telling her how many times a day I indulge and how much food I buy and steal. There's a slight element of bravado—this sense as I talk that I'm the worst of the worst. She's non-plussed but she gets the severity.

"I'd be happy to be your sponsor, Karen, but after hearing how extreme your situation is, I think you'll need more than the one or two OA meetings available each week," she says. "I think you'll need a meeting every day. That would mean going to some Alcoholics Anonymous meetings. It's the same program and many people have dual addictions, so you'll see people from this meeting in AA meetings."

"Do you go to AA meetings?" I ask.

"Yep. I don't throw up but I've been on a weight roller coaster for many years, like many people in OA," she says. "I need as many meetings as I can get to. The support is really helpful. I try to go to a daily morning meeting that meets at seven at a church on Donald Street."

"Can I meet you there this week? I want to get started. It feels like the right thing." I'm not sure it's me talking. Something changed during my three months away, something about acknowledging my need for a different kind of connection with people.

So begins my rocky road to letting go of E&T, acknowledging that my very bad habit is an addiction, and taking the steps needed to give it up. Ever the optimist, before I'm even fully done with step one, admitting I'm powerless over eating and purging, I decide I'll stop everything on my birthday, October 12, less than two weeks after my first meeting. The day comes and goes and I don't stop, but with the support of others, I continue to share in daily meetings despite my failure to will myself to stop.

"White knuckling, we call that," Maria says. "If you continue to share in meetings, read the OA and AA books and work the steps, things will become easier."

I hear the same from many others in the meetings. I enjoy the company and truly like many of the people I meet in the morning meetings.

In one OA meeting early on, I have a particularly meaningful insight while I'm sharing. "It's feeling needy that's the most difficult for me. I hate that I'm so needy, but I am, I feel like I need lots of help. I think I should be OK all alone, but I'm not. That upsets me."

Others share similar things and I realize many people struggle with some of the same things I do. A month or so into my daily meeting routine, after having shared some about my erratic drinking history with Maria, I decide to stop drinking and identify myself as an alcoholic. The night with Paul continues to upset me.

"When I think about refraining from eating and purging, I usually think I'll have a little wine to relax. But that doesn't feel right. I'd be substituting one substance for another," I tell Maria. She suggests I get an AA sponsor in addition to her.

Soon I'm working the twelve steps with Maria, a nurse close in age to me and with Laurie, a sober alcoholic about ten years my junior. These two women, meetings, and working the steps help me gradually let go of E&T over the next several years.

As part of the process of working the fourth and fifth steps, I identify the people I feel I've hurt and make plans to make amends. I write letters to George, Olive B and others I've stolen from, and repay the stolen money. I confess to stealing from the local grocery stores and reimburse them. I pledge to regularly donate money to the local food pantry and volunteer there for several months.

As part of making amends to myself, I tell Laurie about the photos we took for the amputee website and the money I could receive if they're put up on the site. She's incensed.

"You should NOT allow those photos to be published, not for any amount of money. It's about your self-respect," she says. "It was something you did before you realized it was demeaning, before your head was clear enough to make a self-respecting decision."

"Wow. You're pretty serious about that," I say. Part of me wants the money, and most of me knows she's right.

"You bet I am," she says looking directly into my eyes. "You're worth much more than that. It's your decision, but I strongly suggest you walk away from the whole business."

Laurie and Maria stick with me through the next few years of sobriety, when lots of unresolved grief surfaces. I realize I've harbored secret self-pity for many years. During one women's retreat weekend, Maria and Laurie present me with a teddy bear, minus her right leg. We make a short pilgrimage to a nearby tree and dig a hole to bury the leg. It feels like a silly, childish thing to do, but it's a powerful, cathartic experience.

Around the same time, I make another solo performance for a TapRoot production. It's a monologue titled "Lost and Found" that I write after the cross-country walk focused on realizing that what I thought I lost (my leg) was really taken away. The loss went unacknowledged for many reasons, none of them my fault. The monologue goes on to describe the hoops I jumped through to convince myself that nothing had changed, when in fact, many things had changed. It mentions E&T as my main comfort through the years. I deliver the five-minute soliloquy standing, full-front to the audience, covered with a black garbage bag with cut-outs for my head and arms. As the words end, I look down at my one leg, acknowledging that its mate is missing, while I take the bag over my head. The piece ends as I balance on my leg dressed in only my bra and undies. It's about showing myself as I am, acknowledging what's there and hopefully, beginning the process of embracing it.

I make two other short solos. Nine Things and a Thread is about nine physical things—like hopscotch, jump rope, running—I enjoyed as a two-legged child. The thread is the music, the Mickey Hart recording of his child's heartbeat. Grace is a dance I make to a life-size painting David's girlfriend made of me. I have an AA friend make me a mix tape of versions of the spiritual "Amazing Grace." As I crawl on my belly, stand, hop, and maneuver myself around the stage on my one leg, I sing to the lyrics and feel amazingly graced. My self-awareness and compassion for myself and others are growing. I feel more connected than ever to people, places, and things.

I'm beginning a new leg of my journey.

EPILOGUE

The only way to live is to accept each moment as an unrepeatable miracle.

/ Margaret Storm Jameson

FOR THE NEXT TWO YEARS, DAILY TWELVE-STEP meetings would become an integral part of my life. Over the next several years, I would attend a meeting or two a week, until I stopped altogether around 2007. After three years of abstinence from alcohol, and repeated pokes from my brothers about how clear it is to them that I'm not an alcoholic, I now allow myself the pleasure of a glass of wine or a beer whenever the spirit moves me. It hasn't become a problem.

My fear of getting fat after every bite or sip I take diminishes, but food continues to be something I have to be ever-conscious about. Thankfully, over the past ten years, the compulsion to binge and purge has been replaced by a gradual willingness to look honestly at whatever challenges present themselves.

In early 2000, I entered into a four-year program at the Authentic Movement Institute in Berkeley. The practice, which I began in Cambridge at the start of my dancing journey, took me deeper inside where my body, mind, and spirit communicate. It allowed and supported my trip through the long overdue process of grieving the loss of my leg and half my butt and, what was even more difficult, the loss of the body I might have had, and all the fantasies of Miss America and models and slinky dresses and high heels and tap dancing that I had secretly harbored over the years. It opened me to another period of intense dreaming and took me closer to accepting the body I actually have. During one wholly conscious movement session, as I lay flat out on the floor, arms stretched out to the side in a cross-like pose, I had a vivid memory of being strapped down on an operating table. Later, I dreamed of a small girl crouched in a corner of a dark dungeon, and of a young boy I knew in the dream to be my son, locked in a cage. These were startling, yet welcomed images, that provided insight into forgotten aspects of myself that were struggling to be free. My good friend Mary and I have shared weekly authentic movement sessions for the past ten years, traveling from the silliest to the most sacred places and everywhere in between as we move and witness together. This is the ultimate antidote to the sometimes soul-stripping events and activities of daily life, and I am increasing able to bring the playfulness, freedom, and presence I feel during our practice to my everyday interactions.

In January 2001, at age forty-nine, I bought my first house. I transformed the bare front yard into a lush garden of trees, shrubs, and flowers with the help of friends from work and twelve-step groups. I grew vegetables in the backyard. I had yet another short, one-sided infatuation with the man who sold me the house, an OA/AA friend. I shared my feelings with my sponsors and began to understand some of my unfulfilled longings. A few years later, I adopted Annie, a rescue Chihuahua-Dachshund mix. I settled into full-time work.

In 2007 I had trouble with my left hip which doctors said was a result of the forty-five years it had carried the weight of my body. The same doctors recommended I use a wheelchair to preserve the functioning I still had. Much to my surprise, I agreed with little push back. Although I worried others would see me in that chair as lazy and self-indulgent, I also considered my new mode of transportation a fresh adventure and, as always, have found ways to make most everything work. Sitting in the chair provides a much needed rest for my arms and upper body, and encourages me to accept myself as someone who needs help and support. And, unlike many of my years traveling on crutches, I opened to the perks of being alter-abled. For example: being escorted to the front of the line at airports and many other places; offered at the gate, at no charge, the roomier front seats; scoring front-row seats at crowded events, like the Olympic Trials, where others strain to see from the back; and—something that I did enjoy as I softened in my later years on crutches—feeling special and remembered, and being seen as amazing for only just showing up and smiling. Most of us want to be noticed and acknowledged, and I'm happy that I've finally been willing to embrace the positive aspect of the double-edged sword that standing out in a crowd can sometimes be.

In 2012, in celebration of the 25th anniversary of the now DanceAbility International, Alito choreographed an intimate duet for me and Laura, an able-bodied dancer and fellow childhood cancer survivor. The piece was called One Another and as we moved through the landscape of the dance, we were two bodies on three legs, finding ourselves and each other, and delighting in showing off the legs. We performed the duet several times over the next few years, during which time I learned from Alito that performance is not something that must be perfect, like I'd always worried. It's about having a momentary experience and the willingness to share that experience with others. For the first time I was wholly willing to showcase the truth of my body with whoever came to watch, and not cringe at the pictures that documented the truth of that body. I continue to perform the piece once or twice a year with a rotating roster of partners—each one charming and beautiful, and with her own two legs that entwine with my solo leg.

In 2013 Alito and I traveled to Mongolia, the Philippines, and Indonesia as United States Arts Envoys for a month of workshops and performances. In the years that followed, I was part of a larger performance group that traveled around the states. I'm grateful for all of these ongoing opportunities for dancing and sharing and learning.

Gradually, I realized that what I'd worked so hard to hide are the very feelings, pleasures, desires, and interests that make me who I am. What I'd lost all those years ago was a sense of comfort with the truth of myself with my strengths, weaknesses, quirkiness—what others see and like or dislike about me. The curious process of coming out of that hiding, a healing of sorts, is a journey that continues today, full of adventure and surprise.

In December 2016, two weeks after finishing the last chapter of the book, I traveled to Vashon Island for a dance retreat with Karen Nelson, the woman who embraced me twenty-three years before at a dance workshop in Maine. I'd been to two other retreats with her in 2015, with many years in between of not being in contact. The first workshop I attended reminded me of how strong a bond I have with Karen and how attracted I am to her way of working with the dancing body.

One afternoon at that retreat, I had a silly and serious interaction with two women and a Tarot deck. Hannah, the reader, described the cards as a beginner's deck, like Tarot for Dummies. We all agreed there was something both powerful and foolish about the activity, but we each hoped to pull a card that would catapult us into the New Year with something meaningful to ponder.

I pulled the "Power of Joy" card and all three of us giggled with pleasure looking at the rotund laughing Buddha and listening to the reading. It felt so right that I pulled that card—although the part of me that still worries what others think placed herself on alert, lest my ego get too inflated. After all, the Power of Joy—me? If it means I'm enlightened, no way I'm worthy. But in truth, I had been feeling light and joyful since I arrived at Vashon, and for several months before. Something had changed deep within my cells, but I hadn't been able to articulate what it was, or why I suddenly felt so easy with myself.

The next night, December 30, 2016, my Yogi tea tag read, "The purpose of life is to know yourself, to love yourself, to trust yourself and to be yourself." This was exactly what I'd been working, walking, moving, and playing for over the past years! I'd thought finding the purpose of life was an end, a goal to reach, something to attain, but I'm slowly coming to know, deep in my bones, that the purpose of life is the journey, and the joy comes when I embrace each moment of the process. There is no end or final goal or ultimate enlightenment for me. Life itself is all of that when I am willing to be in it with all I've got at every given moment, no matter what.

Later in the weekend, after sharing the tea tag inspiration with the group, I realized that writing this memoir has opened space for subtle, yet amazing, shifts in my inner landscape. The heaviness is gone and I'm easier on myself. There's more joy filling the spaces cleared by sharing my journey in words. It's humbling to acknowledge that I am here in all I've written about. It's the same me typing and reading the words.

The biggest example of this shift is my radically changed relationship with my mother. She'd moved to Oregon in 2002 to be closer to me, and we began to mend our relationship. Ours was a rocky road, and in 2007 she returned to the east coast to be with "her people," but we'd made important inroads. Mainly, we didn't kill each other! Then in 2014 with the help of my brothers, I moved her back to Oregon. She agreed to come after a visit where I saw her losing memory and struggling with daily living. At eighty-nine, she's still physically and mentally strong enough to live in her own studio apartment down the hall from me, but I see her almost daily. Her failing memory means she lives in the present almost exclusively, and this has softened her edges. She's vulnerable, and I recognize myself in her more than ever. I appreciate what she's taught me and, although there are things I'm still sad and disappointed about from the past and in our present interactions, when I'm with her I'm freer of judgment and full of more forgiveness and compassion, for her and for me, than I could ever have imagined.Another Yogi tea tag once declared, "The gate to happiness is self-compassion." So, what is self-compassion? To me it's knowing that with all my idiosyncrasies, oddly-shaped parts, and ever-changing thoughts and emotions, I am enough, just like every blade of grass, mountain range, sunset, and fruit fly. When I live in that awareness, there's endless space inside for worldly compassion, gratitude, delight, playfulness and, yes, the gate to happiness opens.

Funny how you can sometimes find the simplest answers to all of life's quandaries at the end of a tea bag. Funnier still is that my much-loved father spent his working life manning the presses that printed those little tags for Lipton Tea. He may be inspiring these tea tag sayings just for me from The Great Beyond. Ha!

Photos

1952 - Dad & Mom with me in New Jersey

1960 - Hoboken, N. J.

Spring 1963 - Flemington, NJ

August 1970 - Camp Counselor, Spring Valley, NY

June 1974 - Sharon and me, Nursing School Graduation, Rutgers University, Newark, NJ

September 1974 - My wedding to Gene, Flemington, NJ

1974 - My brothers at the the wedding (left to right):
Gerard, me, Billy, and David

Summer 1977 - Cale Kenney and me, Boston, MA

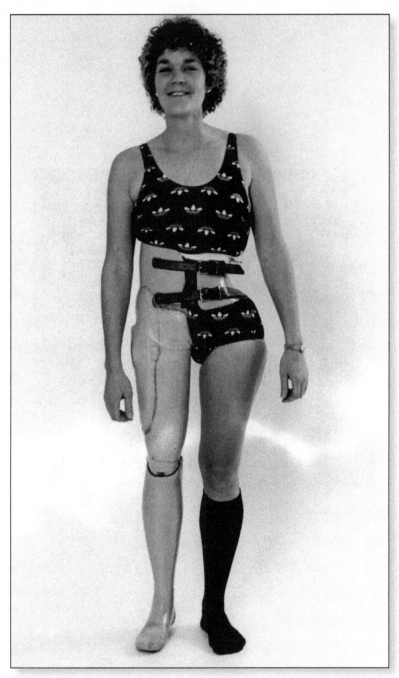

Summer 1977 - My wooden leg, Boston, MA

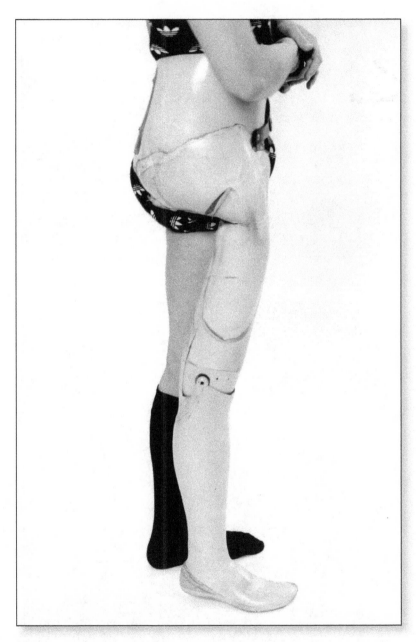

Summer 1977 - My wooden leg, side view

January 1978 - Skiing with other amputees, Jack Frost Mountains, PA

1979 - With friends in Martha's Vineyard, MA

1979 - Martha's Vineyard, MA

1983 - Merrill and me, Connecticutt

Early 1980s - The family without David (l. to r.):
Billy, Mom, Gerard, me, Dad

Late 1980s - Cambridge, MA

1993 - Bathing Beauties, Martha's Vineyard, MA

February 1996 - Diverse Dance, Vashon Island, WA

1998 - Dancing with Body Cartography dancers,
Wellington, New Zealand

1998 - Body Cartography performance with Olive B,
Wellington Fringe Festival, Wellington, New Zealand

Mid-1990s - with DanceAbility in Nicosia, Cypress

June 1999 - Beginning my walk across the United States, Eugene, OR

2013 - Rehearsing with Alito prior to our trip to Mongolia, Indonesia, and the Phiilipines as U.S. Arts Envoys

ACKNOWLEDGMENTS

MANY, MANY HEARTFELT THANKS TO:

Alice Tallmadge for encouraging me to write my story, and suggesting I begin by writing ten-minute memories.

Linda Clare, Cecelia Hagen, and my writing class and writing group buddies for their creative writing knowledge and encouragement.

Mary Seereiter for her commitment to me and our Authentic Movement practice for well over a decade. She may be the most beautiful human being I know—brilliant, compassionate, generous, hard working, and always ready to help in any way.

Alito Alessi for sharing his dancing wisdom and inviting me along on so many DanceAbility adventures.

Karen Nelson for embracing me way back in 1993, and never wavering in her support of what she has always seen as my beautiful, one-legged dancing body. I cherish her ongoing friendship, and the opportunity to continue to learn from her improvisational wisdom and creative dancing ways.

Sadie Iovino and Anne Cole for their friendship and cheerleading efforts.

George Braddock for welcoming me to his home in the early 1990s, and never wavering in his love and support despite my sometimes shady behaviors.

Cale Kenney for standing in as my alter ego, and sharing her unique perspective on one-leggedness with me when I most needed it.

Eva Long, my editor, without whose wise and artistic editing and publishing abilities this project may have never come to completion. Our serendipitous meeting in water aerobics class is in keeping with so many of the other events in the book. She has become a friend, and a trusted partner and true catalyst in the making of this book.

My parents and brothers for always loving and supporting me in whatever way they could.

And all those named and unnamed who have shared in this journey.

> *For all that has been—thanks.*
> *For all that shall be—yes.*
> / Dag Hammarskjold

CPSIA information can be obtained
at www.ICGtesting.com
Printed in the USA
LVHW012031040719
623150LV00002B/345